D1085125

Blacks and the Populist Movement

BLACKS AND THE POPULIST MOVEMENT

Ballots and Bigotry in the New South, Revised Edition

Gerald H. Gaither

THE UNIVERSITY OF ALABAMA PRESS

Tuscaloosa

Typeface: Bembo

∞

The paper on which this book is printed meets the minimum requirements of
American National Standard for Information Science—Permanence of Paper for
Printed Library Materials, ANSI Z39.48–1984.

Library of Congress Cataloging-in-Publication Data

Gaither, Gerald H.
    Blacks and the Populist movement : ballots and bigotry in the New South /
Gerald H. Gaither.— Rev. ed.
        v. cm.
    Rev. ed. of: Blacks and the Populist revolt. 1977.
    Includes bibliographical references and index.
    Contents: Blacks and the Farmers' Alliance Movement : a paradigm for populism —
The search for policy : the roots of racial conflict — Time of trial, time of hope : the
birth of Southern populism — The minority temper : reform spirit during the popu-
list movement — Principles, prejudice, and populism — Theory and practice of popu-
lism : the Atlantic seaboard states — Theory and practice of populism : the gulf coast —
The balance sheet.
    ISBN 0-8173-5188-4 (pbk. : alk. paper)
    1. Southern States—Politics and government—1865–1950. 2. African Americans—
Southern States—Politics and government. 3. Southern States—Race relations—
Political aspects. 4. Populism—Southern States—History. I. Gaither, Gerald H. Blacks
and the Populist revolt. II. Title.
    F215.G23 2005
    320.975—dc22

                                                                    2005003714

Contents

Illustrations

Preface

Ideas and scholarship on the topic of race and Populism in Southern history have continued to flow over the decades. A generation of new scholars has uncovered new sources of primary materials, particularly at the local level. Now, this volume, an extended version of an earlier work published in 1977, incorporates the work of these new scholars and utilizes new methodologies and sources to further assess the biracial complexities of the Populist movement and create a more updated, extended, and intensive portrait of Southern Populism during the last two decades of the nineteenth century, based on these new sources and my added reflections. In the end, however, any reexploration of the subject inevitably leads back to a discussion of what were the different interests and goals of the affected groups, and what were the methods employed by the Bourbon regimes that opposed them and were ultimately accepted by the democratic society at large. There now seems to be a general recognition that the walls between the two races were too high for Populism to have ever succeeded.

Despite this added scholarship and sources, there remains a lacuna in Southern historiography concerning African Americans' role in the South-wide Populist movement. It is hoped that this revised and expanded study will provide a more fully articulated regional portrait of Populism's biracial experiment, pointing out the differences as well as the similarities in patterns of activity. Perhaps the volume may also serve, in some small way, as a stimulus to more scholarship on the subject, which seems to have waned in recent years. Much ground remains to be covered. Furthermore, the volume may offer some additional lessons as twenty-first-century white America confronts, both at home and abroad, an accelerated surge of capitalism accompanied by the difficult absorption of new waves of immigration by people of color and differing religions, a situation somewhat analogous to that faced by the Populists of old.

In evaluating the attitudes of the Southern Populist movement toward

African Americans, modern historians have expressed three divergent viewpoints. The progressive historians of the 1920s and 1930s led by Alex Arnett, John B. Clark, and Roscoe C. Martin, with their studies of individual Southern states, regarded the black man as a puppet, a willing tool with which the Bourbon Democratic opposition emasculated the agrarian movement. The black man, according to this school, was a docile drone who sold his vote for whiskey or a few dollars. His interest was primarily venal and his actions were closely controlled, leaving blacks with few conscious contributions to achieving the democratic promise of events around them.

By the 1950s, however, members of the new consensus school of historiography, led by C. Vann Woodward and reinforced by individuals such as Jack Abramowitz, Lawrence Goodwyn, William Chafe, and Norman Pollack, tended to view blacks as important, more active class allies in the overall agrarian movement. To some such interpreters of the Southern scene, the black person's role within the Populist movement was more important and class interest more driven toward achieving the democratic promise than earlier assumed; and the relationship thus developed—or capable of being developed—between the two races was seen as a viable alternative, an unfortunate road not taken, to the rabid demagogic racism of the early twentieth century. The Black Revolution, it seemed, had challenged our historians to detect a continuous thread of interracial harmony in the American past, particularly in the South where oppression and exploitation of blacks had shaped so much of Southern history.

This interpretation was being challenged by the last decade of the twentieth century by other voices who question the "myth" that a viable interracial coalition could ever have existed between the politically and economically insecure blacks and a more secure white agrarian class. More recently, the existence of any sort of equal, fruitful communication between the races has been challenged, specifically as a result of "institutional racism" in American society. Placing their emphasis more on race than class, such scholars as Charles Crowe, Lawrence Friedman, Burton Shaw, and Robert Saunders set out to dispel the "myth" of racial harmony woven about the early Populist character by the Woodward school.

Yet upon further examination Southern Populism would seem to be a many-faceted crystal that does not fit easily into any set historiographical formula. In technique as well as in approach, this book has pursued a renewed emphasis upon complexity, both individual and regional, to examine what the sociologist Pierre L. van den Berghe called "Herrenvolk democracy"— the vast gap between egalitarian rhetoric, in this case by the agrarians, and the crude contrasts in black-white relations.[1] This volume tests these twin themes and attempts to sort out the myths surrounding Populism and African Americans. Each state and region often had its own distinct pattern of race relations built around individual personalities and issues as well as the degree of crude application of power and corruption these individuals were willing to apply to achieve or retain political dominance. Further, the conflicts between using "self interest" to promote a class movement and the more visceral reaction offered to charges of promoting "social equality" and challenging "white supremacy" were a constant source of personal as well as movement cognitive dissonance.

Populism is still remembered rather romantically these days in the popular press as a noble rising of "the people," and this "New Populism" has resulted in a renewed verbal attack on the growing class and racial inequalities of the American pyramid by such diverse personalities as Bill Moyers, Kevin Phillips, Ralph Nader, Michael Kazin, and Pat Buchanan. Like the old Populism, this new movement often uses the same attractive rhetoric to expose frustrations with the capitalist system and develop a base of working-class support, more often including the growing diverse ethnicity of the American population as the source for this new economic coalition against inequality and injustice. Based on such a foundation of "common interest," it is difficult to visualize the new immigrant Populism lasting any longer than the old—and for pretty much the same reasons. Because of these events and the influx of immigrants from different races and religions, new works on Populist racial and ethnic attitudes could take on a renewed importance.[2] In its coarser, illiberal form, this new, emerging immigrant Populism, like the old, could result in the same old backlash in disguise, for visceral prejudice all too often overpowers economic interests in America. "Race in the South, as in the nation," Carl Degler reminds us, "has always overwhelmed class."[3]

Degler is correct in stressing the continuing power of racist ideas in America—for racism, along with economic differences and the brutal application of power and corruption in politics, precluded the old Populism from effectively uniting groups of deprived people who had only recently been at each other's throats. But for all its ambivalence, its confusion of rhetoric, and social reaction, Populism then as now strongly suggested an abuse of economic power and an overpowering mania for money as the central theme of Southern history; and its legacy survives in a certain school of historians of the South. "The mania for making a fast buck, or even a slow buck, is so widespread in the Deep South today," according to a modern analyst, "that it remains in fact more troublesome than racism; the mind of the South is much more preoccupied with it."[4] In the same view, another observer has concluded that "money rather than ideology had been [the Southerner's] main motivation since slavery."[5] Thus, Populism is an "ism" that has resurfaced in the new millennium in many different forms but in a decidedly more respectable position. It is being driven by the new immigrant influx and, like the old Populism, by self-interests, party realignments, and group dynamics still coming into conflict with the idea of what Lawrence Goodwyn called the achievement of "the Democratic promise." Its proponents' repeated insistence on judging the old movement on the basis of popular images and stereotypes rather than its historical record makes this current trend all the more unfortunate. Perhaps in a small way this book may serve as a corrective and a stimulus to further scholarship on the subject.

Acknowledgments

Any volume covering two decades and the eleven states of the Old Confederacy must of necessity be the product of many minds. While I have relied heavily on manuscripts, newspapers, and magazine articles from the era, I have also relied much on the research of others in fleshing out this updated portrait of Populism wherever necessary. The election data used herein is largely from the University of Michigan's Political Consortium and from the various state agencies that provided election data for their specific states and the years involved. Due to the fraudulent nature of Southern politics during this period, researchers should balance any conclusions drawn against manuscript materials, as I have attempted. I also give particular appreciation to Dr. Sheldon Hackney, who shared unselfishly his statistical data for the development of the election analyses included here.

The limitations of space alone prohibit full reference in the bibliography to the many sources used in the development of this study. Citations in the various chapters have given full reference to the many sources and individuals that contributed to this monograph. Indeed, the many sources used in this volume were so voluminous that they became a separate volume edited by myself and a colleague, Anthony Adam, and published by Greenwood Press. Readers interested in the topic and this era of Southern history should consult this additional text. Sincere thanks are also due to the many librarians at various institutions and states for their assistance in the face of ever-increasing demands upon their patience and stamina. The conscientious and dedicated services of these individuals from all regions have reinforced my belief in the continued existence of "Southern Hospitality."

Special mention must be given some individuals. To my colleague and friend Tony Adam must be given my deepest gratitude, for without his active assistance in the research and editorial reading of chapters in every phase of this revised edition, the task would have been harder and the finished product less worthy and readable. Mrs. Iris Sawyer proved endlessly patient and efficient in typing the handwritten manuscript, on which my handwriting on occasion challenged or defied interpretation. I also want to thank Dr. Omar Ali for permission to reproduce his photograph of the Rev. Walter Pattillo, Dr. Gregg Cantrell for permission to use his photograph of John B. Rayner, and Dr. Merline Petrie for permission to reproduce her photos of William "Gooseneck Bill" McDonald and Alex Asberry. The other photographs are the result of the diligence of my research associate, Tony Adam. Mr. Randy Krumrey and Mrs. Ginger Philips applied modern technology to enhance the photos and produce the scattergrams. Ms. Sue Breckenridge and the staff of the University of Alabama Press have exhibited what Ernest Hemmingway called "grace under pressure" in the preparation of this second edition. Any discussion concerning "grace under pressure" must include my wife, Joan Gaither, whose patience and encouragement made an important contribution to the completion of this volume. Finally, the works of C. Vann Woodward originally inspired this study and helped shape many of my concepts about the racial attitudes of the Populist movement. While I have disagreed with some of his conclusions, this in no way lessens my sense of indebtedness to his early scholarship in further crystallizing and fleshing out the face of Southern Populism and its different racial attitudes in the various states. A major theme of Woodward's with regard to Southern Populism was that race was among the strongest factors affecting political behavior in the South. On this point, all parties could probably agree.

Blacks and the Populist Movement

I

Blacks and the Farmers' Alliance Movement

A Paradigm for Populism

Our fight is a common fight . . .

The last quarter of the nineteenth century was a period of intense agrarian ferment in the South. As cotton and other staple crop prices declined, sometimes below the cost of production, a number of organizations arose to express the discontent and aspirations of the Southern farmer. The Farmers' Alliance was, perhaps, the most important of the lot, at least by the late 1880s. It was the Alliance, the leading incubator of third-party radicalism, that ultimately served as the forerunner of the Populist Party, a political vehicle of agrarian protest.

While the Alliance movement and the Populist Party approached reform differently, the former preferring to work within the Democratic Party and the latter creating its own independent political activity, both nevertheless overlapped in membership. With the failure of one movement to achieve its purpose, the creation of the other began. "Populism in the South," according to the Populist messiah Tom Watson, who never joined the Farmers' Alliance, "was the legitimate offspring of the Farmers' Alliance."[1] Furthermore, because of the extensive carry-over of membership from one movement to the other, the Populist racial ideology was, to a large extent, a transference of attitudes and conflicts into a similar movement, utilizing different means toward accomplishing the same goal: alleviation of agrarian grievances.[2] Because of such an inextricable relationship, the racial ideology of one movement is, indeed, inseparable from a study of the collective whole.

The tradition of organized agrarian discontent began almost immediately after Reconstruction, with disgruntled farmers, spurred on by increasingly depressed agricultural conditions, seeking solace outside the unresponsive Democratic standard through such diverse vehicles as the Greenback Party, the Agricultural Wheel, and the Knights of Labor, all of which had experimented with biracial coalitions. Hard times dogged the agricultural South during the last quarter of the nineteenth century. Dependent largely upon cotton and tobacco for their livelihood, the incomes of both black and white farmers dropped precipitously during the latter part of the nineteenth century. In 1870 cotton prices fluctuated at fifteen cents a pound but had eroded to under five cents a pound by 1898—at a time when it cost around seven cents a pound to produce the crop. There were several other periods during this era when costs exceeded prices. As the region became overly reliant upon two or three staple crops in the postwar economy and was further devastated by the national depression in the early 1880s, poor and middle-class laborers and farmers were particularly hard hit financially. The pattern was common: increased debt led to increased production to overcome declining prices, which led to crop overproduction, but without increased demand, which led to more declining prices, despite record crops. The result was a continuous downward spiral in agriculture and the quality of life with no end in sight. Southern cotton farmers produced in 1894, for example, a record crop, exceeding by two million bales any ever produced, yet they received $50 million less for it than the crop produced in 1862. Hollowness, despair, and a sense of hopelessness increasingly gripped the agricultural community during this period, and economic collapse cut deeply into the lives of black and white alike. In 1860, the income of the average white Southerner was about 72 percent of the national average, but by 1900 it had declined to 51 percent.[3] Because of this common background, Southern agrarians were being forced to consider the practical and necessary advantages—and disadvantages—of working with the region's 6 million blacks in a common brotherhood of poverty.

The Farmers' Alliance originated in Lampasas County, Texas, as early as 1874 or 1875 as a cooperative effort to purchase supplies, furnish effective opposition to land sharks and cattle barons, and prevent cattle rustling.[4] There soon appeared on the scene Charles W. Macune, most recently from Milam County, Texas, a peripatetic man of considerable persuasive abilities and extensive plans and ambitions for the Alliance.[5] Under his charismatic leadership, the organization spread rapidly across the South, introducing itself in Macune's words as "a strictly white man's nonpolitical secret business organization."[6] Despite his strong racial attitudes, Macune believed that the plight of farmers of both races could be improved without engendering the dreaded fear of bringing about "social equality" with the black man. In 1882, the Texas Alliance under Macune's leadership denied membership to blacks partially on the grounds that they were "undesirable" social companions for the whites' wives and daughters.[7] Macune also wished to wage the white farmer's struggle within the Democratic Party, using an Alliance economic plan, especially a Subtreasury Plan in which the central government would build a large warehouse (called a subtreasury) in every county that grew more than half a million dollars worth of agricultural produce a year. The subtreasury would provide government loans up to 80 percent of the value of the crop, store the farmer's surplus crops, and prevent market glut by dumping excess crops and depressing prices. The idea was to stabilize price fluctuations by controlling surpluses and add some steady flow of income to the individual farmer and minimize his need for indebtedness.

As the Alliance spread eastward, it encountered other organizations with similar aims and natures. Obviously, the most expedient process of expansion and growth was a union of forces with these organizations. Perhaps the most important of these mergers was made with the smaller Louisiana Farmers' Union in 1887. With this union the National Farmers' Alliance and Co-operative Union of America, commonly referred to as the Southern Alliance, came into official being. In 1888, a similar merger with the Agricultural Wheel was proposed. After considerable debate, consolidation was finally agreed upon in December, at a gathering of delegates in Meridian, Mississippi.[8] It was also agreed here to support the idea of a separate Colored Alliance to work with the region's 4.5 million black agrarians who were both competitors and members of the agricultural class.

In the early days of the Alliance movement, blacks as potential recruits received only minor consideration. With Reconstruction and the hardening of racial attitudes, the prerogative of the group or individual to openly express economic or political discontent was largely governed by the common denominators of maintaining racial solidarity and loyalty to the Democratic Party in the South, which was regarded as the political vehicle to protect white rights. In the minds of white Southerners, any aberrant action in white ranks that involved organizing blacks was viewed suspiciously as an attempt to revive the "horrors" of black Reconstruction and break the dreaded taboo of introducing "social equality" with blacks.[9] Also, C. W. Macune was a man whose strong racial attitudes, combined with his senior leadership role, hindered closer Alliance association with blacks. It was not only expedient, then, but probably necessary for the Southern Alliance to initially disregard organizing blacks. Conversely, the Republican Party—the party of Lincoln and emancipation—was an important source of support and comfort for blacks. Southern blacks were not, as a group, willing to entrust their fate to the Democratic Party, although some blacks had early flirted with the idea and a few had even been elected to offices on the Democratic ticket. In the South Carolina House of Representatives, for example, between 1878 and 1890, twenty-one black members were elected as Democrats. However, far more black Republicans than Democrats were elected Southwide during this period. The black legislative leadership cadre of Texas, for example, during the postbellum years worked en masse within the Republican Party, with all forty-two of the state's legislators coming from the party of Lincoln.[10] It is not surprising, then, that most white Alliance agrarians were reluctant at first to officially incorporate blacks into their organization despite their common status.

In 1882, the prevailing spirit of racial distrust, Macune's conservative racial views, and a hostile barrage of Democratic propaganda were probably the motivating factors that caused the Alliance to officially restrict its membership to whites and to strongly discourage its membership from becoming involved in or endorsing any "distinct party."[11] While the Alliance chose not to admit blacks into its ranks, with three-fourths of the South's 6 million blacks engaged in agrarian pursuits, blacks found it imperative ultimately to create a parallel organization, if for no other motivation than self-interest.[12] It was impossible for the Alliance to establish a profitable agricultural system in the South while a large black population served as potential competitors and a cheap source of exploitable labor—in essence, agricultural strike breakers. The small white farmer soon realized, whatever his racial attitudes, that he could rise no higher on the ladder of prosperity than his black counterpart. As the *National Economist,* the official organ of the Southern Alliance, observed in 1891, "No one realizes better than [the Southern white farmer], if he allows sharpers to swindle the colored man by paying him excessively low prices for his cotton, by taking advantage of his necessity for money, . . . such low prices will tend to keep prices low until [the white farmers] . . . are compelled to sell . . . and . . . perpetuate the low prices. The fact is that the law of self-preservation compels the Southern white farmer to . . . hold [the Negro] out of the clutches of the exploiter."[13] Thus, while expediency largely necessitated early exclusion of blacks from the order, it also required, both philosophically and practically, that they later be included in the grandiose agrarian plan of salvation. This movement was at bottom an attempt in which one class—the "producers" of wealth, especially farmers of both races—sought to restore Jeffersonian agrarian ideals of an activist central government to better serve the economic interests of the laboring masses.

The Northern Alliance was also instrumental in promoting the idea of a black order in the South. Unlike its Southern counterpart, the Northern Alliance promoted from the outset the philosophy that anyone, regardless of color, should be included in this agricultural "producer"-class movement if born on the farm or involved in an occupation that related to agrarian pursuits.[14] Because of economic and geographical considerations, as well as the concentration of the black population in the South, however, a Northern-based black Alliance would have been of little value from an organizational standpoint. But if blacks, also mired in tenancy and hopelessly indebted to the merchant class, were not included in the overall reform effort, the collective class solution to the farmers' problems would be both practically and philosophically endangered.

Milton George, the founder of the National Farmers' Alliance, the principal organization of Northern and Northwestern farmers, argued that the Southern Alliance, allegedly founded by C. W. Macune, was originally a wing of the National Farmers' Alliance. George asserted that many of the local alliances in the South were chartered by his group, but the split into the Northern and Southern Alliances occurred over the inclusion of blacks into the organization, which the South opposed. There is substantial evidence that George had chartered colored farmers' alliances in the South as early as 1882, the first being formed in Prairie County, Arkansas, in 1882. It does not appear that these colored alliances sustained themselves, however.[15]

As editor of the *Western Rural* of Chicago and the founder of the National Farmers' Alliance, George promoted the delicate task of organizing black Alliance orders in the South. He reasoned that the farmer class should organize to protect its interest and that a working coalition with the black agricultural class could only serve to further this goal. Thus, a combination of self-interest and class-consciousness were the chief progenitors of white interest in the Colored Alliance. Its creation cannot be said to have been inspired by any one single motivation, unless it was the farmers' declining status and economic position.[16] However, a strong sense of *noblesse oblige* permeated the Alliance leaderships' attitudes toward the downtrodden blacks.

One of Texas's worst economic times on record occurred four years after Milton George's ill-fated attempts in Arkansas. The most severe drought in anyone's memory occurred between 1885 and 1887; cotton prices dropped to 8.6 cents a pound, and racial attitudes were hardening. In the midst of dire circumstances, such an agrarian organization was a practical necessity.[17]

The Colored Farmers' Alliance (CFA) was officially founded December 11, 1886, in Houston County, Texas, on the farm of R. M. Humphrey, a full ten to twelve years after the region's white alliance was founded.[18] Attracted by ritual, secrecy, and the possible economic benefits the order might offer poverty-stricken blacks, the membership of the organization at the local level increased rapidly. Like the white Southern Alliance, the Colored Farmers' Alliance was established as "a secret order." There were good reasons to be optimistic about the chance of recruiting black farmers during such difficult times to such an organization that promised relief, since cotton prices had now plummeted to less than it cost to produce it.[19] Within a few days, the CFA had spread to such an extent throughout Houston and neighboring counties that it was deemed necessary to call a convention at Good Hope Baptist Church in Weldon to discuss the possibility of a sub-Alliance merger.

All of this activity took place within a mere eighteen days after the founding of the first local, indicating its appeal to the black agricultural community, as well as the exploitative situation prompted by the agricultural crisis and the drought. The delegates "unanimously agreed" that "union and organization" were absolute necessities to the "earthly salvation of the Negro farmer."[20] The convention also set forth a "declaration of purposes," stating its reasons why a separate Colored Farmers' Alliance was necessary, and outlining goals the organization hoped to achieve. With the adoption of this declaration, the entire convention of "sixteen colored men and citizens of Texas" signed the document and adjourned.[21]

The CFA was well aware of the difficulty involved and the lack of desire by many blacks of integrating with the white alliance, as well as the whites' desire to formally exclude them. Both races recognized the necessity of adherence to the Southern racial norm, be it black separatism or white supremacy; and as such, any organizational integration between the races was highly undesirable to both organizations. A further principle, if not the entire impetus, for this CFA separatism was the increasing emphasis blacks in the 1880s were putting upon self-help, economic development, civic virtue, and racial organization as a temporary tactic to attain wealth and power. In turn, it was believed these virtuous attainments would, in time, result in the subsequent granting of equal rights by whites out of respect for black accomplishment. At bottom, it was the black separatist counterpart to the "gospel of wealth" philosophy that permeated most white attitudes of the period.[22] The economic self-help drive was paramount from the outset in the Colored Alliance, and its concerted economic emphasis was particularly fitted to give the organization an even more conservative cast toward integration than it otherwise would have had at this time. Blacks did, however, make it clear from the very beginning that, as members of the agricultural "producer class," they desired ideological integration and unity of broad purpose with the white alliance, through any means that would be mutually beneficial to both races. One resolution stated rather succinctly:

> That though we are organizing separate and apart from the Farmers' Alliance now existing in Texas, composed of white members, we believe it will be to our interest to work in harmony with that organization. That we ask the members of the white Alliance throughout the United States to aid us in perfecting our organization.[23]

The Colored Farmers' Alliance would be led by an elderly white man who found his calling among Texas's rural blacks. Richard Manning Humphrey, an obscure itinerant Baptist preacher, Confederate veteran, and school teacher from Clarendon County, South Carolina, with a flair for promotion, had attended Furman University before settling in Lovelady, Houston County, Texas, as a missionary to the local black farmers. The son of Irish immigrants, Humphrey was born in South Carolina in 1834 and served as a captain in the Alabama Infantry during the Civil War. Following the war, he moved to Texas, where he taught school and served as an unordained Baptist minister. Described as "an elderly man of large frame and portly person, with plain speech and a free blunt manner," Humphrey was reportedly selected by Colored Farmers' Alliance members in 1886 as their general superintendent because of "his ability and because of their confidence in him as a friend of the race." Little else is known of Humphrey, who faded into obscurity after 1891 with the expiration of the Colored Farmers' Alliance; he died in Texas in 1906.

Privately, however, Humphrey's position was probably to serve more as a white spokesman who could openly express militancy and have access that would be denied to blacks. It was common practice in the South to have racial surrogates, such as Humphrey, serve as intermediaries between segregated organizations such as the Southern and Colored Alliances, a pattern practiced by several state Colored Alliances and later commonly used by the Populists. Only in this way could the dreaded bugaboo of "social equality" between the races be avoided.

According to Leonidas L. Polk, president of the white Southern Alliance, "most of its organizers [were] white."[24] State superintendents of the organization in Alabama, Kentucky, North Carolina, and Virginia were white, but the race of other state superintendents or organizers is obscure. Superintendent Humphrey, for example, had appointed Harry McCall, a white, to lead the Colored Alliance in Alabama; and F. A. Howell, a white, served as manager of the Mississippi and Louisiana orders.[25] As noted, state superintendents of the Colored Farmers' Alliances in Alabama, North Carolina, Kentucky, and Virginia were white, as was Humphrey. The Virginia Colored Farmers' Alliance, for example, initially elected a white president, J. J. Rogers, who served as state superintendent until 1891, at which time he was voted out of office, ostensibly because he had conflict with or ignored the viewpoints of Virginia's black alliance leaders.[26] However, this situation was not true in all states. In Tennessee, for example, whites were barred from any official organizing of Colored Farmers' Alliance lodges unless commissioned specifically by the state's general superintendent.[27] Conversely, the opposite situation apparently occurred in Alabama. A white Texas organizer, Andrew J. Carothers, who came to the state in 1889 expressed his hope "that the

Farmers' Alliance men everywhere will take hold and organize or aid in organizing the colored farmer, and placing him in an attitude to cooperate intelligently and systematically."[28] This indicates, at least in Alabama, that a certain unity of endeavor existed from the start between the orders of both races with regard to recruiting and organizing the black farmer.

In addition to his missionary work, Humphrey brought with him about "twenty-five years" experience in agriculture during which time he had employed "a lot of Negroes, good colored people." It was said that he "used" to be a Democrat although he had voted "a few republican tickets, but mighty few."[29] He was active in the mid-1880s in the Union Labor Party and had run unsuccessfully for Congress in 1888 from the second congressional district of Texas. Lawrence Goodwyn has suggested that Humphrey's involvement with the Colored Farmers' Alliance, in addition to his reform instincts, was partially driven by his personal interest in winning an election seat in his East Texas congressional district. Humphrey won only one county in the 1888 election, one with a large African American population. This resounding lack of success appears to have ended Humphrey's pursuit of further, higher elective office. His opponent, W. H. Martin, had charged Humphrey with "slipping around at night with [a] lantern in his hand to organize the negroes into alliances," which it was alleged was "for mercenary and political ends."[30]

Humphrey was aware of the magnitude of his task as well as the slim chances of making a success of the Colored Farmers' Alliance order. This was, he wrote later, an organization that "had no money, no credit, few friends, and was expected to reform and regenerate a race which, from long endurance and oppression and chattel slavery, had become extremely besotted and ignorant."[31]

Despite such seemingly insurmountable obstacles, Humphrey apparently possessed the necessary missionary zeal, energy, and initiative required of his office. Also, the Colored Farmers' Alliance met a crying need for assistance and organization in the black agrarian community. The order presently began to spread rapidly to other states with newly organized branches adopting the Texas pattern and purpose, adding some slight modifications to fit local needs. By January 10, 1891, the order had members in thirty states, including the entire South, and eleven state associations had been chartered. One can only surmise whether this early success was due mainly to the magnetism of the black self-help philosophy, the organizational talents of Humphrey, the destitute condition of black farmers, or a combination of the three. Urging its members to improve themselves through self-help, Christian character, property acquisition, hard work, economic development, and uplifting of the race, the Colored Alliances echoed the philosophy later made famous by Booker T. Washington and his disciples.

Once the Colored Farmers' Alliance achieved interstate proportions, it became legally necessary to obtain a federal charter. A convention of the various state Colored Alliances was assembled in Lovelady, Texas, on March 14, 1888, to discuss the procurement of this charter. After some debate, it was decided to regard the Colored Farmers' Alliance as a trade union for legal purposes. A charter application was then forwarded to the necessary authorities, using this classification. The federal government apparently concurred with this definition of the order since a charter was granted and duly filed with the recorder of deeds in Washington.[32] Thus, the Colored Farmers' National Alliance and Cooperative Union was born.

Like white agrarians, Texas blacks of that era had developed a number of other similar self-help organizations, including a Colored State Grange organized in Dallas in 1880, the Colored Farmers Association of Texas in 1882, and the Colored Farmers Improvement Lodge in 1887.[33] In addition, a number of states (e.g., Tennessee, Arkansas) had developed Colored Agricultural Wheels. Also, the Knights of Labor were actively involved in biracial activities in several Southern States. Despite the importance of "class and race cooperation," these various agencies also developed rivalries at a time when greater solidarity was much needed.

As the Colored Farmers' Alliance moved toward the possibility of becoming in fact as well as in name a nationwide organization, it encountered a variety of hostile forces and attitudes. A brief examination of selected Southern state orders reveals a number of important points about the movement, not the least being the diverse Southern white attitudes toward the different orders. While little is known about the Colored Farmers' Alliances' organizational methods, it seems probable that they imitated the white Southern Alliances, sending forth organizers in teams, probably recruited on the state level.

ALABAMA

Alabama blacks had expressed little interest in the alliance movement until the consolidation of the Wheel and Alliance in Meridian, Mississippi, in December 1888. At the Meridian meeting the white alliance stated its support for the creation of a separate Colored alliance. Considering the grinding poverty of the region, the concentration of the black population in agricultural pursuits, the cost of producing cotton often exceeding the price received, and this gesture of approval by the whites, it would indeed have been surprising if a separate organization had not resulted. Thus, with white aid and sympathy, Alabama black farmers took immediate advantage of this opportunity.[34]

Black orders came into existence in Alabama as early as January 1889, only a month after the white Alliance expressed the need for such orders. Moreover, by the summer of the same year state membership had reportedly reached fifty thousand. In the formative years of the Colored Alliance, Alabama whites gave their hearty approval of the order.[35] If black farmers could improve their lot, it was thought that it would doubtless yield a rich harvest in white ranks as well. As one newspaper expressed it: "The white and Colored Alliance are united in their war against trusts, and in promotion of the doctrine that farmers should establish cooperative stores, and manufactures, and publish their own newspapers, conduct their own schools."[36] However, this early support for the movement dissolved when the alliances later became associated in the public mind with political developments involving blacks. Any organization of blacks was always suspected of being detrimental to white interests.

The eventual downfall of the Alabama black order was brought about by the purported political complexities of the state alliance movement. The state, especially in the Black Belt, reacted violently against any attempt on the part of blacks to enter politics or to develop any collective efforts that might provide them with political leverage. Because of the "almost paranoid accusations by some Bourbons" as well as a show of disapproval of blacks organizing from the more conservative faction of the white alliance, the Alabama Colored Alliance movement began to decline by 1892.[37]

TENNESSEE

One of the outstanding characteristics of the Tennessee Colored Alliance was its close association with the Colored Wheel. It was reported that "a great many of our [black] brothers belong to both orders."[38] This aspect of the two agrarian movements was unusual, and in most states competition rather than cooperation was the usual pattern between such groups of African Americans. Early efforts to bring Tennessee blacks into the alliance fold were conducted during the summer of 1888 by C. A. Vaughn of Detroit (Tipton County).[39] While the presence of the Colored Wheel prevented the expected membership response to the Colored Alliance, the combined effort of the two orders, nevertheless, achieved a notable degree of general success, reporting 387 Colored Wheels and Alliances by October 1888.[40] These efforts appear to have been concentrated in West and Middle Tennessee, where cotton production was concentrated.

The willingness of Tennessee black farmers to participate in the Alliance and Wheel is attested to many times in the official state white Alliance organ, the *Weekly Toiler*. As one white state lecturer remarked:

> The colored people show an eagerness for information and enthusiasm for our cause and principles, which is unsurpassed by any audience I have ever addressed. I am convinced that the colored farmers of Tennessee, if properly educated will make active working members of the order. The prejudices growing out of their former condition of slavery are gradually disappearing.

He went on to express his hope that "the white brethren will . . . treat them kindly" and show them "that our fight is a common fight for their interest."[41] Again the lure of common benefits served as the core attraction for racial cooperation.

However, the Tennessee Colored Alliance suffered a chronic failing, common to many state alliances—a shortage of funds. While the white alliance permitted black members to trade through their Memphis and Nashville exchanges, it was hoped that the Colored Alliance would establish its own separate business concerns. The *Weekly Toiler* exclaimed that the black order of the state should "blush with shame" at its failure to raise funds to establish its own separate exchange. While the Texas Colored Alliance was reportedly worth $135,000 "above all liabilities," the Tennessee order had not managed to raise a "mere" $10,000.[42] Colored exchanges, based on the co-operative principle, were eventually set up in Houston, New Orleans, Mobile, Norfolk, and Charleston, but never in the Tennessee area. The exchanges secured capital by assessing each member in the territory two dollars. This was at a time when black tenant wages were approximately fifty to sixty cents a day.[43] In light of the Tennessee order's noted enthusiasm for the agrarian doctrines, it seems likely that their failure to establish a separate exchange was due to the membership's financial incapacity rather than any laxity of support.[44] At a time when income was declining, the dire economic plight of most blacks dictated that survival took precedence over membership dues.

Despite this strong dependence on the white alliance for moral and financial assistance, no major rift in policy or purpose initially occurred between the two Tennessee orders. At their August 1890 state convention in Pulaski, the Colored Alliance made clear its plan to "cooperate with the white people of the state." *The National Economist* expressed its belief that the black farmers of Tennessee "under the wise counsels of their grand old leader" Humphrey were "laying a basis for the final adjustment of the race question."[45] Like the Colored Alliance, the white alliance put great stress on economic activity and self-interest as a basis for solving the race question. Underlying all this was the philosophic assumption that wealth and morality would negate racial prejudice. Thus, Booker T. Washington's belief in character, civic virtue, and economic uplifting of the race found an early, comfortable home in the Colored Alliance and other such agricultural improvement societies in the South. Furthermore, its presence and philosophy dovetailed nicely with the old Jeffersonian dream of a self-reliant, independent yeomanry, with independence and civic virtue created by land ownership and cultivation of the soil.

The success of the Colored Alliance and of the Tennessee Alliance movement in general was constricted by the role the black order purportedly played in the state's politics. As in Alabama, the presence of a large, organized group of blacks either incited fears among whites or tempted them to take advantage of blacks as potential voters. Though blacks were never the thorn in the side of Tennessee politics that they were in the Deep South, the Bourbon Democrats nonetheless successfully managed to conjure up visions of black Republicanism in the collective mind of the state's white electorate. Charges were leveled that the Tennessee white Alliance was organizing blacks to create a Republican ascendancy; but in light of the fact that most of the white Alliance members in the state were Democrats, this allegation seems unfounded. Furthermore, John P. Buchanan, the Tennessee State Alliance president, was elected governor in 1890 and carried a strong Alliance delegation into the legislature—yet Buchanan, an expected reformer, was as conservative as the former Democratic administrations.[46] As in Alabama, the supposed interrelationship of blacks, the Alliance, and the Republican Party presented Tennessee's Bourbon Democrats with a potent weapon that proved to be the downfall of the Tennessee Colored Alliance. During the 1890 election campaign especially, there was "a bitter and mendacious war" waged against the alliance, because of its "aggressiveness" for "Alliance principles." Particularly vitriolic against the alliance was Josiah Patterson, the "big brained old champion of Bourbon Democracy," who was a chief contender for the Democratic gubernatorial nomination. Making no appeal to the "ideal one gallus, copperas breeches man with the hoe," Patterson dwelled on the agricultural depression, attributing it to the farmers, and the demagogic rhetoric of maintaining a "white man's government."[47] Charges were successfully made that the Alliance was organizing blacks to create a Republican "ascendancy," but the white Alliance members in the state were mostly local Democrats and did not seek fusion with the Republicans. Furthermore, Tennessee Alliancemen supported the three state laws of 1889 and 1890 designed to disenfranchise black voters.[48] Thus, the assertions of the opposition did not logically follow, but that did not stop the Bourbon Democrats from making the allegation. The Colored Alliance leadership in turn had declared that "we are not for politics [party], we are for the man," preferring to measure candidates by the Alliance yardstick of performance to help the farmer rather than any party label. But how much blacks had turned away from the Republican Party of their fathers in order to elect white Alliance sympathizers is also largely a matter of conjecture.[49] Nevertheless, such volatile charges presented the Bourbon Democratic opposition with a formidable propaganda coup to use against the Colored Alliance. Like its white counterpart, such charges constantly kept it on the defensive and unable to focus its energies primarily on its goals. The enervating effects of this 1890 gubernatorial political campaign took its toll on the Tennessee Colored Alliance membership, which by its own admission had dropped from a July peak of one hundred thousand to sixty thousand members in December 1890, near the end of the political campaign.[50] Further impetus for the Colored Alliance's decline came from white planters in the Memphis area, who successfully resisted black cotton pickers' efforts for a threatened strike to demand pay of over fifty cents per hundred pounds. The Tennessee Colored Alliance's failure to improve its members' desperate lot further resulted in its demise.[51]

SOUTH CAROLINA

In South Carolina, the Colored Alliance movement was inspired by a forerunner, the Cooperative Workers of America (CWA), a loosely based subsidiary of the Knights of Labor operating in several upstate counties in 1887.[52] The Knights of Labor had reached its national membership peak in 1886, with about sixty thousand black members, but the order had started to decline in the South, which undermined these efforts.[53] Black cooperative locals of the CWA were organized in South Carolina in 1886–1887, with the intended goal of securing a higher minimum wage for the state's black agricultural population, reportedly fifty cents per hundred pounds of cotton picked, which sounded much like the goals of the Memphis area strikers. Since any effort to organize blacks was viewed with a suspicious eye, the meetings of the order were kept clandestine and nocturnal, usually held in black churches, with sentries posted to warn the members of any approaching intruder.[54]

Despite these efforts, the movement's activities soon became known and aroused the suspicions of whites, if for no other reason than the unusual and secretive manner in which the meetings were being held. It seems likely that blacks within the group had made whites aware of the meetings. A

South Carolina black teacher observed bitterly that "when anything is gotten up in their [black's] weak judgment for the benefit of their race, there is always some unprincipled person among them . . . ready for sale for a pitiful peck of meal or sack of flour or plug of tobacco."[55] Once knowledge of the group became apparent, old racial fears began to manifest themselves. Was this the root of a black conspiracy? Were there plans to overthrow the state government in one swift move? Fear and paranoia enveloped the white community—a state of mind reflected in an attack on all forms of racial organizations.

During May 1887 in Greenville County, an armed posse of white men took it upon themselves to investigate forcibly the activities of a local black cooperative order that had been secretive in its actions. The secretary was forced to surrender his membership list, consisting of only seventeen names. When each member was interrogated separately, it was discovered that blacks had joined the movement in anticipation of getting their rations at half price and with the possible idea of striking for a wage of a dollar a day. Like the proposed black tenants' cotton picker strike near Memphis in 1891, this effort ultimately resulted in white violence against the black members. The white community initially heaved a sigh of relief that nothing more insidious was planned, but this was presently replaced with white indignation at such proposals. The threat of lynching was imminent; such black insolence could not be tolerated. White wrath soon rendered the state CWA completely ineffective.[56]

In this organizational vacuum the Colored Farmers' Alliance in South Carolina found fertile ground for its beginnings. As early as September 1888, in the immediate wake of the CWA failure, the Colored Alliance made its timely invasion. Under the direction of T. E. Pratt of Cheraw, the order spread throughout the state and by February 1890 reportedly had 237 organized clubs and 30,000 members statewide.[57] Since the general white population of the state initially displayed neither enthusiasm for nor fear of the black order, the Colored Alliance received sympathetic reactions from the white Alliance movement.[58] The Colored Farmers' Alliance was ostensibly perceived as a more conservative organization than the CWA and, working in open consort with the white Alliance, did not raise the same concerns as the more secretive Cooperative Workers of America and the Knights of Labor did among the white population.

Even though the South Carolina Colored Alliance experienced rapid growth up to 1890, the order began to founder seriously by the fall of 1891, the immediate reason again being its alleged involvement in political and economic affairs. During the 1890 election with the rise of Ben Tillman's political machine, the Republicans as well as a faction of the anti-Tillmanite

Democrats, in their desperation turned to the blacks and the Colored Alliance for political support, but with little apparent success.[59] Both sides wanted black votes, and the presence of an economically oriented black organization with the potential of serving as a swing vote—or even a political voting bloc—was enough to create acrimony.

Despite the Colored Alliance's nonpartisan nature in this effort, the existence of a black order in such numbers aroused the political fears of all factions, as it had in Alabama and Tennessee. Further, an abortive attempt in the fall of 1891 to create a general strike among the state's black cotton pickers resulted in a further failure for the South Carolina Colored Farmers' Alliance. This strike, orchestrated by the National Colored Farmers' Alliance, resulted in intense hostility by Alliance and non-Alliance whites and demoralization by blacks after its failure. Following these two ventures, the animosity of the white community destined the South Carolina as well as the national order to oblivion; after 1892, all mention of the organization disappears.[60]

While these three sketches of various state Colored Alliances are hardly definitive, they do show certain general characteristics at the grassroots level. The Colored Alliance attracted early support, often from white Alliance members, rapidly from a broad area in the South. White Alliance members saw their help of blacks as one of common interests, and their approval was often necessary for organization to occur in a hostile white environment. Within months after the first Texas sub-Alliance was founded, locals were to be found in nearby Arkansas; and within months after the founding of the national chapter, state organizations were to be found in widespread areas of the South.

The rapid manner in which these orders came into being was probably due more to the inordinately hard times experienced by blacks and the organization's self-help impulse, rather than to any public relations effort of the central office in Houston County. In chronic debt, black farmers as laborers were at a special disadvantage. Aided by this unfortunate situation, the order symbolized "the substance of things hoped for, the evidence of things not seen" to the oppressed white and black farmers.[61]

An economic self-help motif threaded strongly through early black attraction to the Alliance. During these first organizational years, blacks began to play a more active role in their immediate economic orbit. By the fall of 1891 the Colored Farmers' Alliance alleged "throughout the South [that] the colored man has been able to get more money for his cotton and pay less for his bacon."[62] It is difficult to measure the full extent of black economic development from the scanty literature, but it appears that control—or at least their hopes of it—over the economic essentials necessary for self-help and economic development was increasing, even if economic conditions were continuing to deteriorate. "In various States and Counties," a traveler reported in 1891, "the Farmers' Alliance is attracting attention, many of the Negroes hoping to find relief through it from the bondage of the mortgage system."[63] While progress was slow, very slow, there was a degree of tangible hope with a little proof that the agrarian black masses, through self-help and organization, might rise out of their oppressed economic state. For a brief time the vitality of the black farmers' emphasis on economic self-help and group success did appear to be a viable way, to offer hope, to help reduce prejudice through economic elevation. If the white agrarian refused to grant the South's 6 million black farmers this opportunity, he would ostensibly be forced to pay an increasingly high price in terms of economic disorders that would disrupt the entire price and labor index of the South. Always in the background, the threat of self-interest loomed as an ever-present reminder to the white Alliance that it could not successfully fight the battle alone. In order to prosper, the white farmer reluctantly realized that he "must take with him all engaged in that occupation."[64] It was necessary to organize the producer class for the benefit of all. Blacks were a component of this producer class and must be included.

The Colored Farmers' Alliance depended to a great extent for its survival upon the goodwill of the white South at large. This was necessary because of economic vulnerability and political impotence. Unfortunately, when black Alliance initiative conflicted with what the white community viewed as being in its best interest or threatened social equality and political control, as in South Carolina, the dispute was more often than not resolved using violent confrontations, to the disadvantage of the black farmer. And the stated philosophical common interest of the producer class was also subjected to considerable stress. As William Holmes has succinctly stated: "The Colored Alliance was made up of landless people who picked cotton for white farmers."[65] But small white landholding farmers were the core of the white Alliance, and their primary interest was in gaining greater prices for their *product*. Most Alliance blacks, in turn, were cotton pickers who wanted higher *wages* for their *labor*. When such black Alliance efforts as the proposed cotton picker strike of 1891 came into direct conflict with their white Alliance mentors, the results were less than satisfactory. Strains emerged in the producer class that prevented the necessary agrarian coalition.[66]

Though in theory the Colored Alliances were nonpolitical and nonpartisan, the presence of such a large organized body of potential black voters, with proper manipulation of the all-important race issue, conjured up the Reconstruction specter of black Republicanism and the lingering, paranoid fear of a Republican political coup. By 1890–1891, when many orders had flirted with or participated in politics—or been accused of it—the Bourbons began to subject the Alliance to an intense "ghost dance . . . of 'Negro supremacy.'"[67] By the fall of 1890, an election year in many states, a Virginia Allianceman remarked that "the great gun of white supremacy has been loaded and primed and trained upon our ranks."[68] Race and class coalition interests subjected the Colored Alliance to debilitating forces.

The Bourbons hoped—futilely, as it later developed—that this appeal to poor white agrarian prejudice, always just under the surface, would stem the rising tide of political rebellion in the Alliance ranks. If, as a result of these tirades, the conservative Bourbons could heal the split in white ranks and isolate blacks, a class combination of considerable weight could be removed from the political landscape. Furthermore, a special fear for the Bourbons was that blacks would become the balance of power between two competing blocs of whites. The racial prejudices of the poor whites were courted vigorously in an effort to divest them of any thought of organizing around any ideology except white supremacy. Race was expected to be a stronger deterrent than any proposed class coalition based on economics.

While most grassroots white Alliance members probably at bottom concurred with the hostile racial philosophy of the Bourbons, this was of lesser importance than the fact that the racial and political proposals the Bourbons espoused had come to be an accepted norm of regional conformity. When constructive agitation emanated from the Alliance, especially the black orders, these reforms were often regarded as a political tactic to revive black Republicanism. It was a tactic that had long held sway over the minds of white Southerners and served to keep the Alliance off balance. Denial was not sufficient in itself to prevent repeated frustration. For blacks to become involved in or even merely accused of using political means to achieve their goals usually resulted in internecine strife—at the expense of the Colored Farmers' Alliance in this case. The race issue and related use of inflammatory issues such as the Republican-sponsored Lodge "Force" Bill, a federal proposal to supervise Southern elections, constantly kept both the Colored and white Alliance and the later Populist Party off balance, forcing the agrarians to constantly take a defensive political posture or campaign rather than focusing laserlike on the economic problems which beset black and white farmers alike.

Financial dependence was also a determining factor that militated against the possibility of the Colored Farmers' Alliance's establishing a firm independent policy of self-help. While some state exchanges, notably that in Texas, did achieve a marked degree of financial stability, most, like that in Tennessee, found themselves heavily dependent upon the financial goodwill of the white Alliance. Black initiatives had to be subordinated to white Alliance wishes due to the economic vulnerability of black Alliance members. If the white orders failed to take an active interest in their black brethren, the Colored Farmers' Alliance orders were apt to founder. It should be noted here, however, that the white Alliance leadership, regarding the blacks as "an infant race just growing into manhood," expressed a marked degree of paternalism and *noblesse oblige* for the Colored Alliances.[69] Class- or self-interest, as we have seen, also forced the white rank-and-file to consider rendering aid to the black orders. All elements, despite the diversity of their racial philosophy, had the same stated end in mind: the uplifting of the farmer class through self-help, economic development, and racial organization.

Since blacks as a group were financially destitute and unable to support or establish large separate co-ops or exchanges, it appears that many members of local orders understandably rendered only token financial assistance to their clubs. When wages were fifty to sixty cents a day and exchange dues were two dollars, the daily basics of life had to take precedence. But the appeal of spending meager resources on ceremony and circumstances by some Colored Alliance members resulted in a paternal scolding by the national office in Houston. The *National Alliance,* the official newspaper of the CFA under Humphrey's editorship, counseled the black orders to stop "buying [Alliance] badges and regalia and all that kind of thing" and pay up their dues and subscribe to the paper to keep themselves better informed. While emphasizing the fact that "the [Colored] Alliance was organized to do you good," it was rather sharply pointed out that this had to be a reciprocal process.[70] While the extent of such profligate ceremonial practices is not known, the financial straits of the Colored Farmers' Alliance orders were such that the neglect of only a small parcel of the membership would create financial havoc in any local chapter. Securing capital from a debtor member was always tenuous and provided an unstable cash flow for the organization and seriously undercut its stability.

When viewed with an objective eye, the purported strength of the Colored Farmers' Alliance appears to have been greatly exaggerated. While faulty membership tabulations on the local level and misquoted press releases could have been added to the advertised total, the Colored Alliance administration must take the blame as the chief perpetrator of these claims. Why lie about membership size? Past sizable organizations of blacks had created hostility from the Bourbons. Yet the claims of a large membership could provide influence not proffered to a less expansive organization. Perhaps the temptation proved irresistible, for a pattern of exaggerating membership numbers seems evident. In August 1891, it was reported that "over

2,000 sub-Alliance charters have been issued for Colored Alliances since the Ocala convention [of December 1890]."[71] In June of the same year (1891), the National Alliance reported that "more than 1,600 voters join the Colored Alliance every day that the sun rises.[72] If this astonishing rate of growth had continued for as long as a year, it would have produced approximately 595,000 new "voters"—a sign of potent growth, indeed, if true. If Humphrey authorized these figures—and we must assume he did, as a result of his position—he probably made no personal gain as a result. While such prevarications are "unusual" for a Baptist minister, his only intentions were probably to gain influence and attract prospective members, all in hopes of furthering the order.

Equally as perplexing a problem is the difficulty of ascertaining the aggregate strength and geographic distribution of the Colored Alliance. An 1891 membership analysis by the general superintendent revealed the following breakdown: 300,000 females, 150,000 males under twenty-one years of age, and 750,000 adult males, out of a total membership of nearly 1.2 million "in more than twenty states."[73] However, Colored Alliance president J. S. Jackson reported that the order represented only twelve states but had a membership of 2 million black farmers in December 1890[74]—800,000 more than Humphrey would report nearly a year later (see Table 1 in the Appendixes). The picture is further confused when the *Progressive Farmer,* quoting Humphrey from an interview, credited the organization with a membership of 1.2 million representing thirty states rather than twelve as reported by Jackson. Ironically, these last two statements were made within two weeks of each other! Exact figures will probably never be known, as local chapters apparently did not keep accurate memberships logs.

The discrepancies among these statements points out rather clearly that the true size of the order was probably unknown, even among its own officers. Moreover, in their eagerness to display an impressive total, the officers probably exaggerated their membership claims with the intent of currying political and economic favor. It is highly doubtful that a member, once accepted by the order, was ever dropped from the roll whether his membership was in good standing or not. As previously noted, the dereliction of some members in paying their dues probably detracted from the whole but with no obvious difference being indicated by the officials.[75]

Near the end of 1891, rapid deterioration was evident in the Colored Farmers' Alliance's size and effectiveness. One student has indicated that the order "collapsed about the end of 1891."[76] This viewpoint is further substantiated by a black paper, *The Republican,* which made the comment in January of 1892 that the Colored Alliance went "up like a rocket and down like a stick, a mere pull, a fizzle and she is gone."[77] The Deep South states

TABLE 1

Colored Alliance Membership, 1890

State	Membership		Discrepancy Score
	July 1890	December 1890	
Alabama	75,000	100,000	+25,000
Arkansas	100,000	20,000	-80,000
Florida	20,000	★	★
Georgia	100,000	84,000	-16,000
Louisiana	20,000	50,000	+30,000
Mississippi	60,000	90,000	+30,000
North Carolina	100,000	55,000	-45,000
South Carolina	50,000	90,000	+40,000
Tennessee	100,000	60,000	-40,000
Texas	150,000	90,000	-60,000
Virginia	50,000	50,000	0
Totals	825,000[a]	689,000[b]	-116,000

Source:

[a] *Appleton's Annual Cyclopedia,* 1890, 301.

[b] *Progressive Farmer,* December 23, 1890; *Western Rural,* December 13, 1890, in Saloutos, *Farmer Movements,* 81; *Atlanta Constitution,* December 4, 1890, in Jack Abramowitz, "Accommodation and Militancy in Negro Life, 1876–1916" (Ph.D. diss., Columbia University, 1950), 30.

of Alabama, Louisiana, and Mississippi ostensibly continued their growth, but most other states experienced a rapid collapse in membership, with the home state of Texas reportedly losing sixty thousand members in six months (see Table 1). While the order lingered through 1892, it never again possessed its former degree of importance. After 1892, the Colored Alliance was but a shadow of its former self in both strength and importance.

Although the evidence is sketchy, it appears the Texas branch of the Colored Alliance was still active and viable in the spring of 1892. Alex Asberry, a black Republican legislator in the 1889 Twenty-first Texas Legislature, was ostensibly elected state president of the Texas Colored Farmers' Alliance in early 1892. A newspaper, the *Alliance Vindicator,* was initiated by the Colored Alliance in February 1892, in Calvert, Texas, and edited by Asberry.[78] Robertson County, the home of this activity, was a longtime base for agrarian and other aberrant political sentiments. The Greenback campaigns of the 1880s were strong there, as were the Colored Farmers' Alliance and the Populist Party.[79] Blacks and whites had long achieved an unusual degree of solidarity and a history of working together there on issues of common interest. But even in Robertson County the Colored Farmers' Alliance went into rapid decline and disappeared by the end of 1892. Its seems likely that the Texas Colored Alliance, particularly in this area, was absorbed by the Populist Party. Calvert, Texas, was the home of the preeminent black Populist leader John B. Rayner.[80] Also, the Farmers' Improvement Society, founded in 1890 by Robert Smith, was a growing black self-help organization in Texas and probably siphoned off members from the declining Colored Farmers' Alliance since the two groups shared similar philosophies of black solidarity, self sufficiency, efficiency, cooperating, and teaching moral uplift.[81] This was not an unusual pattern in the post-Reconstruction South, for when one self-help organization formed a working partnership with blacks, or served as an organization of black self-improvement, as soon as the organization deteriorated, another would surface and preserve some on-going voice for blacks.

A combination of factors brought about the downfall of the National Colored Farmers' Alliance. Internal dissension created a certain amount of disunity. As of late 1889, two Colored Alliances were in existence, both competing for the support of the black farmer. Although evidence is sketchy at best, it appears the two groups differed over major issues, such as supporting the South-wide cotton picker's strike and whether to support a third party. Other minor differences existed in the orders, not only in their rituals but in their methods as well. Antagonism between the two groups became so pronounced that it was reported to have "divided our churches, broken up our schools, embittered our communities and created discord in our families."[82]

In early 1890, the two orders decided to compromise. In the discussions that followed, R. M. Humphrey represented the chartered group and Andrew J. Carothers the rebel group. Out of this conference, the proclamation of a merger between the two orders was announced. It was also decided that the national headquarters would remain at Houston County and the official name of the order would be retained as the Colored Farmers' National Alliance and Cooperative Union. February 22, 1890, was set aside as "a day of thanks and prayer" for the merger to be cemented in friendship. Alliance stores and exchanges were also urged to enter into the festivities on this special day of reconciliation. Differences continued beyond these formal arrangements. Carothers, for example, opposed the cotton pickers strike of 1891, which Humphrey supported.[83]

No sooner had this dispute been settled than another schism occurred in the South Carolina Colored Alliance in 1890. Under the leadership of W. J. Grant of Charleston, an independent state group was organized.[84] While little is known about the results of this schism, it appears that it proved to be an abortive effort with few practical accomplishments. It is probable that the South Carolina renegade order, as with Texas, nursed its wounds and returned to the fold. The Virginia Colored Alliance also had rifts within the membership that weakened the organization.[85]

At a time when black solidarity was called for in the agrarian campaign, it is painfully evident that personal grievances, psychological disunity and competing orders created a degree of estrangement within the black agrarian movement. Such divisions of loyalty further served to change the complexion of strained Alliance finances. These small divisions of loyalty and competing groups were important, for they included enterprising black leaders and members who were not afraid to take the initiative. Such a dissident group comprised a significant minority in this as well as any other movement. Divisions between small landowning blacks and black tenant farmers may also have created strains. Like white landowners, black landowners had different interests from the great mass of black landless tenants, the bulk of Alliance members, who lived from hand-to-mouth and whose interest in increased wages conflicted with landed blacks who used their labor.

By the latter part of the nineteenth century, Southern blacks had started to divide into three main social classes. The "highest class" was "composed of farmers, teachers, grocers, and artisans who own their own homes . . . the majority of them can read and write." W. E. B. Du Bois observed that "the careless observer" failed to notice that a class system had developed among blacks since the Civil War, and that the interests of all blacks were not the same. Indeed, landowning black farmers were in the top social class, according to Du Bois.[86] In Virginia during the 1880s, seventeen of the state's black legislators were farmers, representing the single largest occupation among black legislators.[87] In Texas, the same pattern prevailed, with nineteen of forty-six black legislative leaders during the 1870–1890 period listing their occupation as "farmer."[88]

Dire economic circumstances of tenant members and the potential of the order attracted a large segment of the early membership. When cotton cost more to produce than it sold for, small black landowners logically wanted more for their product. In contrast, the debt-laden tenant farmer who picked this cotton sought higher wages—a situation that created a conflict of interests, a sort of agrarian "capitalist" vs. "labor" division in micro-

TABLE 2
Black Farm Ownership, Tenancy
1900

State	Black Population, 1890	No. Farms of Black Farm Owners	No. Farms of Black Part Owners of Farm	No. Farms of Black Owners and Tenants	No. Farms of Black Farm Managers	No. Farms of Black Cash Tenants	No. Farms of Black Share Tenants
ALABAMA	678,489	11,123	2,871	116	72	56,212	23,689
ARKANSAS	309,117	9,991	1,775	175	80	15,842	19,120
FLORIDA	166,180	5,607	851	94	93	5,497	1,384
GEORGIA	858,815	9,547	1,762	66	208	34,728	36,515
KANSAS	49,710	735	371	13	17	229	501
KENTUCKY	268,071	4,240	1,080	8	63	789	4,984
LOUISIANA	559,193	8,460	875	43	79	21,201	27,502
MISSISSIPPI	742,559	18,368	2,459	146	107	57,194	50,405
MISSOURI	150,184	1,901	707	52	37	831	1,425
NORTH CAROLINA	561,018	13,204	4,320	86	121	10,331	26,892

Continued on the next page

TABLE 2 Continued

SOUTH CAROLINA	688,934	15,503	3,376	91	180	42,434	23,817
TENNESSEE	430,678	7,602	1,690	134	82	10,909	13,478
TEXAS	488,171	17,125	2,898	116	91	8,440	36,866
VIRGINIA	635,438	22,809	3,623	134	238	6,891	11,139
WEST VIRGINIA	32,690	477	54	3	8	68	132
TOTAL	6,619,247	146,692	28,712	1,277	1,476	271,596	277,849

Source: STATE LEVEL CENSUS DATA, 1890 and 1900 [Computer file]. ICPSR Study 00003: Historical, Economic, and Social Data: U.S., 1790-1970. Ann Arbor, MI: University of Michigan, Center for Political Studies [producer], 2002. Ann Arbor, MI: Inter-University Consortium for Political and Social Research. [distributor], 2002.

cosm. The producer-class coalition concept seemed attractive ideologically, but in practice the strains of ownership and labor proved divisive. The black leadership of the Texas and Virginia Colored Alliances, for example, were largely small landowners, well-educated for their age and region, while their members were largely uneducated tenants, again a situation that ultimately led to a conflict of interests and goals.[89]

Accordingly, the order was forced to dedicate itself to a great extent to a philosophy of uplifting the small black landowning farmer and the tenant laborer. Behind such a commitment lay a heritage of nearly three centuries of prejudice and poverty, as well as the conflict between labor and capital, which worked against the achievement of such a program of self-interest. Once the organization dedicated itself to such a goal, however, it was forced to produce some tangible results, or obviously it could not long exist. When any institution fails to achieve its expressed mandate, it tends to lose viability. The Colored Farmers' Alliance officials recognized this fact, and their efforts during these years were directed toward achieving some tangible part of this philosophy.[90]

If the white farmer felt the pinch of declining prices, blacks experienced it even more. A slow process of economic erosion and increased indebtedness had mitigated against the possibility of the black tenant farmer developing an adequate financial margin by the 1890s.[91] The presence of the few landed black farmers who did command a comparative degree of prosperity only served to distress the average black tenant farmer. In the spring of 1890, the *National Alliance* noted that many of "our wives are barefoot, our children naked and our home[s] mere hovel[s]."[92] In South Carolina, a hostile critic sympathetically reported that "I have not seen an all wool blanket among them in years. Their clothing is mostly of thin cheap material, especially the women, and children."[93] Testifying before the Senate Committee on Agriculture and Forestry, Humphrey, who had traveled widely among the black communities of the South, noted that "the great majority of the colored farmers of the South . . . and their women spend the season in cotton fields, with a single thin garment, without shoes, and they live upon the coarsest, commonest food."[94] "The Negro and his descendants remain pretty much in the places where they lived when the war closed," a reporter who had traveled 3,500 miles across the South in 1891 concluded. "His wages do not average over fifty or sixty cents a day." "In the Black Belt," he added, "the typical home is a rude log cabin, without windows, and with one door and a stick chimney. The door is usually kept open during the day, in fair weather, to admit light, which at night is furnished by a pine knot. Into such cabins a whole family is frequently crowded." He had "heard of twenty-five persons living in three rooms."[95] In five sugar cane–growing counties of Southern Louisiana in the late 1880s, wages for "husky men ranged from fifty to sixty cents a day lasting from the first gray of dawn to pitch dark." These wages included "five pounds of salt shoulder meat and a pack of cornmeal a week." For "girl or women hoe-hands" the wages were twenty-five to forty cents for the same workday.[96] One Texas newspaper estimated in 1889 that the average black tenant farmer there produced four bales of cotton and two hundred bushels of corn per year. After paying rent and expenses, he made $34 for his cotton and $75 for the corn, or less than $10 a month to live on.[97] In South Carolina the state commissioner of agriculture reported in 1885 that the average wage for a male laborer was 45 cents a day, $8.72 a month, and $90.75 per year with board. In 1891 wages for picking cotton were 30 to 40 cents per hundred pounds.[98] In Arkansas, cotton that had sold for 15 cents a pound in 1870–1873 had by 1894 dropped to 6 cents.[99] By the early 1890s cotton prices had deteriorated to such low levels that even the most efficient farmers could not raise crops at a profit. In essence, the black tenant farmer had his financial back to the wall, and under such arduous circumstances the Colored Alliance membership understandably looked to the organization to provide them with some immediate measure of relief. It had nourished an agrarian philosophy of black self-help and racial self-reliance through economics, but the translation of the rhetoric into reality would require a stronger, more united protest effort than had previously occurred. And the need for immediate relief put pressures on the national and state Colored Alliances to take an immediate unpopular course of action.

There soon occurred an event of such crucial importance that the National Colored Farmers' Alliance could ill afford not to become involved. In the fall of 1891, a number of merchants and planters, notably in the Memphis and Charleston area, agreed to combine themselves into a series of organizations for the purpose of wage and price control. The erosion in cotton prices had put pressure on the merchants and planters as well as the tenant farmers. The ulterior motive behind the formation of these organizations was the further reduction of the wages paid to the cotton pickers of the South.[100] Such a price-fixing measure would increase their profits at the expense of the lower paid, largely black, agricultural workers' wages. Since blacks were predominantly engaged in agrarian pursuits as hired hands, they would be among those hardest hit by the scheme. "Our muscle is our stock in trade," Humphrey said of the Colored Alliance membership, "and . . . labor is the basis of all [our] wealth."[101]

Coming at a time when many black farmers were already living at a subsistence level, any reductions of the prevailing wage scale, however diminutive, would push black agrarians farther down the economic scale of second-class citizenship.[102] As desperate members doubtless expressed their vehement complaints to the state and national chapters, the Colored Alliance was faced with the realization that it must decide on a course of action. If the order failed to aid the black cotton pickers, many of whom were probably members, there could be little doubt about waning interest and membership. Why remain a member of an organization if it is unable to meet your needs? Furthermore, if it became involved in a dispute with the economically powerful white merchant-planter class, it also stood to lose. And since the white Alliance was largely composed of small land-owning farmers who used black tenant labor, wage increases would not be popular with them. The options seemed particularly unattractive whichever course of action the National Colored Alliance chose.

There were several precedents for black agrarian protest in the 1880s.[103] Significantly, their espousal also had almost always been associated with a program demanding higher wages and better working conditions, deriving their inspiration from black self-help, racial solidarity, and in many cases the sympathetic assistance of the Knights of Labor. After 1886 the Knights, admittedly in eclipse, made a major effort toward forging a working alliance with the agrarians, both as a matter of sympathy and because of the need for membership. Thus the black agrarian tendency toward self-help, determination and protest had been exacerbated and made more aggressive by contact with the Knights.[104] It seemed logical that a series of actions would soon occur, given these economic conditions and prior efforts, despite their failure.

A local Colored Farmers' Alliance effort to redress agrarian grievances through self-help and racial solidarity had occurred in Leflore County, Mississippi, during the fall of 1889. The attempt by a black to organize a Colored Farmers' Alliance store and boycott local white merchants who were charging unfair prices aroused considerable ire from whites, who threatened violence and retaliation. As a result of the black's efforts, approximately four hundred Colored Alliance members armed themselves in defense, but the arrival of white national guardsmen reinforced by a local posse overwhelmed them.[105]

The vitality of black agrarian protest was clearly demonstrated by a series of such minor efforts. But it is significant that these efforts were almost always violent, unsuccessful, and never widespread—features that were probably not lost on the National Colored Alliance leadership in seeking a region-wide solution to their members' economic problems. Also, the South, more than any other section, had strongly resisted unionization and strikes. Racism and the conservative temper of the region did not combine to create a hospitable environment for such actions.

After some slight hesitation, the National Colored Alliance decided to support the cotton pickers and proceeded with plans to organize a general South-wide strike on a scale unprecedented in the annals of black history. The chances of success for such a strike were not as remote as they first appeared. Even at this late stage of its development, the order still allegedly had approximately 1 million members; in addition, the crop involved was to some extent a perishable commodity that had to be harvested within a reasonable time. The basic problem, therefore, appeared to be one of success-fully holding out until negotiations were made. But the ability of landless, debt-laden black tenants to hold out for any appreciable period of time was very limited. Resources to sustain themselves during a strike were practi-cally nonexistent, and most of the land and the power were in the hands of the white merchant and Bourbon class. "It is pretty clear," Woodward has concluded, "that as a rule the Negro farmer not only worked the white man's land but worked it with a white man's plow drawn by a white man's mule."[106] Such conditions left the black farmer with little opportunity to express his viewpoint and initiative, or improve his lot by withholding his labor.

The strike plans of the order were clandestine; not even the white Alli-ance was taken into confidence, which suggests a certain lack of solidarity between the two groups despite their purported commonalities of interest. The Texas order first formulated the plan of attack. With September 20, 1891, set as its target strike date, the Texas order agreed not to pick cotton for less than one dollar per hundred pounds plus board. Circulars were then mailed out from the National Headquarters to every sub-Alliance in the South informing them of the proposed strike, what methods were to be employed, and the target date.[107]

The plan, however, appears to have suffered an immediate setback for two major reasons: blacks failed to strike in sufficient numbers, and the tar-get date was not properly synchronized. The Georgia Colored Farmers' Al-liance leadership, with a contingent of landowners, felt the strike would hurt black farmers who owned or rented their land and, as a result, refused to support the strike. Again, interests were at odds within the Alliance, and opposition to the strike surfaced early among black and white Alliance members. Further, black tenants were so vulnerable, being almost totally dependent upon white landowners, that they proved powerless to resist evic-tion or economic strangulation. A minor strike was reported in the area of Florence and Orangeburg, South Carolina, for example, as early as Septem-ber 10, ten days before the Texas strike date.[108] While minor strikes also occurred in areas of Arkansas and South Carolina, a general strike never occurred.[109] The varied maturity dates of cotton throughout the critical area probably explains in great part why the overall strike date was not more closely coordinated. In Arkansas, the strike was forcefully crushed, ending in the death of fifteen strikers, among whom several were lynched.[110] Like other efforts before them, the strike was very circumscribed and hardly disrupted any stranglehold on starvation wages paid to black tenants. By September 26, 1891, the *National Economist* noted that "one thing seems certain, *if a [general] strike was ordered,* it has proven a failure as it certainly deserved to be."[111] Limited funds on the part of the black community and imminent economic coercion on the part of the powerful white merchant-planter class probably contributed to a last minute collapse or withdrawal of the proposed strike.[112] Furthermore, as we shall see below, the white Alliance strongly opposed the strike. The interest of the producer class was in conflict and the coalition was in danger of fracturing.

An independent daily, the *New York Herald,* viewing the whole situation somewhat humorously, remarked,

> This is not what the [white] Alliance expected when it kindly consented to receive colored men as members. A black man's vote being as good as another, when it is counted, it was thought well to secure as many colored votes as possible to take part in the grand strike against capital. But the colored man struck for himself. Who says he never learns anything?[113]

In a bit of ultimate irony, those orchestrating "the grand strike against capital" were now experiencing an attempted strike themselves! The black tenants and white Alliance members did learn something from this truncated effort. Despite Alliance rhetoric about the producer-class coalition, this venture provided a painful lesson about differences within the agrarian movement. Agrarian pursuits among both races harbored different interests, which surfaced when tensions arose from such events. This pattern would repeat itself when other such issues surfaced.

The strike was no laughing matter to Leonidas L. Polk, president of the white Southern Alliance since 1889. He soundly condemned the plan as an attempt by one agricultural group to advance itself at the expense of the whole farmer movement.[114] Coming under attack by the press as favoring the strike in his actions and speeches, Polk acidly replied in the negative, stating that he knew nothing about the matter except what he read in the newspapers. Certainly he did not support the strike. Furthermore, he advised the white farmers to let their crops stand in the field "rather than pay over fifty cents per hundred pounds to have it picked."[115] If blacks and the Colored Farmers' Alliance had any doubts about the lack of agrarian solidarity, the reaction of Polk and the white Alliance members, many of whom were small landowners, must have erased all such concerns.

When all is said and done, the Colored Farmers' Alliance experienced only failure and public disfavor out of this venture. Foremost, the strike had discredited the Colored Alliance and Humphrey in the eyes of the white Alliance, a necessary ally in the broader agrarian struggle. When these results are added to internal dissension between landed and landless, competing organizations, growing political distrust on the part of the powerful Bourbons, growing disappointment and disaffection on the part of the black community toward its program, survival of the order was hardly expected. It seems probable that the last vestiges of the black order were ultimately absorbed into the Populist movement, or local groups with similar aims, such as the Farmers' Improvement Society and the Village Improvement Society in Texas.[116] Some blacks, like their white counterparts, were coming to realize that independent political action was a necessity to achieve their goals. As blacks grew disillusioned with the Colored Farmers' Alliance program of self-help, the consideration of third-party politics as a more viable alternate solution was slowly developing within the inner councils of the Alliance conventions. Central to understanding this slow shift is an examination of the agrarian's search for economic solace through independent political means.

There is little that one can find encouraging in the Colored Farmers' Alliance story, for it is at bottom mostly a story of race, class, and interest conflict (landed vs. landless, black vs. white), organizational failure, and the demoralizing and demeaning effect of repeated promises coming face to face with the distorting power of racism. It is also instructive to question to what degree white Colored Farmers' Alliance leaders actually reflected and represented black interests. In Virginia, and in several cases involving Humphrey, as we shall see, white and black interests sometimes clashed, often to the detriment of blacks. Yet the Colored Alliance's story is instructive because it reminds us that cherished ideals about biracial reform can be compromised rather harshly on the altar of immediate personal need, racial differences and economic self-interest. The Alliance's biracial economic experiment that foundered on the rocks of racism would serve as a role model for the later Populist state and political coalitions that centered around "self-interest;" and the same entrenched differences of race and class would now confront the newly emerging Populist movement. The Alliance view was largely that "like interest," and therefore "self-interest," would rule. Tom Watson articulated this same failed philosophy of "self-interest" for the later Populist biracial experiment.[117]

2

The Search for Policy

The Roots of Racial Conflict

Colored organizations shall prohibit the admission of white men.

It was only natural that the Alliance and the Populist Party, peopled by reformers with their own agendas and prejudices, would be incapable of presenting a unified front against the monolithic merchant-planter-industrialist class. In the South, interracial contact and policy formulation by Alliance leaders increased tension during the movement's political conversion phase. This chapter will demonstrate how the combined forces of violence, party realignment, coalition building, and the absence of a cohesive racial policy undermined the emerging party's effectiveness.

The South in the 1890s witnessed a spurt of racial violence, including an increase in so-called "spectacle lynchings," which coincided with the founding of the Populist Party. Spectacle lynchings often involved ten to fifteen thousand people, with men, women, and children observing what often became a community event. Photographers and reporters would cover the incident.[1] Lynching in the nineties not only took a sharp numerical increase, averaging two hundred victims annually, but added a public viciousness and ritual behavior that included victims being burned alive or mutilated, and even the saving of body parts as grisly souvenirs. Dray refers to such gruesome behavior as "a form of tribal sacrifice," manifested as "an expression of the community's will."[2] A stark but not isolated example of a spectacle lynching was the February 1893 lynching of Henry Smith, a retarded seventeen-year-old black youth, in the rural, poverty-stricken community of Paris, Texas, before fourteen thousand people. The black anti-lynching crusader Ida B. Wells described the Paris lynching in her autobiography:

The [news] dispatchers tell in detail how he had been tortured with red-hot irons searing his flesh for hours before finally the flames were lit and put an end to his agony. They also tell how the mob fought over the hot ashes for bones, buttons, and teeth for souvenirs.[3]

On February 18, 1892, nearby Texarkana citizens roasted a black man named Edward Coy before a crowd of fifteen thousand people. Other examples are prevalent during this period.[4] As cotton prices declined and political turmoil increased with the advent of the Populist Party, the volume and brutality of lynching incidents also rose.[5]

Charles Johnson, a chronicler of this phenomenon, described the effect lynchings had on the black community:

> During and shortly after a lynching the Negro community lives in terror. Negroes remain at home and out of sight. When the white community quiets down, the Negroes go back to their usual occupations. The incident is not forgotten, but the routine of the plantation goes on. The lynching, in fact, is part of the routine. . . . The effect on the children is profound and permanent. After a time the Negro community returns to "normal." Life goes on, but Negro youth "let white folks tend to their business." Contacts with whites are avoided as far as possible. The youth may work for white people, but intimacy is avoided. The Negro servant or laborer continues friendly to his employer. The employer may even be liked and regarded as "good white folks," but ultimate trust is held in abeyance.[6]

Since lynching was a rural phenomenon, occurring in poor districts such as those frequented by the Alliance and Populist Party, poor landless blacks should be receptive to a new party that could offer the security not offered by the dominant Democratic Party.[7] The safest course of action for rural blacks was to support groups that could effectuate protection.[8] However, some blacks abandoned politics as a solution, seeking salvation instead through economic progress, which they believed would reduce racial prejudice.

At this stage, the Alliance was vulnerable to dissolution, not only by newly politicized blacks but by poor and/or liberal Southern whites as well. Regional upheaval could debilitate the movement or, conversely, provide fertile soil for the germination of a third-party reform movement. Any analysis of the Alliance movement, therefore, must consider the conflicts of interest and emerging coalitions exemplified during the order's conventions. The shift of blacks toward Populism was nurtured during this period, despite a tendency toward group separatism and remnant loyalty to the Republican Party.

The deteriorating position of blacks within the Republican Party is worth observing on the eve of the founding of the Populist Party.[9] "At present," Booker T. Washington noted in 1885, "the Democratic Party is composed almost entirely of whites and the Republican Party almost entirely of blacks—it is one race against the other."[10] Blacks as a group were still wedded to the Republican Party in the late eighties, particularly at the national level, but some attraction to other parties was occurring at the local level. Overall, however, blacks were Republicans and whites were Democrats. But the National Republican Party had virtually abandoned black people by 1891, except when it needed votes.[11]

Seeking respectability in the South, Republicans saw blacks as a deterrent to attracting more native white Southerners to the party. Native whites had always been a minority in the Republican Party in the postbellum South, while blacks were the majority. But now, black voting power was threatened as purification of the ballot and disfranchisement became rising themes. If blacks were eliminated as voters, the regional Republican Party would have to attract native whites to survive. A coalition with blacks was not only becoming an unpopular stance but an impractical one as well. Blacks were becoming a liability for the regional Republican Party, but their votes were still coveted by all parties. Nationally, coalition with Northern capitalist business elements gained prominence with Republican leaders. Joseph P. Wilson, speaking before a black convention in Richmond, captured their political plight: "The Republican Party does not know what to do with us and the Democratic Party wants to get rid of us, and we are [now] at sea without sail or anchor drifting with the tide."[12] As blacks struggled to come to terms with these events, a certain element still searched for a political vehicle that would provide solace.

T. Thomas Fortune, the leading black journalist of his day, claimed that "none of them cares a fig for the Afro-American" and suggested that "another party may rise to finish the uncompleted work" of Liberation.[13] Republican repudiation, worsening economic conditions, and rising violence hastened some black interest in the incipient Populist Party as an alternative.[14] While many blacks, primarily in the urban middle class, looked toward wealth accumulation, frugal virtues, and character development, others maintained that meaningful participation in politics was essential to alleviate the evils of the day. Populism eagerly offered to be that vehicle, since attracting black and white votes from both parties would be necessary to win elections.

As the Alliance grew, the question surfaced about the need for a centralized third party to battle the Democratic Party, which was unresponsive to reform platforms, despite promises to the contrary. The two regional Alliance orders met in St. Louis in December 1889 to discuss the possibility of consolidating the Northern and the more fractured and radical Southern Alliance movement. At this meeting, according to one observer, delegates from twenty-eight states represented over two million black and white constituents, "all acknowledging the same evils to exist and seeing the necessity for the same remedy." With "shoulder touching shoulder as brothers," they proceeded to discuss the knotty problems of unification.[15] But at this stage, the idea of a third party was still largely anathema. Charles W. Macune, the first white Southern Alliance president, who was succeeded in 1889 by North Carolinian Leonidas L. Polk, continued to express his opposition to a third party, as did Polk. Like many white agrarians, Macune had long preferred to work within the Democratic Party,[16] and his influence proved an effective barrier against others wishing to cast their lot with a third party.

Although agrarians of both regions called for planting "the white rose of peace on the grave of sectionalism," at St. Louis mutual policy agreement proved difficult.[17] Three major sectional controversies surrounded the question of consolidating the two orders: the name of the proposed order, the exclusion of blacks as members by the Southern Alliance, and the Southern policy of maintaining strict membership secrecy. Before the St. Louis meeting, the Southern Alliance had changed its name to the Farmers' and Laborers' Union and subsequently elected new officers and drew up a new constitution. The Northern Alliance objected to the new name and suggested instead the National Farmers' Alliance and Industrial Union, "possibly to satisfy the Wheel or to offer a bait to the forces of labor."[18] The problem of nomenclature was readily solved, and the Southern Alliance incorporated the new name into the constitution. Because it "was a condition thought necessary by the brethren from the Northwest," the Southern Alliance was also willing, under duress, to remove the word "white" as a membership qualification, leaving to each state any decision about the eligibility of blacks as members. However, only whites would be allowed to serve on the powerful Supreme Council, the legislative body of the National Alliance. As a final concession, the Southern Alliance acquiesced to the proposal that blacks be allowed even into the sacred Supreme Council if it would help facilitate consolidation.[19]

A more formidable obstacle than race to the Southern Alliance was membership secrecy. On this point the South remained adamant. Both the Southern Alliance and the Colored Farmers' Alliance had been founded as secret organizations. Without secrecy the Southerners felt that they would be infiltrated by hostile elements and be unable to attain their goals. Experience indicated that infiltration by unfriendly elements such as lawyers and merchants had been prevented through limiting access and maintaining membership secrecy. "Attend one of our county conventions," a York County, South Carolina, Alliance leader maintained, "and you will see the whole affair manipulated by a mere handful, they mostly merchants and lawyers, who are well alert for their own interests, and are well-tickled at how easily they have made dupes of us."[20] By monitoring the membership and carefully limiting application to the farmers' "natural allies," the Southern Alliance had a more protective hold on its membership than the Northern Alliance. Almost anyone in any profession could claim to be a "farmer," but their interests could be antithetical to the farmer. Strong membership limits were a necessary component for the organization to survive and remain focused. All further attempts at concession ended in stalemate at the 1889 St. Louis meeting, the question of secrecy being "the sole cause."[21] Interestingly, whites were more adamant about secrecy than racial integration.

Representatives of the National Colored Farmers' Alliance from Tennessee, Florida, Texas, Alabama, Mississippi, North and South Carolina, Kentucky, and the Indian Territory were in session at St. Louis in 1889 at the same time as the two white Alliances. Committees were exchanged with various white organizations as a gesture of friendship. The Colored Alliance was "extremely delighted" with its white visitors, regarding them in Colored Alliance Superintendent Humphrey's words as "ministers of light and salvation" to the black race.[22] St. Louis leaders pointed out the possible contributions of biracial cooperation, despite the continued emphasis on separatism and segregation as a solution to the race problem. Humphrey espoused a program of economic cooperation between the two groups as he spoke before the white bodies. Blacks, he noted, did not deny that a large percentage of the goods bought and raised by the two races were in common and, as stated at the Meridian meeting in 1888, there should be race cooperation as "mutual interests may demand."[23] The threat of self-interest always loomed as a reminder to both races that they could not achieve a program of agrarian reform separately. A further indication of biracial cooperation was the offer by Milton George, editor of the *Western Rural,* to do all the necessary printing for the Colored Farmers' Alliance at no cost.[24] However, this emphasis on economic reform and class cooperation did not diminish several efforts toward racial separatism and at St. Louis in 1889.

The old shibboleths of race, party loyalty, and sectionalism, as well as the Southern disposition for secrecy, precluded further consolidation of agrarian interests at this time. Of all these reasons, it seems strange that secrecy rather than racism was the greatest obstacle, and the Southern delegates were the most intransigent on this point. On the other hand, according to Woodward, "the old bloody-shirt feeling was more prevalent among the Northern delegates than among the Southern."[25]

If sectionalism was more prominent in the North, certain observers believed they saw its decline in the South. It was now some twenty-four years after the Civil War's end, and a new generation who had not personally experienced the hostilities was now on the scene. In the black community, a new generation who had not personally experienced slavery was also now present. "Hostility to the Northern people has almost disappeared," Lord Bryce commented of the white Southern climate.[26] Less optimistic but still hopeful, Macune more correctly prophesied that sectionalism would continue but added that it would "assume a different form from that which has so long afflicted the [Southern] people, and have another purpose." In varying degrees, these predictions were both true, but dissatisfaction with existing conditions was not yet sufficient for the races to bolt the established parties and would force Southern agrarians to adopt a conciliatory tone. Furthermore, the Southern Alliance's larger membership (some three million alleged members) gave it a controlling position in the Alliance's decision over a third party—which it now opposed.[27] The failure of the white orders to unite negated the first steps toward organizational integration of the two regions in their fight for common agrarian ends.

Black agrarians took matters into their own hands to improve their lot. The Georgia Colored Farmers' Alliance implemented a plan to establish a black land investment company. This land investment plan was put into action by Georgia delegates on their return from the convention, and by May 1890 a number of such land investments were in operation in the state.[28] Also, Colored Farmers' Alliance members' preference for prosperous black landowners as their local leaders added impetus to such ventures.[29] The impulse for land ownership was very strong among landless blacks, and such activities fed a strong desire among them. Samuel Barrows found "thousands of instances," particularly in the upper Southern states, where blacks were becoming farm owners and householders."[30] As a group, blacks thirsted for land and education, part of the growing philosophy of self-help and economic elevation prominent in the decades following the Civil War.

Despite the willingness of the Southern Alliance to compromise with the Northern Alliance over segregation, the Colored Farmers' Alliance nonetheless did not wish to consolidate with its white Southern counterpart. At its 1888 convention, the CFA adopted a resolution "that white organizations shall positively prohibit the administration of colored men to membership, and colored organizations shall prohibit the admission of white men to membership."[31] This unwillingness to admit white members suggests a suspicion of how their presence would affect black goals, which often differed with those of whites. While reasserting this philosophy of black separatism at St. Louis in 1889, the CFA reaffirmed its wish to establish "the most intimate confederation with the white Alliance."[32] While the two groups could work together, trust was still not such that the CFA wished to completely merge. And quite aside from the policy of economic cooperation, it is interesting to note that the Colored Farmers' Alliance continued its earlier policy of separatism despite the white Southern Alliance's willingness, albeit reluctant, to change its membership qualifications. On the surface, this separatism may seem to indicate a reluctance among blacks toward class cooperation, but it actually represents a strong grasp of reality, for it embodied a distinction between economic self-interest, the sensitive race question, allegations about introducing social equality, and the need to control the membership in order to effectively promote the group's own agenda. The policy also was realistic in that no Southern state Alliance voted to include blacks as members.[33] Achieving common economic goals was paramount, and racial integration would only create an issue for the Democrats.

Both races at St. Louis were farsighted enough not to open themselves to the charge of promoting social equality leveled by their Bourbon critics. Furthermore, the white grassroots members' own regional and lower-class prejudices made it difficult to translate their membership principles into practice. Like everyone, they craved social acceptance, which would prove difficult with their proposed compromise on interracial cooperation. "The color line cannot be rubbed out," Terence Powderly of the Knights of Labor exclaimed of the South. Speaking before the St. Louis convention, he added that "the Southern people are capable of managing the Negro question for themselves." Repudiating any suggestion of social equality, he suggested that blacks be protected when they become "a lever with which to oppress the white man."[34]

If nothing else, the St. Louis meeting demonstrated how far the Southern Alliance would compromise to implement economic reform. These practical, hard-pressed farmers wanted to improve their class and personal prospects; prejudice could yield few financial returns. Open challenges to racism were downplayed, subordinated to economic self-interest. Alliance leaders understood that interracial cooperation was necessary, but overcoming the prejudices of the rank-and-file would prove difficult.

It is significant that the racial and sectional unity theme was not totally abandoned at St. Louis but subordinated until reconsideration at Ocala, Florida, on December 2, 1890. Although all three Alliances debated their desire for reform, the Colored and Northern Alliances were too skeptical of white Southern domination to welcome unification unreservedly. Realistically, in a movement still so shaky, much could be gained through longer exposure to agrarian poverty, as class interests and racial conflicts could be mitigated by more economic suffering. Landless tenants would suffer even more as crop prices continued to fall. The only way out was for them to raise more staple crops, produce fewer subsistence crops to feed themselves, and borrow more on future crops to pay the rising tide of debt.

An earlier cynical outburst by the editor of the Greensboro, Georgia, *Herald* captured the farmers' forced dependence on cotton:

> Oh, yes, Farmers, cotton is King! A merchant in this city sold some cotton in Savannah last week at 4¼ [cents a pound] that he bought last September, and he lost $20 a bag on it. But still cotton is king. Meat is ten cents cash, corn going up gradually, cotton down; but the Farmers don't need such trifles: cotton is just the thing of course: men, women, and children and horses and mules can eat cotton and grow fat on it. Put in more cotton Farmers. Four or five cents a pound now, who knows but what it will open next fall at three cents! Plant more cotton—plant all cotton and get rich.[35]

Farmers were pressured to raise more cotton to pay off their rising indebtedness, but overproduction forced prices down. That farmers under such circumstances would seek scapegoats and see conspiracies is understandable. The miracle is that they were not more irrational and racist in their behavior.

Delegations from all the Southern states were present at Ocala, with expectations of later arrivals from as far away as California. The Floridians extended generous hospitality to the convention. Free entertainment was available, trips to local points of interest were organized, and a thousand boxes of Florida oranges were distributed among the guests—all of which was capped off by an elaborate display of local products.[36] The Colored Farmers' Alliance also held its annual meeting at Ocala, but the black delegates assembled in a separate body.[37] On their arrival, CFA delegates were greeted with the usual committee visitations from the various white organizations, bidding them welcome. In return, the Colored Farmers' Alliance appointed committees to visit each of these white Alliance bodies to express their good will and fraternal regard for these orders. Now that economic conditions had worsened since the previous year, at Ocala the black delegates seemed more interested in a confederation, rather than a fully integrated organization, with the white Alliances. The CFA proposed to these various white committees that they form a confederation "for purposes of mutual protection, co-operation, and assistance." This was readily agreed to by the white orders, and a joint session met to discuss the proposal. An agreement was reached and "heartily endorsed" by all.[38] Each organization pledged itself for "common citizenship . . . commercial equality and legal justice" toward all men, black or white. In a burst of optimism, Superintendent Humphrey announced that "this agreement will be known in future ages as the burial of racial conflict, and finally of race prejudice."[39]

In turn, the Supreme Council of the Southern Alliance unanimously

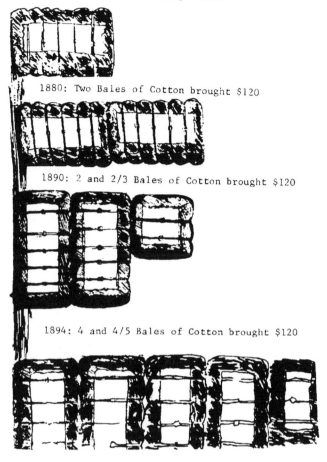

1870: Bale of Cotton brought $120

1880: Two Bales of Cotton brought $120

1890: 2 and 2/3 Bales of Cotton brought $120

1894: 4 and 4/5 Bales of Cotton brought $120

Fig. 1. Post–Civil War deflation (*People's Party Paper,* October 5, 1894).

adopted the following resolution: "We recommend and urge that equal fa-cilities, educational, commercial, and political, be demanded for colored and white Alliance men alike, competency considered, and that a free ballot and a fair count be insisted upon and had for colored and white alike."[40] With this statement, the Alliance supported the Jeffersonian concept of good moral character ("competency considered") as a necessity for political par-ticipation, and that those lacking sufficient virtue and intelligence made poor citizens and voters, regardless of race. But despite the leaderships' rhetoric about more interracial cooperation, such statements could not mask internal conflicts. As racial self-interests increased stress within the move-ment, the shakiness of the alliance soon surfaced. Despite its earlier support for political equality, the white Southern Alliance adopted a resolution on the second day (December 3, 1890) which "most soundly condemned" the "Force" Bill as being "partisan in spirit . . . and . . . partisan in application."[41] They declared it

> Resolved . . . that we do most solemnly protest against the passage of the Lodge election bill, and we most earnestly petition our Senators to employ all fair and legal means to defeat this unpatriotic measure.[42]

Under the "Force" Bill, Federal supervisors would be given power to pass on qualifications of challenged voters, control registration of voters, and decide between federal and state differences over election results. Given lingering though exaggerated fears over a return to "Black Reconstruction," white Southerners' reaction was not surprising. According to Woodward, "The Lodge bill caused more alarm and excitement in the South than any Federal measure since 1877."[43] However, the Colored Farmers' Alliance, while normally subordinating political to class interests, supported the Republican-sponsored bill as a measure of receiving fair treatment at Southern polls. It was not surprising, therefore, that on December 5, 1890, the CFA delegates unanimously adopted the following resolution: "That we, the delegates of the National Colored Farmers' Alliance do hereby . . . urge upon Congress to pass the Lodge election bill, and let it apply to all sections."[44] While not entirely satisfied with the proposed bill, black delegates "wanted something guaranteeing every man a free vote and an honest count."[45] While both groups could embrace Jeffersonianism, whites realized that its application required an activist federal government, but only to guard basic American values that economic monopolies such as banks and railroads had endangered. The franchise was the bailiwick of state and town governments and sacrosanct against Federal encroachment. In contrast, Southern blacks knew their social and economic advancement depended on Federal voter protection against local authorities, as well as receiving fair wages for their labor. Neither saw a problem in an activist central government helping secure economic rights, but Southern white agrarians were hesitant about giving more political power to the region's black population. Alliance leaders of both races might support biracial equality in convention assembly, but their opposing stands on the "Force" Bill suggests problems would arise when delegates returned to their local chapters and tried to form a united front against the ruling elite.

When faced with common economic problems, however, the alliances united. The Colored Farmers' Alliance entered a strong protest to Congress concerning the passage of the Conger Lard Bill, which was designed to check the adulteration of lard. The Conger Lard Bill attempted to impose taxes on the production of vegetable oil to elevate its cost and make it less competitive in comparison to the higher prices of animal fats. Cottonseed, "the colored man's crop," was widely used as an admixture to pure lard and had reportedly dropped from twelve to fourteen dollars a ton the previous year to six to nine dollars at the time of the Ocala meeting. Taxes on top of declining prices would further depress the profits Southern farmers received from cottonseed. "No legislation ever introduced into Congress, with the exception of the laws fastening slavery upon us," according to Colored Farmers' Alliance president J. S. Jackson, "has been so injurious to the colored race as the so-called Conger Bill."[46] Southern Alliance members also expressed opposition to the bill.[47]

But conflicts of interest existed between the two orders concerning other economic issues. The Subtreasury Plan, a proposed federal network of warehouses that would allow farmers to store crops, provide low-interest loans, and release products slowly on the market to prevent market glut and depress prices was approved by both organizations, but the Colored Farmers' Alliance adopted a more radical position in favor of a single tax, whereas the Southern Alliance desired a graduated income tax. Superintendent Humphrey, in his annual address at Ocala, "came out distinctly in favor of a single tax on land." This concept was also advocated by the Knights of Labor present at Ocala, represented by Terence V. Powderly and A. W. Wright of Toronto. More specifically, it was Wright who promoted the single tax philosophy of Henry George to the black delegates and "they swallowed whole" the idea.[48]

Henry George, author of the bestseller *Progress and Poverty* (1879), had developed the socialistic single tax concept as a method of ultimately turning land ownership over to the community rather than the individual. Under his system, all landowners would receive an income created by social and economic conditions rather than by their own efforts, and a single tax on landowners would be used to run all functions of government. As a landless debtor group, Southern blacks were responsive to programs that would prevent land monopoly by a rich, privileged class. Under George's influence, black author T. Thomas Fortune argued that "land is not property; can never be made property . . . the land belongs to the sovereign people."[49] This is one of the few times that the Colored Farmers' Alliance responded with a radical thesis of class conflict between largely white capital and black labor.

Conversely, the Southern Alliance, primarily composed of middle-class white small landholding farmers and merchants, was leery of the single tax, which inhibited any closer union between the two orders. Simultaneously, the Southern Alliance Subtreasury Plan received only minor support from the black delegates, who believed the government should "take care of the product[s] of our labor."[50] These issues are particularly significant, because it was this gap between small landowning whites and the largely landless black masses that made it impossible for the doctrine of class development to be practically acceptable to both groups. On certain issues where interests were similar, the two organizations agreed. For example, both Alliances advocated the abolition of the Louisiana Lottery, believing its existence would lead all farmers further into debt.[51] But, in general, the differences over race and landed versus landless groups created tension and conflict.

The threat of independent political action, latent since the St. Louis convention, became a crucial issue at Ocala, as had been predicted. Southern Alliance delegates, unlike those present from the Midwest and the Colored Farmers' Alliance, objected to forming a third party, preferring to work through the Southern Democratic Party. The Colored Farmers' Alliance, however, under Humphrey's control favored a third party. "From the very first," he announced, "the Colored Alliance has been strongly in favor of the third party movement."[52] Humphrey overstated the black delegates' support for a third party, but black criticism of the Republican Party and its abandonment of them was significant by the 1890s.[53] Blacks, according to Humphrey, were willing to withdraw from the Republican Party because of a "lack of justice" resulting from the inequities in the allocation of political patronage and a pro-business Republican Congress increasingly opposed to the black farmers' interests.

Blacks had become disillusioned not only with the Republican Party but with politics itself. One contemporary scholar and officer of the Alliance estimated that "at least 70 percent of the Negroes refrained from voting in the election of 1890." J. H. Turner, a native of Georgia and National Secretary-Treasurer of the National Farmers' Alliance and Industrial Union, said "the Negroes as a class" had "taken very little interest in politics for several years. They have lost their former faith in politics and politicians, which was very natural to one acquainted with the fact that they had always been loyal [Republican] partisans, and for their devotion and zeal they had been paid off with a few appointments as postmasters in, most generally, third or fourth-class post offices." Turner further added that "judging from the utterances of their leaders, they are willing and anxious to sever all past party affiliations, and join hands with the white farmers . . . looking for betterment of their condition."[54]

Political patronage was an important factor in the relationship between blacks and the Republican Party, but the national party was transforming into a conservative pro-business organization that wanted little to do with Southern blacks as the century waned. By 1890 the Colored Farmers' Alliance, discouraged by the Republican Party's increasing lack of interest in Southern black issues, was more receptive to political insurgency than the white Southern Alliance. The frustration of black political ambitions and patronage diminution drove some blacks toward a third party that they hoped would meet their needs. Still, the old Republican Reconstruction coalition that included blacks in its ranks still held a magnetism for most blacks, particularly in presidential elections. Also, blacks had to be very cautious in their commitments, because a coalition with the Alliance and later the Populist movement, if it failed, left them open to severe recrimination.

The question of forming a third party resulted in a compromise at Ocala. Despite the urging of the black delegates, except Georgia Colored Alliance State Superintendent E. S. Richardson and the white Kansas delegation, most of the white Southern delegates agreed with the position of Alliance President Leonidas L. Polk, who succeeded Macune in 1889. Polk urged caution on the third-party question, suggesting that "the greatest and most essential need of our order" at this point was "education"—by which he probably meant creating greater awareness "among the masses upon those questions which mostly relate to their interests."[55] In short, most Southern white agrarians in 1890 were neither ready nor willing to bolt the Democratic Party and challenge the region's racial orthodoxy. It was officially decided to postpone a final decision on the third-party question until February 1891. While independent political action was not totally agreeble to all factions, black or white, at this time, independent political thinking had certainly taken on new warmth by early 1891.

The most conservative black elements, such as the Mississippi Colored Alliance and the Georgia Colored Alliance, were as yet not in favor of a third party. Although they wanted "the common good . . . benefit of the farmer and national reform," they believed that this could best "be brought about by our own choice of candidates."[56] At bottom, like their more conservative white counterparts, they believed it was a question of the right men with reform ideas working through the establishment, primarily the Republican Party in the case of the blacks and the Democratic Party in the case of the whites.

Racial cohesion also prevented quick development of a third party. "In the South," a Georgia paper explained, "whatever may be the [harsh] condition of affairs, the farmers and the Alliance men are compelled by [racial] circumstances to carry out their views and reforms through the Democratic Party. There are some things more important than reforms that merely affect the pocket."[57] These and similar warnings about the South's need for racial orthodoxy filled the columns of Southern papers, testing the sincerity of the white farmers' belief in white supremacy and the Democratic Party when confronted with poverty. Also, the recent 1890 elections had initially reinforced the white view that agrarian reform could still be accomplished within the Democratic Party.

Controlling no fewer than eight legislatures, four governorships, and numerous minor offices throughout the region, the Southern Alliance endorsed and continued to embrace the existing political system during the months immediately following the 1890 election. For example, the Georgia Alliance had captured 182 of the 219 seats in the state legislature. Alliancemen captured 52 seats in Florida's 100-seat legislature, and in Alabama, although Alabama Alliance leader Rueben F. Kolb lost his bid for governor, the agrarians elected 75 of 133 legislators. James S. Hogg and Benjamin R. Tillman won gubernatorial positions in Texas and South Carolina respectively by uniting with Alliance forces, and in Tennessee J. P. Buchanan was elected governor by the farmers with slightly less than half the posts in both houses filled with agrarian sympathizers. All in all, the 1890–91 election was victorious for the Alliance, or so it initially seemed. If agrarian legislative reform depended on the election of Alliance supporters, then positive results for the farmers should follow the 1890 results. But agrarian needs remained unfilled by Democratic politicians elected under the Alliance banner, as they did not or could not deliver. Also, Alliance members elected to state legislatures—Georgia being an excellent example—remained philosophically loyal to the Democratic Party and its conservative Bourbon pro-business principles and were not dedicated to agrarian political or economic reform for either race. For blacks, the Alliance legislatures of the early 1890s passed a number of discriminatory laws. For example, the 1891 Georgia Alliance legislature revived the use of the whipping post, provided that black and white prisoners could not be chained together, and passed a Jim Crow law for railroads. In Tennessee, Farmers' Alliance legislators helped vote in laws that partially disenfranchised blacks. Texas Alliance governor James Hogg asked his Twenty-Second (largely agrarian) Legislature to pass a law that required separate coaches, or coaches with partitions, for blacks and whites. Clearly the Alliance legislatures were a disappointment to white and black farmers.[58]

On the whole, the accommodators dominated the Ocala meeting, but the process of working within the two major parties proved a failure. Once the 1890 elections were over, Southern Alliance members found they had little control over the regular party legislators they elected. According to the Reverend J. L. Moore of Crescent City, Florida, superintendent of the Putnam County Colored Farmers' Alliance, "The wily politicians see and know that they have to do something, therefore they are slipping into the Alliance, and the farmers, in many instances, are accepting them as leaders; and if we are to have the same leaders, we need not expect anything but the same results."[59] It became obvious to some agrarians that they must create their own third party if they truly wanted to achieve reform. These were the conditions that ignited the Populist movement. Some blacks and whites now embraced, albeit reluctantly, the third-party idea, but the 1890 Ocala meeting suggested that black delegates were more receptive to a new party than the whites in attendance.

A recapitulation of the nature of the Alliance movement reveals several defects that would make interracial cooperation difficult, if not impossible, in the emerging Populist movement. First, the Alliance failure reveals the lack of interracial class-consciousness among the poor and disadvantaged of the South, one of the very un-Marxian burdens of Southern history. The stress of Jeffersonian ideals and rhetoric about a common producer class that included blacks was beyond the permissible boundaries of acceptable dissent in the South. True, for a time it seemed that the agrarian movement might succeed in creating a genuine class coalition among blacks and whites, but in the end this was eroded by racism, antithetical interests, and economic expediency. When it came to specific issues such as the "Force" Bill, the cotton pickers' strike, higher wages vs. high prices, or the single tax vs. the graduated income tax, racial differences quickly surfaced. Ultimately, this black–white coalition was driven by self-interest, in which race rather than economics dictated the direction that would be taken. Both the Alliance and Populist membership, according to Woodward, were "always more interest-conscious than class-conscious," but in the case of black and white, as we have seen, the interests were often contradictory.[60]

From the outset the white agrarian movement largely comprised "employing farmers," particularly in the case of the leadership, whose main endeavor was to abate the steady deterioration of their middle-class economic position as producers. Indeed, they were often only one step away from sliding into the economic morass occupied by the landless black masses. Conversely, blacks employed as toilers were understandably less concerned with pursuing policies that were contrary to their group interests.[61] A coalition composed of blacks who sought more compensation for their labor and small land-owning whites who conversely sought more for their products and oftentimes hired these same blacks as laborers seemed destined to fail. The hostility of the Southern Alliance toward the 1891 cotton pickers' strike indicates that black laborers were welcome as long as they promoted or enhanced the interests of their white mentors and made no effort to better themselves outside the white paradigm.

Secondly, the Alliance experience reveals how reform rhetoric would transform under practical application. Poverty, suffering, and hostile public opinion can erode lofty-sounding principles and enhance racial orthodoxy and conformity to regional norms. Farmers of both races had been forced to shift from subsistence crops to more staple crops, such as cotton, as prices declined and debt burdens grew. Both races believed, among other things, that the root of all their evils was the *shortage* of money. Although both black and white agrarians were avowed inflationists, at bottom their positions were at odds: blacks, as tenant laborers, sought to reduce their accumulated debts, while whites sought higher prices for the products.

A small group of black landowners—probably no more than 10 percent of the total Southern agrarian black population during this era, as leaders of the Colored Farmers' Alliance—were also at odds on occasion with their largely black tenant membership. In 1880, 9.8 percent of blacks owned land in South Carolina, Alabama, Georgia, Louisiana, and Mississippi. However, only 7.3 percent were farm owners. In the lower South as a whole, only one out of five black farmers owned their land a half century after freedom (see table 2 in the Appendixes).[62] However, the black desire for land ownership was prominent among rural and urban blacks in the postwar South.[63] In 1889, a North Carolina black emigration convention captured in proper perspective these differing racial and class interests when it attacked the Southern Farmers' Alliance for keeping wages low and inhibiting black political rights.[64]

Thirdly, the Alliance's biracial experience illustrates dramatically the fragility of Southern racial liberalism, which is often fused with both liberal and illiberal tendencies. Thus, while the small-farm, landowning white agrarians perceived the evils of a planter-banker-industrialist coalition, they also saw nothing morally wrong with promoting their own self-interests over those of the biracial agrarian class. Espousing a Jeffersonian motto of "Equal Rights to All and Special Privileges to None," the Southern Alliance's sentimental appeals to conscience and class were not characterized by a revamping of actions that conflicted with their regional orthodoxies. When self-interest conflicts with idealism, it generates the crassest sort of opportunism and racism. Such was the case with the agrarian coalition when crucial episodes and issues exacerbated the simmering tensions and contradictions. These conflicts of interest would continue to surface when the Populist movement sought to consolidate these two racial groups on the basis of "self-interest."

Lastly, and perhaps most important for the emerging Populist movement, the Southern and Colored Farmers' Alliances disagreed on the two major political issues of the latter nineteenth century that offered substantial aid and comfort to downtrodden blacks: the Blair Education Bill, designed to reduce illiteracy through the use of federal appropriations to the states, most of which would go to the South and benefit blacks; and the "Force" Bill, which was designed to protect black voting rights.[65] Ultimately, the National Republican Party also failed to pursue both issues to passage, further suggesting party abandonment of Southern blacks.[66] Republicans, particularly at the national level, were growing increasingly silent about outrages and disenfranchisement tactics against Southern blacks. The Civil Rights Act of 1875 had been declared unconstitutional by a Republican Supreme Court in 1883, and in 1890 the Republican Congress failed to pass the Blair and Lodge bills. By 1888, lily-white factions of the Republican Party, largely seeking to purge the party of blacks, also had started to make their appearance in the South, reflecting an increasingly hostile public opinion toward blacks. This silence on black rights and protection was increasingly rooted in the national realignment of the Republican Party around Northern industrial rather than Southern agrarian interests and black votes. The growth of industrialism in the New South resulted in less dependence on black and agrarian votes and more concern with developing party strength around Northern banking and industrial interests, which dominated Southern industry. Sectional reconciliation resulted in a compromise and then an acquiescence on passage or enforcement of anti-Southern legislation. These changing attitudes and conditions meant that Southern blacks seeking solace for their deteriorating conditions increasingly would not receive it from the national government or the Republican Party but had to develop new alignments themselves within the region. Outside interference resulted in anti-black prejudice.[67] As Booker T. Washington, the ultimate compromiser, astutely pointed out, any effort at reform had to emanate from within the South.[68] Any outside efforts tended to promote organized resistance.

Indeed, given the political nature of Southern race relations, it was unlikely that attitudes toward the Lodge and Blair bills were unusual. Rhetoric about a producer-class coalition by the Southern Alliance did not capture the varied economic interests and shifting political emphases of blacks and whites. If one examines the rhetoric of the Alliance and later Populist Party, it would appear that here was a call for one people united around an agrarian coalition who would extend equal and exact justice to all—that there would be no white, no black, no East, no West, but one common united group opposing injustice. But when confronted with specific issues, it is evident that tensions and differences underlying this agrarian coalition put increasing stress along racial lines. But racial divisions were also found along economic and class lines, to a limited extent, with landless blacks desiring more for their wages, and small landowning whites wanting more for their products. The role an activist central government would play in this agenda also found stark differences. Such a coalition would find great difficulty in supporting a common political end and practically applying the principles and precepts laid down in their platforms. Time would reveal that the emerging white Populist movement was faced also with these same obstacles in its effort to form a political coalition with blacks.

3

Time of Trial, Time of Hope

The Birth of Southern Populism

> The argument against the independent movement . . . may be boiled
> down to one word—nigger.

The Alliance's drift into third-party politics was inevitable. From the movement's inception, members of both races believed only an independent party
could promote agrarian reforms. The experience of the Colored Farmers'
Alliance in Alabama stands as a case in point. Organizing in the state in July
1889, a segment of the organization under Frank Davis, a successful black
farmer, sought to confine the Alliance to business and eschew politics. Conversely, a more radical, primarily landless black group resorted immediately
to politics but were "dispersed" by the more conservative group.[1] Such conflicts between solvent landowning blacks and the landless majority under-
score the oppositional interests within the black community. The same
conflicts also occurred between those who wanted a third party and those
who wanted to remain wedded to the two old parties. Although the evidence is fragmentary, it appears that landowning blacks were less receptive
to the idea of a third party than were landless groups.

In some ways the most interesting part of the Alliance movement was the
gradual change in its attitude toward embracing a third party. Prior to the
Alliance experience, other post-Reconstruction precedents created a heightened awareness of biracial politics as a potent reform force for the farmers—
notably the Agricultural Wheel, the Louisiana Farmers' Union, the Knights
of Labor, and the biracial Greenback-Labor campaigns of the 1870s and
1880s.[2] These movements had "few successes," as Carl Degler has pointed
out, but nevertheless undermined the restrictive effects of the Democratic
Party on the white Southern agrarian mind. In short, Populism was not a
sudden political aberration but the culmination of a pattern of agrarian
protest that had existed at least since Reconstruction.[3]

The Democratic Party, however, represented the dominant political ideology of the white South throughout the final quarter of the nineteenth
century, and as such, the majority of the South's white inhabitants were sure
to follow in whatever direction it moved. By the same token, in whatever

direction the party refused to follow, the South would not long continue. "To be anything but a Democrat," Tom Watson later lamented, "was in public opinion to be a traitor to the section and the white race."[4] You "may strike the wife of your bosom while her arms are locked in love's embrace about your neck, or your little child as it lisps its evening prayer at its mother's knee," one former Georgia governor declared, "but for God's sake, don't strike the dear old Democratic party."[5] John B. Rayner, a black Texas Populist leader, observed that "The faith the [white] South has in the Democratic Party is much stronger than the faith the South has in God."[6] This extremist faith is understandable when examined as something other than a uniquely political mechanism. As one Democratic North Carolina editor explained:

> The Democratic Party at the South is something more than a mere political organization striving to enforce an administrative policy. It is a white man's party, organized to maintain white supremacy and prevent a repetition of the destructive rule of ignorant Negroes and unscrupulous whites. . . . The safety of the South . . . as well as the conservation of free institutions on these shores depends upon the strength, unity and perpetuity of the Democratic Party.[7]

Most whites seem to have taken for granted that the Democratic Party was a racial necessity. "In the South," a Georgia paper pointed out, "whatever may be the condition of affairs, the farmers and the Alliance men are compelled by circumstances to carry out their views and reforms through the Democratic Party. There are some things more important than reforms that merely affect the pocket."[8] These and similar public warnings filled the columns of Southern newspapers, testing the white farmer's belief in white supremacy and fears of social equality. Reviewing the primary sources of the period, the number of warnings about the "Negro question" and "social equality" voiced by white Southerners is outstanding. George Washington Cable commented on the white South's "absurd visions of all shantytown pouring its hordes of unwashed [black] imps into the company and companionships of our own sunny-headed [white] darlings." "What utter nonsense," he further added. "We may reach the moon someday, not social equality."[9] Furthermore, blacks expressed no interest in social equality, always drawing a distinction between political and social equality. For example, South Carolina black congressman Joseph Rainey noted, "I am content to be what I am as long as I have my rights." Indeed, "I prefer to choose my own associates."[10] Some whites, such as Georgia native J. H. Turner, the secretary-treasurer of the National Farmers' Alliance and Industrial Union, argued that "the poor negro . . . neither needs nor wants . . . social equality," to no avail.[11] A sexual inference is sublimated—if blacks could enter the voting booth or a railroad car, they could also enter your home and violate your wife and daughter. The horrors of miscegenation also fill the literature of the period. Writing in 1922, W. E. B. Du Bois observed: "There is no doubt that at the bottom of the race problem in the United States is the question of 'Social Equality,' and the kernel of the 'Social Equality' question is the question of intermarriage."[12]

Alliance leaders, Populists, and blacks repeatedly challenged these accusations. "In fact," a white Alabama Populist asserted, "we are further from advocating or practicing social equality, than any ballot box stuffer alive. Our objection does not relax at the going down of the sun. We have got no children at the Tuskegee normal school or kindred there."[13] Rayner frequently opened his speeches by pointing to his light skin and exclaiming that this is what he had received from the Democrats![14] Maud Cuney-Hare, the light-skinned daughter of black Texas Republican leader Norris Wright Cuney (himself "the acknowledged mulatto offspring" of a white planter and a slave woman) and a mulatto mother would on occasion pass for white and enter segregated transportation facilities—an act that must have provided her with private satisfaction, being only inches from individuals who would have treated her differently if they had known she was black.[15]

In substance, allegiance to party and race was touted as more important than allegiance to principle and economic well-being in the South of the 1890s. But whereas most whites leaned toward the Democratic Party, blacks remained loyal to the Republican Party at both the Southern and national level. Such was the mystical legacy of Lincoln and emancipation that few Southern blacks failed to vote Republican. As Frederick Douglass said during the 1872 Republican Party Convention, "the Republican Party is the ship, and all else is the sea."[16] That rhetoric still resonated with the black masses, even though the reality was otherwise. Only four years after Douglass's pronouncement, representatives of the two major parties would broker the presidential election and send Republican Rutherford B. Hayes to the White House in exchange for the removal of federal troops from the South, which in turn opened the floodgates of Southern electoral fraud that returned Democrats to power. By the 1890s, national Republicans were dismissive of Southern elections and had developed new party allegiances based along urban and business lines that could keep them in power at the highest levels. "For almost half a century after the end of Reconstruction in 1877," Degler has observed, "not a single Republican presidential candidate was able to carry a state of the former Confederacy."[17] Yet Southern blacks remained loyal to the Republican Party. With the races split along party lines, third-party success required attracting enough black voters from the Republican

Party and white voters from the Democratic Party, without alienating either race.

The South's rigid value structure offered few opportunities for an individual to buck the tide of political solidarity and racial pride. White and black Southern farmers were subject to the same prejudices as their urban peers. Charles Nordhoff, a Northern reporter writing in 1875, described the poor whites and "wool-hat boys" who resided in the piney woods, mountains, and coastal plain South:

> The numerous classes of poor white farmers are a kind of people unknownst among us. Settled upon a thin and unfertile soil; long and constantly neglected before the war; living still in a backwoods country, and in true backwards style, without schools, with few churches, and given to rude sports and a rude agriculture, they are a peculiar people. . . . They are ignorant, easily prejudiced, and they have since the war, lived in dread of having social equality with the negro imposed upon them.[18]

Democrats could easily promote fears of "social equality" and "Negro Domination" among such people. Hardscrabble whites could be swayed to take their social and economic frustrations and fears out on the region's blacks. The main difficulty any reform group faced was in convincing the region's economically disinherited, black or white, that it was in their self-interest to vote as a coalition along economic and political, not racial, lines. Rigid racial priorities had long driven political inaction in the South and an allegiance to the status quo. Racial solidarity was more important than political reason or economic reality.

Finally, one must note the psychological and compensatory role conformity played in Southern politics. In the face of insult, conformity provided dignity; in place of accusations of "Negro supremacy" and "social equality," it provided acceptable arguments and group acceptance. Discussing the Southern white farmers' dilemma of "revolt or conformity," Woodward has stated:

> Changing one's party in the South of the nineties involved more than changing one's mind. It might involve a falling off of clients, the loss of a job, of credit at the store, or of one's welcome at the church. It could split families, and it might even call into question one's loyalty to his race and his people.[19]

Faced with strong opposition from powerful authorities, Southern Populism's even limited success is surprising. Equally harrowing were the experiences of insurgents of both races and the psychic strains they encountered in their daily lives. As Milford Howard, a Populist senator from Alabama, lamented:

> It will give you some idea of this bitterness when I state that my own father would not hear me speak and said he would rather make my coffin with his own hands than have me desert the Democratic party. This has been more than thirty years ago but some of the old feeling still slumbers and I have never been and never will be forgiven for my fall from grace.[20]

Describing his third-party experience, Howard "doubt[ed] if in all the political campaigns of this country there was ever as much vituperation, filth and vindictiveness unbottled as was ever turned loose upon [my] head" as during this era.[21] Similarly, in Georgia, Tom Watson's brother was secretary of a meeting that publicly denounced Watson as a traitor.[22] In his private journal, Watson describes the constant threat of injury he faced as a Georgia Populist:

> It was almost a miracle I was not killed in the campaign of 1892. Threats against my life were frequent and there were scores of men who would have done the deed and thousands who would have sanctioned it. Fear of the retaliation which my friends would inflict prevented my assassination—nothing else.[23]

Such actions also constituted an integral part of the experiences of less ordinary folk involved in the movement. In Guntersville, Alabama, for example, a group of Alliancemen who had brought their produce to market were greeted by local housewives as "nigger lovers and nigger huggers." In disgust the farmers gathered up their produce and "reported to their families and neighbors the estimation placed upon them by much of the populace."[24] Even the institution of marriage was not sacrosanct to Populism's enemies. At the marriage of Populist leader "Mary-Ann" (Marion) Butler to Fannie Faison in Raleigh, North Carolina, in the fall of 1893, the newlyweds were escorted from the church to the local depot by a jeering mob of Democrats beating tin pans. The hecklers wondered how any "decent woman" could go so far as to marry a Populist.[25]

The sacred, like the secular, promoted conformity in racial and political matters. Southern white Protestantism had long adhered to a narrowly conceived evangelism that eschewed Populist ideals.[26] To church leaders, Populism challenged the hegemony of traditional religion in Southern life and, as such, orthodox religion condemned the reformers.[27] In Nolensville, Tennessee, the Reverend Douglas Anderson preached a sermon to the church's third-party brethren, urging them to "abandon their evil ways and return to the fold of the Democratic Party before it was too late."[28] To escape such invectives, some churches were almost exclusively composed of Populist memberships.[29] A Raleigh religious publication despaired of the "suffering in the land" but did not think Populist interference could provide a solution. "The poor ye have with you always," it insisted.[30] The Populists were well aware of the intimate connection between the pulpit and the politician, and of the reasons for it. "Too often," one Populist declared, "the modern money changer and usurer pay the bulk of the preacher's salary."[31] Another third partyite had a more cogent explanation: "Most preachers," he bluntly asserted, "are Democratic."[32]

In the black community as well, many professionals spoke out against the reform efforts. Most black preachers were Republicans, and the symbiotic relationship between the segregated black church and politics presented a challenge to the newly emerging Populist Party. Politicians of all parties sought to "hire" (often literally) black preachers to proselytize and turn out the black vote for them, as their endorsement or withholding of support had significant effect on election outcomes. "The democrats have hired such of our ministers as they could to go work among our people," a black Georgia Populist exclaimed. "Who ever heard of the like before—white democrats hiring colored men to vote the Republican ticket?"[33] The more common tactic was for Democrats to hire black preachers to turn out the black vote, for a price, to vote for the Democrats. It was also not unusual for blacks, following a night of revelry, to be escorted in groups to the polls on election day by such leaders to vote for selected candidates. It is true that some, perhaps many, blacks during this period sold their votes, but it is also true that whites bought their votes. Populists were at a disadvantage in this arena, since the more affluent Democrats could better afford the use of such surrogates and attract the more powerful and persuasive of the preachers. Black teachers, also dependent on their livelihoods from the white community, followed the same pattern as the preachers.

Given the white power structure, black dependency on whites, and the nature of Southern race relations, it was unlikely that many black preachers and teachers would openly support the Populist Party. However, black preachers such as the Reverend Walter Pattillo of North Carolina, Reverend H. S. Doyle of Georgia, and John B. Rayner of Texas, repeatedly show up as spokesmen in state Populist circles, suggesting they gained more from their efforts to support the movement than from the pecuniary efforts which characterized most politics of the day. However, such efforts would make them and their organization vulnerable.

The struggle for control of the Southern black mind by black leadership coincidentally heightened during the rise of the Populist movement. In addition to the traditional influence of preachers and teachers, radically diverse black leaders arose with their own agendas for the salvation of the race. Frederick Douglass, long the voice of the black community, would be dead by 1895. In his place, T. Thomas Fortune, Alexander Crummell, Bishop Turner, and others would argue separatism, direct action, or expatriation as solutions to the race problem. But above these, Booker T. Washington, following his 1895 Atlanta Exposition speech, captured the imagination of the Southern agrarian by stressing hard work and accommodation rather than political gain. White and black could find comfort in Washington's vision of industrious black farmers and industrial workers uninterested in rising much beyond their station in life. Simultaneously, the growing tendency was to look toward "the better class of whites" to provide protection.[34] The growing acceptance of white hegemony from Democrats and the increasing abandonment by Republicans made political activity for blacks outside the mainstream less attractive, and economic and moral endeavor the areas for more focus.

Such stories are frequent in the Populist literature. Any connection with the Populist movement, whatever one's race, could bring ostracism down on one's head. These successive waves of ostracism fed the white farmers' pessimism and finally led many of them down the road of race hatred, while blacks migrated to the Midwest and North in search of more politically amiable climates. Tom Watson's conversion from racially liberal Populist spokesman to rabid race baiter in a few years can be explained in part by the corrosive effect such experiences had on his already fragile psyche.[35]

In addition to the Southern quest for regional solidarity, external events also forced the closure of political ranks. The Democratic propaganda machine received unintentional but much needed invigoration through the well-meaning efforts of Henry Cabot Lodge, a young Harvard–educated Brahmin Republican Congressional representative from Massachusetts. At the request of President Harrison, Lodge introduced on June 26, 1890, a bill designed to supervise federal elections.[36] While the bill's passage would have ensured increased unbiased federal monitoring of voting in local elections, the measure was obviously aimed at the South, where the black vote had long supported the regional Republican Party. Democratic officials normally controlled the local polling places, which gave rise to anti-Republican and -third-party fraud. The fewer black voters, the better chances for Democratic victory. Degler has estimated that probably no more than 20 percent of Southern whites voted Republican even during Radical Reconstruction.[37] Federal correctives had long been contemplated by Republicans, and after the congressional election of 1888 they believed that such a proposition could now be passed.[38] In brief, the Lodge Bill stated that when fifty persons in a county or five hundred persons in a district signed a petition that unfair election methods were prevalent in their area, federal authorities could intercede and supervise the federal elections.[39] The Lodge "Force" Bill, as it was quickly tagged by the largely Democratic opposition,[40] passed the House on July 2, 1890, but failed to reach the Senate until the Fifty-first Congress, where it was defeated by a coalition of Western "free silver" Republicans and Southern Democrats.[41] The price the Democrats paid for this, it was alleged, was their vote for the "Free Silver Bill" in Congress.[42]

Despite the vehement denials of Lodge, the bill quickly developed an image in the South as a "Force" bill and a "Bayonet" bill, intended to place "a bullet behind every ballot" cast in the South. In the public discourse of the times, any federal involvement figured as a preemptive blessing at best. Reminders of black Reconstruction legislatures received wide press coverage, and writers exhorted the region to turn inward to its own political defense. Campaign propaganda combining blacks and the "Force" Bill flooded the region. The result was a reassessment of individual regional loyalties—a demand for greater political solidarity and racial orthodoxy to oppose federal intervention. In short, it was necessary to close ranks, because white solidarity was more important now than any nonracial issues. Since memories of the Civil War and Reconstruction were still fresh, the Democratic leaders saw before them a chance to regain their foothold among the dissatisfied agrarians. And it worked to an amazing degree. The "Force" Bill's introduction was a case of particularly bad timing for the emerging Populist Party, for it gave the Democrats a potent issue to keep white voters in the Party. "The only argument on which the Democrats depended for results in '92," according to one Populist, "was the Force Bill." "The argument against the independent political movement in the South may be boiled down into one word—nigger," according to Tom Watson on the eve of the party's emergence.[43]

The defeated South had developed a mythical sense of history. The past was glorified to bolster the values of the present, with an emphasis on retaining the status quo and racial orthodoxy while exalting the "Cult of the Confederacy." Post-Reconstruction writers invented a white elite that was right and true, supported by happy slaves and faithful retainers. The myth threatened to become an end in itself. Using these fictions in their defense, the Bourbons sought during the upheaval from the 1880s to 1900 to create a state of mind for a solid South that demanded political and racial conformity as a fulfillment of this ideal. The Bourbon investiture of sanctity in regionalism and the Confederate past robbed the Populist movement of

The Colored man in the picture is not Dead, but Asleep, and he has a Ballot for "Harrison and the Force Bill" in his hand. He pretends to be Dead, but he will be Awake in time to cast that Ballot in November.

Fig. 2. The Democrats campaign with the cry of "Negro domination" (Marmaduke J. Hawkins Collection, State Archives and Library, Raleigh, North Carolina).

its greatest efficacy. The tragedy of Southern Populism is that while both groups looked backward for their ideal state (Jeffersonian and Jacksonian democracy for the Populists), the mythical South proved more magnetic to many white agrarians than the romantic agrarian ideal. Such issues as the "Force" Bill, "Negro domination," and social equality resulted in a reflexive sense of regional loyalty, of racial and political discomfort for many white Populists. Consider the admonitions of W. J. Cash:

WHAT THE FORCE BILL MEANS

Fig. 3. The "Force Bill" revives Reconstruction fears of black domination in the South (Marmaduke J. Hawkins Collection, State Archives and Library, Raleigh, North Carolina).

The eyes of his old captains were ominous and accusing upon him. From hustings and from pulpits thousands of voices proclaimed him traitor and nigger-loving scoundrel; renegade to Southern Womanhood, the Confederate dead, and the God of his fathers; champion of the transformation of the white race into a mongrel breed. And in his own heart, as he gazed upon the evidence, it was, in ninety-nine cases out of the hundred at least, echoed and confirmed—fearfully adjudged true.[44]

"Perhaps only a Southerner can realize how keenly these converts to Populism must have felt their grievances," John Hicks has observed.[45] Degler, not a Southerner, also recognized in his study of Southern dissenters that in the case of the South "the past limits options for change in the present." As the Alliance and the Populists attempted to escape, or recapture, their past, "circumstances, events, and common experiences" made change or return to a more ideal past exceedingly difficult.[46]

Southern Populism's growth was marked by constant attacks from those who saw agrarians as a threat to the status quo. "The one [lasting] fear of the people," said Tom Watson, evaluating the failure of the movement, "was federal interference with our local concerns [the threat of a "Force" Bill], and the consequent uplifting of the Negro [the threat of "Negro supremacy"] into a position of political influence."[47] Democrats based their early attack against the third-party movement on these two basic issues. If Professor Hicks is correct that only "perhaps half" of the white Alliancemen supported a third party while the rest were unwilling "to risk the reality of white supremacy," then the Democrats were successful in preventing voters from leaving the established order.[48]

In the eyes of the political insurgents, the "Force" Bill was proof that New England planned to revive Reconstruction and spur racial hatred in the South.[49] "The cry of Negro domination in Mississippi and a demand for a force bill in Massachusetts," one agrarian constituent angrily reported, "are activated by similar desires and continued for similar ends."[50] If the sections and races would "pull together," the "nefarious schemes" of the politicians to revive "the gory ghost of sectional estrangement" would be to no avail.[51] The Populist and Alliance groups' need to respond to these issues constantly kept them off-balance and diverted voters' eyes from the economic issues upon which they wished to concentrate.

In January 1891, the *National Economist,* the official organ of the Southern Alliance, in an effort to answer the Colored Farmers' Alliance's support for the "Force" Bill, promised the black voter "something better than the Lodge Bill." Reaffirming the promise to stand by the Ocala pledges of equal educational, commercial, and political facilities for both races, it further pledged to "guarantee the colored voter more [economic] justice than has ever been shown him by any association or party"—all without the need of a federal election bill. "During the past few years," the *National Economist* continued, "a silent but potent force has been at work . . . , trying to bring about a [better] condition of affairs between the races."[52] This statement was probably motivated by the Alliance's growing political aspirations more than any desire for biracial economic-class unity, given the history of the segregated Alliances. The federal government, white Alliance-

men and Southern Populists asserted, should focus on alleviating agricultural distress and leave political matters to the South and the state. In consequence, economic advancement rather than political involvement would
uplift the black race. Southern equal educational opportunity and other reforms were also possible without federal legislation. As Booker T. Washington argued, "My faith is that reforms in the South are to come from within.
Southern people have a good deal of human nature. They like to receive the
praise of doing good deeds, and they don't like to obey orders that come
from Washington telling them that they must lay aside at once customs that
they have followed for centuries, and henceforth their [sic] must be but one
railroad coach, one hotel, and one schoolhouse for ex-master and ex-slave."
"Reforms are to come from within," Washington warned, "since Southerners don't like to obey orders that come from Washington, D.C., telling them
that they must lay aside at once customs that they have followed for centuries." [53] The support of the federal government on such issues was almost
certain to doom them to failure. Further, regional pressures for conformity
had squashed a long line of earlier attempts to reform the South. [54]

Although the Colored Farmers' Alliance strongly supported passage of
the "Force" Bill, there was no solid black or white South on this or other
issues. The heterogeneity of the black population made for disagreement
over what changes were wanted or needed most. The growing division of
the black community into three primary economic classes diffused black
opinion about how to solve "the race question" and what was in their best
interest. Rarely will those who subscribe to reform be unanimous on how
it may best be brought about. In this context, the "Force" Bill did not win
approval from all quarters of the black community.

Some blacks and whites believed that discrimination would end only
after they first improved their economic condition through an assertion of
a segregated black self-help philosophy, as articulated by Booker T. Washington and his disciples. This viewpoint placed minimum value on political
activity and insisted first on patience, industry, and moral and economic elevation. [55] In many ways this largely educated, middle-class, and urban black
class espoused much the same role for the federal government as did white
Populists: federal interference would inflame the race issue and rupture any
good feelings that had developed over the decades. A Louisiana black opposed the "Force" Bill "because it is fraught with danger to the Negro;
because it will be the means of rupturing those good feelings which are at
present existing between the two races; because, in fact, it is but an incentive
to bring about a war of races in the South." If it was passed, he predicted,
the result would be a "massacre" once the federal government tried to en-

force the measure in the South. A black lawyer from Florida asserted that, "there is not an honest, intelligent and patriotic colored man in the South, who has the interest and welfare of his race at heart and sincerely desires its permanent prosperity in the Southern States, who can conscientiously endorse . . . the Force Bill." Such a bill "would place the negro population in a very serious position in the South. They would have all odds against them." He further added that "no force bill, under the present circumstances, can place the race in that exalted position in the Government which it craves," and "no Congressional interference can better the political condition or affairs in these [Southern] states."[56] Senator John Morgan of Alabama presented a petition from a group of blacks who denounced the Bill. Washington also took a public stand against the Bill.[57] A number of prosperous blacks in Atlanta, including well-to-do merchants, were reportedly indifferent or opposed to the Bill.[58] Even W. E. B. Du Bois asserted that the "Force" Bill was based on "the erroneous assumption that law can accomplish anything. . . . We must ever keep before us the fact that the South has some excuse for its present attitude. We must remember that a good many of our people . . . are not fit for the responsibility of republican government." He added, "When you have the right sort of black voters, you will need no election laws. The battle of my people must be a moral one, not a legal or physical one."[59] North Carolinian J. C. Price, president of the Afro-American League, the National Equal Rights Convention, and Livingstone College also opposed the bill, but the man Du Bois classified as the "new leader" of blacks died of kidney failure in 1894 and was replaced as the nation's leading black spokesman by Booker T. Washington soon afterward.[60]

According to Meier, "articulate black opinion was all but unanimous in support of the Force Bill of 1890."[61] However, this does not appear to be true in the South. More affluent blacks "simply thought and acted like most Americans—particularly Southern Americans of the age."[62] Economic self-interest could and did transcend race unity—blacks would weigh the benefits of direct political action against financial self-interest along class lines. To infer that all blacks were receptive to reforms that delineated into the Populists' "predators vs. producers" worldview is to say that race crystallizes politics into simple propositions based on class or economics. For example, "the Virginia Colored Alliance did not generally perceive its primary objective to be that of a class struggle with all Farmers."[63] The emerging Populist movement dismissed far too easily these vital elements of intraracial dissimilarity, class, and economic difference, and thereby self-interest politics, that impacted black receptivity to reform, particularly among the leaders. Neither class nor racial appeals captured everyone. These different interests and black self-determination shaped both black and white actions beyond the appeals to class cooperation and help explain the failure of Southern Populism.

Despite these differences, however, by the early 1890s some white and black farmers no longer believed that the Democratic and Republican parties would help them. This slight shift in attitude and the alignments of the Populist revolt were rooted in the slow reorientation of the black and white farmers' attitudes since the 1880s. By the early months of 1891 it was a psychological if not a physical fact that a new party was being seriously considered in the South. The dialogue carried on in the Farmers' Alliance literature of this period reveals a mood of criticism and political introspection as well as discussion about a potential third party. "Through sheer blind adherence," one North Carolina farmer sadly commented, "we hate to go back on it [the Democratic Party], no matter what an extent it has gone back on us."[64] Without acknowledging it, many white farmers battled internally over the questions of "Negro supremacy," federal election interference, "social equality," and the effects of a third party on these issues. In essence, their problem was one of conflicting loyalties—they had to choose between their own needs and those of the South and Democratic Party (or the Republican Party in the case of blacks). Belief in one, however, conflicted with belief in the other; the inevitable result was a period of confusion and indecision. The Northern Alliance was simultaneously engaged in similar introspection and was taking stock of the political weaknesses and economic deficiencies of its region. Furthermore, the Northern Alliance, unlike the Southern order, contained energetic men and women who had long worked for a third party.

The question of a third party had been raised at the 1890 Ocala meeting among the diverse groups, but no formal agreement had been reached. To stay a hasty move, the Ocala delegates decided to assemble in Cincinnati on February 23, 1891, for the express purpose of discussing the third-party issue. The date was later changed to May 19 when it was discovered that it conflicted with the meeting of the Kansas legislature.[65] On the fateful day, "all of the political odds and ends of the country" assembled in Cincinnati. Of the estimated fourteen hundred delegates, the Southern delegation numbered a mere thirty-six. Of this number, twenty-one were from Texas, while Alabama, South Carolina, Virginia, and North Carolina had no representatives.[66] The imbalance in delegates was a telling sign in itself. Furthermore, the support of the Southern Alliance with its larger membership of some three million members was necessary if a third party was to succeed.

The extremely small number of Southerners at Cincinnati was probably due to two factors. First of all, the agrarian South was still not psychologically ready to divorce itself from the Democratic Party. Secondly, and more immediately related to the small delegation, was the Southern Alliance's lack of finances. The attempts at economizing by the delegates was evident. "All the second and third class hotels," one newspaper correspondent reported, "are filled to overflowing."[67] A Georgia politician later estimated that "there are not one-half of the farmers of this country who can save enough money to make a trip to a convention once a year."[68] The later Populists continued to confront financial problems throughout their existence and found them acute when they competed with the more affluent Democrats in later political campaigns. The lack of money and political patronage was a particularly thorny shortcoming in political campaigns, for political patronage was an important element in attracting black political support.

The few Southern delegates who attended the convention, much to the dismay of the Northern Alliance, were the most conservative element there. The combined anti-third-party element of the convention, through a bit of oratorical chicanery, attempted—unsuccessfully as it soon proved—to divert the impending political question by organizing a filibuster around those issues that did not involve the third-party question. Ironically, one of the major leaders of this effort was James B. Weaver, later the unsuccessful Populist presidential candidate of 1892.[69]

Unlike the Ocala convention, at Cincinnati there was no planned segregation of the Colored Farmers' Alliance delegates who attended the meeting. Such "liberal" actions, however, immediately aroused the resentment and suspicions of the white Southern delegates. Long exposure to the threats of "social equality" as a campaign issue, coupled with a growing pattern of *de jure* segregation in the region, prompted the Southern delegates to work for a segregated seating plan. To achieve this purpose despite their small representation, the minority Southerners proposed that a unit rule be adopted for the gatherings. Under this plan, the various organizations would meet separately, discuss the issues, and cast a single vote for the measure before them. The negative vote by other delegates and organizations for this proposition further raised the worst fears of the white Southern delegates. As the measure was overwhelmingly defeated, the Southerners realized that, in the final analysis, the question of a third-party coalition with the North could involve more than just politics. These suspicions must have been even more pronounced when Terence V. Powderly, the Grand Master Workman of the Knights of Labor and a well-known Northern labor leader, spoke out for equality of opportunity, and justice for both black and white laborers of both sections. The racial creed of the South, as the Southerners viewed matters, would receive little consideration if a North-South coalition materialized.[70]

Symbolic efforts were made, nonetheless, by both sections to reduce the sectional and racial hatreds caused by the Civil War. One of the most touching of these acts was the clasping of hands by a Union and Confederate veteran on the center stage, while a black delegate stood in the background between these two former enemies.[71] This black man was named Savage, "a smart Negro politician" who had come from North Carolina to be with "the people." He had been noticed by a Saginaw, Michigan, Allianceman who had been greatly impressed by his political astuteness. The white Allianceman managed to secure a place on the rostrum for Savage, and he made a "slick" speech to the audience.[72] Despite Savage's various talents, he found himself unable to pay his railroad fare back to North Carolina. Again employing his oratorical ability, Savage, expressing great loneliness for his home, made an impassioned plea to the convention to help him out of his financial predicament. A hat was passed and several small coins were collected. Savage then commented that if it had not been for the problem of finances, many more of his race would have attended the meeting. After his short speech, "much cheering" for the Colored Farmers' Alliance and the work it was trying to accomplish in the South followed. Savage, after a final expression of his gratitude to the delegates, took his leave.[73]

The primary purpose of the Cincinnati convention, according to Ignatius Donnelly of the Northern Alliance, was "not . . . so much to proclaim a [political] creed as to erect a banner around which the swarming host of reform could rally."[74] The movement was still fluid and had not crystallized views toward a third party. A necessary prelude to reform was the need to establish a program around which all elements could agree and coalesce. A sharp division of opinion, however, quickly developed among the delegates over the question of a third party. Despite the vigorous urgings of the third-party advocates, even the most aggressive of the delegates stopped short of final commitment, believing that "the people" needed more political education before they could be induced to leave the Democratic Party.[75]

Since the Southern Alliance would constitute the balance of power in any farmer coalition, the radicals at Cincinnati courted the favor of the Southern delegates. The hopes of the third partyites, however, were soon dimmed when a letter from Southern Alliance President Leonidas L. Polk urged the convention to give the people more time to decide on the political question. The reading of this letter, one paper reported, "was received with painful silence" by the delegates. Since "it was President Polk . . . more than to any other single individual" to whom the Alliance "owes its existence," his opinion carried substantial weight with the members.[76] For all practical purposes, Polk's letter brought closure on the third-party question. The Northern delegates quickly realized that the political question was settled, at least for a time. Reaffirming February 22, 1892, at St. Louis for the next convention, the gathering adjourned, with few tangible results to its credit.[77]

If the Southerners assessed the Cincinnati meeting in terms of future racial politics, they knew that they would have to reorient their personal racial philosophies to accommodate blacks within the movement—if they combined with the Northern Alliance. However, although Republican politics demonstrated the viability of racial accommodation as a political device, the concept was not yet manifest in Southern Alliance thinking. The Southerners approached racial accommodation warily, suggesting only that at best blacks be permitted segregated roles, with political activity relegated solely to whites. This system would hardly have given blacks a sense of belonging. But to understand the problems of accommodation, one must measure how preemptive the black presence actually was in the face of regional prejudices.

It is against the background of increasing political ambitions and hostility that the South's third-party ideology at Cincinnati must be viewed. As Democratic propaganda increasingly called for political and racial solidarity within regions, frustration with the Democratic Party as a party of reform boosted feelings toward political insurgency. Despite agrarian racial antagonism, the prospect of reform strengthened the belief in a third political party that would champion the farmer. Discouraged as the farmers were, the acceptance of a third party would depend upon its regional approval.[78] While Southern insurgency grew, it made sense to nurture agrarian protest to a point where the farmer would finally strike out in anger. Grassroots voters of both races needed to be brought to the point where they would vote for their pocketbooks over their prejudices. This, the Alliance felt, was where the emphasis should be placed—not on the racial philosophy of the Democrats.

The movement's racial attitude at this point can be gleaned from the literature of the period. "A third party will accomplish what millions of money and tons of blood have failed to do," reported one South Carolina optimist. "It will solve the race question."[79] Expressing distaste for the political "tricks of the past," one North Carolinian believed that:

We have a prospect of being permitted to vote truly for equal rights. The giant born a few days ago in Cincinnati will sweep the fields and the hollows. Empty names of past political parties, along with their

"bloody shirts" and "niggers in the woodpile" are no more to be
adored; measures, not men, are to be advocated.[80]

The *Alliance Vindicator* of Sulphur Springs, Texas, a CFA newspaper edited
by Alex Asberry, black president of the Texas Colored Alliance, believed that
the campaign to "suppress personal, local, sectional and national prejudice"
had been so successful that "only a few" people still clung to the old ideologies. "These will in time," it was predicted, "become educated up to the
point where they can comprehend the situation" and the "cloak" of color
will no longer be an "index to his character."[81] Ideas on the eradication of
racism, class solidarity over political solidarity, and independence of thought
would continue to grow as tensions increased.[82] Accepting the region's racial
orthodoxy was one of the burdens that Populists always were tempted with
as they presented their unconventional formula for biracial political and economic cooperation to the region. Obliged to court the black vote out of
self-interest as well as a natural component of its Jeffersonian class coalition,
white Southerners were troubled by the incompatibility between self-interest and societal demands. Racial accommodation, in the incipient stage at
this point, was a necessity for the movement during the next decade. As John
C. McLaren, a white Populist leader from Alabama, expressed it, "we are the
only party that is in fact a friend to the colored race, and we are so, not from
choice, but necessity."[83] Perhaps, after all, racial barriers could fall if the
practical reasons and the nature of their collective actions could be explained to the membership, as well as the region.

One reporter described the St. Louis convention of February 22, 1892, as
"an assembly of cranks composed of long haired men and short haired
women" where "all sorts of ism's struggled for recognition."[84] Since the
third-party question had been officially deferred until this meeting, it was
only natural that agitation on the question soon resumed. The division between Southern white and black delegates over the third-party question is
worthy of special recognition. R. M. Humphrey, general superintendent of
the Colored Farmers' Alliance, was now regarded as a somewhat unsavory
character by the Southern white delegates since he had authorized the unsuccessful black cotton pickers' strike the previous fall. Aware that the question of supporting a third party would be a major issue at St. Louis, Humphrey, perhaps in an effort to boost his declining popularity in the white
community, had engaged in a bit of political skullduggery to ensure that
the Colored Farmers' Alliance vote was cast according to the dictates of
white Alliance opinion.

At the Indianapolis meeting of November 1891, Humphrey had inquired
of J. L. Gilmore, a white man from Georgia and a third-party proponent

who had only recently emigrated from England, if he would "look after the colored work" in that state for him. Gilmore readily agreed to this request and added that he would also lecture to the Colored Farmers' Alliancemen whenever it was agreeable to his white constituents. Following the meeting, Gilmore was commissioned as a state lecturer for the Georgia Colored Farmers' Alliance.[85] Part of the state's white order, led by Gilmore's Tattnall County Alliance, feared that the Georgia white delegation to the St. Louis convention would be packed against favoring a third party. Thus, anti-third-party men now had numerical superiority in the Georgia delegation. Leonidas F. Livingston, a small planter from Newton County and leader of the Georgia Alliance, had packed the Georgia delegation with opponents of a third party. E. S. Richardson, superintendent of the State Colored Farmers' Alliance and a Livingston supporter, did the same with his delegation. By manipulating the CFA vote, this minority pro-third-party faction saw a chance for the opinion of the state's whites in favor of a third party to be successful, at the expense of the black order. Preparations were made for Gilmore to represent this pro-third-party element at St. Louis. As soon as the prevailing white pro-third-party opinion was made known to Humphrey, he immediately forwarded Gilmore a letter appointing him proxy for the entire Colored Farmers' Alliance, including the Georgia branch, and instructing him to cast the state's eleven CFA votes for a third party.[86] With the appointment of Gilmore, the situation changed numerically.

Opposition to a third party was not new to the Georgia Colored Farmers' Alliance. As early as 1890, the Georgia Colored Farmers' Alliance, or some of its leaders, opposed forming a third party—which Humphrey supported. At Ocala, the National Colored Alliance had officially voted down a motion supporting a third party. However, certain individuals had endorsed the third party. But E. A. Richardson voted against and later opposed formation of a third party in Cincinnati on May 19, 1891, as well. He had also opposed the cotton picker's strike. His actions represented what he regarded as the broader interests and wishes of the Georgia Colored Farmers' Alliance membership and white partisans opposed to a third party. Richardson appears to have been supporting Livingston, who opposed a third party, against Tom Watson, who favored a new party. But the machination of Humphrey and others was an attempt to get Georgia blacks to go along with their white Alliance colleagues in supporting a third party.[87] At the St. Louis conference, Humphrey packed the National Colored Farmers' Alliance delegation with pro-third-party white men, an action contrary to the organization's charter, which forbade integration, but one that would ensure him convention victory.[88] A further indication of Humphrey's character was his commercializing of the individual black delegate's credentials, selling them to the white delegates for fifty cents each.[89] If the ninety-seven votes of the National Colored Farmers' Alliance were cast in favor of a third party at St. Louis, the chances for its enactment would be greatly enhanced.[90] Even if the black delegates favored a third party, these sorts of covert activities seemed unlikely to elicit their support.

The Georgia Colored Farmers' Alliance appears to have been the most provoked of all the state orders as a result of its delegation being packed with white men and their votes being forcibly cast. Perhaps since Richardson opposed a third party, this was a long-standing political enmity finally surfacing between him and Humphrey. In protest, the Georgia Colored Farmers' Alliance refused to participate further in the convention's proceedings. Immediately upon their departure, Gilmore, with astonishing insouciance, cast the state's eleven votes for a third party. At this point, only five other members of the National Colored Farmers' Alliance were still present, which allowed Gilmore to also assume control of the remaining eighty-six votes for the third party. Word passed from delegation to delegation what had happened. Blacks learned that Gilmore, a white man, could cast their vote because of Humphrey's covert proxy deals. In a display of protest and rage, the entire black delegation walked out of the convention, warning the white delegates that even if a new party was formed, it would receive no black votes.[91]

The Georgia Colored Farmers' Alliance further protested that they had not only been treated in a demeaning manner, but that Gilmore had also persuaded them to pay his way to the convention. Gilmore promptly retorted that "not a Negro paid a cent of my expenses" to St. Louis and "if they said so, they lied."[92] It was apparent that Humphrey and Gilmore had won the day for a third party at St. Louis against the black delegations. The actions of Humphrey, Gilmore, and the other white Alliance members who permitted this fraud against the Colored Farmers' Alliance delegates testify that blacks had no real voice in national agrarian politics. Pre-convention voting also suggests that CFA members may have been more reluctant to bolt the Republican Party than were whites to leave the Democratic Party. While it is possible that white convention leaders thought they were doing what was best for their black brethren, it would seem nevertheless that stripping the Colored Farmers' Alliance of its vote against a third party would offer few inducements for the black voter to join the new party. Finally, there was a valuable lesson for the blacks in these backroom deals. As a white employed spokesman for black agrarians, Humphrey could not deny the power of race in the South, and facing white ostracism, his siding with white pro–third partyites against black anti–third partyites demonstrated that biracial coalitions could not be sustained on the basis of agrarian sentiment and appeals to conscience. In short, Humphrey probably simply lacked the psychic strength to withstand the pressure of race, as did most Southerners.

The St. Louis brokering was not the first time that Humphrey and his white protégées had gone against the wishes of the CFA membership. A similar incident occurred with the Virginia Colored Alliance during the prior year, when Humphrey and the white superintendent of the North Carolina and Virginia Colored Farmers' Alliance, Joseph J. Rogers, seemed more attentive to white Alliance concerns at the expense of the Colored Farmers' Alliance as well as how operation of the Colored Alliance Exchange at Richmond should be handled. Humphrey's sympathies again seem primarily with white concerns. As a final straw, Rogers absconded with the Virginia Colored Farmers' Alliance Exchange funds. This behavior by Humphrey and other white CFA leaders suggests questionable loyalties, even when they were being paid to represent their black members.[93] Additionally, the assumption that what was good for whites was good for blacks indicated that black voices were secondary to whites'. Although agrarian leaders argued a common class bond between the races, the built-in conflict of interest between propertied whites and landless blacks manifested itself as the Alliances transformed into a political movement.[94]

Not all topics provoked racial and political hostility at St. Louis. In a ceremony reminiscent of Cincinnati, a symbolic burial of sectional hatred was performed for the benefit of the delegates. "If the common people could win victories on the battlefield," predicted the *National Economist* in describing the ceremony, "they can win greater ones at the ballot box."[95] This touching scene was followed by the "weak voice" of one T. A. Powell, singing "United We Stand, Divided We Fall" to a guitar accompaniment. As he finished, shouts of "let's shake hands" arose from the audience, but few delegates participated, suggesting a less than enthusiastic endorsement of national unity. Suspicion of some of the proposals by various groups inhibited greater unity. However, E. C. Cabel, a black delegate from "Kansas City and Virginia," was brought forward on the rostrum and asked to shake hands with some of the white delegates from both sections. Due to the large crowd, he was able to shake hands with only those persons at the front of the platform, but he performed this service with joviality, laughing throughout the whole process.[96]

White Southerners, evaluating the convention's political temperament, took issue with the more radical statements and proposals around with which they were expected to unite. Part of the problem was the wide variety of ideologies present, especially amongst the Midwestern leaders, who pushed planks not related to agrarian reform. The suffragist groups, for example, demanding the vote for black as well as white women, aroused the ire of all sections.[97] On the second day of the convention, Mrs. Mary Lease, the Kansas Alliance feminist firebrand, proposed to no avail that the delegates abolish the sex line "as has been done to the color line."[98] Furthermore, the pledge of Ignatius Donnelly "to wipe the color line out of politics" also held overtones of something beyond political sentiment for blacks.[99] Southerners desired major economic reform, in addition to political reform that retained local privilege, but they balked at those proposals that suggested stronger political and social assimilation of blacks beyond the range of political expediency. Poor rural white Southerners would not embrace these measures. Southern leaders also knew that the Bourbons would use these issues to galvanize the region's potential voters against the movement.

While even the most reform-minded white Southerner looked askance at wholesale social participation for blacks, the need for black leaders within the movement was recognized. If blacks were expected to vote for the newly formed Populist Party, their leaders must hold positions of responsibility within the party hierarchy. Building on the earlier efforts of the Knights of Labor and other groups, some agrarian leaders sought to construct a practical party framework that would include both races. But the Populists would face the same problems as other independents since Reconstruction.[100] Such controversial Alliance slogans as "equal rights to all and special privileges to none" were part of the folklore of reform traceable back to the ages of Andrew Jackson and Thomas Jefferson. But even a charitable view of the gap between agrarian rhetoric and reality at St. Louis hardly pictures an uncompromising biracial alliance by the white South, the actions of Superintendent Humphrey aside.

Other difficulties soon arose from the white Southern delegates having limited black participation. On the second day of the convention, one black, W. H. Warwick of Virginia, rose "in a dignified but extremely earnest manner" and pointed out that the CFA was receiving inadequate attention from the largely white assemblage. If black votes were to be coveted, then visible black participation was required. Perhaps the conflict with whites the prior year over activities of the Virginia Colored Farmers' Alliance had incensed Warwick. White agrarians could not have it both ways. Subsequently, Warwick demanded that such policies of exclusion be halted. A white delegate at the rear of the convention "flippantly" suggested that Warwick be made assistant secretary—a position of little power but prestigious enough to blot out the accusations of racism and exclusivity leveled by Warwick. Seeing the need to provide blacks with a substantive role, "the convention took the suggestion seriously." It was, surprisingly enough, a white delegate from Georgia who moved that the Warwick's nomination be made unanimous.

Immediately, however, an Alabama delegate rose in protest, not because a black was nominated he said, but because of the call for a unanimous vote. The motion of the Georgian was then put before the floor and a great "aye" resounded, the objector from Alabama signifying the only "no" in the whole house.[101] J. Brad Beverly, a prominent white delegate from Virginia, later denied reports by the Associated Press that the election of Warwick was a joke.[102]

Taken out of context, such acts suggest that blacks were to have active movement roles. However, the contrast between this symbolic act and Humphrey's earlier treatment of black delegates is obvious. This call for the election of a black official is not as callous as the earlier capture of the CFA vote for the third party. In fact, one must wonder if convention delegates were in earnest in electing a black assistant secretary, a largely symbolic position, or whether this act was a concession to obtain black cooperation and votes. Perhaps white Southern delegates reasoned that political tokenism was a necessary evil, no matter how distasteful it might be, to protect the white farmers' interests. If the Populist movement could not offer patronage to attract black leaders and voters, perhaps the next best thing would be participation in the councils of the agrarian movement. This struggle was analogous to the regional Republican Party's development of "Lily-White" factions that wanted to bring respectability and more white voters to the Southern wing. They wanted—and needed—black votes, but substantive black participation in Republican Party affairs was not desired.

By the time of the St. Louis meeting in 1892, many Southerners realized that agrarian reform would not be forthcoming through the Democratic Party. The election of several candidates in 1890–91 on the Alliance platform had proved futile, since upon election the candidates did not live up to their promises when measured against the Alliance yardstick. Some of these legislatures even passed legislation detrimental to black interests. As a result, the Southern and Colored Farmers' Alliances went into rapid decline after 1891. In addition, heightened financial difficulties pushed many disgruntled farmers into the third-party movement. The Mississippi River flooded each year from 1891 to 1893; the boll weevil made its appearance in 1892. Cotton prices continued to fall; foreclosures and mortgage and tenancy rates increased as the lien system tightened. Black and white alike suffered. In Georgia, Texas, and Tennessee, for example, the tide of debt had been on the rise since 1889.[103] By the fall of 1891, the Tennessee Alliance movement was near collapse because of debt. A quarter of the members had dropped out of the movement, probably because of an inability to pay their dues.[104] Just as the National Alliance was forced into exerting financial pressure against the Tennessee order, agrarian life became further entangled in a web of personal and organizational financial problems by 1892. The Alliance was incapable of solving agrarian problems, either because existing governments were too powerful or so-called "Alliance Legislatures" had not voted in the reforms. Another solution seemed necessary.

Since the Populist Party had existed de facto on the local level in many states as early as 1891, third-party reform began to receive more favorable comment in the South. By the time of the St. Louis conference, a sizable segment of the white agrarian South began to see a third-party presidential nomination as a necessity. The economic pinch seems to have been the chief motivating factor, although disillusionment with the Democratic Party contributed to the mood. According to Hicks, perhaps half of the white Alliance members gave the new party their support. Henry Demarest Lloyd, radical journalist and author of the famous tract *Wealth against Commonwealth,* asserted that "one of the principal sources" of the Populist Movement "was the Farmers' Alliance." No one knows how many Alliance members joined the Populist Party, but if principle were the determinant, it would have been a majority.[105]

The national Republican Party after 1891 had for all practical purposes abandoned blacks in the South, except when it needed their votes. "By 1893," Stanley Hirshon has written, "the race question as a political issue was dead and national solidarity was to a large extent achieved, but at the expense of the Southern Negro."[106] Southern blacks were less privy to patronage, and when they were, the press and white community reacted negatively. Further, the Southern wing of the party sought respectability and more white voters. If black voters were being eliminated, they needed to be replaced by native whites, but the "Negro Party" found recruiting native white Southern members difficult. Several Southern states developed Lily-White factions that sought to make the Republican Party a white man's political instrument and purge blacks. And as the Republican Party became less hospitable toward blacks, the only real alternative in the South was the Populist Party, if blacks wished meaningful political participation. But would a new third party be able to deliver on its promises? Caution was necessary because blacks, being vulnerable, had more to lose than whites by supporting the new party if it failed. Since the Populist Party needed votes and blacks needed a receptive party, the two groups seemed an ideal match. The Populists could offer blacks little if any patronage and lacked the finances to court voters, so political participation was their best option. But the Populists also had to attract not only large numbers of black voters but also significant numbers of white voters, a dilemma faced by the Republican Party. The third partyites needed to straddle the race issue yet attract black and white voters to a new coalition based on, in Tom Watson's words, "self-interest." Would it work?

The step preceding political reform for the third party was a national nominating convention. The responsibility of selecting the place and date for the occasion was delegated to a five-man subcommittee at St. Louis. Omaha, Nebraska, in the heart of the depressed Midwestern farm belt, was selected as the site of the convention, and the symbolic date of July 4, 1892, was set to convene the new Populist Party and nominate national candidates. As an obvious symbol of the new party's patriotic fervor and crusading spirit, the membership eagerly seized upon this date to declare to the country their political independence from the two old parties.[107]

The delegate selection process also represented the party's split from traditions. Each state would select eight at-large representatives and four from each congressional district. The number of delegates to be present at Omaha, it was eagerly noted, was 1,776—a most appropriate figure given the date and purpose of the meeting.[108] The agrarians were openly announcing their independence from both old parties and striking out on their own. Whether this total was by design or accidental is unknown, but the chances against such a random total leads one to suspect that it was incorporated to add symbolism to the occasion. Furthermore, since the Populist Party constantly spoke of itself as a reform movement seeking to return to the principles of Jefferson and the Declaration of Independence, the promise held in such a gesture could hardly fail to be noticed by the news media or associated in the mind of prospective recruits.[109]

When the Omaha convention convened in the summer of 1892, approximately 1,400 delegates were present, more than 300 short of the magic number of 1,776.[110] Perhaps this shortfall was an ill omen about the future of the new third party. Indicative of the South's changing political sentiment toward a third party was the presence of large delegations from all the states but South Carolina,[111] an exception probably due to the influence of Ben Tillman, who had failed to bolt the Democratic Party in South Carolina.[112] Since Tillman was the undisputed leader of his state's agrarian movement and was supported by the South Carolina Alliance, very little would attract South Carolinians of third-party leanings to Omaha.

Even though there was "no musty prejudice or caste system" at Omaha, blacks had little representation at the convention. Only four black delegates are reported, one each from Kansas and Virginia and two members with the Texas Committee.[113] Undoubtedly, travel costs and distance kept many black as well as white delegates away, and perhaps some black delegates were still discouraged over the negativity of the St. Louis meeting. Since the majority of the black representatives at St. Louis had not supported the third-party movement, it is possible they were unwilling to listen to any proposition in favor of political insurgency.

A great stumbling block in the official formation of the Populist Party had been the white South's conformist psychology toward the cry of "nigger domination." While white Southern Populists intended to keep blacks socially and, to an extent, economically subordinate, the potential of the black vote as the balance of power in close elections did not escape the white farmers at Omaha. According to the Columbus *Advocate,* a black paper, the insurgent South had decided that:

> The Negro will vote. That was the edict issued by the Southern delegates at the Omaha convention. One of the national committeemen said, we shall vote the Negroes and their votes will be counted. We know how to control and handle the Negro. Already 400,000 black men have been enlisted in this organization.[114]

White Populist comments that they knew "how to control and handle the Negro" may have caused blacks to pause and reflect before joining such a party.

Leonidas L. Polk had pledged that the white Alliance would protect blacks and "see that they are allowed to vote. . . . They are largely in this movement, and will be an important factor in the campaign next year."[115] The *Omaha Daily Bee* confirmed that "these former Democratic leaders now say that the votes of these people shall be cast and counted. . . . The old democratic managers . . . have completely changed their attitude toward the colored voter."[116] The new third party of necessity produced attitudes favorable to the survival and development of the black vote—if blacks voted Populist. But the basic outlook for grassroots white agrarians remained unchanged: the black man was free to vote and would receive white agrarian protection provided his vote aided his white mentors.

Perhaps white Populist leaders rationalized that what benefited one race would benefit the other. If blacks were to benefit as members of the agrarian class, it was only right that they participate and, of course, vote Populist. Consequently, Populist rhetoric was pragmatic as well as idealistic, but was at all times primarily tailored to the time and place. The main attraction to the movement for lower-class white and black Populists was the alteration of the status quo, and Populist leaders spoke of better economic conditions for all. Further, agrarian class rhetoric included rural blacks as an essential and compatible part of the reform movement's philosophy and underpinning whenever black votes were needed. Although grassroots white Populists might hate the idea of significantly raising black economic status, many Populist leaders understood that the necessities of the age demanded that racial etiquette yield to political expediency. In a sense, Populist leaders subordinated race and place to class and the "self-interest" of an agrarian coalition as the central theme of the movement. Populist leaders pointed out to blacks that they were already in economic slavery via the tenant system, lien laws, debt, peonage, and so forth, but that the Republicans and Democrats also kept them in political slavery. "Sockless" Jerry Simpson had earlier predicted that "they [blacks] will vote for us" and that a biracial "farmer class" would constitute a potent voting force in the South.[117] "The forces of reform" would not quit until there were "equal rights and equal privileges securely established for all the men and women of this country."[118]

The delegates gathered at Omaha clearly viewed themselves as a class separate from the goldbugs of the country. "From the same prolific womb of governmental injustice," they declared in their platform, "we breed the two great classes—tramps and millionaires."[119] Ideologically, a more fundamental dichotomy than the Southern race issue brewed among the radicals. The white farmers viewed themselves as society's underlings and included in this class the black man.[120] American society by the late 1880s had split into distinct economic divisions with increasingly little interaction between classes, and the more forward-thinking political agitators understood that defeat of the capitalist bosses would require a coalition of men and women of all backgrounds and races. But to succeed, coalition politics requires all sides to set aside differences both short- and long-term. A new national party as proposed in Omaha would force delegates to abandon personal and societal prejudices to an extent not asked by earlier third parties. Appeals to common class and agrarian interests had failed repeatedly in the post–Civil War South when the Democrats played the race card, of which they were masters.

Polk's untimely death in the spring 1892, just prior to the Omaha convention, was a serious blow to the Populist cause, especially in the South. His nomination as Populist presidential candidate at Omaha seemed assured, which would have placed the South in a leadership position with the party. For it was Polk "more than any other single individual" who had created the Alliance and made it a force to be reckoned with during this era.[121] Also, his proven leadership skills and presence would have motivated more of the South's fence-sitters to support the Populist Party. As early as the St. Louis meeting of 1892, the Colored Farmers' Alliance was reportedly beginning to support him, for which they received praise from the white delegates.[122] The CFA seemed willing to forgive Polk's strong opposition to the failed 1891 cotton picker strike and the "Force" Bill.

Whether Polk's nomination would have created a more favorable climate for blacks in the Populist movement is conjecture, but judging from his past statements, he had little sympathy for blacks. While Polk had, in his own words, spent some of the "sweetest" hours of his early life with his "old black Mammy" and "little colored playmates," he nonetheless regarded the black race as "an incubus—a solid barrier" against the forces of progress in the South. Although he had "naught but feelings of kindness" for blacks, he supported black colonization and would gladly "hail with delight and rejoicing his peaceful departure" from the region.[123] Polk actually formulated a plan to rid the South of blacks. First mentioned in Mississippi in 1891, the plan outlined the creation of a separate state in the West, Texas preferably, where a large uninhabited parcel of land would be cut up into forty-acre plots for black homesteads. To prevent unscrupulous whites from taking political advantage of the settlers, any white man who ventured into this "reserve" would be disfranchised and disqualified from holding office.[124] While Polk intended to present his plan before the Supreme Court in hopes of having it legally implemented, it appears that he made no real efforts toward this end.[125] It is interesting to contemplate what position on colonization Polk would have taken had he lived and been nominated as the Populist presidential candidate in 1892. If he had then won the election, the question becomes even more tantalizing.

Polk's thinking was not unique to his age. Various ideas had long been discussed among whites and blacks as part of the solution to the "Negro problem."[126] Every black leader of consequence had flirted with or was receptive to the idea of colonization by the time of the Civil War.[127] Although the war blunted the migratory urge, at least temporarily, it flared back up again within the decade, stimulated by persecution, migratory impulses to less worn-out lands in the West, recruitment by labor agents, and the hope of a better life.[128] By 1882, blacks by the hundreds were "turning their faces to Arkansas and Texas."[129] In North Carolina, future Texan and Populist leader John B. Rayner was making his way West in 1881, as were hundreds of black laborers seeking relief from indebtedness and harsh tenancy agreements.[130] In Georgia, "certain colored agents," notably Bishop Henry M. Turner, were urging flight to Liberia or the West.[131] Such precarious circumstances and the approval of departure by leading blacks and whites produced an increasingly restless migratory urge among lower-class agrarian blacks, prior to and during the Populist era. According to the Reverend H. N. Payne:

Much as the colored people are attached to the places where they grew up, thousands of them would gladly go to Arkansas, to Texas, or to any other place where they could better their condition; but they cannot raise the money to emigrate and must stay and suffer where they are.[132]

The internal migrations, notably to Kansas in the early 1880s, produced several initially successful all-black "states" or towns, including:

The town of Judson, on Johnson's Island on the Mississippi River a little north of Memphis, in which there is not a single white man, the owner ruling out the inferior [white] race. There are in the town six stores, a few shops, two churches and a school. The island, the soil of which is quite rich, is eight miles long.

Judson, the owner of Johnson's Island, thus had "his own country" composed solely of blacks.[133]

The 1894 state platform of the Alabama Jeffersonian Democratic–Populist fusion group took a clear stand in favor of voluntary black colonization to lessen the number of blacks in the state.[134] The increased migration in the last two decades of the century was "correlated with the agricultural unrest associated with the rise of the Farmers' Alliance."[135]

Polk's death opened the door for other men of ambition and initiative in both sections to vie for the coveted Omaha third-party presidential nomination; however, his death left the South with a lack of suitable candidates, thereby increasing the North's ability to drive deeper into the political leadership of the movement. With the removal of the Southern-supported Judge Walter Gresham, primarily by his own efforts, "there was none so eligible as General James B. Weaver of Iowa" to head up the third party.[136] The selection of Weaver from the Northern Alliance, combined with the death of Polk, undoubtedly encouraged more liberal political and social expression than would have otherwise been the case if the more conservative Polk had lived.[137] The South, frustrated by its failure to lead the party's crusade, now had to be courted in order to offset any charges of regional domination. Sectionalism manifested itself in several earlier Alliance national meetings, and its impact was still present in 1892. In order to counterbalance the nomination of General Weaver, "General" James Field, a one-legged Confederate veteran representing "the best and ruling element of Virginia Populism," was accorded second place on the National Populist ticket.[138] While Field's selection related to the convention's aim of developing political unity, it was also probably political opportunism, an attempt to halt further deterioration of sectional unity and resentment over the selection of Weaver.

Weaver's Civil War record against the South was particularly distasteful to many in the region. He reportedly had instituted a reign of terror during his Civil War occupation of Pulaski, Tennessee, robbing, imprisoning, and executing soldiers and civilians. During his later campaigns these allegations would come back to haunt him.[139] Polk's selection would have created some of the same problems since he was a Confederate veteran, but his past leadership reduced the potential damage. Moreover, the Southern Alliance was not heading up the party's ticket, which made the national ticket less palatable in the South. With a third-choice national ticket, sectional rivalries, and the race question, the Populist Party entered the political arena.

In the post-Reconstruction period, Southern white agrarians clung to the idea that reform could be realized through the established political order, namely the Democratic Party. But that view transmuted into the Populist axiom that reform could not be achieved through the existing political system by men who viewed change as a threat to their own peculiar interests and security. In short, reform would emerge only through the efforts of an economically and politically deprived class who forced desired changes to grow into a full-blown third-party movement. "This reform commenced where all great reforms commence," General Weaver observed, "among the poor. Necessity is not only the mother of invention but reform also."[140] Reform was seen as less a stage in the development of Populism than an essential condition for its inception. "No reform ever occurs in old organizations," asserted a Populist organ.[141] To Populists, the entrenched political system sought to protect its ill-gotten gains against "the people."

Despite initial appearances to the contrary, there was no guarantee that blacks would join the Populist Party in large numbers. Despite their repudiation by the Republicans and the Democrats, the disenfranchised historically were unwilling to openly experiment with and incorporate change. Blacks as victims understandably feared the power of change. Those who had the power to make change, such as the Bourbon Democrats, could also create more conflict. And the recent tide of lynchings had coincided with such change in the blacks' environment and resulted in the exercise of repressive justice when change was introduced.[142] As John B. Rayner expressed it: "The Negro is the most conservative of men, he fears change, because he fears the power able to produce changes."[143] The idea that a new, unproven third party could deliver on its promises was a matter blacks needed to ponder seriously, for to support a failed party left blacks more vulnerable than ever. The promotion by such middle-class black leaders as Booker T. Washington of moral uplift, spiritual and economic improvement, and economic progress as solutions to the race question gathered momentum by this point.

At the outset, most third-party movements find it difficult to build and maintain strong, widespread membership bases at the grassroots level. To evolve, these organizations must appeal widely to specific interests before they can forward their reform planks. If the movement is incapable of building and maintaining a large active member base, a more powerful organization, such as the Democratic Party in the South, can sway public opinion against reform and maintain the status quo. Alternately, the established organization can co-opt enough planks from the third party's reform platform to forego any need for full-scale reform in the public's eye. In the 1890s South, the Democrats could institute enough reforms to satisfy most white voters, regardless of class, and thus undercut the larger arguments of the Populist Party. If enough white voters were satisfied with establishment efforts and accepted the Democratic proposition that Populism would give more power to blacks, the movement would wither on the vine. In short, black rights could be advanced if they could anticipate the needs and help direct such reform-minded movements, but their efforts could as easily be for nought.[144]

Black interests were not being fulfilled by the Republican Party. A Georgia black man who endorsed the Populist Party captured his race's interests, which focused on economics and not social equality. "But I tell you what we do want," he informed the Populists:

We want equal rights at the ballot box and equal justice before the law; we want better wages for our labor and better prices for our produce; we want more money in circulation to pay for our labor and our produce; we want to lift the mortgage from the old cow and mule which they have carried till they are sway-backed; we want to school our children, and we want a chance to earn a home."[145]

The *Atlanta Constitution* observed in October 1890 that it was a "curious fact" that some blacks were now entering politics, still seeking to find a voice that would improve their economic condition.[146] But blacks were pragmatic and cautious in their expectations of the third party. Whereas white Populist leaders had lofty Jeffersonian ideas for the party, blacks were pragmatists. Throughout the Populist campaign of the 1890s, blacks called for equal rights and equal justice from a system which provided little of either. Better wages, debt reduction, the desire for land ownership and education—these were things blacks wanted. For the new party to attract black voters, it must offer some combination of these.

One correspondent with an eye to the Populist Party proclaimed that "all political progress is made through new parties. All new parties in America," he further commented, "have believed in the equality of man before the law, and while new, they have made such progress as has dimmed in some small degree the separating lines of nationality, race and color."[147] At the outset of any movement, a philosophic base and a certain amount of idealism is necessary to gain the attention of and convert new members. The promise of economic relief, however, probably interested the grassroots following more than any vague philosophy or idealism.[148] Despite an increasing emphasis on political conformity and racial solidarity, the third-party movement continued to grow after the Omaha convention. Ironically, the very pressures designed to break up the movement instead created a feeling of class unity among the agrarians. The cry against social injustice, human indignity, and fraud at the ballot box, and for the chance for an economically frustrated class to enjoy the fruits of their labor motivated Southern Populism. "Social justice, emotionally approached," according to one historian, "became the religion of the movement."[149]

To a considerable extent, the Southern white Populist attitude toward blacks can be contrasted between a short-range emphasis on self-interest and political expediency on one hand, and a long-range identification with the goals of American society on the other—what Lawrence Goodwyn called "the democratic promise." In its Jeffersonian aspirations, if not so much in actuality, the egalitarian Populist creed must have created ambivalent feelings toward blacks in the minds of the white agrarian reformers from the outset. This seems particularly so for the more articulate and educated Southern leaders who voiced an egalitarianism that they rarely practiced. In actuality, two types of ideological dichotomies concerned blacks—between the sections and within individuals themselves. In the first, conservative white agrarian Southerners stressed economic and financial development by an activist central government, believing that what benefited whites must of necessity benefit the blacks. The Northern Alliance and blacks, on the other hand, additionally stressed political rights supported by a centrist government, as well as civil rights for blacks. In the second, distinctions existed within the South between those who relied upon the economic self-interest approach and those such as Tom Watson who initially also championed black political rights. Consider Watson's comment on equal justice for all men: "I believe in the Jeffersonian creed with all my heart, and think that all the aims of good government can be covered by that one sentence. EQUAL AND EXACT JUSTICE TO ALL MEN!"[150]

Holding to both ideologies created a cleavage within the Populist movement, with the grassroots members clustering around a conservative philosophy of self-interest and racial solidarity, while white Populist leaders fostered a more "radical" political philosophy around the race issue. In this realm of ideas, we will review the thoughts and actions of minorities during this period of Populism's ascendancy.

4

The Minority Temper

Reform Spirit during the Populist Movement

All the Negro wants is Protection.

In order to understand the white Southern Populist attitude toward blacks, it is necessary to examine the movement's concept of agrarianism, the social ethic, and the application of power in politics. Conversely, the mood of the black community was in flux at this point, wavering between two antithetical arguments on the future of the race. This chapter will examine how attitudes of both races combined to form the uneasy coalition of third-party politics of the late-nineteenth-century South.

Populist rhetoric propounds an agrarianism translated through a Protestant concept of wealth achieved through honest work and virtue by an independent hardworking Jeffersonian yeomanry. With religious fervor, Populists quoted Jefferson and Jackson as their ideal economic paradigm and as the source of answers to their questions. Their use of these doctrines was not always accurate, and they overlooked Jefferson's view that "the government that governs least governs best" and Jackson's hard money philosophy. But the enemies were always the same—big business, big industry, big government. Speakers invoked Jefferson as the champion of the little man in opposition to federalist policies dating back to Alexander Hamilton. The theatrical Texas Populist James H. "Cyclone" Davis often brought a copy of Jefferson's writings to the speaker's platform. Davis was, in the words of Henry Demarest Lloyd, "tall and thin as a southern pine, with eyes kindled with the fire of the prophet, a voice of far reach and pathos, and a vocabulary almost every word of which seemed drawn from the Gospels or the denunciating psalms." "We will now look through the volumes of Jefferson's work and see what Mr. Jefferson had to say on this matter," Davis would thunder to his audience. Comparing Grover Cleveland to Hamilton, Davis declared that "The crowd that takes their politics from Alexander Hamilton is the crowd we have got to beat." Expounding on "Hamiltonian ideas," he would conclude with this analogy: "Jefferson opposed; so do the Populists."[1] The Populist mission was, in the words of future North Carolina Populist senator Marion Butler, a search for "the principles of true Democracy represented by Thomas Jefferson and Andrew Jackson, and for the principles of true Republicanism, as represented by Abraham Lincoln."[2] But according to Cantrell, Populists actually looked back to the Whig Party for their more historical and intellectually precise views, despite their rhetoric.[3]

To the average Populist, the great contrast between his past and present status paralleled a decline in morality and virtue. Society was deteriorating because agrarian values were displaced by corrupt, immoral urban moneyed interests who preferred personal gain over the nation's moral health. Populism saw itself in the broad romantic reform tradition in which agrarian values were pitted against the dehumanizing components of commerce and industry. British and American writers well before the Civil War idealized the rural life while demonizing the city, and the Populists in that sense were no different from their reformist predecessors. Their use of the past augmented with historical precedents was meant to counter the charges of radicalism by their critics and provide grounding for their arguments. In substance, much of the Populist rhetoric was an indictment of the present using the agrarian past as a model.[4] And like their predecessors, Populist leaders were often more well-to-do than the masses they wished to help, which often blinded them to the realities of day-to-day economic suffering. It is understandable that grassroots members sought scapegoats in history and saw exaggerated evils as targets for their frustrations. The channeling of their frustration toward blacks as scapegoats would not be an unexpected response and would later be indulged in by such Populists as Tom Watson.

While condemning the intrusion of monopoly and its successful regional coalition-building, Populists paradoxically sought to alter the course of history through similar tactics. The Southern political strategy would be based on racial and regional combinations cemented through the common interests of an agrarian labor class. The urban working class was included at least philosophically in this coalition but was never a major component, save in select cities. Inherent in Populist rhetoric was the theory of a "natural harmony of interests" between black and white members of the agrarian producer class. As one white Texas Populist expressed it, "They are in the ditch just like we are."[5] Of this biracial strategy, Tom Watson had further added the view that "Self interest always controls."[6] But as earlier Alliance episodes foretold, racial interest could be in opposition to class interest. If blacks and agrarian whites formed a natural coalition, it stood to reason that their economic interests were identical: uplifting and elevating this class in society. This simple classification included also Western agrarians and urban laborers, again on the basis of working class and interest politics.[7] Furthermore, Populists believed that such a political combination would eventually succeed and that right would triumph. The natural order of things, temporarily out of balance, would regain equilibrium.

Excoriating the money worship of the Capitalists, Populist speakers preached agrarian economics to their audiences, both black and white. Money was not the root of their evil—the *shortage* of money was the problem. As such, both black and white Populists were inflationists. An unnatural monopolistic force controlled society, which explained their poverty. The producer class was being deprived of the fruits of its labor, while the wealth accumulation of the plutocrats revealed that "there is something radically wrong in our industrial system. There is a screw loose. The wheels have dropped out of balance."[8] The farmers' inability to feed their families by their own labor was proof that the system was not working. In substance, the Populists felt that they had "moral wealth" on their side; principle and virtue would win in the final showdown, unless some artificial restraint on the system prevented it from working as it should. But the agrarians believed they would win if they remained faithful to their doctrines. "The People's Party," according to Marion Butler, "is distinctly a party of principle; and our principles are all that we have. We are like a woman who has nothing but her chastity; when that is gone, everything is gone."[9] "Hard times, then," said one popular writer,

> as well as the bankruptcies, enforced idleness, starvation, and the crime, misery, and moral degradation growing out of conditions like the present, being unnatural, not in accordance with, or the result of any natural law, must be attributed to that kind of unwise and pernicious legislation which history proves to have produced similar results in all ages of the world. It is the mission of the age to correct these errors in human legislation, to adopt and establish policies and systems, in accord with, rather than in opposition to divine law.[10]

"To tell the truth," one Populist organ remarked, "we are opposed to and hate wrong—hate injustice, fight oppression and tyranny, and condemn the corrupt use of money, and we propose to fight for the right."[11]

Populists, along with other *fin de siècle* reformists, lambasted the dehumanizing effects of a postbellum industrial society controlled by bankers, middlemen, and monopolists and encouraged by the laissez-faire policies of the federal government. They believed society's moral fiber degenerated as a result of this corrupt money class, and that moral degeneration, according to the Populist platform in 1892, portended "the destruction of civilization, or the establishment of an absolute despotism."[12] An activist central government was needed to right these wrongs. Here the Southern Populists differed somewhat with their Midwestern counterparts in the degree of federal intervention they desired. Federal legislation designed to interfere with local racial practices was not desired by white Southern Populists, who instead proposed reforms in the political, economic, and racial arena that were more compatible with their environment. The use of the federal government to protect black rights troubled white Southern Populists and conflicted with the views of their black target constituents.

The Populist conception of the role of the federal government intertwined with a belief in self-reliance and virtue found in the writings of Ralph Waldo Emerson and Booker T. Washington, and with the development of a nation based on knowing one's place in society. Populist leaders idealized a society in which all men, no matter what their race, would be given a chance to rise economically as far as their merits and character would take them. Thomas Nugent, a studious, soft-spoken lawyer, judge, and twice Populist gubernatorial candidate of Texas, had a strong faith in the improvability of man. His speeches were laced with quotes from Jefferson, Paine, Kant, Mill, Edward Bellamy, Herbert Spencer, and David Ricardo, among others. He wanted to Christianize the political order, make social Christians of men, and he wanted to use the Populist Party to gain his ends. Differing from many Populists, he did not expect to secure complete justice by political action or institutional reform, although he believed that these could alleviate wrongs.[13] In Alabama, Joseph C. Manning, a Populist writer and orator variously referred to as "the Apostle," "the Clay County Evangelist," and "Evangel Manning," preached "the gospel of human brotherhood," expressing a deep commitment to a free ballot and "a fair count to all parties." Like Nugent, Manning was a humanitarian, and he remained constant throughout his lifetime to his idealism and the expression of his principles.[14] While Nugent and Manning were more racially liberal than other Southern Populist leaders, they were not alone in their beliefs. To the Populists, economic and ethical reform would be realized through the federal government. Concern for the economic welfare of all and a higher form of individual behavior toward one's fellow man would solve the race problem. White Populist speakers often spoke and wrote paternalistically of blacks, whom they felt were slowly evolving into maturity. As an obligation of birth, white Southern Populists expressed responsibility for helping them advance. However, black advancement would be limited to a lesser rung on the social ladder than that achieved by Southern whites, and in this belief they found agreement with the accommodationist teachings of Washington and the Tuskegee school.

Populism's ideological and intellectual foundations combined the idea of a social democracy with the Social Gospel, to be demonstrated by reform activity "that would cast down the mighty and exalt the humble."[15] Like many Social Gospelers, Thomas Nugent stressed sociotheological values and felt that the Biblical expression "Thy Kingdom Come" was in the incipient phase. Although he "never expected to live on earth to see the full day," he believed nonetheless that he "lived in the morning of the coming light."[16] Dr. Cyrus Thompson, president of the North Carolina Farmers' Alliance and Populist Secretary of State, was likewise committed to the Social Gospel ideal that the contemporary church should become "a manifestation of . . . divine life flowing into human history." Making no apology for his much criticized philosophy, he explained that as a Christian it was "un-Christly" to "disregard . . . man's daily needs until he is pauperized and unmanned." Thompson felt that "you cannot . . . render Him acceptable service save by doing, in a charitable way, service to His children here."[17] Another Populist preacher considered "the principles of the Omaha platform" to be "in perfect harmony with the ten commandments, and the application of true Christianity [i.e., Populism] in civil government." If Christ "didn't teach and practice pure socialism, he didn't teach and practice anything."[18]

But Southern Populists as a group never believed in socialism any more than in pure laissez-faire capitalism. White Southern Populist leaders framed arguments that sounded both traditional and reformist yet fit within the racial imperative of white supremacy, in order to retain the party's white grassroots faithful while attracting voters from all races and parties. In a critique of Southern politics, a Louisiana Populist preacher argued that "the people" could not be socially and morally wrong and politically right. It was "God's will that man establish God's Kingdom"—socially, morally, religiously, and politically—here on earth.[19] Southern Populists, conforming to the ethics of the Social Gospel, castigated the political and economic system for its incompatibility with Christian principles toward man. The competitive capitalistic spirit of the Gilded Age made men dishonest and heartless, whereas Populism, centered on the Christian state, hoped to create a new climate in which oppression of the poor of all races would be alleviated.

Though effective in creating an awareness of poverty and the problems of modern industrialism, Populism was seriously flawed philosophically. As George Tindall has observed, the Populists' "one critical blind spot, one fatal naiveté" was their "unwillingness to face the fact of agricultural overproduction." Given that market control was in the hands of the merchant-industrial complex, the individual farmer continued to plant crops without thought of the larger picture of price fluctuations. As product flooded the market, farm profits dropped and decreased the profit margin at the lowest levels of society. From 1870 to 1891, "commodity prices declined persistently as a consequence of over-production and deflation."[20] It would be another half century before the federal government would formulate a program that offered practical remedies to such problems. Surrounded by hunger, white Southern Populist leaders seemed incapable of understanding the relationship between overproduction, race, social control, and poverty.[21] As they could not (or would not) make these associations, Populist leaders sought metaphysical answers to practical problems. God would not allow such injustice to continue, and Populism would serve as God's agent to right such wrongs. They believed in a moral agrarian imperative of divine sanction and a human stewardship of virtue. It was in the natural order of things and their destiny. The 1892 Populist presidential candidate, James B. Weaver, noted that Populists "were of a religious character," like the camp meeting of old.[22] "Their earnestness," according to the leading conservative Democratic paper of Texas, "bordering on religious fanaticism, has a touch of the kind of metal that made Cromwell's round heads so terrible a force. . . . It would be supreme folly to despite and belittle a movement that is leavened with such moral stuff as this."[23] In its mind, Populism, through the tribunal of divine sanction, would be the human gyroscope that would reestablish the agrarian ideal, whose workings had been deranged by the emergence of capitalism after the Civil War. Faith in Divine Justice, however, was no match for the market process and those who controlled crop pricing, shipping, agricultural lending, and other economic factors that brought about the rise of Henry Grady's New South philosophy.

The religious spirit filled Southern Populism. At Populist meetings, James Weaver observed, people "wept and shouted, forgave their neighbors and shook off their old party sins."[24] A Louisiana Populist organ admonished its readers that "To register [to vote] is the religious duty of every reformer."[25] In Alabama, Joseph Manning preached "the gospel of Populism";[26] Harrison Sterling "Stump" Ashby, a Methodist minister with a fondness for whiskey and popularity with the ladies, possessed "the oratorical rhetoric of an evangelical revivalist" and had no peer on the hustings.[27] He was a "stump" speaker who, when he brought his full oratorical power to bear, was a remarkable advocate for the Populist cause throughout the South. Indeed, partisan clergymen were not reluctant to invoke religion in the name of party. One preacher in Alabama, for example, made a political speech to "prove to the people that Christ was one of the third party."[28] A Tennessee Populist saw "the finger of God in every thing and ready to help the good [all] the time."[29] At an Alabama tent revival, one Populist in his enthusiastic fervor shouted "Hurrah for Kolb," the Populist gubernatorial candidate, rather than "Glory Halleluiah"; the result was a break-up of the revival.[30] A North Carolina Populist stated that he "literally" believed that there was no problem "in statesmanship" for which an answer could not be found in the Bible.

"Life would not be worth the struggle of maintaining it," he added, "if one calmly concluded that wrong, even in this world, could permanently keep under the right. It would destroy . . . the belief in God's government of the world." If things were left in His hands the people were sure to win "at some time."[31] Lawrence Goodwyn in his *Democratic Promise* has persuasively argued that Populism created a "movement culture" that incorporated family, faith, and friends, whose cloistered spirit and passion kept the movement alive during its darkest hours.[32] "Like 'hard shell' Baptists," according to one newspaper, "they have faith in their principles, and the torture of the rack could change but very few of them."[33] The idea that agrarians were the chosen of the earth was nationwide and deep-seated, certainly not confined to Southern Populism, but among no other stratum of the South's population was it more pronounced than among the Populists.[34]

Also running throughout Populist doctrines was, in the language of Richard Hofstadter, "the dualistic version of social struggles," resulting in a simplistic dichotomy of right versus wrong, moral versus immoral.[35] "A thing is right or wrong, no matter what you believe about it," a Louisiana agrarian organ asserted. "All the people in the world believing a wrong would not make it right."[36] Delineating the conflict between Populist and non-Populist, Populists divided the world into the "masses" and the "powers" and believed the movement's solidarity would achieve agrarian reform. The masses, of course, were always in the right, as long as they held to Populist ideals. "It is a struggle," said "Sockless" Jerry Simpson, later Populist candidate to the United States Senate, "between the robbers and the robbed." [37]

The Populist worldview was quite simple:

There are but two sides in the conflict that is being waged in this country today [declared a Populist manifesto]. On the one side are the allied hosts of monopolies, the money power, great trusts and railroad corporations, who seek the enactment of laws to benefit them and impoverish the people. On the other are the farmers, laborers, merchants, and all the other people who produce wealth and bear the burdens of taxation. . . . Between these two there is no middle ground.[38]

Blacks were at least rhetorically included among the "people." "We are a unit," the *Louisiana Populist* observed, "from Maine to California, having one faith, one Lord and one baptism."[39] Populism made symbols of both capitalism (e.g., immoral, wrong) and agrarianism (e.g., moral, right) and was in itself a manifestation of how Populist agrarianism transmuted into a belief in moral stewardship.

It is not surprising that conservative Southern leaders and writers saw in Populism's feverish rhetoric the genesis of regional confrontation, particularly when race was injected into the equation. The established white Bourbon leadership understood that the reform movement aimed to upset their stable, conservative society, increasingly wrapped in a cocoon of conformity. White reform movements could be rendered ineffectual merely by a show of power or co-option of reform planks, but a biracial coalition could put the numbers on the side of the reformers and potentially shake up the status quo. In response to Populist rhetoric, the establishment developed its own mantra to keep blacks and whites from uniting, recalling "Black Reconstruction horrors" and the introduction of "social equality" if Populism prevailed. It was an astute tactic that constantly kept the Populists on the defensive and that ultimately proved fatal. Whether conservative rhetoric was introduced purely for inflammatory effect or out of genuine conviction, it prevented wholesale apostasy from Democrats or Republicans, black or white.

The contrast between the promise of the agrarian myth and their present wretched circumstances understandably made grassroots Populists disgruntled and conspiracy-minded, seeing malevolent forces behind their ills. An Alabamian noted that his was "naturally one of the richest states in the Union" in farm lands, crops produced, minerals, and such. "Notwithstanding all this, we are about the poorest people on God's green earth. Why it is?"[40] "What was wrong with agriculture?" was a common theme in Populist literature. The harder farmers worked, the worse off they became. Typical was a farmer with a wife and five children in Grant Parish, Louisiana. After working hard during the growing season and selling the proceeds, the family members now "find ourselves thirty-nine dollars and fifty-four cents worse off than when we started at the beginning of the year, after consuming the fifty-seven dollars and twenty cents [mortgage] interest."[41] Year after year increasing debt coiled slowly around the farmer, creating the "anaconda mortgage system" that choked the life out of the agrarian South. Railroads as well as supply merchants were especially singled out for vilification. In his earlier years John Sparkman, later a U.S. senator, interviewed an aging Alabama farmer who recalled instances in which producers had shipped huge carloads of goods to market, only to be later presented invoices indicating that money was still due for shipping charges in addition to the total proceeds from the sale, already consumed by transportation costs. Another farmer related an instance in which a carload of horses was sent from one point to another and the proceeds from their sale was ten dollars less than enough to pay the freight cost. Another recalled that "first class" farmhands working "from dawn to dusk"—fourteen to fifteen hours a day—with forty minutes off for lunch received forty cents a day and dinner or forty-five cents if one furnished his own lunch.[42] "We are chained to the soil with long weary hours of toil before us," a Populist organ lamented, "and we are to every trust and combination of gamblers in the products of our labor a legitimate prey."[43] White and black suffered alike, and Populist leaders like Tom Watson would focus on common misery and enemies to temporarily mold biracial coalitions.

In counterpoint to the New South Creed, the agrarians were constantly frustrated and understandably despondent over the relationship between their individual efforts and resulting compensation.[44] Jeff Wilson, a tenant character in *In the Land of Cotton,* Dorothy Scarborough's novel about cotton-growing in the Brazos Valley, expressed the average Populist's feeling of fatalism and frustration: "If I was to start to hell with a load of ice there'd be a freeze before I got there."[45] Paradoxically, for the Populists agrarianism still held as much resonance as ever, despite daily evidence to the contrary. They were more focused on the "unnatural constraints" placed upon them by this new industrialized society than with the shortcomings of the ideal itself.

In a society that taught that hard work and frugal living would invariably lead to success, Southern Populists stood in stark contrast to the Horatio Alger myth. Their insistence on the virtues of work, morality, and religious values accommodated itself closely to the ideals necessary for success by popularizers of the concept.[46] However, the harder agrarians worked, the more they suffered disproportionately to their efforts. In substance, they saw themselves as playing the game of success strictly by the rules yet failing to achieve economic advancement. The Populist worldview became distorted by their experiences and lack of success. Why was this happening to them? What was wrong with agriculture? Weren't they supposedly among the anointed of the earth? Perhaps the answer to the problem was in the myth itself, which addressed success in an urban milieu to the neglect of the rural life. The myth also responded to the migration from farm to city by Northerners and Southerners alike. How could you keep them down on the farm when pay and living conditions were so much better in the big city? The agrarians fought a losing battle from the beginning against the juggernaut of urbanization, and blacks who remained on Southern farms would suffer the most.

Some members of the movement believed their opportunities had been restricted by the conspiratorial behavior of "the international money power." Ignatius Donnelly, one of the most prominent Populists nationally, asserted in 1892 that "a vast conspiracy against mankind had been organized on two continents, and it is rapidly taking possession of the world. If not met and overthrown at once it forebodes terrible social convulsions, the destruction of civilization, or the establishment of an absolute despotism."[47] It was not enough to be aware of the existing conspiracy; it was necessary to study these historical plots to better recognize and defend oneself against their effects. According to a Louisiana third-party member,

> Populists are not prophets, but they have studied the great conspiracies that have been and are still being formed to sap the wealth of the nations of the earth, and they have so familiarized themselves with the rise and downfall of nations, that they are able to read "the hand-writing on the wall" as fast as the conspirators put it there.[48]

Conspiracy was an important factor in the Populist mind, particularly at the grassroots level, and its fantasies surely reflect the ideas of some of our own contemporaries.[49] In the case of Populism, the mood was more causal than symptomatic, and it provides us with a concrete example of what can happen when people are impoverished and insecure. However, the breaking point that distinguished Populism from other reform movements was its failure to distinguish between conspiracy *in* history and history *as* conspiracy.[50]

While the worst forebodings of Southern Populists were not realized, a perusal of their day-to-day experiences can generate sympathy and understanding from the most hostile of critics, however untenable their views may appear on balance. Southern Populist leaders, particularly blacks, remained pragmatic despite doctrinaire ideas about agrarianism and democracy. But their failure to quickly effect change made it all too easy for their unlettered white followers to seek a scapegoat. As they were doing their part, failure was not their fault. It must be some force in their environment. The Bourbon Democrats took advantage of the farmers' frustration with a campaign to convince white Populists that their attempted political coalition with blacks could bring about terrible social and political consequences, and that following the white Democratic line would not only be in their individual self-interest but in the interest of the white race as a whole. Also, repeated ballot box fraud using black voters to sway elections must have influenced rural white voters that blacks were malleable and untrustworthy.

Examination of the Southern Populist mind must also take into account the mood of the black man, particularly since Populism sought to coalesce both races under a single reform banner of a "natural harmony of interests." To white Populists, blacks came to symbolize parity in political competition, as they constituted the balance of power in many electoral contests. Populists needed to attract votes from both Democratic and Republican

Fig. 4. A vote for Grover Cleveland would bring financial and racial ruin to the South (*Weekly Toiler,* November 2, 1892).

constituents, and blacks, disillusioned with the Republican Party, were a potential voting bloc as well as a natural agrarian coalition partner. Populism had to create significant defections of voters to win at the polls. The movement felt it must make deep inroads into the black voting pool to succeed, and it was not surprising that blacks were encouraged to join the party.

That farmers both black and white would be swayed by Populism is understandable, for it sought to prove their moral superiority and promised to improve their economic status. But black party loyalty was also colored by the increasingly hostile white public mood of the era. As the postbellum South reinvented itself, blacks found their paths strewn with more violent obstacles and personal pitfalls such as lynching, political circumscription, and growing formalized segregation than whites. In this atmosphere, Populism needed to offer some tangible inducements to the peculiar interests of a people increasingly victimized by intolerance. Thomas E. Miller, a black representative from South Carolina, provided a superb summary to the House of Representatives on what reforms Southern black farmers needed most during this period:

There are other things more important to us [than holding office]. First is the infernal lynch law. That is the thing we most complain of.

It is a question whether when we go to work we will return or not. Second, they have little petty systems of justices who rob us of our daily toil, and we cannot get redress before the higher tribunals. Third, we work for our taskmasters, and they pay us if they please, for the courts are so constructed that Negroes have no rights if these rights wind up in dollars and cents to be paid by white task-masters. . . . Yes, gentlemen, we want office but the first and dearest rights the Negro of the South wants are the right to pay for his labor, his right to trial by jury, his right to his home, his right to know the man who lynches him will not the next day be elected by the State to a high and honorable trust, his right to know that murderers shall be convicted and not elected to high office.[51]

Thus, the impetus for black support centered around four major points: economic betterment, protection of person, a share in the patronage, and actual involvement in the political process. Perhaps most immediate of these was protection of person.

Although lynching was the most newsworthy form of violence against Southern blacks, especially for the Northern press, minor attacks and threats against individuals were commonplace and varied from locale to locale. These elements of violence required blacks to cultivate certain forms of protection. One segment of the black community regarded it as "the duty of the state" to "throw the law's strong arm of protection around the Negro."[52] But having often faced state and county officials who regarded white-on-black violence as the natural order of things, blacks soon despaired of any political redress of grievances. To many black leaders, the explanation was obvious:

Because of coveted advantages intended to be gained influential leaders among the whites of the State have either directly or indirectly advised or allowed to be taught that any treatment of the negro would tend to impress him with the white man's superior power in a conflict of force is justifiable.[53]

As such, some middle-class blacks looked to "the better class of whites" for protection and repudiated federal intervention or politics for solace. Blacks must first elevate themselves morally and economically before politics would be an instrument for salvation. A South Carolina black minister declared:

I hate the mean, vacillating [federal] government which, if it finds that one or a part of the citizens are not wealthy or educated, throws her back on them when they cry for redress for their grievances, and says: "Had you staid [*sic*] in your right place you would not need the arm of the law; those who are murdering you and cheating you are your best friends."[54]

But by the 1890s, Northern Republicans were tired of the problems associated with Southern blacks, and despite the increased violence they left the white South to do pretty much as it pleased.[55] Blacks were openly divided over which road would ultimately prove the most beneficial. To some the answer was simple: politics had brought ruin on the race, and moral, civic, and economic uplift were required before political rights would be forthcoming. Therefore, politics must take a back seat to self-improvement. A Tuscaloosa, Alabama, black preacher, the Reverend A. L. Phillips, believed that "once we have set aside all political considerations and social fears, we will find that the essence of the whole matter" would be how the two races "behave" toward each other. "Political expedients are at best," he added, "mere temporary aids."[56] The black editor of the *Knoxville Gleaner* suggested that "Christian education and wealth is [*sic*] the colored man's only savior." These two things would do more "to adjust his station" presently than any other.[57] "Take politics in small doses without any shaking," another black cautiously advised.[58] To these accommodationists, their station would improve via the good graces of the "better class of whites" obligated by birth to watch over and protect blacks.[59]

But for more militant blacks, the necessity for political participation remained constant, although truncated. To those whites who insisted that political participation would beget social equality, these blacks advocated a type of separate-but-equal doctrine, providing for political participation but allowing social separatism. A Georgia black, J. W. Caner, a legislative spokesman for the Colored Farmers' Alliance, summed up this argument:

We don't want social equality. All the Negro wants is protection. You white people attend to your business and let us alone. . . . The politicians and lawyers say you must keep us Negroes down. But that is not right.[60]

The Reverend J. C. Price, president of Livingston College, astutely observed: "The position that political and civil equality carries with it . . . [social equality as] a consequence is contrary to the experience of all men, and especially to that of southern white men."[61] The *Richmond Planet,* one of the major black Republican newspapers in the South, reiterated this view with the comment that "the colored people of the South have no desire for social equality" but do favor their "civil rights and political equality" before the law.[62] "Separate the races in everything that looks like social intermingling, but in God's name treat us fairly," a black religious organ pleaded.[63]

In their approbation of social equality, middle-class blacks emphasized the religious and social goals of a socially separatist black bourgeois respectability in this life and heavenly salvation in the next, which they believed morality, industry, and economy insured. Like white Populists, blacks developed a pragmatic philosophy, which was still fluid in view of the region's increasingly hostile environment. Some of the more militant black middle class, such as Bishop Henry Turner of Georgia, did not believe that whites would ever grant blacks social or political equality; and, on contemplation, he was not "certain that God wants them to do it."[64] A few blacks disagreed. "If we are not striving for equality," John Hope said in 1896, "in heaven's name for what are we living."[65] Blacks were divided on their means for the advancement of the race, and it would not be until Booker T. Washington's emergence as a leader in 1895 that the rural black community would coalesce around a single philosophy. But by that time, Southern Populism was in decline.

Part of the problem involved a question of semantics. To most whites, black political involvement implied "Negro domination," whereas for blacks it meant equal participation in the existing political process.[66] Equally as potent a term was "social equality." As August Meier has observed: "Most Negroes interpreted social equality as meaning simply intimate social relationships which they did not desire, though most whites interpreted it as meaning the abolition of segregation."[67] Racial interpretation strained the political ambitions of blacks and the emerging Populist movement and kept the gulf between the races open. Thus, political and social ideals themselves became clouded even further with ambiguities and were transformed as they were taken up by both groups and revised with the Populist revolt.

Much black resentment and frustration centered on their shrinking share of the patronage and opportunities needed for political advancement. Many of their grievances focused on Republican federal appointment policy:

The colored people of the South are beginning to realize with a vengeance that President Harrison has a southern policy. They say "Ham wants pie, but he can't even get the crumbs that fall from the [Republican] table."[68]

Increasingly, officeholding and patronage for blacks on the state level also diminished. Without patronage, blacks lacked incentive to follow the Republican banner. Simultaneously, the 1890s saw white Republican resentment of black political participation reaching the critical point. In one election campaign after the other, Republicans had to deal with voting irregularities, violence, and smear campaigns, and soon after the end of Reconstruction the national Republican leadership decided to refocus its energies on becoming the party of the businessman rather than the savior of Southern blacks. So-called Southern "Lily-White" state groups openly sought to expunge blacks from the party except when their votes were needed. Respectability became a dominant theme of the Republican Party. In Virginia, William "Boss Billy" Mahone, a white Republican and father of the earlier Readjuster Movement, in a summary of Republican racial policies noted that blacks "have been made to understand that they must take a back seat and let their white bosses and political masters run the political machine and have all the offices."[69] Also the Republican Party was in a rapid decline throughout the South, with only three Republicans left in the Virginia General Assembly by 1891—none of whom were black.[70] In Texas, it was suggested that the "Republican party . . . , to merit the respect of mankind must be in the hands of the [white] race."[71] The "white Republicans have been traitors to us," a black convention in North Carolina declared, and "the [black] backbone of the Republican party, got nothing" in the way of patronage.[72] In varying degrees this story was true in the remainder of the Southern states, as the Republican Party, particularly the Lily-White component, sought to make itself "respectable" to the region's white constituency. John Lynch, the black Mississippi congressman, spoke of the motivations behind this "small but noisy and demonstrative class . . . comprising about fifteen percent" of the Republican Party in the South:

> What those men chiefly wanted and felt the need of for themselves and their families was social recognition by the better elements of the white people of their respective localities. They were anxious, therefore, to bring about such a condition of things as would make it possible for them to be known as Republicans without subjecting themselves and their families to the risk of being socially ostracized by their white Democratic neighbors. And then again those men believed them, and some of them still believe or profess to believe, that Southern Democrats were and are honest and sincere in the declaration that the presence of the colored men in the Republican party prevents Southern white men from coming into it.[73]

By the 1890s, both major parties had given up on improving the economic and social lot of Southern blacks but used them at will when elections rolled around. T. Thomas Fortune, one of the foremost black leaders of the day, bitterly remarked of the parties, "none of them cares a fig for the Afro-American" and predicted that "another party may rise to finish the uncompleted work" of emancipation.[74] Gauged by the vacuity of contemporary Southern politics, the future seemed to hold promise for the emerging Populist Party if whites could suppress their racial prejudice sufficiently to attract a black following. Could they develop a biracial coalition based on forwarding practical economic remedies within a moral framework? Above all else, given the philosophies of the two groups and the realities of the region's culture, Populism could make deep inroads into Southern politics through a coalition with the black voter. New ways could be offered to the region's disinherited of both races. Indeed, their philosophies were at the very center of this promise.

5

Principles, Prejudice, and Populism

Wipe out the color line, and put every man on his citizenship.

"It is altogether probable," Woodward contended, "that during the brief Populist upheaval of the 'nineties Negroes and native whites achieved a greater comity of mind and harmony of political purpose than ever before *or since* in the South."[1] Portrayed as a thoroughly good man with a strong moral philosophy and sense of justice, the white Populist instinctively knew right from wrong and tried to develop his relationship with his black counterpart in the face of regional adversity. Woodward's earlier (1938) excellent biography of Tom Watson painted the Georgia Populist with the same rose-tinted brushstrokes.[2] In fairness Woodward never claimed that this prototype held true for all white Populists, although some historians reached this conclusion. To these historians Populism was a road not taken for Southern race relations—a lost opportunity for racial brotherhood in the South. Consider the summation of Jack Abramowitz:

> The collapse of Populism in 1896 put an end to a movement that had every chance of producing a truly emancipated South in which the Negro would have been accorded a respectable position which might have broken down hostility and suspicion between Negro and white.[3]

Lawrence Goodwyn echoed the belief that "In the South, the Populist era was one of those moments in American history when things could have changed somewhat."[4] But racial prejudice in the white Southern Populist camp doomed any biracial reform efforts from the start, and it is questionable to what extent biracial rhetoric was sincere or merely politically expedient. This chapter examines the nature of prejudice among white Southern populist leaders and followers to determine if and why blacks were welcome in the movement.

Out of context, the progressivism of some white Southern Populist statements is an impressive prototype for liberal racial attitudes. Watson, for example, articulated the Southern Populist core biracial philosophy which he hoped would unite blacks and whites in a common bond and goal:

> My [black] friends, this [1892] campaign will decide many things, and one of the things it will decide is whether or not your people and ours can daily meet in harmony, and work for law, and order, and morality, and wipe out the color line, and put every man on his citizenship irrespective of color.[5]

The first platform of the 1892 Louisiana State People's Party, in a sympathetic appeal to the black voter, also promised fairness and appealed as did Watson to their "self interest":

> You colored man . . . you must now realize that there is no hope of any further material benefit to you in the Republican Party, and that if you remain in it, you will continue to be hewers of wood and drawers of water in the future as you have been in the past.[6]

A judicious selection from the rhetoric of Populism could give a moral coloration of racial equality to the movement. Upon closer inspection, however, the facts of Southern Populism rebut the romantic fallacy of uniqueness and concern for racial equality. As we saw earlier, the Alliance's actions did not always square with its rhetoric—particularly when white interests conflicted with black interests. Economic interest constantly clashed with class and racial interests, and despite Alliance and Populist ideology to the contrary, race and class were all too often the final determinants of agrarian actions.

In the initial spread of Alliance and third-party ideology across the South, many white farmers argued that blacks should be excluded. But the more pragmatic leaders recognized that the black vote held the balance of power necessary for reform. Recognizing the internecine strife that could result not only within the movement but within the South itself (because of white sensitivity to the race question), H. L. Loucks, president of the Southern Alliance and a strong supporter of the third-party movement, cautioned that "we must make reform by the ballot exceedingly slow in the Southern states where the Negro vote is an important factor." While venturing the opinion that "a majority of the white men in the South believe in our principles," the difficulty, he predicted, would be in convincing them to vote their principles over their prejudices when blacks were involved politically.[7] As interest in a third party grew, basic changes in racial thinking slowly developed. Southern Populism's psyche always suffered over race. Although the movement harbored such "libertarians" as Tom Watson, the change in official ideology probably resulted more from expediency than racial liberalism.[8] If white Southern Populists could only win through a coalition with black voters, they would include them in their ranks—but only as long as they were a political asset.

In formulating the official racial creed, white Southern Populists soon realized that their political support lay in inverse relation to the concentration of the black population, the two general exceptions to this rule being Virginia and Tennessee, which never were Populist strongholds.[9] Therefore, in order to control the Southern political machine, it was imperative to control the Black Belt. Through sheer weight of numbers, for example, blacks controlled a bloc of sixteen counties in Texas. Moreover, in as many as fifty Texas counties, their ballots served as the balance of power when the white vote was split.[10] In the same manner blacks controlled sixteen counties in eastern North Carolina and due to their numerical concentration could determine results in at least thirty-two other counties; and as late as 1896, blacks held an electoral majority in twenty-six Louisiana parishes.[11] In varying degrees, this situation was also true of the remaining Southern states.[12]

Most white Southern Populists realized that they must choose between conformity to regional prejudice and their desire to implement agrarian reform principles. It seemed, however, that one must come at the expense of the other. "For no matter what the Populists may think on general principles," one Virginia Democratic paper warned, "they will have to face the fact that a vote for the third party will mean a vote for Harrison and the Force Bill; a vote to bring [black] Reconstruction horrors upon the South."[13] Perhaps the most significant obstacle the Populists faced may have been psychological. They had to choose between principle and prejudice, and the problem of race was directly involved in both cases.[14]

Openly expressed racial attitudes were not always an adequate measure of the white Southern Populists' true feelings toward blacks.[15] "The regions where Populism made its strongest appeal," Woodward reminds us, "were the very regions that found it most difficult to overcome racial feeling."[16] By dramatizing racial tensions, a well-disciplined Democratic Party machine could retard any election alliance based on the Populist appeal to "harmony of interest" between the races. Carl Carmer's *Stars Fell on Alabama* captures this racial cleavage as an upland white Populist prototype expresses his deep-seated attitudes:

We don't like niggers in this neck o' the woods [Tom Nabors explained]. We ain't never liked 'em. I can remember my father standin' on the mountain where you can look off down toward the Black Belt an' the flat country an' sayin': "Them black bastards is takin' the food out 'n our mouths. We oughta be down there workin' that black land but we got too much pride to work for nothin'." They're down there sharin' the good things with the rich while good white folks in the hills have to starve.[17]

In addition, the proposed class-reform movement was blunted by the South's mixture of race and politics, which could easily result in reaction rather than reform. "I'm a Democrat, because my daddy was Democrat, and I'm g'wine to vote agin the Nigger!"[18] The interpretative problem for the historian lies in the fact that while the leadership's official creed was obvious on the surface, the prejudices of the grassroots members were rarely expressed in print.

Despite the necessity that party members suppress personal prejudices, racism surfaced at times. "This is a white man's country," one Virginia Populist bluntly asserted, "and will always be controlled by whites."[19] The "People's Party in this state," according to a Louisiana Populist organ, "is a white man's party, as evidenced by its vote in every election since its organization and by the utterances of its platforms, press and speakers in this State."[20] The same paper commented further: "If you want white supremacy join the Populists[;] if you want to go into a party that acknowledges its failure to even exist without uniting with the negro, then follow the modern *so-called* Democracy."[21] It "is a condition and not mere sentiment that confronts us here in North Carolina," said Polk about the third-party question. "We cannot afford to risk Negro supremacy here."[22] An Alabama Allianceman of Populist principles suddenly exploded that he was thoroughly "disgusted with all the [third party] rot carried on . . . and the effort to drag the Alliance into a third party movement that wants to affiliate with Negroes, carpetbaggers, and Republicans."[23] In Comanche County, a later Populist stronghold in West Texas, all of the region's blacks were driven out in 1886 because of the criminal acts of a black minority; a signboard was posted in DeLeon to warn all future blacks who might desire entry into the area: "Nigger, don't let the sun go down on you in this town."[24] Prejudice lurked within the inner psychology of the movement, although it was occasionally curbed at the urging of the more visionary leadership in favor of political expediency. The twin currents of racism and agrarian-class egalitarianism flowed side by side, eventually resulting in a fundamental split in the Populist psyche. The Democratic opposition found positive pleasure in the white Southern Populists' dilemma. "Mr. Scipio Africanus," according to one Louisiana Democratic organ, "ought to know that Mr. Populite loves him less than any other white man on earth, but is willing to go into a deal with him to defeat the Democratic party."[25] Henry Lincoln Johnson, a prominent black Atlanta attorney, similarly berated Populist biracial efforts as a sham. "The intelligent negroes of Georgia know that there is far more hate and spleen against the negroes in the populist camp than in the democratic."[26]

By the 1890s blacks had become political symbols calculated to keep white agrarians in the white supremacy camp. The repeated use of the "nigger" theme in the region's political campaigns exacerbated postbellum fears of black domination. "Nigger, nigger, nigger is its [the Democratic party's] only cry," a white North Carolina Republican shouted in frustration over his opponents' successful appeal to race.[27] "Heavens," a Louisiana organ exclaimed in exasperation, "how we would enjoy a rest on the 'nigger' question! It seems that four-fifths of the State [newspapers] can't come out without a longwinded article . . . with the negro as their target, and what's more, they have been at it for the lord only knows how long."[28] Democrats successfully used race-baiting against previous political insurgents, and the threat of black domination was used to attract or retain most of the region's white population to their party. It was no surprise, therefore, that the race question was the central issue used to erode the Southern Populist movement. By fall 1892, Tom Watson, who tried to transcend the race issue and articulate an alternative line of biracial development for the Populist Party, concluded that "the argument against the independent political movement in the South may be boiled down into one word—nigger."[29]

Populist racial rhetoric was forced by political expediency to stop short of frankness, but there was also a clarity in some less-publicized actions. It remains to consider a select few who embodied the sublimated racial attitudes of Southern Populism. Two-time Texas Populist candidate for governor Thomas Nugent did not extend fully his concept of the Social Gospel to blacks.[30] "My idea," he asserted, "is that segregation as far as possible is best for the negro."[31] Consonant with this philosophy, Nugent openly supported segregation of prisons, railway cars, and schools.[32] James H. "Cyclone" Davis, Texas Populist candidate for attorney general in 1892 and a Ku Klux Klan sympathizer, clearly stated his opposition to social equality and miscegenation:

The worst sight of social equality to be seen in this land is the sight of a sweet white girl hoeing cotton in one row and a big burley [sic] negro in the next row. Talk of social equality, when your industrial system forces a good woman's precious Anglo-Saxon girl down on a level with a burley [*sic*] negro in a cotton row. Oh, my God! and this in a free America![33]

But even this passionate statement was little more than a denial of the Democrats' charge that black political participation would lead to social equality. This passion for segregation was also demonstrated in Alabama, where a "Separate But Equal Accommodation Bill" was "passed without opposition by both Democrats and Populists." "The unanimous vote on the Jim Crow seating bill of 1891," according to Sheldon Hackney, "indicates that there probably were no significant differences between the Democrats and the Populists on race relations." Furthermore, he found "no objective difference between the two parties on racial policy." "In fact," he adds, "thousands of ordinary white Alabamians voted Populist without abandoning their belief in white supremacy."[34] A comparable Jim Crow bill was passed by the Alliance Legislature of Georgia in 1891, supported by Alliance and Populist votes.[35]

Equally noteworthy was Tom Watson, who courted the black vote.[36] Like white Populist leaders throughout the South, Watson was caught in a delicate balance between attracting both white and black voters to the new party, and that problem would in part spell Southern Populism's ruin. A scrutiny of his roots indicates that he "shared the obsessions of his peers in a hatred of Reconstruction and black aspirations and in a consistent devotion to white supremacy. Nothing in his career prior to 1890," according to Crowe, "would lead one to suspect him of racial heresy or a radical future."[37] For a brief period in the early 1890s, Watson's rhetoric overflowed with pleas for racial brotherhood against the dominant powers. Numerous critics have attempted to explain his wild psychic swings between 1890 and 1894, but from today's vantage point Watson's bout of racial liberalism is suspect. By 1894 he supported segregation laws for public accommodations, denied favoring jury service for blacks, opposed racial equality, and took an ambivalent stand on lynching.[38] If, as one historian has asserted, "Georgia Populism was Tom Watson, and Tom Watson was Georgia Populism,"[39] his earlier career was a shallow foundation upon which to erect biracial Southern reform.

A mixture of white supremacy and political expediency resulted in an agrarianism molded by pragmatism and opportunism. Philosophically, the Alliance and Populist movements incorporated a strong sympathy for the downcast and underprivileged and a concern for the human condition. But this concern was tinged, as it was throughout the nation, by the prevalent racial orthodoxy of the era. With the popularization of the racial theories of Louis Agassiz and others, Americans came to accept their Manifest Destiny as benevolent overseers of the non-Aryan world. Whereas landowning Anglo-Saxon males governed society, with blacks and women in comfortably subordinate roles, the end of slavery, rise of industrialism, repositioning of women's "place," and the influx of "non-white" (i.e., Asian in the West, Eastern European in the North) cultures challenged white conservatives and liberals to reevaluate the meaning of democracy and equality. What we now call "liberalism" and "racism" could easily go hand-in-hand down the path of reform. Even George Washington Cable, one of the most outspoken Southern "liberals," would only go so far in his cry for black rights. In the Southern agrarian movement, white leaders understood that blacks must accept a subordinate position in society and the party. This subservient role reinforced the white Southern Populists' sense of stewardship for blacks.

Stewardship would rapidly morph into legalized means of maintaining the separatist status quo, and as a group white Southern Populists would differ little from their Democratic colleagues in this area. As early as 1890, racial conservatives were highly visible in the Georgia agrarian revolt. The 1890 "Alliance" legislature passed one of the nation's earliest Jim Crow laws but also appropriated eight thousand dollars to create a new black school in Atlanta.[40] Interestingly, Tom Watson voted against state appropriations for black schools and colleges on the premise that the state was already committed to other costly public ventures and could not afford these outlays.[41] Indeed, Watson's record is a mix of actions that would neither attract nor sustain black support. In this manner, he was no different from many other individuals. Dr. S. W. Johnson of Appling County, later a Populist candidate, introduced a bill in 1891 to establish Jim Crow railroad cars in the state. To many conservative agrarians, this was "a bill that should stand as a lasting monument to his name and statesmanship." Watson's *People's Party Paper* supported the law on the basis that it would prevent race riots and protect blacks from "insults, etc., by rough, card playing, drunkenness, etc., in cars provided for the colored people," concluding that "no one can fail to see the propriety and necessity for such a law."[42] As in the Southern Alliance's opposition to the Blair Bill and Lodge "Force" Bill as instruments that would disrupt peaceful race relations, conservatives regarded legislation that limited racial contact as conducive to avoiding racial conflict.

Such attempts at racial proscription were usually met by black protest, and Johnson's bill was no exception.[43] "These exhibitions of prejudice," according to the *Savannah Tribune,*

are simply an expression of hostility injected by the white farmers of the South into the great currents of passing political opinion. They represent the feeling of the agricultural class always more strongly wedded to the old ideas and less susceptible to the newer teachings of an enlarged and progressive humanity. They have their origin in an order dominated from its incipiency by a feeling of enmity to the Negro.[44]

Black protest however meant little to Southern legislators, and the support of white Populists for anti-black legislation underscored the basic problem of biracial political reform in the region. The Douglass Incident of 1892 would drive the wedge even deeper.

In an extraordinary move that resounded in the nation's black and white press, President Grover Cleveland invited black Republican leader Frederick Douglass and his white wife to the White House for dinner. For the Democratic administration in Washington, the symbolism of the event would hopefully bring more black voters into the Democratic fold. Southerners saw the event in a different light. At a speech before the 1892 Populist convention in Atlanta, the Reverend Sam Small, a one-time alcoholic and now an ardent Prohibitionist, attacked the Democrats' breakdown of racial social barriers:

> Grover Cleveland invited that leader of niggerdom, Fred Douglas, to his dinner table. I might excuse him for getting the nigger into the house for supper, but when he invited the low [white] wife to go there, it is more than I can stand.

The two black delegates attending the convention, R. J. Matthews and John Mack, apparently did not comment—at least openly—on the good reverend's opinions, but they must have raised concerns about white Populist attitudes toward blacks who were openly seeking African-American votes.[45] But such rhetoric by white Southern Populist leaders, particularly in front of black delegates, suggests a lack of racial and political sensitivity in a movement seeking to develop a biracial political coalition. And when words failed, white Georgia Populists turned to violence, intimidation, and fraud to defeat the Democrats.[46] If white Georgia Populists' rhetoric is compared with their overall *methods,* it appears their actions differed little from their opposition. These actions suggest even more the Populists' practical attitude toward blacks.

Louisiana agrarians also promoted increased circumscription of social relations between the two races. An 1890 bill that required mandatory racial segregation in railroad coaches was "with few exceptions" supported by the Farmers' Union, including its ex-president John M. Stallings. Furthermore, the Farmers' Union selected as its official state organ the *Shreveport Weekly Caucasian*—hardly a title to attract black support.[47] How much these incidents affected attempts toward biracial coalition is open to question, but they probably made it difficult for blacks to distinguish between friend and foe. However, such actions bore the impress of a white agrarian attitude about the desired relationship between blacks and whites and the prevailing social order. Louisiana as we shall see later is an unusual case study, as the state then (as now) divides itself between New Orleans, arguably then the most racially liberal and "European" of all U.S. cities, and the more traditionally separatist western and northern rural communities where Populism flourished. It is interesting to note that Populism had little support among New Orleans blacks, but the city's biracial dockworkers' unions demonstrate not only the willingness but the ability of lower-class whites and blacks to unite for economic justice against the white city fathers.

Hostile Populist racial attitudes also can be found in Virginia. Edmund Randolph Cocke, grandson of the distinguished Virginia statesman Edmund Randolph and Populist candidate for governor in 1893, urged in 1891 the repeal of the Fifteenth Amendment on the assumption that "depriving the negro of suffrage . . . might have a good effect." This was, he added, "the only solution to prevent troubles."[48] Cocke's viewpoint here would grow popular throughout the South as the century came to a close. Continued rhetoric about the need for "purification of the ballot" and removal of blacks, immigrants, and poor whites was necessary to achieve that desired end. Furthermore, in the face of massive electoral fraud and corruption, the belief grew that voting was not a "natural" right of all persons but a "privilege" that should be limited to persons of good character, competence, education, and property ownership, among others. Furthermore, white Virginia Populists did not subscribe with enthusiasm to social mingling between the races even in political situations. In a description of a political rally, the Populists lamented that the Democrats served food for both races and they "ate side by side, shoulder to shoulder."[49] As Charles Wynes has shown, by 1893 white Virginia Populists openly rejected blacks as political allies, believing they would prove more of a burden than a benefit, and blacks responded by failing to attend state Populist conventions or providing political support for the movement. Earlier coalition efforts between the Southern and Colored Farmers' Alliances had also suffered strains.[50]

Reviewing regional political rhetoric, no clear pattern of actions or attitudes arises between blacks and Democrats, Republicans, or Populists during the early nineties. Variations are found within all parties in microcosm as well as regionally. All parties could be paternalistic or neglectful of black interests at times. Part of this attitude is attributable, as Woodward observed, to the ongoing formalization and legalization of segregation in the 1880s and 1890s in the South. In the five sugar cane producing counties of Southern Louisiana, for example, wages for blacks and whites during this era were equally subpar: twenty-five to forty cents a day.[51] A Northern reporter found blacks and whites living side by side during this era in neighborhoods of Montgomery, Alabama.[52] Some coastal cities developed separate but highly successful business and residential communities that coexisted harmoniously until the politics of the late 1890s. Thus, housing, wage disparity, and segregation had not occurred firmly in areas that in later years could be very hostile to blacks. While "separate but equal" transportation facilities were quickly becoming legalized in the 1890s, other patterns were still in flux. The rising "Cult of the Confederacy" mythicized an Old South of apolitical subservient black and gallant white men of the planter class who protected "Southern Womanhood" against the occasional renegade black or lower-class white. The cult arose in part as a reaction to the growth of industrialism and diminishing prospects for staple crops (particularly cotton) in the "New South," partly as a means of reestablishing a hierarchy in which every person knew his or her place, partly in reaction to growing Northern and Western economic dominance, and partly as an answer to the spread of U.S. imperialism that was leaving the Deep South behind. When they thought about the racial question, political parties argued shouldering "the white man's burden" and maintaining white supremacy. Thus, no clear pattern in race relations existed, as Woodward has observed. If there was a difference, it was in degree and not kind.

All in all, the Populist record in the region is not what its proponents claim it to be, but neither should it be read with complete contempt. If a charitable view is taken of the inevitable gap between their rhetorical aspirations and the political practical possibilities of the Deep South, the Populists were not failures. But the pattern was not Populistic alone, and this blurs the Populist portrait. Region-wide variation rather than consistency was the pattern in race and political relations. Thus, the overall pattern of Southern race relations at this point was one of *diversity* rather than one in which any clear distinction can be drawn between Populist and non-Populist, black and white, and to some extent, the differing classes. The political order that Populists advocated was too remote from the diversity of human nature and social and legal patterns to be practical. Southern race relations and behavior depended on local social and individual attitudes and actions concerning black-white relations, though invariably paternalistic. Studies in microcosm have found wide variations, some areas extending political benefits to blacks and others denying these same rights.

In this light, it is necessary to examine in further detail the discrepancy between Southern Populism in theory and practice as outlined by Woodward and his proponents. According to this school of thought, blacks were not put off with nominal duties and peripheral appointments but were taken into the inmost councils of the Populist Party. They served with Southern whites as members of state, district, and county executive committees and delegations to national conventions. Black and white campaigners spoke from the same platform to audiences of both races, and both had their places on official party tickets. Populist sheriffs in some counties saw to it that blacks appeared for jury duty, and the Populist editors sought out achievements of blacks to praise in their columns.[53] But, again, the pattern was not Populistic alone but marked by locale, individual attitudes, and lack of specific incidents that precipitated racial violence and dissolved calm. Although he cites specific examples and ideas of black participation, Woodward's conception of Populist actions remains in the traditional white liberal mold: he associates the meaning of static biracial involvement with the democratic process, an assumption that bears investigation.

Black participation in Populist conventions varied considerably from state to state during the initial People's Party gatherings in 1891–92. "You look over the large assembly and find very few of my people represented in this great movement," an angry black delegate charged at the Populist convention in Dallas.[54] In Virginia, it is unclear if any black delegates were present at all.[55] The Arkansas Populists had 11 blacks among the 170 delegates in attendance.[56] The North Carolina Populist convention, according to the *Wilmington Morning Star,* had only "a few negro representatives," although over half the delegates were reportedly ex-Republicans.[57] In Georgia, the state Populist convention attracted only two blacks, although two years later black representation increased to twenty-four.[58] The high point of early black participation in the South was reached in Louisiana, where twenty-four black delegates attended the state Populist convention.[59] Alabama and Mississippi effectively circumscribed any black participation by refusing to seat black delegates.[60]

The number of blacks at various state Populist conventions thus varied greatly, but in all cases they were deprived of the substance of power. In the case of the earlier Alliance movement, black interests were often sacrificed to group interests. Controlling delegates and voting blocs was as necessary for Populists as it was for other parties. The most effective technique used by the white delegates to prevent a potential black power bloc was to assign black representatives as delegates for the state-at-large.[61] By failing to appoint blacks to a particular district-at-large, the opportunity to develop a viable concentrated base of grassroots support was eliminated. This dilution decreased the voice of blacks and increased that of whites who hoped to solicit black votes against token black delegations. With whites controlling the reins of power, meaningful black participation in the convention process was blunted almost entirely from the beginning. From this vantage, merely having black representatives on hand appears laudable at first blush, but suffers when actual black opportunity to make meaningful change is examined. In substance, this situation was also true in the Democratic and Republican parties. The comparison here between the actions of many state and local Republican conventions during this era is instructive. Southern white Republicans wanted black votes but not black power in their conventions. Both parties found the still-enfranchised black an awkward but necessary component of Southern politics.

A more personal explanation for Woodward's thesis seems plausible. Living in the midst of the civil rights era stimulated the social conscience of transplanted Southern liberals such as Woodward, who participated with Martin Luther King Jr. in the march on Montgomery, Alabama. "There we were," Woodward recalled, "walking down that highway to Montgomery. I looked over to the side of the road, and I saw the red-necks lined up, hate all over their faces, distrust and misunderstanding in their eyes. And I have to admit something. A little part of me was there with 'em."[62] For a moment here, one can picture Woodward as a late-nineteenth-century white Populist faced with the same vulgar personalities he observed on the road to Montgomery. If blacks and whites were living side by side in Montgomery during the 1890s, was it not possible that such racial behavior could again be introduced?[63] In his writings, especially his collection, *The Burden of Southern History,* Woodward addresses the problem of conscience plaguing the South and the white Southerner's preoccupation with guilt and the reality of evil. The desire to find an earlier version of the civil rights revolution and project one's own views on the past are a part of being human and simply reflect the flaws of all human beings when confronted with such challenges.

In his assertion that "Populist editors sought out achievements of Negroes to praise in their columns," Woodward adds yet another dimension to the Populist portrait.[64] This is one of his most explicit expositions of Populist actions and, like previous statements already examined, demonstrates the centrality of his belief in the People's Party as promoter of a liberal tradition in Southern history. It is perhaps his highest tribute to Populism that, in the face of racist allegations, it had the chance to use racial propaganda as a weapon and largely rejected it. But if white Populists sought to enlist the support of blacks to get themselves elected—or if the failure to use propaganda revealed a genuine desire to extend justice to blacks—the same actions were appropriate in both cases. The motivation for these actions is the catalyst for judgment, and that is too uncertain to determine.

Despite Woodward's contentions, however, Populists protested the role of blacks in their newspapers. The "Douglass Incident" is a good example of this negative Populist line. When Cleveland invited Frederick Douglass, his white wife, and black child by a previous marriage to four different mixed social affairs at the White House, Populists charged that the president was advocating social equality between the races. Under strong pressure from his fellow Republicans to condemn Cleveland, Douglass nonetheless praised the Democratic president for being "brave enough when public sentiment set against me" to invite him not once "but many times" to the White House.[65] Since the condemnation of Douglass "partakes of personal character and appeals to the prejudice of race," the *National Economist,* the primary Populist organ, made it clear that it would not print such a story except that "numerous requests" from grassroots subscribers had demanded it.[66] The editor's claim is specious, however, and instead suggests that Populist leaders could just as easily use newspapers to tacitly agree with the grassroots members on race questions without actually saying so outright.

Cleveland came under further attack because he had reportedly signed a bill in 1884, while governor of New York, that made provision for "mixed schools." Paradoxically, the statute concerned integration of *black* schools in New York, providing "for the education of pupils for whom admission is sought without regard to race or color." This, the Populists charged, was "proof" that Cleveland "committed himself to both the principle and policy of 'mixed schools.'"[67] The usual pattern in Populist papers presenting this story was to print a verbatim extract of the statute, with the conclusion that this was tangible "proof" of Cleveland's integrationist attitude. "I do not believe in Grover Cleveland's plan of treating the negro," Tom Watson declared. The result of such a policy would be "eternal discord" between the races.[68]

This viewpoint was not inconsistent with the views of many middle-class accommodationist blacks and whites of the day who believed that actions which brought the two races into closer contact would disrupt the good relations being developed by the two groups. Such policies would not solve the race problem but instead stir up racial conflict. It would be hard to overemphasize the Populist opposition to interracial association on a social basis. This oft-quoted New York statute was singled out to make this fact glaringly apparent. "Socially, I want no mixing of the races," Watson proclaimed. "It is best that both races should preserve the race integrity by staying apart." To a group of Atlanta blacks he sternly advised, "Let the whites dwell to themselves to have peace and happiness. [Populists] will not have social equality."[69] The attitude of Watson and other white Populists was summarized by a white North Carolina Populist: "We have no advocates of social equality with the Darky. All parties want their vote on a pinch. Now let the poor Negro alone."[70] Reverend H. S. Doyle, the black Georgia preacher who campaigned widely for Watson in 1892, expressed the limitations of the biracial venture: "Mr. Watson's position was that, in politics, the color line should be wiped out. He especially emphasized the word 'politics.' His enemies misrepresented him, and claimed that he was preaching the doctrine of social equality."[71]

It is clear that Democrats, Republicans, and Populists of both races as a group did not advocate "social equality," however it was defined. Almost all whites and a growing core of the urban black middle class were coming to believe that, in the face of growing conflict and the fact that blacks were not going to disappear as a race or a population, this method of race relations was the most viable option.

A third issue that received extensive press coverage during this period was the appointment of black diplomats to what Watson characterized as "white countries."[72] These pronouncements particularly centered around the proposed 1893 appointment of C. H. J. Taylor, "Cleveland's pet Democratic Negro from Kansas," as minister to Bolivia.[73] However, the Senate refused to confirm his appointment. A proponent of the "economics before politics" point of view later popularized by Booker T. Washington, Taylor was a former United States minister to Liberia, having been appointed in 1887 by Democratic President Grover Cleveland. An articulate middle-class mulatto lawyer, he had opposed the back-to-Africa element and Radical Reconstruction and urged blacks to eschew politics to prevent racial troubles.[74] A supporter of Cleveland, Taylor suggested that if blacks refused "the olive branch of political peace offered by Grover Cleveland . . . then by all means disfranchise them, and that speedily."[75] Here, then, Taylor was supporting in some degree the growing groundswell for "purification of the ballot" by eliminating the voting power of the illiterate black masses. Taylor's appointment to Bolivia was opposed by a faction of Senate Republicans, and his candidacy was subsequently withdrawn. He was then made register of deeds in Washington, D.C., where, according to a hostile Populist press, he would have "a few white girls" serving as "stenographers for his 'nigger' clerks." There is "certain to be a scramble" by Southern white "ladies" to serve as stenographers, it was cynically charged.[76]

A similar Cleveland appointment involved Harry Clay Smith, a black from Birmingham and editor of the *Cleveland Gazette* who was made consul at Santos, Brazil. The Populists charged that the Democrats had selected a black over their "own kind" to fill a position formerly held by a white diplomat. All this, it was charged, at a time when seventy thousand white Democrats desperately needed the president's endorsement for a diplomatic post.[77] Watson opposed such black appointees because it would break down the social barriers, thereby permitting blacks to eat, sleep, and mingle with whites.[78] Again, "social equality" would beget political equality, which would result in blacks being elevated to a status which was unacceptable to the white South.

A final racial issue receiving broad coverage in the mainstream Southern Populist press concerned a visit from a Massachusetts legislative delegation to Virginia's Democratic Governor Charles O'Ferrall. Included in the delegation was Robert Teamoh, a black. O'Ferrall asserted that he knew nothing of Teamoh's presence until the arrival of the representatives, whereupon he "merely" performed his official duties of mingling with the delegation. He reportedly "regretted the circumstances," but that was not enough for the white Populist press: the fact remained that "he performed the act."[79] Describing the incident, Watson stated: "Teamoh was there in great shape. He drank with the proudest, ate with the most select, and wiped his distinguished lips with O'Ferrall's napkins just as if he had been at it all his life."[80]

O'Ferrall's contention that he was unaware of Teamoh's presence in the delegation appears to have been manufactured ex post facto for public consumption once the incident received unfavorable notice. The Virginia delegation included John Mitchell Jr., prominent black editor of the *Richmond Planet,* an influential black newspaper throughout the South, who arrived with the mayor of his city. Mitchell was included in the local entourage as a social companion for the visiting black delegate and dined at the governor's mansion with Teamoh.[81] He "stretched companionable legs under the same mahogany," Watson asserted, "and forgot the toils of political war in a feast of brotherly love."[82] Ridiculing the episode, Watson added: "Mitchell saw, ate, and drank along with the Massachusetts delegation, the Governor and the Governor's wife, *just as natural as if he was a human being,* and Governor O'Ferrall hasn't found it out as yet."[83]

Such comments represent an essential part of the African American experience in the South during this era. This lack of ambiguity on black equality and humanity on the part of white Populist editors reveals the pervasive racism that potential black Populist recruits would face. The pattern of thought and events developed in this chapter has by no means exhausted the collection of racial events surrounding Southern Populism.[84] However, it is hoped that it has been sufficient to stir the historiographical dust surrounding the portrait of Populist racial attitudes laid down earlier by those historians who presented too sympathetic a portrayal of white Populist rhetoric. But there was a racial maturity and progressivism to Southern Populism even in its hours of peril that testifies to the validity of the Woodward Thesis. Populists did not, for example, often make blanket indictments about blacks as did their opponents but concentrated largely on specific personalities and events. In these incidents, Populist rhetoric was not knee-jerk racist but rather colored by political expediency. The attack on C. H. J. Taylor stands as a good example. Although a Populist candidate for the Kansas legislature in 1892, Taylor called the financier and railroad magnate Jay Gould, one of the Populists' major opponents, "as great a benefactor and philanthropist as the world has ever seen."[85] In addition, Taylor defended Cleveland, whom the Populists regarded as their political nemesis. Denouncing Southern Populists as "shabby, shiftless" and not "as good as any kind of negro," Taylor responded to the defeat of Alabama Populist gubernatorial candidate Reuben Kolb with obvious pleasure.[86] Such sentiments certainly prompted later Populist outbursts against Taylor and provided a rational basis for Populist actions. Purity of motive cannot overlook the practicalities of everyday political life even for a reform party. It would be a mistake, then, to attribute Populist attacks on particular black personalities solely as appeals to race prejudice.

The pattern of actions outlined by Populist sympathizers was not Populistic alone. The political and social views of such individuals are too sharply delineated and are intellectually precarious if not factually untenable. To make such stark dichotomies is to overlook the power of personalities, individual actions, local patterns, and racial harmony in microcosm. It would be a mistake to equate region-wide white Populist support of black political participation much beyond the perspective of immediate class interest and reform. To be sure, Populism would not pass the current tests for racial militancy and liberalism, and nowhere did it approach the millennium in race relations, even at its height, that its defenders imply. Compared with their contemporaries, Southern Populist leaders were often no better or worse than fellow reformers in their racial attitudes and at least on par with many Republicans and Democrats.

We may now pass to another aspect of Populist thinking, the biracial philosophy. Populist leaders understood the need to attract both black and white voters, and their biracial philosophy become an essential part of the reform compromise. But Populist thinking also completely rejected social equality and stressed a subservient political role for blacks within the movement. Every one of the previously examined incidents aptly illustrates this point. The sincerity of white Southern Populist convictions on this point seems unimpeachable: political equality could never be allowed to beget social equality; it would be an "unnatural" function of the social order. Just as much as it was a part of the "natural coalition" of the agrarians to include blacks in the producer class, such concerns did not override racial views concerning "natural inferiority" that took precedence over economic circumstances and individual views among blacks and whites. If anything, Populist adherents, particularly at the grassroots level, were more vehement on this point than their opponents. Perhaps the attacks of their opponents also exacerbated this tendency in Populist actions, making it into a sort of defensive mechanism, or perhaps poverty forced them to seek scapegoats for their circumstances. It is a wonder that white and black Populist leaders balanced grassroots white racism and black suspicions toward Southern white politicians. Readers who have not visited the primary sources of the period will find it difficult to understand that these few publicized outbursts by the Populists were, on balance, very moderate by the standards of the age. Further, they seem more defensive than offensive in nature.

To sum up the racial philosophy of Southern Populism is not simple. The following might be tentatively offered: the reformer cooperates biracially in a class sense, due to agrarian Jeffersonian underpinnings, during the political process insofar as it makes his movement more effective in the struggle against the established order. However, he is antagonistic to "social equality" and strongly opposes such "unnatural" egalitarian tendencies as being harmful ultimately to the welfare of both races. Thus, political equality does not nor does it need to beget social equality between the races. One is possible without the other. It remains now to turn to the application of this philosophy to local political affairs.

6

Theory and Practice of Populism

The Atlantic Seaboard States

Self interest always rules.

To those unfamiliar with the region's history, the late-nineteenth-century South seems a stereotypical monolith of drawls, good ol' boys, and white-suited planters smiling benignly at their black fieldhands. In truth, the region was a crazy quilt of wealthy and poor populists, impoverished patricians, outspoken and accommodating black leaders, booming industrialization, and rural poverty. Southern Populism localized and transformed itself to fit the needs of these various constituencies, which in turn prevented the fledgling party from coherently uniting to fight the ruling elite. The following chapters examine each of the three main regions in which Populism was active and raise questions as to why the movement attracted blacks in one area and not another.

VIRGINIA

In Virginia, after initially flirting with the idea of a biracial coalition, the Populists disassociated themselves from blacks and their votes. Blacks, in turn, long oppressed by personal and political prejudice, did not respond in significant numbers to the third party in Virginia.[1] J. Brad Beverly, former Alliance leader and a Populist, said of Virginia blacks:

> The Negroes to some extent voted for the Populists if there was no Republican candidate, but they always voted the Republican ticket if there was one. The Negroes were very unreliable, their promises amounted to nothing. They could be bought for money or whiskey. Major Mann Page told me of an amazing experience. A Negro leader had promised to support him and did not. Page reprimanded him, and he replied, "Major Page, don't you know that God made the Negro for sale to the highest bidder?"[2]

Some black votes could be purchased, but white Populists lacked the capital and influence with black leadership to attract sufficient black votes. The failure of blacks to support the Populist Party in Virginia only added to the growing view that eliminating the black vote would reform the political process. Virginians were more concerned with eliminating fraud and purifying the ballot through suffrage restrictions than with protecting the rights of the lower classes of either race. A growing view in Virginia and elsewhere, as a reaction to rampant corruption, was the idea that universal suffrage was not a "natural" right of all but a "privilege" extended to some persons on the basis of such matters as character, competence, and education.

Virginia Populists at the outset attempted to organize blacks on the precinct level. Votes of any persuasion or color were needed by the new party to offer a credible challenge to the Democrats. In the summer of 1892, Charles Pierson, editor of the *Virginia Sun* and Populist state committee chairman, urged each precinct committee to "have one or more colored citizens on it to look after the colored vote."[3] In short, the initial approach by Virginia Populists was to bring blacks into the fold using local black leaders. By fall 1892, Virginia Populists, responding to increasingly hostile Democratic opinion and race-baiting, shifted to a policy of organizing segregated black Populist clubs. The strategy was simple: seek out the most influential black in the community, secure him as a convert (which generally meant providing some financial remuneration), and then proceed to build grassroots support from that point.[4]

This pattern was not unique to the Populists or to Virginia politics but was widely practiced by all parties throughout the South. Turning out the black vote was normally preceded by nocturnal barbecues, and black leaders—or white plantation owners—accompanied black tenants, now "voters," to the polls to ensure that they voted for the "correct" candidate. Afterward, these same blacks were taken to other polling places and forced to vote again. Voting one's tenants was a common practice by white landowners throughout the South, including Virginia. Thus, Virginia Populism's early success with black voters depended on persuading them to vote in their favor, overcoming their own racial prejudices—no mean feat—and voter fraud. Unlike Georgia, where Populists and Democrats both resorted to fraud, intimidation, and violence, evidence does not suggest the same methodology by Virginia Populists, although Democrats certainly used fraud widely. By 1893, however, the Virginia Populists had repudiated the idea of securing the black vote, regarding it not worth pursuing.[5]

In their denunciation of Populist efforts to organize blacks, Virginia Democrats as always had raised the old political shibboleth of "Negro domination and rule," warning the white population that "every vote cast in the South for the third party will be a Republican vote by proxy, tending to encourage the Negro to another effort for supremacy."[6] These charges received added impetus with the skillful development of a "Cult of the Confederacy," which had developed by the 1890s under the aegis of the Democratic party.[7] Virginia, the cradle of the Confederacy, provided fertile ground for Democrats to wave the "bloody shirt" and warn of disaster if blacks and Populists were allowed to unseat the Democratic majority. This blind devotion to the "Lost Cause," bolstered by the racial issue, laid a firm foundation for the absolute loyalty being demanded of the white voters to the state's Democratic organization—an obstacle that Virginia Populists failed to surmount, either psychologically or politically.

A factor that further reinforced the issue of party and race solidarity in Virginia politics was the presence of William "Boss Billy" Mahone, characterized as "the best-loved and best-hated character in postbellum Virginia politics."[8] The Democrats had passed over General Billy Mahone for governor in 1877, and he consequently bolted and founded the Readjuster Party. Mahone, with a group of black lieutenants, united black and white voters in a biracial political movement in the 1880s that challenged ("Redeemed") the Democratic Party in Virginia, and his successes had encouraged other dissidents to challenge Democrats in various Southern states.[9] Foreshadowing the Populists, Mahone had shown it was possible to successfully unite black and white in a political movement to defeat the Democrats. The suggestion that this effort might be replicated by the Populists was a propaganda tactic that helped Democrats undercut Virginia Populism and any biracial coalition. The fear of "Mahoneism" when coupled with the race issue was a threat Virginia Democrats could use in stifling the Populist movement.

Although he had suffered a substantial loss of power and prestige by 1890, Mahone nevertheless retained a power base in Virginia politics until his death in 1895. To Virginia's movement, his very presence and symbolic value were still significant, since white opinion had come to hold that "the man blessed with a white cuticle is false [to his race] if he does not in this emergency cooperate with the Democratic party."[10] "Mahoneism" and Populism in Virginia became jointly associated in the public mind. As one newspaper expressed it, "The [Democratic] party . . . , is the very life of Virginia."[11] And it needed the public to continue its unflagging support. In the Virginia of the 1890s, as elsewhere in the South, voting Democratic was portrayed as not so much a matter of politics but as a test of race loyalty and a defense of white civilization. Ironically, it was this very gap between white and black that made it impossible for Virginia Populism to be acceptable to either group. Tom Watson had warned about and fought to overcome this racial chasm; in Virginia it was not to be.

Faced with this situation, informed Virginia Populists had by 1893 given up the notion of soliciting the black vote and sought rather to dispel the belief that they desired black support or votes. John Mitchell Jr., the black editor of the *Richmond Planet,* observed in the hotly contested 1893 gubernatorial campaign between Democrat Charles T. O'Ferrall and Populist Edmund Randolph Cocke that "the colored people were practically ignored by the Populists." If the white Populists wished to attract black voters, Mitchell added, then their "platform must furnish strong inducements" to African Americans.[12] But these efforts were never forthcoming, certainly not after 1893. Ironically, Virginia blacks at this point, with their desertion by the national Republican Party, were probably open and receptive to political arguments from Populists or Democrats. To be tagged as "the nigger party" would prove, Virginia Populists came to believe, more of a political liability than an asset. As a result, about two-thirds of the black voters stayed away from the polls during the 1893 election. This was particularly notable in the Southside, which was Virginia Populism's stronghold and also contained Virginia's Black Belt and the bulk of the black vote.[13] After 1893, however, there were few serious efforts by Virginia Populists to bring blacks into the party. As John Mitchell Jr. succinctly stated: "The Populists cannot carry Virginia without the aid of the [black] Republicans. It seems useless to deny that fact."[14] But after 1893, Virginia Populists made no more major appeals to blacks, and as Mitchell predicted, the Populists never carried Virginia.

Yet while white economic advancement, self-help, and reform were paramount in Virginia's Populist ideology, some observers believed they still saw an underlying hint of desired political amalgamation with African Americans. For the white population, the ever-present apprehensiveness about reviving black Mahoneism and the earlier Readjuster Movement was such that the fears of the white voters were easily intensified, further driving an ideological wedge between the two races. Taking note of these conditions, Sheldon has rightfully concluded that "the election of 1892 made apparent once more the fact that economic issues must remain subordinate to the racial problems . . . so long as the Negro was a potential factor in [Virginia] politics."[15] But that was to change shortly, with the passage of the Walton Act in 1893, which essentially disenfranchised Virginia blacks.

Philosophies of racial chauvinism and political solidarity, however, were but part of a larger complex of problems facing Virginia Populism. The Democrats, determined to retain their hard-earned supremacy, still employed the corrupt methods learned in Readjuster days against Mahone and the blacks in order to ensure their claims to victory. The *Virginia Sun,* the official Populist paper of the state, lamented that "never were such bacchanalia of corruption and terrorism" seen as in the 1892 campaign in Virginia.[16] Especially notable were the fraudulent voting practices. The Populists had "no doubt at all" that they had been deprived of victory in at least four congressional districts by Democrats who went "through precinct after precinct" and threw out the Populist returns.[17] "Devotion to fraud and perjury," the *Richmond Times* declared, "was set as the standards of the Democratic faith . . . as if, forsooth, principle and not principle were one and the same thing."[18] The *Times* further claimed that fraud and arbitrary action by local Democratic election officials resulted in the entire vote of 31 of 98 voting precincts in the Fourth District, which voted Populist, being thrown out in the congressional election of 1894.[19] The Democratic governor frankly admitted in 1895 that previously "there had been much confusion and disorder at the voting places and that large sums of money had been used in every election to corrupt voters by all political parties, and men's ballots had been purchased like stock in the market."[20] But to their credit the Virginia Populists, while not pure, never engaged in the degree of fraud, intimidation, and violence used in other states by both parties, particularly the Democrats. Further, Populism "was only a minor eddy" in Virginia politics, never becoming a major political force in the state. Their failure—or choice—not to form a biracial coalition probably helped doom the People's Party in Virginia to an early decline.[21]

The gubernatorial election of 1893 between aristocratic Populist Edmund Randolph Cocke and Democrat Charles T. O'Ferrall represented the "last, almost desperate bid for state control" by the Virginia Populists—an attempt to blend the state's heterogeneous white elements into a workable political machine.[22] In that summer, blacks' almost total indifference toward the Populist Party was made conspicuously clear to all when not a single black member attended the gubernatorial nominating convention![23] Even those Democrats who had loudly lambasted the Populists with the race question regarded this absence with surprise, inasmuch as all party conventions usually contained a few blacks. But the decision was clear by 1893: blacks were not welcome in the Virginia Populist Party. Their presence was regarded as more of a burden than a benefit, the cost of their vote was prohibitive in attracting native whites, and their presence did not provide a remedy among the agrarian coalition.

Cocke's racial attitudes had been made clear as early as 1891 when he suggested that Congress repeal the Fifteenth Amendment, since "the only solution to prevent troubles . . . , is to disfranchise the Negro."[24] The irony that befell Virginia Populism was that it contained such patrician names as

Page, Beverly, Cocke, Ruffin, and Harrison, who represented the "better class of whites" to whom many middle-class blacks were looking for protection and direction. This mechanism for political accommodation to turn Virginia Populism into a biracial instrument of third-party revolt was never utilized in the state that most looked backward toward a Jeffersonian ethos.

Although Virginia Populists early attempted to disassociate themselves from Republicanism, blacks, and Mahone, the loose lips of "Boss Billy" succeeded in placing the two parties in the same camp—at least in the mind of the white electorate—when he indicated publicly that he "favored any ism that will bust the Democracy."[25] Since the minority Republicans decided not to nominate a ticket in 1893, Mahone's open admiration of the Populist platform merely confirmed the suspicions of many whites, adding flames to the already heightened political atmosphere and concerns about the revival of "Mahoneism" and the Readjuster Movement. In the minds of Virginia whites, Mahone's open admiration of the Populists confirmed a long held belief that "the Republican Party in Virginia is the snake and the Populist Party is the toad just about swallowed already."[26] The fear that a Populist-Republican fusion would return Mahone to power, and with him the despised black, was a strategic propaganda position for Democrats to hold, for with it they could further cut the legs of white support from under Virginia Populism. But Mahone's indirect endorsement still appears to have helped the Populists in 1893. Regression analysis indicates that almost every Populist vote cast in 1893 came from the same voters who four years earlier had voted for Mahone.[27] Mahone's followers and Virginia Populists had many of the same grievances and enemies, and it is understandable that the voters supporting each movement highly overlapped.

It was unfortunately under such conditions that the national Populist movement ill-advisedly chose to attach import to the 1893 Virginia election, arguing that it could win in a state that had traditionally served as a political leader in the South. While the state movement suffered from a shortage of money, there is evidence that ample operating funds for the campaign were furnished by the National Committee, out-of-state sources, and Western silver interests. Now desperate for support, the Populists proceeded to "beat the bushes" for political discontents who could provide them with votes.[28]

A factor that should have been in the Populists' favor was the state's rising agricultural problems, accentuated by the Panic of 1893.[29] But Virginia was more of a border state than a "typical" Deep South agrarian state. Business and industry had grown considerably since 1880, which gave them unusual power and growing political clout in the state. By the 1890s, Virginians identified less with the Populist agricultural revolt than did their less well-off fellow Deep South comrades. As Virginians suffered less, as a rule, the state had a less-responsive third-party constituency than other Southern states. However, the material change in the state's economy was becoming obvious by the fall of 1893. By the following spring, conditions had reached the point where black votes "could be cornered at half price." In the fall election, Democrats took advantage of blacks' destitute condition and "for a consideration," purchased their votes.[30] The party that offered itself as the harbinger of political reform and advocate of "a free ballot and a fair count" found such actions reprehensible and, to its credit, largely repudiated fraud and corruption.

Indeed, Populist emphasis on moral sentiment and class development as concomitant to political activity encouraged whites' disillusionment with blacks for debasing the election machinery. To the Populists, widespread purchase of black votes by Democrats proved how a corrupt ruling power backed by business and upper-class interests exercised undue influence on the political process. Populists believed such actions were detrimental to black self-interest and inconsonant with the imminent conflict between capital and labor. The natural coalition of agrarian interest groups supporting Alliance and Populist dogma presumed that the biracial farmer class would battle for reform, which was not always so; Virginia stands as a glaring case in point in the Populist revolt.[31]

When the 1893 election was over, O'Ferrall emerged the victor by the largest majority of any gubernatorial candidate in Virginia's history, with 127,940 votes to Cocke's 81,239.[32] With this crushing defeat, the Populist cause not only in Virginia but throughout the South suffered an irreparable blow. The Populists' attempt to make Virginia a symbol was prescient of the movement's ultimate failure. An analysis of the 1893 election reveals that white Republicans split their vote almost equally between the Democratic and Populist parties. Nearly two-thirds of eligible black voters boycotted the polls, according to one estimate, with a sizeable portion of the remainder voting for the Democrats. Kousser has observed that "almost every vote" the Populists received in 1893 came from persons who had backed Mahone, four years earlier, and many of them were blacks.[33] It would appear therefore that the failure of blacks to support the Populist cause helped cost them the 1893 Virginia election.[34] It is difficult to gauge whether Populist appeals to blacks would have made a difference in the outcome, but if so, it probably would only have been a difference in degree, not result.

Economic expediency as well as political despair and the growing economic and political power of the Democrats prompted Virginia blacks to revise their traditional policy of voting solidly with the Republicans. With the failure of the Republican Party to make any nominations for either the General Assembly or the gubernatorial office in 1893, African Americans were left pretty much at the disposal of the Democrats. Virginia Democrats in 1893 took advantage of the cry for election reform with its demands for "purification of the ballot" and passed the Walton Act, which provided for a publicly printed ballot on which neither party names nor symbols were present. Voters were given two and one-half minutes to mark lines through names of candidates for which they did *not* want to vote. The law was not enforced very strictly among whites but was applied very stringently to black voters. Illiterates, of which many were black, were "assisted" by constables, who were always Democrats. The Walton Act virtually ended black suffrage in Virginia.[35] As such, Populist pursuit of the black vote after 1893 virtually ended. Those blacks who did vote after 1893 largely supported the wealth and power of the emerging pro-business Democrats who could benefit them.[36] Any attempt by blacks to give tangible expression to their views through their own legislators had further been eliminated by the removal of the last African Americans from the Virginia State Senate in 1891—the first time since 1867 when blacks were not represented in the state.[37] In turn, the successful Democratic exploitation of the racial issue and "Mahoneism" helped force the Populists to stop short of openly soliciting black support, concluding that its overall value in repelling white voters would be substantial.

One of the ironic burdens of Southern history is that Democratic appeals in Virginia to the race question ultimately resulted in the subsequent inclusion after 1893 of substantial numbers of blacks under the Democratic banner.[38] Political suppression, economic expediency, and political despair had forced blacks, poor in both spirit and finances, to support their worst enemies or not participate in the political process, in order to garner benefits from the powerful of the state. The Negro Democratic League of Virginia expressed this attitude when it advised blacks to vote with "that class of white people that own and control everything."[39] Although Democrats made bold use of the race issue against their opponents, they were not yet willing to forfeit such a bloc of voters, no matter what their color. As a result, "large numbers of Negroes turned to the Democrats in furtherance of what appeared to be their best interests."[40]

Blacks split over what political strategy to adopt under such circumstances. Consider the course of political action advocated by T. Thomas Fortune, black editor or the *New York Age,* who did not deem "it binding upon colored men further to support the Republican party when other more advantageous affiliation can be found":

No colored man can ever claim truth fully to be a Bourbon Democrat. It is a fundamental impossibility. But he can be an independent,
a progressive Democrat. . . . [He] must think less of the party and
more of himself, give less heed to a name and more to principles. . . .

When colored voters differ among themselves find themselves on
both sides of the local political contests, they will begin to find themselves of some political importance, their votes will be sought, cast,
and counted.[41]

It is difficult to ascertain the extent of the defection among Virginia blacks,
but the attitude of all parties toward blacks in Virginia by the mid-1890s
was about the same: they either bought their votes, largely in the case of the
Democrats, or desired their votes but not their presence, as was the case
among the Populists, and increasingly so, the Republicans. By 1902, their
vote was not significant in achieving a Democratic majority.

Although the Virginia Populist movement was never strong, it was a mere
shadow by 1896. What vitality remained was sapped by the Democrats
through the following tactics: "First denounce it, then accept its platform,
and then force the party out of existence."[42] This strategy was effective not
only in Virginia but in the remainder of the South. Whether the movement's
failure to encourage black participation in Virginia would have prevented its
decline seems doubtful in light of the effects of the Walton Act. With the
death of William J. Mahone in 1895, the Readjuster threat was also dead.
During this same year, Frederick Douglass also died, leaving a vacancy in
black leadership nationally which would shortly be filled by Booker T.
Washington. For Virginia blacks, the twin blow of Mahone's and Douglass's
deaths, coupled with the earlier Walton Act, would largely eliminate blacks
from the political equation in Virginia until the mid–twentieth century.

NORTH CAROLINA

To what extent the decline of the Republican Party in the South directly
influenced black defection to the Populist cause is difficult to evaluate, although in North Carolina, at least, party disunity over the racial issue probably drove a number of Republicans into the Populist ranks as early as
1892.[43] North Carolina blacks, unlike their Virginia counterparts, voted in
large numbers before 1900 and, as in Virginia, ballot box stuffing appears to
have been less extensive than in other Southern states.[44] While internal
feuding might have caused some black Republicans to defect, the large majority remained loyal Republicans, partly because of the prospect of social

ostracism from members of their own race.[45] Since white North Carolina Populists were as a rule "avowedly anti-Negro,"[46] and they did not anticipate or solicit black votes in some cases,[47] it is unlikely that the party ever received much support from the black community in North Carolina. Yet only in North Carolina would Democrats lose control in the 1890s, primarily due to Republican and Populist fusion. And it was also home to two of the most prominent and competent Populists, Leonidas L. Polk and Marion Butler.

North Carolina blacks' consistent loyalty to the Republican Party, despite the abuse they suffered from many of its white members, is one of the complex phenomena of the state's history. Tar Heel blacks emerged from slavery with a lack of skills, education, and independent spirit, making them malleable to the needs of the Republican leadership. Also, the symbolism of the Republican Party as "the party of liberation" attracted blacks committed to it as the party of liberty, democracy, and independence, despite growing evidence to the contrary. Observing this state of mind in the black community, an unfriendly white North Carolina judge recalled that during this period blacks "exercised no choice at all" in their votes but "voted precisely as automatons" under the tutelage of the Republican Party.[48] White Populists were not unaware of this political current. In an early analysis of the various types of voters within the state, the *Progressive Farmer,* a leader among Southern Alliance farm journals, spoke of the "voter of rather dark skin" who has been branded "straight ticket R. P. [Republican Party]" in several places. Around this voter's neck was fastened "a party collar" to which was attached a "chain," a link of which was passed through the black's nose with a white Republican leading him about and vigorously applying the "party lash" to his body—which was covered with "a bloody shirt" that had not been washed in years.[49] Four years later another white Populist similarly wrote that "The Negro is as close under the repub. as ever, voting against his own interest as well as ours. This state of affairs has no future."[50] All in all, black loyalty to the Republican Party in North Carolina as a vehicle for political protest ultimately failed to result in increased rights. As a group, North Carolina blacks did not see it being in their best self-interests to vote Populist.

But there were exceptions. The Reverend Walter A. Pattillo of Oxford, North Carolina, was, according to his biographer, "the principal leader of the black Populists in North Carolina." A former slave who received a theology degree from Shaw University, Pattillo worked tirelessly for the black Baptist Church and served as a lecturer and elected state organizer for the Colored Farmers' Alliance in North Carolina. Like his black counterpart in Texas, John B. Rayner, originally from North Carolina, Pattillo was "an extraordinary mass organizer." He worked to secure the "middle ground," according to his son, in order "to relate to both the black and white communities." Unlike many of his race, Pattillo early advocated a third party and was one of only three national representatives of the Colored Farmers' Alliance on the credentials committee of the St. Louis convention in 1892. But for all of Pattillo's efforts, blacks in North Carolina remained largely wedded to the Republican Party, and only through fusion with the Republicans did Populists enjoy much benefit of the black vote in North Carolina.[51]

With the rise of the third party in North Carolina, Democrats attempted to solidify the white population around the old political rally cries of white supremacy and "Negro domination."[52] The possibility of fusion between the Populist and Republican elements in 1894 was not lost on the Democrats, who planned to duplicate their 1892 victory in any way possible, even if it meant the open solicitation of black votes. Populists by 1894 were seething against the Democrats, to the extent that they were now willing to work with the despised Republicans and blacks to win at the ballot box.

North Carolina Democrats won an easy victory in 1892, capturing both the legislature and the governorship. For example, the vote for governor was: W. P. Exum, Populist, 47,840; David M. Furches, Republican, 98,684; and Elias Carr, Democrat, 135,519. The Populists carried only three counties. It was not lost on the Populists and Republicans that their combined vote total exceeded that of the Democrats, suggesting the need to work together in order to be successful at the ballot box.[53] With the white vote split, all camps soon recognized the political value of the black vote as the balance of power and proceeded to court it with equal vigor. And since blacks were predominately Republican, it would primarily be through the aegis of the Republican Party that these benefits would be enjoyed by either of the other two parties—unless fraud were employed.

Showered with racial epithets in 1892, the Populists eagerly seized the opportunity to ridicule the Democrats about their hunt for black votes, taking obvious pleasure in noting that the Democrats no longer referred to "the coons" and "the brutes" but spoke benignly of "our colored brethren" in their campaign speeches. Also, Democrats openly appealed to black leaders and candidates, liberally purchasing the support of black preachers, hoping thereby to deprive the fused Republican-Populist coalition of black votes. Populists charged, probably truthfully, that the Democrats planned to "kill off" politically these black candidates after they received the black vote.[54]

While exaggerated, the Southern Democratic attitude toward blacks was portrayed by the *Progressive Farmer* in a post-election parody of the 1894 opposition's political naiveté. In a humorous exchange between two "court-house politicians" ("R" representing the Populist viewpoint and "B" the Democratic attitude), the paper revealed a prototype of fixed political principles and pragmatism in Southern politics. The Democrat opens the conversation by lamenting that "the nigger voted ergin us" in the 1894 election, sadly concluding that "it iz a downrite disgrace ter be beat by nigger votes."

> R says—"But it is entirely honorable to beat the other side with the help of Negro votes."
> B says—"But of course it is. If enough niggers had voted with us Dymakrats ter beat you fellers it would hev bin awl rite, but I dont like ter get beat by folks what ain's got no souls."
> R says—"Certainly you dont. In your estimation, no one, white nor black has a soul unless he voted the Democratic ticket."
> B says—"Oh yes. The colored folks whut voted the dymakratic ticket hes souls, but them whut voted for the cooperative Fusion ticket haint got enny souls."[55]

Fusionists understood that Democrats would use fraud and corruption against them. As early as January 1894, perhaps more in satire than in earnest, in anticipation of this problem Marion Butler's *Caucasian* offered a "prize" of twenty-five dollars for the best method of ensuring a fair and honest election that fall.[56] If the Democrats could not secure the black vote, the Fusionists loudly proclaimed, they would suppress it; a Democratic paper, the *Charlotte News and Observer,* countered indignantly that "In a few Negro counties, it may be that the Negro vote has sometimes been partially suppressed, but this has never occurred in more than eight or ten counties and it is a base slander [for the Fusionists] to charge otherwise."[57] It is difficult to judge the degree of political corruption from the charges in the literature. But the open admission by the Democrats that the black vote had "been partially suppressed" in "eight or ten counties" suggests Democrats relied upon fraud and corruption to remain in power. Following the election of 1894, however, the Populists charged that the Democrats had stolen forty thousand votes and still lost the election.[58] Despite claims to the contrary by a contemporary historian, it cannot validly be said that "there is no reason to think that there was wide-spread fraud" in the 1894 election.[59]

The 1894 election in North Carolina, despite widespread fraud, represented one of the better showings by the Populists in the South. Indeed, North Carolina was the only state in the old South in which the Democrats lost control in the nineties. This victory was the result of fusion between

Republicans and Populists—many of the former being blacks—against the Democrats. Republicans and Populists avoided their 1892 mistake and agreed upon a single ticket, except in the case of governor, lieutenant governor, and auditor, on which both parties would be represented in 1894—thus, the emergence of the "Fusion ticket" in North Carolina. As in Virginia, the Democratic Party in North Carolina by the mid-1890s was a party in transition, increasingly identified with business interests and "hard money" issues. In 1894, the Democrats had no clear state-oriented reform program and were regarded as a "do-nothing" party. With an unfocused Democratic effort and Populist-Republican fusion, the outlook was good for the coalition. When the 1894 election was over, the Fusionists had won control of the state legislature, elected the two United States senators and a majority of the representatives. Perhaps the highpoints of the 1894 legislative coalition were the election of Marion Butler to a six-year term in the United States Senate and filling a second vacancy, caused by the death of an incumbent Democrat, with a Republican. The 1894 Fusion ticket carried thirty-one counties, whereas Populists carried only three in 1892.

The North Carolina Populist Party continued its campaign against corrupt election practices after the 1894 campaign. Viewing the situation from the vantage point of the 1896 election, William A. Guthrie, the party's gubernatorial candidate, added that there were some "localities" in North Carolina where elections were "reasonably fair," but "taking the state as a whole" there had not been "a fair state election in over twenty years."[60] Democrats, "by some hook or crook . . . , will get the legislature," a disgusted correspondent from Farmville informed Marion Butler.[61] From Mecklenburg County came reports of "a most tremendous fight against fraud and rascality."[62] The "cry of 'nigger'" was the "cowardly subterfuge" used by local Democrats "to deceive men into voting for a party with a record as black as hell." In the Charlotte area, after "many voters were unjustly erased from the Registration books and our election box broke up," Democrats moved in and "reorganized" the election machinery, excluding Populist votes in the recounting process.[63] Walter R. Henry, a lawyer and Populist candidate from Mecklenburg, discovered a Democratic plan to keep blacks "from the ballot box" by intimidating or arresting "two or three hundred negroes" who had registered to vote but had not paid their taxes, which was "a misdemeanor." Blacks, who would likely be unable to pay the fine, would either "run away to avoid arrest" or else be incarcerated during the election process. These votes were "important" to the Populist victory in that area, but "the negroes [were] sent to jail on frivolous charges."[64] From the Sixth District came similar reports by an angry Populist candidate who had lost to the Democrats because of election fraud. "Whenever a man gets to *stealing*, whether it be *bonds or ballots,* he has gotten as low as a human being can get." Such actions:

> make my cheek blush with shame when I think that *Southern white men* have sink [*sic*] so *low* as to steal votes. Before the war the "nigger" stole from the 'old master' but since the war old master, the *high-toned and honorable gentleman,* has gone to stealing from the "nigger." Oh! What a fall was that!![65]

Republicans, long accustomed to working with the black voter, took it for granted that the development of the black vote would require certain concessions, such as black candidates on the ticket, patronage, and funds to purchase ballots. In Alamance County in the eastern part of the state, for example, where blacks constituted "the majority of the Rep. party," blacks made clear their demands: "They want recognition—a County Com.— magistrates and jurors."[66] While the Populists inwardly opposed blacks as officeholders, they outwardly agreed to this prospect to gain political ascendancy. But it was more difficult to keep the rank-and-file in line when blacks were so intimately involved in politics. Race relations became more and more strained. One former Democrat who became a Populist did not "imagine" that his future "political affiliations" were "to be governed by a party [Republican] who in my own state is three-fourths black." To the grassroots Populist following, association with a party that "set forth and passed [resolutions] in Negro school houses in the dead hours of night" was not a pleasant thought.[67] Democrats skillfully played the race card, charging Populists and Republicans with encouraging social equality, intermarriage, and political "debauchery." Populists were both angered and embarrassed by use of the race issue. From Alamance County came comments from other disgruntled Populists: "If to vote for [Daniel] Russell and a Republican Legislature is to bring the negro into the front in political prominence, the Alamance Pops don't want [it]."[68] Heartened by the prospects of victory from the 1894 Fusionist election, however, most white Populists remained silent, although they refused to publicly endorse the black candidates on the ticket.[69]

Populists who formulated the coalition ticket with the Republicans shared few basic principles or party traditions with their allies. The Fusion ticket was largely a marriage of convenience brought about by hatred of a common enemy—the Democrats. Republicans generally favored sound money, the gold standard, a protective tariff, banking legislation, and other legislation partial to the business community whereas Populists wanted government ownership of railroads, telephone and telegraph companies, and free and unlimited coinage of silver—policies almost diametrically opposed to the pro-business, non-inflationary principles of the Republican Party.[70]

Since the Fusionist ticket represented two distinct political philosophies, this relationship harbored from the beginning a degree of dissent and antagonism. And when the race question arose, both parties revealed rifts. The example of Andrew D. Cowles, a white Republican leader from Iredell County, stands as a case in point.[71] Cowles, who strongly opposed fusion on the grounds that it would lead to an erosion of Republican principles, expressed his belief that:

> There is not a plank in our platform on which the Populist Party would stand, and not one in theirs on which a Republican should stand. *Expediency is the only bond of union.* I have tried to reconcile it with conscience and principle. I can't do it. Being as I am, Republican to the core, I can't be a Populist even skin deep.[72]

Not everyone thought Populists and Republicans made good allies. "I have always thought that the natural alliance was between Dems. and Pops in the fight," the Populist candidate for state auditor, Hal Ayer, observed, but the Democrats "force us to fight them."[73] Yet principle was often the public campaign sentiment espoused for the continuation of this mesalliance. "Everyone must admit that such a fusion for such common interests is not only legitimate but of the highest importance," a Populist campaign pamphlet asserted. Populists and Republicans must in good faith "unite to secure a free ballot and a fair count."[74] Ironically, political expediency held the two groups together to achieve their principles. To the Populist, Jeffersonian principles were paramount, whereas the big business-oriented Republicans favored Hamiltonian principles.

The absence of clear-cut issues, the difficulty of uniting with old enemies, and the heightened use of the race issue at least initially created apathy among the voters, particularly regarding national questions. The national Populists, seeing that the Democrats held doctrines much like their own in 1896, had accepted Democrat William Jennings Bryan as their 1896 presidential candidate, primarily because of his stand for farmers and workers and because of his advocacy for free silver. Bryan stampeded the convention into nominating him with his populist "cross of gold" speech. This national alliance of agrarian interests and big business was a crushing blow to many Southern Populists, black and white. "So deep were the resentments aroused by four years of war against the old party in the South," Woodward has observed, "that fusion with Democrats had become more abhorrent to many Southern Populists than fusion with Republicans."[75] In 1896, Bryan by a convoluted compromise ultimately became the presidential nominee of four parties or factions of parties (Democrats, Populists, Prohibitionists, and Silver Republicans) while William McKinley, the ultimate winner, represented the Republicans. A complicated Fusion agreement was finally worked out in September at the state level between Populists and Republicans, with each having separate nominees for governor, lieutenant governor, and auditor, but generally supporting a common ticket for the legislature.[76]

As the 1896 election approached in North Carolina, the turmoil and rancor so obvious in previous elections was not initially producing hysterical responses. Indeed, just the opposite response was true. "I have never seen so much indifference" from "the voters in my life so near a Presidential election," a correspondent reported from the Piedmont area. If there was "any real difference" between the three parties, it was that "the Rep. are in better shape than either of the other parties."[77] Republicans were better funded, which they used in part to "turn out" the black vote. A Farmville Populist also observed that "our people are surely lacking in enthusiasm" over the national ticket with William Jennings Bryan.[78] The voters were further confused by the statewide amalgams on the local level. In the Newton area, a Populist leader cried out in dismay and utter confusion: "I am confronted in my Disct. with Republican-Populist fusion in some counties and Democratic-Populist fusion in others[;] it seems that a great many [voters] look no further than their local [conditions]." An analysis of the situation revealed that "This state of affairs exists to some extent all over the state"— and so it seemed.[79] In Rockingham County, it was reported that "we have fused with the Democrats [and] some of our Pops have kicked against it and wanted to fuse with the Republicans. But I think it will be all right."[80] Populist gubernatorial candidate William A. Guthrie observed from the coastal area that "Our folks have up to date generally fused with the Republicans."[81] In the La Grange area, however, Republicans expressed reservations about fusing with Populists.[82] Much of this shifting around was due to parochial loyalties, personalities, and prejudices, but much was also an attempt to find some political and economic relief at the local level. In the following months this state of affairs made a concerted statewide campaign almost impossible for the Republican-Populist fusionist ticket—or so it seemed at that point. Under such circumstances, blacks were as much the victims of confusion, changing loyalties, varied interests, and shifting emphases as their white counterparts. Their deteriorating status in the Republican Party and loss of patronage angered blacks and made their vote an uncertain prospect, and it was getting harder to control—even under Republican leaders who were normally able to exert significant influence over the course of black support in the Tar Heel state.

The advance of business and industry in North Carolina by the mid-nineties gave Democrats considerable economic power. And power and money were proving attractive to some blacks. "In the quest for full citizenship," Elsie Lewis has concluded of middle-class blacks of the era, "those Negroes who were articulate exhibited no concern for any issues that did not affect their status. They ignored or failed to understand the great issues of the economic revolution that was transforming America and creating complex new problems."[83] In short, self-interest among middle-class blacks was increasingly taking precedence over the principles and loyalty to the party of Lincoln that had long sustained black voters.

By the 1890s, middle-class black leaders throughout the nation openly flirted with Democrats "to procure a job or to attempt to gain favor with the white community."[84] Always tactful, this group quietly sought to cultivate the sources of white power as a means of redressing personal or racial grievances. The "best thing for the colored people to do," according to black Baptist minister Garland H. White, "is to unite with the governing class of white people in this section who are Democrats whom we have to depend upon in emergency."[85] A black spokesman far more prominent nationally, President Joseph Charles Price of Livingstone College in Salisbury, North Carolina, believed that blacks "would do well to harmonize with that element . . . , even at the sacrifice of nonessentials" such as political involvement as much "as is consistent with the instincts of mankind."[86] Price also argued that social equality must not be the aim of his people: "I say that the Negro has no idea that in seeking his political and civil rights he is seeking an arbitrary social equality with any race. . . . The Negro does not seek in other races what he does not have in his own, notwithstanding; the whites are disposed to put all Negroes in one class."[87] Furthermore, "The Negro does not desire and does not seek social equality with whites. Such an equality does not obtain among Negroes themselves. . . . the social tendency is not possessed by Negroes."[88] To distance himself from social equality would raise his merit in the eyes of the business leaders of the community. These expressions show clearly the growing allure of the white Democratic power structure on the party loyalty of middle-class blacks who were in turn increasingly seeking a conciliatory policy with the white South. But many black agrarians remained loyal to the Republican Party, particularly where national elections were concerned, well into the next century, not only in North Carolina but elsewhere.

Understandably, many blacks were uncertain whether the historical animus between white untutored grassroots Populists and blacks would allow any common ground from which to launch a campaign against the Democrats. To compound the dilemma, both races were also driven by factionalism over local issues, personalities, and the neat separation of state and fed-eral issues around which the fusion maneuver depended. Blacks in the Sixth District were "split all to pieces" over "free silver," although "4 to 1 say they will vote for silver" and support the Populists over the Republicans in the event fusion failed to materialize.[89] In the Burgaw area, Populists were cer-tain they could "divide the negro vote with the republicans in this county from president down to say nothing of the gains we shall make from the democratic ranks."[90]

A goodly number of blacks and whites—not only in the Tar Heel state but elsewhere as well—were also split in their support of "the Great Com-moner," William Jennings Bryan, as the 1896 Populist presidential candi-date. On closer examination, the reason for this division among blacks be-comes clear when Bryan's attitudes on race relations are surveyed. He shared a contradiction with the Populists: his much-vaunted talk about "letting the people rule" and "defense of human rights" did not always square with his actions toward blacks and other minorities.[91] In the matter of black educa-tion, Bryan, during his first term in Congress, had developed a substantial middle-class black following through his promotion of educational oppor-tunities "for the race." This support centered around his "generosity of heart and earnest eloquence" in supporting an 1892 bill proposed by Henry Cheatham, a black Republican Congressman (1889–93) from North Caro-lina, "to aid in the establishment and temporary support of common schools." Inasmuch as it was "designed particularly to promote the interest of the colored people of the South," blacks wanted the bill passed. Although Bryan gave the proposal his "best" efforts "from first to last," white Republican opposition ultimately defeated the measure.[92] Conversely, in discussing black political rights, Bryan freely and openly used the common clichés of the day about disavowing "social equality" and the "excesses of the black legis-latures" during Reconstruction.[93] At best, his insensitive racial remarks about such matters must have made it difficult for blacks to discern the difference between friend and foe. Generous and broadminded in some respects, Bryan, like the white Populists, was not unique in his racial thinking. In this re-gard his position was consistent, for he had said "essentially the same things at the turn of the century that he was saying in the 1920s."[94] His advo-cacy of limited political rights for blacks understandably did not result in blacks voluntarily supporting him in large numbers. North Carolina white Populist leaders had come to believe that "we will get very few negro votes for him unless we can get some money from the national committee."[95] Essentially, black support for Bryan would rest upon profit rather than prin-ciple.

It seems ironic that despite such widespread disunity between the races and the political parties Guthrie could optimistically predict in early October that "Democratic leaders now see inevitable defeat in the State staring them in the face."[96] His comments proved prescient; despite all the twistings and turnings during the campaign, Guthrie had summed up the situation perceptively. Discouraged as they were by the trend of events, black and white agrarian voters alike, when confronted with the choice, still supported the Fusionists and their program in their eagerness, or bitterness, to overturn Democratic hegemony.

In the 1896 North Carolina campaign, Fusionists won the governorship and increased their numbers considerably in the House and slightly in the Senate.[97] The total state vote was the largest on record to that time, with a voter participation rate of 80 percent, a feat not since duplicated. Partly as a result of 1894 Fusionist election reform, voter turnout increased 7 percent in 1896, to 85.4 percent.[98] Republican gubernatorial candidate Daniel L. Russell carried 44 of the state's 96 counties and received 59,000 more Republican votes than the party's gubernatorial candidate received in 1892. Much of the success of the Republican and Fusionist ticket was due to the large black vote that turned out in the Black Belt of the eastern counties.[99] Populist candidates carried only Sampson County, losing 16,000 votes statewide from the 1892 election. Republican Russell was elected governor by a vote of 153,797 over Democrat Watson's 145,266 and Populist Guthrie's 31,143. At the national level, William Jennings Bryan carried North Carolina by a 19,000 vote majority over Republican William McKinley who won the national election—Democrats and Populists fused in favor of Bryan.

Sweeping the opposition before them, the Fusionist ticket in both 1894 and 1896 enjoyed remarkable political success in North Carolina.[100] While the Populists reaped the benefits of black voting power along with their Republican allies, it is highly doubtful that the election results can be interpreted as a widespread acceptance by blacks of Populist principles. A close examination of the local election results in 1896, for example, reveals the continued presence of the mass of blacks in the Republican Party. In the 1896 election, 59,000 more Republicans voted than had voted four years earlier; a substantial part of this increase was due to the added support of blacks in the eastern area.[101] In substance, North Carolina blacks as a group were never very enthusiastic about the prospect of fusion with white Populists, and the election results are simply a manifestation of this feeling. Paradoxically, the Republican Russell had on several occasions openly heaped abuse on blacks, and a goodly number of black leaders had voiced their objections to his candidacy, openly supporting Guthrie.[102] Yet in the final analysis, the black masses loyally supported the Republican cause—although aware of its inconsistencies—in order to ensure its success. Thus, most North

Carolina Populists, black and white, voted "Republican" in 1896, and for the first time since Reconstruction, Republicans elected a governor, Daniel L. Russell—with the Fusionists increasing their majorities in both houses of the legislature.[103] Blacks had responded not to a new set of agrarian Jeffersonian principles, or to having been turned away by the open prejudices of Russell, but to an old code of party prejudice and loyalty. "It appears that the [North Carolina] Negroes committed political suicide," Helen Edmonds has concluded, "by continually supporting the Republican party."[104] Blacks, as a group, retained their commitment to the Republican Party largely because of its symbolic value as the party of black liberation, and because the alternatives with the Populists and Democrats were, on balance, viewed as less positive. In this sense, their actions were rational and based on limited choices available to them, however unappetizing.

A central theme in Populist philosophy was that "a free ballot and a fair count" would first be necessary before the people could attain their objective of economic reform at the ballot box. The early attempt by the Alliance and such agrarian leaders as C. W. Macune and L. L. Polk to seek needed reforms through the Democratic Party failed. This necessity of initially reforming the election machinery and cleaning up the election process was reinforced and in turn strengthened by the widely held philosophy of advancement and reform through class solidarity and an agrarian coalition. The subsequent use of this power in politics would be used by the third party to undermine "the money power." Democrats subjected the Populists and Republicans to such a campaign of filth, vituperation, and hate, primarily centered around the race issue, during the Fusionist period in North Carolina that hatred of the Democrats united the minority parties to drive them from power. Josephus Daniels, Democratic editor and author from the state and no friend of blacks, later refuted Democratic charges of "Black debauchery" during this era, concluding that "All Negro legislators were not peanut munching apes. . . . There were definitely superior men among the Negro leaders after the war. In politics, however, they were black and that was enough."[105] But exploitation of the race issue lingered in state politics, fueled by the "New South" business class, which understood the power of rhetoric to destroy biracial coalitions among agrarians. Discouraged as they were by election fraud, it is not surprising that the North Carolina Populists sought to minimize corruption in the state's political system. In its 1892 state platform, for example, the People's Party included a plank to "deplore the corrupting use of money in elections as tending to degrade manhood and to corrupt the ballot-box, and . . . to subvert the rights of the people at the ballot box."[106]

The 1894 platform carried a stronger, more extensive statement about corrupt election methods "concocted and executed by the Democratic machine of this state."[107] With the advent of the 1896 election "a free ballot and a fair count was yet more to be desired than free silver." It was "the main issue." Free silver was "drink and lifeblood" of the party, but "the privilege of a vote and that vote being counted was greater still."[108] In the final analysis, North Carolina Populists were never able to reform the election process, particularly at the local level, and as such were unable to sustain their own interests politically or morally. This fact necessitated a party of principle joining with a party of often opposing interests, using black votes to ensure political success. As illustrated above, voting fraud was rampant, but while the Populist class-struggle was blunted somewhat in North Carolina, the specter of "Negro domination and rule" as a result of these successful efforts was revived by the Democrats.

The Populist experiment in North Carolina proved a mixed blessing for blacks. The Fusionist effort revived flagging black political interest and party interest in black votes. However, it is uncertain how much of this energized vote can be attributed to fraud versus individual political participation and choice. It does seem clear, however, that the Populist-Republican fusion in North Carolina, for all its inconsistencies, prolonged and perhaps even increased the black vote for a brief period—all at a time when other Southern states were reducing black voting power. By 1895, eight of the eleven states of the Old South had adopted secret ballot laws. Georgia and South Carolina respectively had implemented a poll tax and the notorious eight ballot box law, which achieved the same purpose of reducing black voting power. The result was an earlier, sharper reduction of black votes in other states of the Old South. Only North Carolina with its Populist-Republican Fusion majority in the legislature had no such laws.[109]

But by 1898 the Democrats had managed to develop unprecedented organization, correspondence, publicity, and stump speaking into a white supremacy campaign. In the Democrat-controlled 1899 General Assembly, they proposed a suffrage amendment, which would be voted on by the people in the August 1900 state election. The amendment carried by a vote of 182,217 to 128,285. Ironically, counties with large black populations voted for the amendment. With the unlikelihood that blacks voted for their own disenfranchisement, fraud had largely eliminated the black vote in North Carolina by 1900.[110]

On the downside, although Populism attracted a few vibrant black leaders like the Reverend Walter Pattillo, most blacks remained loyal to the Republicans. Their increased political presence, combined with electoral success, brought about a worsening of race relations and a revival of black rule and Reconstruction fears in North Carolina that culminated in the Wil-

mington Race Riot of 1898. White supremacy and black disenfranchisement campaigns were hastened by these actions, and by 1900 North Carolina blacks had ceased to vote in large numbers, and the "race question" was
easier to use on insurgents by the newly dominant Democratic Party.[111] As
the new century dawned, blacks were no longer a factor in North Carolina
politics—and neither was the Populist Movement.

SOUTH CAROLINA

South Carolina presents a significantly different political picture from either
Virginia or North Carolina. The state had early moved towards disenfranchising its black and poor white populations, which would leave power in
the hands of the white Democratic educated few. The vehicle for South
Carolina's political change was "the eight ballot box" law passed in 1882.[112]
Under this system, the voter had to deposit correctly separate ballots for
president, governor, congressman, and so forth in each of eight separate
boxes. If a ballot was not placed in the correct box, it was not counted.
Ballot boxes were constantly shifted back and forth by Democratic election
officials to prevent illiterate voters from being informed by literate individuals outside the polling place in which box to deposit their votes. Illiteracy
was a serious problem, with 55 percent of South Carolina blacks being illiterate as late as 1900, compared to only 12 percent of whites. Additionally,
enforcement was more rigorous in the case of blacks.[113] Such confusion
greatly reduced the black vote, eliminating much of it and discouraging
others.

Into the morass of state politics stepped the quasi-Populist Democratic
political boss "Pitchfork Ben" Tillman.[114] The triumph of the Tillman machine in the 1890 election put an end to almost all Populist and black political participation in South Carolina. In his first-term inaugural address of
1890, Tillman made clear the dominant ideological position he and his
agrarian following had toward blacks. Even though "we come as reformers,"
he said "this administration represents the triumph of [white] Democracy
and [white] supremacy over [Negro] mongrelism and anarchy." While there
"never was any just reason why the white man and the black man of South
Carolina should not live together in peace," it must be recognized by all
whites that "the intelligent exercise of the right of suffrage is as yet beyond
the capacity of the vast majority of colored men."[115] Tillman resented being
called a Populist, according to his biographer: "He did not favor a third
party; he ignored many of the reforms demanded by the Populists; his bid
for Western support *did not violate* Southern prejudices." He "denied the
charge of Populism, identifying himself as a Democrat of the school of

Jefferson and Jackson." Paralleling the Farmers' Alliance's early desires, here was a white man who remained within the Democratic Party, brought some relief to white agrarians, and opposed uniting with blacks. This appeal to grassroots whites would undercut any appeal to South Carolina Populism.[116] Also, unlike other Deep South states, South Carolina developed no strong Greenback or Independent movement for Populism to build on. It was soon clear to all that this new white proletarian political force represented white agrarian hostility toward blacks. Black votes would not be sought, because suffrage would be eliminated. And so it was, for the most part.

Once established, the Tillman machine within the state Democratic Party negated the broad policy of biracial agrarian class-interest articulated by Tom Watson. Yet some white South Carolina Populists believed in a class-consciousness that extended beyond Tillman's racism. J. W. Bowden, the Populist manager of South Carolina, wrote that:

> We are not [openly] considering the negro. This is a question the ne-
> groes will have to settle for themselves. I have reason to believe that
> thousands of them will not go with the Republicans any longer. Es-
> pecially do I believe this will be the case among the Colored Alli-
> ance.[117]

Thus, while white South Carolina Populists soft-pedaled their interest in the black vote, they understood that coalition with black agrarians was possible, if only blacks would make the first move. What role blacks would play in the movement was anyone's guess, and "by the end of the eighties," George Tindall has observed, "the Negro vote had been all but eliminated as a factor in the state's politics."[118] Such statements as Bowden's indicate, however, that regardless of Tillman, biracial agrarian class-interest was not totally dismissed by the state's whites, but also that the state's agrarian movement was seriously ruptured by the split in party racial politics. Defeating the Tillman machine would dominate South Carolina opposition politics for years, with results that proved even more disastrous for blacks in the state.

As for the prediction that blacks might support the Populist Party in South Carolina, the evidence again indicates that they generally remained loyal to the Republican Party. The Republican vote had been cut from 91,870 in 1876 to 13,740 in 1888. The party in South Carolina, more so than in many other states, thus depended on blacks for its membership. However, viable black votes for any party were few. Furthermore, blacks remained loyal to the Republican Party. The fact that many blacks could still look to the Republican Party for their salvation—despite the rising element of "Lily-Whiteism" in the party—shows how completely they had absorbed the ideological myth of a liberating Republicanism.[119] Also, it reflects a firm grasp of reality because of limited options with the other two parties. If the Republican Party had betrayed South Carolina blacks, the options with the other two parties were each less attractive.

The Colored Farmers' Alliance in South Carolina would seem to be a potent vehicle for Populists to appeal to black voters. But the political outlook of the organization is epitomized by the actions of George Washington Murray, "the Republican Black Eagle." By "no means a bad-looking colored man," Murray was described as having a "cannon-ball head" and a hue as black as "the ace of spades." While enjoying a close association with the Colored Farmers' Alliance, he rose from the Republican ranks and was elected to Congress in 1892 as a representative of "the toiling and producing millions, who are neither gold bugs or silver bugs." In short, the black agrarian masses that Populists sought to attract in other states. Despite the abuse he suffered, Murray remained in the Republican Party, serving as the last black Congressman from South Carolina.[120] Like Frederick Douglass, who had been disappointed by the Republican Party in the latter years of his life, Murray remained faithful to the party until his death, although he did not always agree with it—nor it with him. As such, any Populist appeal to the black voter would not be aided by the Colored Farmers' Alliance or black politicians such as Murray. Moreover, the state's Colored Farmers' Alliance, serving as a possible entree for Populists to the black vote, went into a state of decline in 1891, and from all appearances had probably disappeared by 1893.[121]

The Tillman machine and the Democratic Party served largely to fulfill the white agrarian reform impulse in South Carolina. Somewhat like Virginia, South Carolina Populists were never a very potent force, and blacks were not an active component.

GEORGIA

Up to this point, the commitment of the white Populist movement toward blacks had been either almost nonexistent or mercenary. In Georgia, however, one can trace a positive ideological affirmation through the early days of the movement's rise under Tom Watson to its decline in the late 1890s. "To the colored man the People's Party in Georgia," one correspondent correctly asserted, "is largely what the Republican Party was to him in this nation thirty years ago."[122]

From the very first, Georgia Populism's racial ideology conflicted with the Democrats' more mainstream racial policy, which reflected an anti-black social bias. Temperamentally conservative racially, white Democrats could not understand and therefore would not forgive members of their own party or race who deserted their ranks to join a party that openly trafficked with blacks. The Georgia Democratic message was fairly consistent: whites splitting their votes would mean blacks would become the balance of power in any election. Blacks would then want social equality. The more palatable option, they argued, was to stay in the Democratic Party and remain loyal to white Southern civilization. Class grievances, it was emphasized, were not sufficient to bolt the Democratic Party.

Of those who promoted common class grievances, few if any were more respected by blacks than the charismatic Tom Watson. The ideological foundation of the state's third-party racial philosophy, indeed the region's, was essentially the work of this one individual. Moreover, the influence of his personal charisma on African Americans cannot be ignored when evaluating the various political forces that attempted to promote an ideological cohesion and coalition among the state's black population. Watson early became the strongest advocate of a pragmatic but realistic racial policy encompassing five essential considerations aimed at benefiting both races at the expense of neither. By promoting his program, based upon reform and stimulating the passion for personal progress, Watson prophesied that "the People's Party will settle the race question":

> First, by enacting the Australian ballot system. Second, by offering to white and black a rallying point which is free from the odium of former discords and strifes. Third, by presenting a platform immensely beneficial to both races and injurious to neither. Fourth, by making it to the *interest* of both races to act together for the success of the platform. Fifth, by making it to the *interest* of the colored man to have the same patriotic zeal for the welfare of the South that the whites possess.[123]

The official racial ideology, its interpretations, and its application to the Populist racial dilemma were formulated by the movement's leadership. Watson, a wealthy Georgia planter and state representative (1891–93), early served as the official racial interpreter of the order and offered up the published biracial vision of the movement in its formative years. Intellectually, Watson was capable of being such a biracial philosopher and visionary; even more perhaps than his followers, he had an instinct for the practicalities necessary for political reform and was well read and successful for his milieu. In an 1892 article in the *Arena*, Watson set forth the official ideology to consolidate the South's poor black and white agrarian class of the South.[124] The polemics of the race question, he argued, had been resorted to for so long by both major parties "until they have constructed as perfect a [political] 'slot machine' as the world ever saw." A polarization founded on the basis of race had created conditioned political responses on the part of the South's electorate. On the basis of this campaign issue, Watson lamented, "We have a solid South itself, a solid black vote [Republican] against the solid white [Democrat]." His critique of existing arrangements went on to point out the loss of autonomy of both races, and that solving the economic problems of both races necessitated a reappraisal, a reorientation of their thinking and their voting together to improve their condition. What would break down such a rigid value structure and pattern of response? The answer was clear: it was in their "self interest" to make these changes, "and self interest always rules." However, self-interest was to remain the fatal flaw in Populist coalition building. Class unity requires sublimation of the self for the good of the whole, but any argument to self-interest automatically assumes that individual or sectionalized rights precede those of the class. Such thinking would also hold true for the ruling classes, particularly in North Carolina, where it was in the self-interest of the Democratic policymakers to give a remarkable degree of political power to state blacks. But for the lower classes, self-interest could not transcend race in most cases, although the Knights of Labor and New Orleans dockworkers had limited success in class coalitions.

Because of "the sharp and unreasoning political divisions" maintained by the racial issue, "a new party was necessary" to break this pattern of thought control. But how could Southern Populism entice the traditionally Republican black into voting with the poor white farmer? "Their every material interest is identical," Watson replied.[125] Here Watson proposed the practical lessons learned from the Alliance experience; but the interests of black and white were not always the same, as the Alliance experience had proven. Rhetoric conflicted with reality, but Watson felt otherwise. Therefore, "granting to him [the black] the same selfishness common to us all . . . would he not act from that motive just as the white man has done?" Watson's philosophy on biracial politics was best revealed in his view as to what motivated the average voter. Only a foolish optimist, he believed, would deny the dark realities of personal interest at the bottom of all human nature, regardless of color:

> Gratitude may fail; so may sympathy and friendship and generosity and patriotism; but in the long run, *self interest always controls*. Let it once appear plainly that it is to the interest of a colored man to vote with the white man and he will do it. Let it plainly appear that it is

to the interest of the white man that the vote of the Negro should [and must] supplement his own, and the question of having that ballot freely cast and fairly counted, becomes vital to the white man. He will see that it is done.[126]

While the Populists generally reacted favorably to a policy of black suffrage, particularly when blacks were voting for the third party, they nevertheless viewed their black counterparts as inferior social allies. At their meetings and gatherings it was not unusual that blacks were segregated, or at least separated themselves.[127] Like many of its contemporaries, Populism associated the meaning of American democracy with a parochial interpretation of the ethnic and social order, which had at its core white supremacy. "Anglo Saxons, whether Populist or patrician," Richard Hofstadter reminds us, "found it difficult to accept other peoples on terms of equality or trust. Others were objects to be manipulated—benevolently, it was often said, but none the less firmly."[128] White Populist reaction to the new political coalition with blacks was as diverse as the criticisms of American life that had provoked them, but their agreement on the rejection of social equality was near consensus. Reflecting the prejudices of their culture, they subordinated such concepts as natural rights and Jeffersonian virtue to the more immediate interest of practical politics. "The question of social equality," Tom Watson and the Populists constantly emphasized, "does not enter into the calculation at all. That is a thing each citizen decides for himself."[129] The opposition, however, spun the question of racial equality from a social into a political issue: granting civil equality to blacks, the Democrats charged, would open the door to social equality, with catastrophic results for the Anglo-Saxon race. The subtle warning was that the integrity of white civilization would be called into question if whites didn't stand together and oppose such a biracial malignancy as Populism. Poet James Weldon Johnson noted: "Through it all I discerned one clear and certain truth: in the heart of the American race factor the sex factor is rooted; rooted so deeply that it is not always recognized when it shows on the surface."[130] And this reasoning enjoyed, generally speaking, widespread belief and acceptance in the white South, particularly among the region's agrarians to whom the Populist leadership were appealing.

The "Minnesota sage" and Populist crusader Ignatius Donnelly captured in his novel about the South, *Doctor Huguet* (1891), the Southern white Populist leadership's view toward blacks, articulated by Watson one year later. Indeed, the passages are so close in wording and viewpoint that one strongly suspects that Watson's shopworn personal copy of *Doctor Huguet* was a primary source for his *Arena* article:

Doctor Huguet: "Political equality does not imply social equality, or physical equality, or moral equality, or race equality."

- "Because a man votes for me at the polling place, it does not follow that I must take him into my house, or wed him to my daughter, any more than those same results follow because we breathe the same air."

- "The black man's interests are the same as their's [Southern whites]. He needs prosperity, growth, opportunity, happiness. So do they. He wants to see the robbers struck down. So do they. He desires all that civilization can give him—all that belongs to him. So do they."

Dr. Huguet encourages Southern whites to adopt a policy of *noblesse oblige,* just as many white Alliance and Populist leaders adopted toward blacks: "But are we only to do justice only to our superiors, or our equals? If so it yields us no honor, for our superiors and our equals are able to enforce justice from us." "Generosity," he continues, "can only be exercised toward those less fortunate than ourselves. Power has no attribute grander than the god-like instinct to reach down and lift up the fallen."

Donnelly's novel was not only prescient and prophetic but clearly seems to have influenced Watson's thinking. Concerning social equality with blacks, "That is a question each person decides for himself," Watson noted in emulation of Doctor Huguet. Both Donnelly and the Southern leaders defined the biracial political philosophy at the core of Southern white Populism.[131]

Out of an eventual consolidation of the two races on a platform of self-interest Georgia Populists hoped to weld their party into a strong political force. As a fledgling party, Populists needed every vote they could muster to defeat the Democrats—a fact that did not go unnoticed by the blacks. "The People's Party," one black newspaper noted, has "from the very *necessities* of the situation . . . delivered the colored voter in Georgia from political bondage."[132] Since the Democrats branded everything hostile to them as pro-black, they served in an indirect manner as one of the best propagandists to introduce Populism among the black masses. In addition, the assimilation of a small faction of discontented Republicans, along with such minor black leaders as the Reverend H. S. Doyle, R. J. Matthews, and John Mack, provided other positive forces to attract the black vote.[133] Perhaps the best known black leader who worked for the Populist cause in Georgia was the Reverend H. S. (Seb) Doyle, a Methodist minister, who was active in Watson's campaigns and made sixty-three speeches in 1892.[134] John Mack, who attended the 1892 Populist convention, seconded W. L. Peek's nomination for governor, an unheard-of feature in Georgia politics of that period.[135]

As Democratic hostility became more intense in the 1892 campaign, the heightened racial consciousness caused by hostile propaganda required a further explanation about Populist solicitation of black support. "Why cannot the cause of one [race] be made the cause of both?" Tom Watson inquired of the white community. "Why should not a colored farmer feel the same need of relief as the white farmer? Why is not the colored tenant open to the conviction that he is in the same boat as the white tenant?" Watson, voicing the feelings of many white Populists, could "see no reason why I am less a white man—true to my color, my rights, my principles—simply because black people are convinced that our platform is a fair one and will vote for me on it."[136] By emphasizing the philosophy of self-interest, the Populists created a defense mechanism that would not only stimulate but defend the sentiment of common class grievances.

Watson held that the two races were logically bound together by economic ties and that self-interest was not unique in Southern history. In Georgia, Sidney Lanier had called for a united front between black and white farmers as early as 1880. Predicting the "obliteration of the color line" and its subsequent political implications, Lanier's argument of class-consciousness and self-interest foreshadowed Populism by over a decade.[137] The epochal Populist campaigns of the 1890s appear to be miscast by some historians in terms of racial uniqueness. Rather, Populist class-consciousness sentiments appear to be the culmination of a philosophy that grew upon a tradition that had existed for at least a decade before the birth of Southern Populism.[138]

That Georgia Populists, especially Watson, were making an open appeal for the black vote was obvious from the birth of the party. It may also have been a necessity since, in the case of Watson's Tenth District, blacks outnumbered whites. If the new party could not draw black votes, the chances of victory were substantially reduced. "I want to say," Populist gubernatorial candidate W. L. Peek said of the political implications of this policy, "that the nigger has been in [Georgia] politics since the war and will be there until the last trump[et] has sounded. The only trouble in this case is that [the Democrats] think [the Populists] will use the Negro vote."[139] Using the 1892 People's Party convention in Atlanta as a platform to make these remarks, Peek, in a dramatic incident that served not only as a test of his political courage but also of his determination to solicit the black vote, allowed black Populist leader John Mack to second his nomination for governor.[140]

On the surface, Populist racial sentiments appear laudable, but the true measure of this policy was the extent to which they were applied and hence strengthened the Populist organization in Georgia by attracting black votes.

Above and beyond its rhetoric, Populist actions provide ample reasons for blacks to distrust Populist overtures. The 1892 ticket included no blacks among the list of Populist candidates. Furthermore, only "two lonely and isolated blacks," John Mack and R. J. Matthews, out of a total of 160 delegates were present at the state Populist convention in Atlanta.[141] Finally, anti-black statements from many white Populists heightened the suspicions of blacks. Fostered on the tradition of race-baiting, many Populist candidates, according to black Republican senatorial aspirant W. H. Styles, "were in the front rank when that army of oppression came against the negro."[142] The sudden outburst of Populist "egalitarian" rhetoric understandably was not sufficient to alleviate black suspicions of past hostilities. And the number of blacks not voting Populist later on, despite the efforts of Watson and others, revealed the extent to which Populists failed to attract large numbers of blacks.

Generally outspoken against proposals for fusion with other parties as Populists had done in North Carolina, Georgia Populists missed a grand opportunity in 1892 to attract a large mass of black and white voters by failing to make greater efforts to enlist Republican support, seeking instead to appeal to blacks through the Colored Farmers' Alliance, which had long opposed a third party.[143] In this sense they failed to broaden their voter appeal but remained loyal to their Populist Jeffersonian principles. Even after the Republican convention had refused to nominate its own candidates, Tom Watson rejected unequivocally any fusion proposal. "My policy is for a straightout fight. I whip the other fellow or he whips me. . . . [N]o republican must vote for me under the impression that I am heading for the republican camp."[144] This aspect of Populist strategy in Georgia highlights one of the difficulties faced by many idealistic third-party movements—the failure to broaden the base of support in the formative stages to include a constituency whose appeals differ somewhat from the party platform.

Despite the flurry of Populist rhetoric preceding the election, the traditions that clustered around state and local election practices were not suddenly transformed. "The size of the colored vote for a particular candidate might depend primarily upon the personal popularity of that man with the Negroes and upon his record in matters relating to the colored people, regardless of his political label," writes a modern authority on Georgia politics.[145] In this respect, Georgia blacks differed little from the mass of black voters in most other Southern states, particularly in elections at the local level. Blacks were much less likely to desert the Republican Party at the national level, and the magnetism of the Republican Party was still considerable, despite the tendency on occasion to "vote for the man." Furthermore, under such circumstances the notorious anti-black records of some

Populist leaders offered few inducements for successfully soliciting black votes.[146]

In the last months of the 1892 campaign, a small group of prominent black leaders found the record of Democratic gubernatorial candidate William J. Northen more appealing on racial matters than that of Peek, the Populist nominee. Particularly appealing to blacks was Northen's opposition to lynching. Blacks were concerned with personal protection and legal rights, and Northen's open opposition to violence against them was magnetic. Even before the state Republican convention decided in August not to nominate a slate of candidates, "Northen Clubs" were being formed by blacks. It was William Pledger, the black Atlanta attorney, who spearheaded this campaign for Northen among the black leadership class who would in turn enlist the support of the masses. Following the Republican decision, a group of black delegates, most of whom were members of the State Central Committee, openly endorsed Northen.[147] "We . . . prefer in the campaign to follow the plan mapped out by Hon. W. A. Pledger and vote for Governor W. J. Northen."[148] In the face of this endorsement, Pledger predicted that Northen would be re-elected by a majority of 40,000 votes. Pledger's estimate was extremely conservative, for when the 1892 gubernatorial votes were totaled Northen received 140,432 votes to Peek's 68,990. Peek lost 50 to 80 percent of the black vote, failed to attract much of the state's 40,000 Republican votes, and failed to attract strength in those areas where the Alliance was strong. Peek believed he received about 50 percent of the black votes cast, but Shaw believes he received "as little as ten thousand" and Kousser has concluded Peek received only 20 percent.

The center of Populist voting strength was Tom Watson's Tenth District, where blacks outnumbered whites. The legislative results were equally discouraging, with Populists only electing sixteen members. The Democrats won every congressional seat in Georgia! Fraud and violence were rampant, although it appears Peek was not swindled out of a victory against the popular Northen, but Tom Watson probably fell victim to fraud in his Tenth District. Two years earlier, he had carried the district by a 210 to 1 majority, but in 1892 as a Populist he was defeated by "the most outrageous of corruptions." It was hard for the new party to be inspired by such disastrous results, when the movement began its venture with such high hopes and expectations. Many Populists blamed blacks for these dismal results. "Them doggoned Democrats outcounted us," Peek responded the day after his defeat. "They juggled with the negroes yesterday and the day before, and they just outcounted us." Populists were angry and highly suspicious of such election results; and fraud using black votes as well as blacks actually voting for Northen over a natural coalition ally of agrarians created frustration. Because hopes had been so high, the loss was so much more shattering.[149]

The key portions of Northen's record that captured the black imagination concerned added educational appropriations, promise of an anti-lynching bill, and a strong anti-lynching stand.[150] Working within the established power structure, Northen could deliver on his promises to blacks—he felt violence against blacks was not worthy of whites and would erode their civilization.[151] In turn, Populists sought to establish a new power base and could do little more than make promises. Politically, blacks have usually been pragmatic in their ideologies with regard to eliminating discrimination.[152] Voting for Northen over Peek was simply a practical choice, given the records of the two men and the likelihood they could and would deliver on their promises. Also, Peek's past record with blacks was far from exemplary. In 1887, for example, he had introduced the infamous "Peek slave bill," a piece of legislation that would have jailed tenants, primarily blacks, who failed to fulfill their contracts to their landlords. The result of such antitenant legislation, which Tom Watson, a planter, also supported, would have been the reestablishment of a debtor's prison. Wanting to control a supply of cheap labor, such proposals—which failed to pass—could only erode black support.[153]

It is of interest to note that the legislation supported by Peek and Watson surfaced in a different form in 1903. A resurgent Georgia Democratic legislature passed a new crop lien law in which tenants who did not fulfill their contractual obligations in essence committed fraud. Tenants could not move away from the land until their obligations were fulfilled. Since black tenants were more easily exploited than whites with this new bill, owners tended to replace white tenants with black tenants, who were often old Populist prototypes. The white yeomanry resorted to violence against black tenants who replaced them in a short-lived system called "whitecapping."[154]

The Democrats were not slow in taking steps against the new political party in 1892; the old pattern of using various forms of fraud and corruption was repeated. And the Democrats were skilled and experienced in such matters. Populist protest was stifled under the guise of white supremacy, the fear of a second Reconstruction and black rule, and ironically fear about the corrupt use of the black vote. Bribery, corruption, fraud, and violence, in turn, largely negated rebellious blacks' response to Populist principle over party loyalty. At least fifteen blacks and several whites were killed during the 1892 election.[155] According to Professor E. Merton Coulter, a careful historian of the Georgia scene,

> the [1892] election throughout the state was a pathetic example of the venality that often accompanies the rule by the people. Negro voters were bought and sold like merchandise and herded to the polls like so many cattle. They were fed at barbecues and made drunk and *penned*

up to prevent them from voting if they could not be otherwise controlled. Most of them who voted were in the hands of the Democrats.[156]

But the pattern of corruption was not Democratic alone. *Purchasing* of
votes, as Coulter observed, was common, but *coercion* of the black vote was
also common by both parties. Consider Shaw's summary description of the
machinations of both parties during this era in Georgia politics:

> Third-Party men complained that Democrats often compelled black
> tenants to vote for the Democratic ticket, a practice called "voting my
> boys." Thus a man with twenty tenants could cast twenty-one votes
> for the candidate of his choice. But many Populists landlords were also
> guilty of such chicanery. The evening before the election, they assem-
> bled their hands and treated them to cigars, cheap whiskey, and a bar-
> becue. Soon everyone was roaring drunk, and by morning few were
> in any condition to cause trouble. They climbed or were loaded into
> wagons that took them to the polls. The landlord then kept watch to
> make certain that all his ballots were counted. Afterward his voters
> staggered back to the wagons and were driven to another polling
> place.[157]

Such activities identified the dynamics of Southern politics during this period and led to cynicism by white Populists about the system, further feeding the public demand to "purify the ballot" and restrict the suffrage. Such
scenes also fed the growing viewpoint that voting was not a natural right
but a privilege and should be connected to character, competence, education, and property ownership.

That even the Populist philosophy of class interest did not override black
venality and white corruption is exemplified by a black Populist from Zei-
gler, Georgia. Unable to restrain his indignation, he lamented that the "price
of Negroes had depreciated in the last 40 years." Even though he had "personally" sold for fifteen hundred dollars in the 1840s, he saw one black in
the 1892 election "bought" for a glass of cider, a second for a "two-for-a-
nickel" cigar, and a third for a pint of peanuts. With the price a vote should
command, it was obvious, he concluded derisively, that blacks "are holding
themselves too cheap." Available in bountiful supply, black votes generally
sold from three to ten dollars, the price advancing as the election neared its
end. One Democratic faction openly boasted of purchasing 1,100 black
votes to defeat the Populists.[158] Lacking the finances, Populists were unable
to respond in kind. But corruption was not Democratic alone. Shaw has

Fig. 5. The Democratic attitude toward blacks before an election (*People's Party Paper,* September 21, 1894).

aptly documented that "the Populists used the same methods as their opponents." They "used the same techniques" of fraud, swindling, and corruption in Georgia as the Democrats but were apparently less successful or skilled at such practices. "Populists had assumed that blacks would throng to the new party," Shaw concluded, "yet from all over the state reports came of blacks at the polls, bribed and drunk, voting again and again for the Democrats." [159] Such sights must proved bitter to voters of all complexions and parties about the state of democracy and the need to "purify the ballot" and reevaluate who was entitled to vote.

Perhaps the degree to which corruption and violence occurred in the 1892 election is best illustrated by the case of Augusta, a part of Tom Wat-

Fig. 6. The Democrats attitude toward blacks after an election (*People's Party Paper,* October 5, 1894).

son's "Terrible Tenth" District. A deputy sheriff was killed by the secretary of a local Populist club. Out of an area that possessed a total voting population of 11,466, the district's total vote was 12,558. Investigation revealed that blacks, transported from South Carolina in four-horse wagonloads, had added in excess of 400 ballots by Populists and more by Democrats, to the overall Tenth District total. One Democrat later admitted to dressing black women as men, filling them with liquor, and voting them throughout the Augusta area.[160] "Lying, red whiskey, and counterfeit bills . . . have ran [*sic*] the thing over us" one white Populist painfully concluded.[161] The *People's Party Paper* provides an incisive criticism of the political techniques used by the Democrats in the 1892 election and the inability of the Populists to overcome such lawlessness:

> The leaders and newspapers of the Democratic party have touched a depth of infamy in this campaign which is almost incredible. They have intimidated the voter, assaulted the voter, murdered the voter. They have bought votes, forced votes and stolen votes. They have incited lawless men to a frenzy which threatens anarchy. They have organized bands of hoodlums of both high and low degrees to insult

our speakers, silence our speakers, rotten-egg our speakers, and put lives in danger.[162]

When General James B. Weaver, the Populist presidential candidate, and Mary Elizabeth Lease, the Kansas feminist firebrand, campaigned in the state in September, they were met by "howling mobs," angry and boisterous crowds shouting vituperations and filth and reportedly throwing rotten eggs. Reports of intimidation, shootings, deaths and related activities were common in 1892.

Like the Populists, Republican President Benjamin Harrison was unable to overcome his loathing of such election practices in Georgia and other Southern states. Learning of the widespread fraud and violence, Harrison asserted that "I have washed my hands of the south. It is a land of rebels and traitors who care nothing for the sanctity of the ballot, and [I] will never be in favor of making an active campaign down there until we can place bayonets at the polls."[163] The national Republican Party abandoned blacks to the white South and the dominant Democratic Party.

The Democrats also resorted to the use of the highly sensitive "Force" Bill issue, loudly predicting "Negro domination and rule" and the revisitation of a Second Reconstruction upon the South if whites split their vote. Fears of the "Force" Bill and its impact, according to one Populist, had prevented three-fourths of the white Democrats from defecting to the Populist camp.[164] While this claim is obviously exaggerated, many whites doubtless did refrain from splitting their votes when the disturbing memories of Reconstruction days were revived.

The Georgia election of 1894 proved even more venal than its predecessor. In Watson's Tenth District, fraud was so obvious that Watson's opponent, Major James C. Black, the election winner, resigned and a new election was held, but Watson was again defeated. Major Black conceded that his first victory was "shrouded in doubt," and so it was. Fraud committed against Watson was outrageous. In Richmond County, for example, Democrats had hired blacks who voted "again and again" for Major Black. In a county where only 11,240 people had paid the poll tax, Black alone received 13,750 ballots. And so it was throughout the "Terrible Tenth" District.[165] "In this election," Coulter tells us, "the Negro vote was so corrupted as to make an unbearable stench to all men in both parties."[166] Arnett has described it as "the most exciting as well as the most degrading election since the overthrow of the 'carpet-bag' government."[167] Shaw more benevolently characterized the 1894 election as "a humiliating victory for the Democrats."[168]

The introduction of a poll tax also kept poor whites and many blacks from the ballot box. In 1894, 62 percent of blacks did not vote. That same year, only 15 percent of blacks voted Populist, and Democrats recorded 23 percent of the black vote, although fraud accounts for part of that total. Yet Georgia was one state where Populism fared better than many of its sister states despite low black and Republican turnout. In Georgia gubernatorial contests during the 1890s, Democrats won by a five to three margin.[169]

How to explain Democratic success in 1894, considering Watson's popularity? While the Democrats had, in general, retained control of the political machinery in 1892, it was evident that an effort would be necessary to retain their power two years later. Economic conditions had been made worse by the Panic of 1893, and cotton was now selling for less than five cents a pound. Property values were down, and wheat bread was a delicacy tasted only on rare occasions. Hard times, it seemed, should have made Populism more attractive in 1894 and victory possible.[170] In order to head off the Populist challenge in the state, the Democrats selected more and better men to represent them on the local level. In addition, an effort was made to undermine local Populist organizations by wooing their abler men back into the Democratic Party.[171] Since Republicans made no nominations in 1894, their potential voter base, which contained large numbers of blacks, was now available to both parties.

During the 1894 campaign, Democratic leaders agitated frantically for blacks to pledge their support to their "personal and political friend[s]" in the party.[172] On the other hand, they continued to clamor about "Negro domination" and social equality if the Populists were allowed into the political circle. Their underlying motive was to garner both the black and white vote by appealing to both races—or parts of both—until after the election, and then to shift back to the characteristic white supremacy orientation of the party. Both disenchantment and expediency caused the Populists to wax bitter toward their Democratic opposition's maneuvering, since in the main, their official racial ideologies were poles apart.[173] In moments of despair, Populists were moved to acrimonious criticism of blacks when they became an unwitting instrument for politicians. Expressing futility, the *People's Party Paper* concluded that "a Negro lost his African origin if he voted right [Democratic] and took on the scent of the rose-geranium if he could chatter Democratic gibberish. A Democratic ballot made [them] color blind and a Democratic speech from ebony lips lent sweetness to the desert air."[174] If reform drives were paramount in the movement's political ideology, the sweeping corruption of 1894 merely reinforced the increasing prejudice toward blacks.

With little or no abatement, corruption was practiced as in the preceding election. Vote buying was prevalent, with the more affluent Democrats purchasing the most for a dollar apiece. In Watson's "Terrible Tenth" District, one Democratic candidate reportedly received three thousand votes from five hundred blacks "who practiced this fraud" for ten cents a vote![175] "I think that the stench from the 10th District will fill our nostrils for a generation to come," one Georgian said. "It will be held up to the nation for decades to come as proof positive of the fraud and violence of Southern elections."[176] In Dalton, it was somberly reported that "the Negroes went solidly against us on account of bribes mainly."[177] Another constituent was "perfectly outraged" at the "simply monstrous" frauds in Richmond and Hancock counties. If the "reported vote" of 15,000 from Richmond County was correct, he asserted with acumen, the population would be 105,000. But "in my opinion" there were not "over 2,000 legally qualified voters" in the whole county, despite the approximate total of 15,000 votes.[178] "We had to do it!" contended one prominent Democrat. "Those d——Populists would have ruined this country."[179]

Of course, there was a basic problem underlying much of the corruption that did not escape the most astute contemporaries, including many Populists who sympathized with blacks. The black man's faith in the class denominator of Populist ideology was frequently negated by white Democratic control of the rank-and-file black's vote. In the 1892 election, for example, it was reported that blacks were "bulldozed, intimidated, driven from the polls, and in some instances, shot for attempting to exercise the right of citizenship."[180] White employers, who were in the main Democrats, would oftentimes threaten to "turn the Negroes off the place" if they did not vote Democratic.[181] Blacks were also considered "incapable" of voting competently without some restraints—an inherited popular suspicion held over from the early days of Reconstruction when blacks were identified as slavish tools of carpetbagger governments. More than any other group, the black member of a perennial debtor class was subjected to economic and physical coercion by employers who compelled him to conform to Southern white majority opinion—notably, Southern white *Democratic* opinion.[182] The obvious result of such actions was not only to make a mockery of public elections and increase cynicism about the process, but to give expression to Democratic demands for unilateral conformity to the principles that the party deemed as representative of Southern politics.

The 1894 election was certainly not a victory for Georgia Populists, but it was not a total loss. They polled 44.5 percent of all votes cast, elected five senators and forty-seven representatives to the Georgia legislature.[183] But Watson lost again in the "Terrible Tenth" District. Black support for the Populists was strongest in the Third and Tenth congressional districts, and Kousser believes "Perhaps a majority of the Negroes who participated in

1894 cast Populist ballots."[184] Yet ballot box stuffing, fraud, and intimidation resulted in the Democrats "attracting" more black votes in the nineties than did the Populists. The 1894 election would also prove the watershed for black voting power for years to come. Following this election, a voter registration law passed in 1895 put more restrictions on requiring proof that the poll tax was paid before voting, which diminished opportunities for blacks to make an unrestrained voting choice. Black voting diminished again in 1896 and subsequently lost more influence; one indication of this is that W. H. Rogers of Macintosh was the only black to win a seat in the Georgia legislature between 1902 and 1908.[185]

Under the cover of national indifference, political standards and ethics, not only in Georgia but in the rest of the South, had gone by the board or were so flagrantly violated in the name of white supremacy that they ceased to be binding. Since Populism and the race issue aroused white Democrats much more than the enervated endeavors of a dying Republicanism, white Populists were forced into dissipating much of their reform energy toward fighting the corruption of the opposition, thereby taking an inactive defensive stand. By the mid-1890s it could truthfully be concluded:

> Heretofore the Negro has been the man against whom the frauds of the South have been directed. Now it is the white [Populist]. If when white man proposes to divide in that section of the country which has for years been called "the solid South" the same frauds are resorted to continue this [white] solidarity, and the North yields to it, then we must expect that solidarity to endure through time.[186]

MISSED OPPORTUNITIES

The challenge the Populists presented to the political status quo in the seaboard states represented the spirit of a discontented agrarian reform class seeking an identity of interest with blacks. Self-interest was adopted as a rallying cry because it appealed not only to individuals but groups as diverse as white agrarians and downtrodden blacks. But the neutrality of its supposed detachment from prejudice failed to come into play. Populism had started with the hope and promise of reform, but its purported sense of class-consciousness failed to emerge for several reasons. Foremost, Populists were generally deprived of the black vote as a result of corruption and because of the traditional loyalty of the black masses to the Republican party. As a general rule, blacks also were not responsive to the idea of fusion with Republicans and Democrats, and when Populists did enjoy the fruits of the black vote, it was because African Americans added their weight to the Republican contributions.

Secondly, one of the outcomes of the Populist campaigns from Virginia to Georgia was the awkward choice taken by more and more blacks—particularly in the middle classes—of voting Democratic as a result of their instinct for preservation and self-interest. In Georgia, a state sometimes portrayed as the archetype of the Populist biracial experiment, blacks openly supported such Democratic gubernatorial nominees as William J. Northen and W. Y. Atkinson because of their past records of accomplishment fighting violence against blacks. Whether such votes were given or taken is not clear, but one thing is clear: Democrats received the benefit of the black vote. But in the 1893 Virginia gubernatorial election, Populists, according to Kousser, received 49 percent of the black vote, which they did not solicit. Undoubtedly, the failure of Republicans to present a candidate, and their open admiration of Populism, added to their black support. In North Carolina's controversial 1896 gubernatorial election, Republicans received 59 percent of the black vote, but Populists only received 8 percent. In South Carolina's 1894 gubernatorial election, Populists only received 5 percent of the black vote. Kousser estimates that "at least 60 percent" of black males failed to vote in Georgia and South Carolina in the hottest elections of the decade. Less than 40 percent of blacks voted in North Carolina and Virginia.[187] What emerges most clearly from these accounts is the dilemma of a party that could never quite achieve the delicate balance between a suspicious black ally and whites, mostly farmers, who were confronting their personal prejudices. Such chasms proved too deep to surmount.

Although Populist leaders promoted the illusion of biracial interest, they were unable to translate their rhetoric into practice. In contrast, the Democrats provided a stabilizing function, however repressive, on the prevailing order. To blacks, accommodation was a viable alternative to violence. In other cases, both sides employed coercion and vote purchasing was common, most successfully by the Democrats. Tom Watson articulated the Populist biracial philosophy of self-interest but ultimately maintained that the political good that benefits the individual ("self-interest always controls") is greater than the interest that benefits the class. It logically follows that black accommodation to the Democratic order was quite consistent with this philosophy. Put in a less pleasant way, the hostile spirit of the age demanded that they yield to political expediency. In cases where they did not yield, fraud and coercion provided the Democrats with the same benefits of the black vote. In the final analysis, Populists lost because of the black vote, however it was gained.

In the Atlantic seaboard states, many blacks who should have shared the economic values of Populism often rejected the Populists' facile class expression of self-interest and Jeffersonian yeoman commonality of interest, even when unrestrained. This further supports the view that some blacks, when unrestrained, found the values of white Populists antagonistic to black interests. In North Carolina, for example, the loyalty of blacks to the Republican Party was substantial. It is revealing of the relationship between the two races and parties that it was often blacks who demonstrated a lack of sympathy for fusion between Republicans and Populists. The old inspirational tradition of Republican association with emancipation continued to run strongly in the minds of the black masses, even at a time when such a body of beliefs was on the wane politically. It is important to remember also that in this period a growing segment of the Republican Party, the Lily-Whites, appeared increasingly as one of the subverters of black rights. Conversely, black loyalty served only to provoke Populist antagonisms as they observed blacks as a source of assistance, both willing and unwilling, go to the political forces that were frustrating them. Such party loyalty severely strained the expression of class loyalty by white Populists, particularly the untutored following, and in this way perhaps served to ultimately exacerbate racial resentment.

There was, of course, a reactionary potential in the Populist myth. This came into full glare in South Carolina particularly, where the forces of tradition were violently antagonistic toward Populism as a symbol of radical social upheaval. In the presence of such prescriptive forces, Populism generally enjoined in its literature the principle of biracial class-consciousness and did not cultivate widely blacks as sources of voting potential. In Virginia and South Carolina, the Populist Party was, in racial terms, conservative. The failure of the Populists to successfully solicit, enlist, or enjoy in large numbers the support of blacks foreshadowed the gradual disappearance of the party in the Atlantic Seaboard South. It remains to study the nature of the difficulties faced by the Populists in the Gulf Coast South.

7

Theory and Practice of Populism

The Gulf Coast

The Democrats succeeded in maintaining white supremacy with Negro votes.

Like the Atlantic Coast states, those of the Gulf Coast saw their share of reformist third-party activity during the post-Reconstruction decades. And similarly, each state's ruling elite addressed the question of reform differently, sometimes attacking and sometimes co-opting the movements to their advantage. Electoral fraud was also prevalent, but the unique political and social conditions of the Gulf Coast states preclude any one simple answer as to why the Populists were not more successful than they were. This chapter examines the Populist challenge to the established order in the three major third-party strongholds of the Gulf Coast area—Alabama, Louisiana, and Texas—and sheds some light upon the conflicts and differences that emerged as this movement sought to achieve reform.

Populism arose in the Gulf Coast largely due to severe economic conditions. According to a former Alabama governor, "The origin of the Populist movement in Alabama was the low price of farm produce and poverty of the people. They were fighting and did not know where to strike."[1] Compared with other radical movements in the postbellum South, Populism pitted a lower-class agrarian population against an increasingly urban industrial society. The significance of this rural challenge to the region's growing industrial class was not lost on Alabama historian William Garrott Brown, a contemporary observer of this tumultuous period. "I call that particular change a revolution," he recalled, "and I would use a stronger term if there were one; for no other political movement—not that of 1776, not that of 1860–1861—ever altered Southern life so profoundly."[2] To another historian, however, race impelled the movement: "the negro, more than any other factor, was responsible for the Populist party in Alabama. Economic questions fell into the background."[3] Race was a central component of Gulf Coast Southern Populism, for blacks and their role in the election process had to be "reformed" before economic reforms could be achieved.

ALABAMA

Alabama, like Georgia, had divided along class lines by the late 1880s, with a growing industrial base in coal and timber production pushing aside a weakening agrarian power base. Postbellum sectional bitterness between northern hill-country farmers and the wealthier Black Belt crystallized during Reconstruction. "No love was lost," observed C. Vann Woodward, "between Black-Belt gentry and hillbilly commoners." The aristocratic William Alexander Percy, in his *Lanterns on the Levee* (1943), captured this class and sectional hostility in the Mississippi Delta: "I can forgive them as the Lord God forgives, but admire them, trust them, love them—never. Intellectually and spiritually they are inferior to the Negro, whom they hate."[4] Poor whites complained that the counties in North Alabama had rescued the Black Belt from "Negro domination" during Reconstruction, but they in turn failed to receive their fair share of political influence.[5] And it was among these and other impoverished white farmers that Alabama Populism registered its strongest appeal. The sectional basis of the state's movement was thus laid early and, in the face of growing economic discontent and declining prices in the eighties, the transition from the Farmers' Alliance toward an organized third-party political effort as a means of ameliorating the distress will become clearer as the story develops.

In the years following the Alabama Constitution of 1875, race was a strong adhesive power for white political solidarity in Alabama, but sectional and economic grievances, as well as biracial coalitions, came to the surface at times in the form of Republican, Greenback, and independent candidates, as well as the Knights of Labor and the United Mine Workers. As all of these organizations served as a biracial prelude, Populism is miscast, then, as a unique interracial movement in Alabama.[6] These early efforts faced the same white supremacy campaigns as would Populism, and organizers met with varying degrees of success because of that.[7] Bourbon Democrats and editors succeeded in identifying blacks in the public mind with corruption, corrupt "nigger rule," and Republicanism. There were enough nuggets of truth in these charges to drive a wedge between the lowland Black Belt and white agrarian Democrats in North Alabama. The ruling Bourbon Democrats used well the threats of black rule, which obsessed the white agrarian mind. Nevertheless, while earlier political and labor revolts failed, Alabama Populism benefited from the radical tradition of interracial coalition building of its predecessors, a feature that was absent in South Carolina. Also, the Colored Farmers' Alliance in Alabama had reached an estimated membership of fifty thousand by 1889 and could be used to challenge Bourbon Democrats.[8]

With rising economic discontent and declining prices among farmers, the times and conditions were right in the 1890s for the disruption of Alabama politics. According to Albert Goodwyn, Populist congressman and gubernatorial candidate, the farmers organized the Alliance "for the purpose of ascertaining the cause of such abnormal [economic] conditions, and to find a remedy for them. After much discussion they concluded that these conditions were *political,*" with the result being the formation of the Populist Party.[9] Convincing white farmers to support a third party was not easily accomplished, however. State Democratic Party leaders sought to overcome grievances to a degree to disengage the movement, but a discontented agrarian faction nevertheless formed a splinter third-party variant called "Jeffersonian Democrats," which remained at one and the same time both in, but not of, the Democratic Party. Although their name suggested a potential allegiance with the Populists and their Jeffersonian ideals, the Alabama Jeffersonians never fully merged with the Populists, though they voted along Populist lines.[10] Primarily out of party loyalty, "the majority of them never departed in the least from their ancient allegeance" to the Democratic Party and "held fast to the side of their 'old captains,'" according to W. J. Cash. "And those who did go in for Populism, the greater number continued to exhibit that lack of intense enthusiasm."[11] Populists simply could not convince Jeffersonian Democrats to split completely from their party, and that failure as much as anything else contributed to the movement's decline in Alabama.

What we begin to see in Alabama is the growth of a class order, not one solely of economic making but one that evolved out of the regional, political, and geographical order of things. North Alabama hill-country farmers complained of the control of state politics by the machine bosses in the Black Belt, a cry similarly echoed in Louisiana against New Orleans politicos. Farmers knew that fraud played a major part in their inability to elect their supporters to state office, and the initial interest in ballot reform partly explains the rise of Populism in the state and the difficulties it faced. "Running throughout Alabama Populism was," according to two modern analysts, "a trend of a free ballot and fair count, perhaps the central theme."[12] Alabama Populist Joseph C. Manning "was so thoroughly imbued with his mission that he concentrates every energy in promulgating ballot reform and doctrines." Manning was confident that "an honest election is of paramount importance" to the Southerner. Reuben Kolb, Alabama Populist leader and twice-failed gubernatorial candidate, contended that honest elections were "the paramount issue" in the state's campaigns.[13] His reasoning was abundantly clear: "Until a fair and honest election is assured, no [economic] reforms, however needed can be instituted."[14] Economics was, therefore, subordinate to the more pressing question of election reform. Lawrence Goodwyn has asserted that the Alabama Populists, particularly their stand-ard-bearer Reuben Kolb, placed so much emphasis on "a free ballot and a fair count" that it diverted attention from the party's economic goals, which did not allow it to create the necessary magnetism found in states like Georgia and Texas.[15] In this sense, he suggests that this fixation helped bring about the movement's demise in Alabama. Furthermore, Alabama Populists were never imbued with the zeal for dynamic change that was found in other states.[16]

The Alabama gubernatorial election of 1892 represented the first major election around which the reform element could rally. Democratic incum-bent Thomas G. Jones sought reelection, and he was opposed by the Populists allied with the dissident Jeffersonian Democrats and their candidate Reuben F. Kolb, former commissioner of agriculture, watermelon farmer, and suc-cessful pioneer in scientific agriculture.[17] The realignment resulted in a campaign that was particularly virulent, a fact recognized by the state's his-torians. "The resulting contest for the nominations and then for governor," according to Sheldon Hackney, "was probably the most scurrilous on record in Alabama."[18] The state "had never witnessed a more acrimonious or ex-citing campaign," Rogers has written.[19] Summersell called the 1892 elec-tion "one of the most controversial in the history of Alabama."[20] The po-litical schism polarized the populace. Summersell has captured the mood:

> Electioneering in 1892 was rough. Speakers were booed down. Preach-ers who differed with their communities were sometimes fired. Mer-chants lost business after political arguments. It was reported that Guntersville lost about $8,000.00 in business when Kolb supporters in Marshall County adopted the slogan "Down with the Town Clique." Friends and close relatives disputed and parted company, and boycotts and social ostracism were weapons in the fray. In Athens Jones was hanged in effigy. P. G. Bowman of Jefferson was preaching a doctrine of "ballot, bayonet, and blood."[21]

In this highly emotional campaign, both parties openly sought the much needed black vote, and the Populists also received Republican votes. But the Populists' pursuit of black votes was doomed from the start in their choice of gubernatorial candidate. As an active "Redeemer" during Reconstruc-tion, Kolb reportedly bragged about "suppressing Negro votes," but once the "white voters . . . repudiated him" in later years he "turn[ed] with open arms" to the blacks whom he had earlier spurned. Furthermore, Kolb was an apostle of "white supremacy."[22] In January 1892, before he broke with the Democrats, Kolb had "exhibited a sense of intolerance and hatred to the black man," in a recent speech, the black-owned *Huntsville Gazette* contended.[23] By July, however, he openly sought black speakers to proclaim him from the hustings during his campaign. At Talladega, his audience listened to a black speaker for over an hour; at Greenville he was followed on the platform by Ike Carter, a local black.[24] At Gordon in Henry County, Kolb and a black third speaker, L. W. McManaway, were unable to speak due to agitators hurling eggs at them.[25] Kolb also had two blacks, "Professor Cooper" and Lewis Bostick, on the campaign trail flashing "what it takes to make the mare go."[26] In short, by purchasing black votes and preachers to turn out the black vote, Kolb was using the same tactics employed by his Democratic opposition. The problem of interpreting Kolb's actions is made even more vexing by his eagerness for black votes on one hand and his reluctance on the other to admit blacks to the party organization.[27] As a further indication of party attitudes, not a single black Populist candidate was offered in 1892.[28] Black voter participation was acceptable but black candidates posed too much of a liability to the party and potential white voters. In his attitude toward blacks as candidates and participants in the party organization, Kolb differed little from other Southern Populist leaders.[29] Alabama Populists did not advocate political equality but encouraged political participation by blacks primarily limited to the exercise of the suffrage to achieve "a higher civilization and citizenship." However, Populists did not believe extending political rights to blacks would logically extend to social equality, as the Democrats charged.

The Jeffersonian Democrats went further than the Populists in seeking the black vote. The 1892 party platform contained a so-called "Negro plank" designed to attract the black vote as well as to publicly explain their position toward black participation to skittish native white voters:

> We favor the protection of the colored race in *their political* rights, and should afford them encouragement and aid in the attainment of a higher civilization and citizenship, so that through the means of kindness, better understanding and more satisfactory condition may exist between the races.[30]

Blacks desired stable race relations and protection of their political rights, but could Populists deliver on their promises? To drive home further their appeal, the Jeffersonians focused critical attention on the thirteenth plank of the Democratic platform:

We favor the passage of such election laws as will better secure the government of the State in the hands of the intelligent and the virtuous, and will enable every elector to cast his ballot secretly and without fear of restraint.[31]

The Democrats' appeal to restricting the ballot to "the intelligent and the virtuous" meant, in simplest terms, that most blacks should not have suffrage rights since they allegedly did not possess nor demonstrate intelligent use of the ballot. Yet blacks were still voting, and so both parties openly sought black votes. Clearly, the Jeffersonian-Populists strongly appealed for the black vote. As a new reform party, Populists needed every vote to challenge the Democrats. In addition to lofty-sounding principles, Populists did on occasion employ limited economic inducements to get black votes, usually paying up to a dollar per vote. Since this sum was equal to two days' wages for a field hand, the Populists were to some extent successful, but lack of funds and Democratic control of the election machinery were immense disadvantages.[32] As such, Democrats were much more successful in their purchase of the black vote.

Democrats also openly appealed for the black vote in much the same manner as the Populists. And blacks sought stable race relations and the elimination of violence, which only Democrats could deliver. Both candidates maintained separate clubs for black and white supporters of their respective parties.[33] Like Kolb, Jones had his share of black speakers and purchased votes. Dr. C. N. Dorsett, "a successful practitioner, a man of property," and a prosperous black Republican from Montgomery, publicly endorsed Jones as did a number of other prosperous, prominent blacks from Mobile and the counties of Elmore, Pike, Lee, and Russell.[34] As in other states, prominent and more prosperous middle-class blacks were turning to the Democrats to ensure stable race relations and to further their own best interests, which could only be fulfilled by the dominant Democrats. In substance, both parties sought with few distinctions to harvest black votes yet maintain a basic commitment to white supremacy and social inequality. Summersell suggests Jones was more successful in attracting black voters: "Conservatives seemed to corral Negro votes with more grace and fewer repercussions than did the Jeffersonians."[35] It is not surprising that the more wealthy and powerful Democrats were able to keep the majority of the black vote. On August 1, Thomas Jones was reelected governor with 126,959 votes to Kolb's 115,552.[36] Alabama Populists had polled 48 percent of the vote in 1892, and their presence greatly increased voter turnout in the election. Voter turnout increased from 57 percent in 1890 to 71 percent in 1892.[37]

The charges of election fraud were rampant—some accusations palpably false and others of substance.[38] Kolb carried thirty-seven counties but only five in the Black Belt. He claimed that 70 percent of the white votes in the state were cast for him. With a margin of only eleven thousand votes, Jones only carried twenty-nine counties, eight out of the Black Belt, and with a narrow margin. Kolb's counties had a white–black ratio of better than two to one; Jones' counties had a black–white ratio of better than three to one, and more than four to one in the counties with the densest black population. A good case can be made that black votes, voluntary, forced, and bought in combination, elected Jones governor in 1892. Indeed, scholars are still divided over who actually won the 1892 Alabama gubernatorial election. Hackney believes Kolb "would have won in a fair election in 1892"; Rogers "seems certain" that Kolb was "legitimately elected but counted out."[39] Clark's figures "do not bear out this conclusion."[40] Probably the most honest conclusion was presented by Summersell, who believes that "it is still not possible to give a yes or no answer to the question, 'Was Kolb counted out?'"[41] The *Nashville Banner,* a strongly partisan Democratic paper, captured a common Southwide viewpoint of that day: "It is needless to attempt to disguise the facts of the Alabama election. The truth is that Kolb carried the state, but was swindled out of his victory by the Jones faction, which had control of the election machinery and used it with unblushing trickery and corruption."[42] Despite the wrangling, Democrats understood the need for quieting the race issue. In his acceptance speech, Jones stressed the need for harmony between the races.[43]

As a result of widespread fraud, the election dilemma is probably unsolvable; yet it is significant that the election heightened an old pattern of intrastate sectionalism between the Black Belt and the largely white hill-country of North Alabama. An analysis of the election returns indicates that Kolb's support was strongest in the hill country, whereas Jones received more black votes than Kolb in the Black Belt.[44] Thus, the voting pattern was along traditional geographic lines of hill country vs. Black Belt. It has been estimated that Kolb would have been elected by a majority of seventeen thousand without the huge black vote received by Jones.[45] Black Belt counties provided an incredible portion of black ballots—70 percent in Dallas County, 87 percent in Wilcox County, and so on. Overall, of those counties with a two-to-one black majority, Kolb carried only Macon County, where Booker T. Washington's Tuskegee Institute was located. There is no tangible evidence, however, of activity on Washington's part for Kolb.[46] Indeed, no evidence exists of Washington ever openly supporting the Populist Movement. While Kolb lost the governorship, many Populists were elected to the legislature, preventing a Democratic attempt to disenfranchise persons who

A. IS A MOVABLE - SLOT IN BOTTOM OF BALLOT BOX.
B. WIRE TONGS TO CATCH BALLOT
C. RECEPTACLE UNDER BALLOT BOX AND INSIDE OF TABLE TO DUMP THE BALLOT IN.
D. FOOT TREADLE WORKED BY ELECTION MANAGER

Fig. 7. Populists' conception of fraud at the ballot box (*People's Party Paper*, September 28, 1894).

did not own at least forty acres of property worth $250.00. The 1892 election proved to be the high point of Alabama Populism, and by 1894 the movement was already on the decline in the state.[47]

As in Georgia, the Alabama Jeffersonian-Populists' failure to win the 1892 election was so demoralizing that it was difficult for them to pick up the pieces and reassemble them for the next campaign. These were crucial formative years for the Alabama Jeffersonian-Populists, for they needed to develop their organization to prevent the loss of potential white voters. The Panic of 1893 added to the party's problems. The number of farmers becoming tenants and sharecroppers increased from 21 to 34 percent over the course of the 1890s.[48] Eight-cent-per-pound cotton in 1892 dropped to five cents a pound by 1894.[49] The situation was further complicated by the stigma attached to third partyites as traitors to the ideals of white supremacy and the Democratic Party's emphasis on government by the intelligent and the virtuous. Paradoxically, the Democrats managed to secure a landslide margin in the Black Belt counties yet transfer to the Jeffersonian-Populists in the public mind the stigma of racial treason. This had the dual effect of identifying the Democrats as the white man's party while serving notice that a Populist victory would have the same perceived negative consequences on Alabama politics and society as had Black Reconstruction.

Caught up with the image of scalawags, many grassroots whites were reluctant to oppose Democratic wishes when they involved cooperation with blacks and Republicans.[50] The existence of the Jeffersonians indicates how reluctant some whites were to depart the party. Whites generally incorporated the idea of black incapacity to govern and feared unrestrained black participation as leading to a challenge to white civilization. Such fears emboldened Democrats to attack adversaries with these views, constantly keeping them on the defensive.

As the 1894 election approached, the Democrats again appealed to the same old racial patriotism of saving the state from black control. The conglomerate of reformers met in February and renominated Kolb as the Jeffersonian-Populist Party candidate. To further complicate the election, Alabama Republicans suffered an interparty factional dispute between the Lily-Whites and the Black and Tans. In substance, the division was a struggle over black or white control of the party. Since 1888, the Lily-White faction had been led by Dr. Robert "Bob" A. Moseley Jr., who favored cooperation with independent parties and the Populists in particular. The Black and Tan faction was led by William "Bill" Stevens, a black barber from Anniston, who favored a straight-out Republican ticket. As in the 1894 North Carolina election, many blacks were leery of fusion with Populists or Jeffersonians who did not have a history of favorable relations with blacks. Stevens had been a black leader during Reconstruction and in subsequent years had allied himself with Independents, Greenbackers, and the Alabama State Labor Party. During this time, however, he had developed a well-deserved reputation as a somewhat unsavory character and opportunist whose loyalty was purchasable. His reputation made the Populists suspicious of his motives to work with them. In turn, Stevens was suspicious of the white hill-country Populists, with their longstanding hostility to blacks, doubting their promises of political equality with blacks.[51] By the 1894 convention, the political division grew into open hostility between Stevens and the Populists. As Stevens attempted to enter the Jeffersonian-Populist convention, he was unceremoniously ousted by force. In turn, he then led the Black and Tan Republicans against endorsement of Kolb and threw his support to William C. Oates, the "one-armed hero" of the Civil War who was nominated as the Democratic gubernatorial candidate. The Lily-White Republicans in turn endorsed Kolb, a move certainly not designed to attract black support to the Populists. Many middle-class black politicians, teachers, lawyers, ministers, and editors—the opinion leaders in the black community—subsequently gathered around Stevens and endorsed Oates.[52] In turn, Populists openly ridiculed Stevens:

O did you see Billy Skaggs, upon his toe,
Lift Billy Stevens through the Wigwam [hotel] doe;
O, did you see Bill Oates in big alarm,
Lift Billy Stevens under his arm.[53]

In addition to receiving Lily-White Republican support from the Moseley faction of the party, Kolb approached the Republicans for a much-needed campaign contribution. Democratic papers picked up this and gave it wide prominence as anti-Kolb propaganda among white voters. Thus, in two classic campaign mistakes Kolb had managed to alienate many blacks and whites. It is impossible to tell how much money Kolb received from the Republican Party, inasmuch as Republican papers tended to maximize the figure ($50,000) while Populists tended to downplay the amount received ($5,000).[54] Receiving money from the Republicans and support from the Lily-Whites made Kolb anathema to Alabamans in 1894. Aware of their experience with vote fraud in 1892, the Kolb supporters again made a "free vote and an honest count" their foremost demand in 1894.[55]

The 1894 Jeffersonian Democratic-Populist state platform included a strong declaration in favor of black political rights, but with some clarification about their moral exercise of the suffrage. With some ambivalence about being after the vote of a group of individuals widely perceived as corrupt and immoral, or as an object to be manipulated, the ticket declared:

> As Thomas Jefferson was opposed to any restriction upon the suffrage of men, so are we, except it be for some grades of crime, among which we would place the purchase or sale of a vote, or other interference with the honest expression of the will of the people at the ballot box.[56]

Cognizant of the popular viewpoint that blacks as a race had not yet evolved to the point where they had the capacity for the intelligent exercise of the ballot, this statement suggests that Populists believed the failure to exercise the ballot responsibly was grounds for elimination of eligibility. They were quite conscious that it was the sale and purchase of black votes in the Black Belt that had cost Kolb the 1892 election.

Closely connected was the question about the future of the black vote. "On one point all agree," Populist William Skaggs concluded, "and that is that the ballot has been a curse rather than a blessing to the Negro."[57] To bring about an end to election corruption, the Jeffersonians had proposed on two occasions, once in 1892 and again in the spring of 1893, that a white Democratic primary be established. On both occasions, the Democrats refused the offer.[58] To counteract this, the third partyites then made an open appeal to blacks to stay away from the polls. Moseley and the Lily-Whites circulated a petition in the Black Belt urging blacks not to register. Skaggs claimed that "less than one percent of those of voting age actually registered." A Democratic paper claimed that not more than 20 percent of Alabama blacks registered, while a Jeffersonian paper advised blacks that the best thing they could do "in the coming registration and election is to keep hands off and let the white voters settle the matter themselves."[59]

All of these actions, however, were to no avail. In the Black Belt counties, blacks were added to the registration lists and their ballots cast by the Democrats when they were not even near the polling place on election day.[60] Furthermore, dead blacks and fictitious names were added to the voting lists.[61] Other votes were simply and blatantly stolen. In Tuscaloosa County, for example, ballot boxes from Blocker's Beat, a strong Populist section of the county, contained no ballots whatsoever when they were opened.[62] The Democratic explanation was that it was "more humane to manipulate the ballot against the Negro than to use brute force to drive him away from the polling place."[63] In substance, fraud was a more viable alternative than violence and regarded as less harmful morally than brute force.

In view of such widespread tactics, it is not surprising that Kolb lost the 1894 election. The vote was 109,160 for Oates and 83,394 for Kolb.[64] Again, the Jeffersonian/Populist/Lily-White Republican coalition had lost the governor's race but did well in local legislative races, winning nearly a third of the seats in the House and Senate. However, the total vote fell from a total of 242,483 in 1892 to 192,554 in 1894. The Populist vote in 1894 had dropped more than a third from its 1892 level. According to one analysis, the Alabama Populist Party had lost 15 percent of its 1892 supporters and virtually all of its black votes. Black voting percentage dropped 22 points from 1892 to 1894 and remained at below 50 percent thereafter. The 1893 Sayre Election Law, which prohibited assistance in marking ballots, disenfranchised thousands of illiterate blacks and whites and "was largely responsible for the decline of the Populists and the decrease in Negro turnout after 1892."[65] The most dramatic drop in voting had occurred in the predominately white hill-country counties. While Kolb carried thirty-four of sixty-six counties, these wins were by very narrow margins. In contrast, Oates's margin was substantial in the Black Belt.[66] The Democrats also moved toward adopting many of the Populists' more popular issues, such as openly supporting free silver.[67] This was a common tactic used by Democrats throughout the South. The intrasectional parallel between Jones's 1892 lowland Black Belt vote and Oates's hill-country returns was apparent. Again, the overwhelmingly lopsided Black Belt vote and fraud used there in favor of Oates ensured his victory. In Mount Willing, Lowndes County, for example, Oates received more votes than there were inhabitants—black, white, men, women, and children.[68] The ballot stuffing was so blatant that open rebellion was contemplated. On Inauguration Day, Kolb and his supporters marched up Dexter Avenue in Montgomery, threatening violence if Kolb was not inaugurated. Met at the capitol by the militia and the police, Kolb counseled patience, "Let us be peaceable, and justice and right will reign in Alabama," he said.[69] Like his party, Kolb believed that justice and truth would ultimately prevail in such contests. Politically impotent, Kolb could do little more than urge the formation of "honest election leagues" to ensure that fraud would not be employed in the future.[70] Such losses blunted upcountry white agrarian idealism.

As indicated earlier, 1892 marked both the launch as well as the climax of Populism in Alabama, and subsequent campaigns were little more than a repetition of fraud and Black Belt votes against the state Democratic machine.[71] In the case of blacks, the third partyites were placed in a peculiar position. On one hand, as noted in their 1894 platform statement, they believed strongly in the sanctity of the ballot for all people; on the other hand, continued black participation ensured their inability to win control of the state government and implement reforms. This problem was not only moral but political. "Purification of the ballot" would be necessary for Alabama Populists to win. Also, blacks, as part of the Jeffersonian agrarian class coalition, served the special interests of the money power in disregard of their best interest. To some Populists, disenfranchisement of blacks represented a necessary reform of the electoral process.[72] A continued theme throughout this period in Alabama politics was the need for a constitutional convention to settle the question. Consider the opinions of one agrarian organ:

> There is but little doubt now that there will be a Constitutional Convention. The last election has convinced all that a large proportion of the Negro vote is purchasable, and that much of the opposition to their disfranchisement will cease. The only thing in the way is how to do it without disfranchising a large number of whites. Purchasable votes mean that the dollar and not the man is to rule, and we think a law should be made disfranchising all who sell or buy votes. We would not object to a Constitutional Convention, if we could have a fair election in choosing delegates.[73]

Running throughout this argument for purification of the ballot also was an appeal for white unity. Even though "the classes" are divided "by the accident of fortune," a Jeffersonian newspaper added that "they are still bound by the same pure blood." There was also strong opposition to disfranchising any hill-country whites through a constitutional convention. "No disfranchisement except for crime of a single white man must be tolerated."[74] The third partyites also wanted to prevent the subsequent "setting up of one class of whites over the other class and pulling down another class to the level of the negro." They adamantly believed that a constitutional convention should "save all [whites] or save none."[75] According to I. L. Brock, a Populist editor, "the Populists always were willing and ready for the negro to be disfranchised if it could be done without disfranchising the white man."[76] Such prominent Alabama Populist leaders as Kolb, Manning, and Skaggs came slowly to an acceptance of black disfranchisement as a necessary means of "purifying the ballot." Without such reform, the goals of the Populists would be unattainable. Indeed, a significant portion of the third partyites had by the mid-1890s come to believe that "we are not bound to count the negro in the horoscope." The black man was now recognized as a "nuisance" to "honest endeavor" and to "hard won achievement"—a peril to civilization. He "will be disposed of at an early day as an abnormal political force broke loose from its moorings and careening through the land without license."[77] One proposed manner of "disposal" was through the setting aside of a separate state for the exclusive use of blacks. As early as 1894, the Alabama Jeffersonian-Populists had endorsed such a scheme in their convention.[78] Emigration also seemed to some impoverished blacks their only salvation from increasing white economic, political, and racial militancy. A contingent of Alabama blacks had already chosen Mexico as the site of their new nation.[79] The Jeffersonian-Populists' open endorsement probably added some encouragement to such unlikely ventures.

The increasingly hostile tone of Alabama race relations during this period ensured that some steps would lead to the almost complete elimination of black voting. The 1901 Alabama constitutional convention, which had no black or female delegates, assembled amid a Southwide drive to eliminate blacks from the voting lists. Beginning with the Mississippi constitutional convention of 1890—which enacted poll taxes and literacy tests for prospective voters—five states (including Alabama) drafted new constitutions as vehicles of disfranchisement: South Carolina (1895), Louisiana (1898), Alabama (1901), and Virginia (1902). Another belt of upper South states—North Carolina (1900), Georgia (1905), and Oklahoma (1910)—accomplished the same purpose through amendments to existing constitutions. Florida (1889), Tennessee (1890), Arkansas (1891), and Texas (1902) eliminated black voters by way of new state laws imposing a poll tax as a condition of voting.[80]

Eventually the 1901 constitution would eliminate two-thirds of all voters in Alabama. In Alabama, as elsewhere, the way to ensure that black votes would not be stolen was to make sure that blacks could not vote. Following the 1901 Alabama constitutional convention, the racial differential in voting was marked. By 1906 only 2 percent (3,654) of adult male blacks were registered to vote; conversely, 83 percent (205,278) of whites were registered. These figures would remain pretty much the same in Alabama and elsewhere in the South until the black voter drives of the 1960s years.[81] Politically, the Alabama blacks' role had been largely played out by the turn of the century, and the agrarian counterrevolution was brittle for the third partyites; Alabama Populism after 1894 had become an abortive crusade. The party persisted, but the potential for any spectacular political assault had long since been eliminated. Insofar as the term "Populist" was used, it had become a confession of defeat rather than a potent threat to the existing order.

LOUISIANA

Many of the same problems that mystified a generation of Alabama farmers were familiar, even elementary, to Louisiana Populists, and it is not unimaginable that citizens of the nearby Pelican State read the Alabama third-party papers that traced their experiences. Vote fraud and corruption could easily be documented by third partyites who saw the same malaise inherent in the Louisiana system.

But Louisiana is unique among Southern states in many ways, and those factors have influenced the rise and decline of Populism and other reform movements until today.

Louisiana's racial complexion in the 1880s revealed a curious disparity in black voter registration in comparison to its neighbor states. Indeed, black voter registration outnumbered whites up to 1890, although the two races were roughly equivalent in population.[82] Although there was considerable coercion, discrimination, and political manipulation, blacks during this era still voted to a much greater degree than is often recognized. A formal system of race relations had not as yet been firmly established, and blacks still retained enough organization and leadership to force politicians to come to terms with them.[83] Since black voter registration was abnormally high, this was also a further incentive for whites to seek or control black support. City life in particular, with its closeness, blurred racial distinctions, undermined intolerance, and allowed areas such as New Orleans an interracial freedom not enjoyed in the rural South. Black ballots offered an obstacle to segregation, and until blacks were largely disenfranchised by the state constitutional convention of 1898, municipal politicians in Louisiana sought black votes.[84] "Everybody wanted" the black vote "and everybody was soliciting it," a contemporary recalled.[85] Unlike many other Southern states, a factor that also allowed black voters to retain a significant role in Louisiana politics was their ability to divide their votes and turn out in large numbers for elections. The state's Republican Party, often stereotyped as "the party of the Negro," rarely received over 50 percent of the black vote; furthermore, even this percentage of black commitment was on the decline by the late eighties.[86] As a result, white factions openly vied for black support. Unlike in other states examined, Louisiana blacks did not have permanent friends, such as the Republican Party, but were more prone to pursue class- or self-interest.

Upper-class conservatives in Louisiana rarely practiced the subtle philosophy of *noblesse oblige* that other aristocrats in the post-Reconstruction South used to attract black support.[87] When necessary, violence directly involving upper-class white conservatives effectively accomplished the same purpose in the end. Less violent methods were also equally applicable. For example, Democrats controlled the election machinery and, when necessary, stuffed ballot boxes and employed intimidation and violence to secure a winning margin of votes for the Democratic ticket. Planters commonly voted their tenants early and often. For whatever combination of reasons, the Bourbons could claim " 'lots' of Democratic [Black] voters throughout the state."[88] Between these two competing white factions, the Populists would need to launch a vigorous campaign to capture the black vote, which still held the balance of power in Louisiana during the 1890s. Such a campaign was the key to destroying the power of the dominant conservatives, assuming that blacks would be allowed to vote unmolested and that they could be persuaded to support the agrarians.

Populism had entered Louisiana by the summer of 1891. As in Alabama, the small economically aggrieved white farmers of the northwestern upland parishes had been particularly receptive to Populist doctrines.[89] These rustics regarded themselves as the true inheritors of the Jefferson-Jackson tradition. They also harbored an antipathy toward the downstate Bourbon Democratic politicians, particularly in New Orleans, who controlled state economics. Corrupt machines established by these same politicians subjected the farmers to harsh programs and legislation not designed to alleviate agrarian grievances. According to one portrait, nine-tenths of Louisiana Populists were "true American citizens of Caucasian blood." Furthermore, many fought in the Mexican War and "nearly all" who were old enough were "good confederate soldiers"; moreover, "until a few years ago they were enthusiastic Democrats." However, Populists did not fear a repetition of the excesses of black Reconstruction. During "the dark days of Radicalism," when the lowland parishes were "in the hands of negroes," it was these same men, they asserted, who had "helped to redeem the state" for the same groups they were now turning against in an agrarian revolt. "If it had not been for the white men in the South who are now Populists, the Republicans would indeed now have 'black heels on white necks.'"[90] Primarily composed of the "little one to five bale farmers" in North Louisiana centering around Winn Parrish, the movement was strongly marked with the Baptist religion and a personal sense of history.[91] The inefficacy of the post-Reconstruction political structure resulted in an agrarian frustration that had now become the focus of their political activity.

The catalyst for Populism in Louisiana was a People's Party convention held on October 2, 1891 at Alexandria. Seventy-eight delegates from seventeen parishes attended, including Isaac Keys and another black Allianceman from the state's Colored Farmers' Alliance.[92] On October 3, the party presented a campaign "Address to the People of the State of Louisiana People's Party . . . Irrespective of Class, Color, or Past Political Affiliation." This first platform tried to capture black votes from the Republicans:

> You colored men . . . you must now realize that there is no hope of any further *material* benefit to you in the Republican party, and that if you remain in it you will continue to be hewers of wood and drawers of water in the future as you have been in the past.[93]

Aware that black votes alone were insufficient to accomplish an agrarian revolution, the People's Party platform also included a plank designed to test the power of white supremacy on the minds of white Louisianans, a factor that rendered past movements ineffective. Pointing out the malignant results of "uninterrupted Democratic rule" in the state, third partyites contended that, in words reminiscent of Tom Watson's 1892 speech in Georgia:

> The specter of negro supremacy has been used to keep you in the toils of the scheming machine politicians as effectively as the vodou [*sic*] is employed to terrify the credulous negroes themselves.[94]

The party made a strong appeal to its members to assert their rights against conservative domination and "not let the scarecrow of Negro domination longer drive them to the Democratic wigwam."[95] No nominations were made at the Alexandria meeting; those would come later in February.

Meeting again in Alexandria, the nominating convention had increased to 171 delegates, including 24 blacks. This high number of black representatives is reflective of the Louisiana blacks' willingness to split from the state Republican Party. Significantly, two prominent blacks, Charles A.

Roxborough and L. D. Laurent, were placed in nomination for the office of state treasurer.[96] Both were well-known black leaders in the state, and their endorsement would go far in ensuring a degree of much-needed black support for the new party. A long-time, highly visible leader in the Louisiana Colored Farmers' Alliance, Laurent had been a delegate to the Ocala meeting in December 1890 and had been designated to attend the St. Louis convention in February and the Omaha meeting in July 1892. As early as the Ocala meeting he had backed the proposal for a third party.[97] His presence at the state party's first convention, then, was not surprising. During the summer of 1890, Roxborough had resigned from the Republican Party, labeling it an organization dedicated to white supremacy. Like other state branches of the Republican Party in the South, Louisiana Republicans were not looking favorably upon a black presence in the party, and blacks were open to an alternative. Would it be the Populist Party? Paradoxically, in his letter of resignation, Roxborough had hinted that blacks might support the Democrats although, like the Republicans, they were oriented "towards that same goal—white supremacy."[98] In either case the choice was not bright for blacks. The presence of the Populist Party presented an alternative hope, a more viable choice to blacks, and blacks offered Populists much needed votes. The endorsement by these two prominent black leaders and the black votes they could bring undoubtedly would help the Populists present a more serious challenge to the Bourbons.

Both Roxborough and Laurent withdrew their names from nomination, however, on the suggestion of other blacks present that "it was not the proper time" for black political candidates in Louisiana. The presence of blacks in a prominent positive role in the new party would provide the Democrats with a potent weapon to use against the Populists. As befitting their prominent station within the black community, however, both men were subsequently placed on the Populist State Executive Committee.[99] Conscious of the critical role blacks would play in forthcoming elections, Populists presently added an even stronger plank in their bid for black voters. Clearly the presence of black delegates in such large numbers and the need for their votes forced the new party to encourage their participation:

> We declare emphatically that the interests of the white and colored races in the South are identical, and that both would suffer unless the disputed control of our government were assured to the intelligent and educated portion of the population. Legislation beneficial to the white man must, at the same time, be beneficial to the colored man. Equal justice and fairness must be accorded to each, and no sweeping legislation should be allowed bearing unjustly on either.[100]

The Alexandria convention represented a high point for black representation and participation in the new party in Louisiana. Robert L. Tannehill, a politically unknown, untested, and colorless personality, was nominated as the party's first gubernatorial candidate for 1892. The only previous office he had held was sheriff. Needing strong candidates to attract support for the party, his selection was a poor choice for the party in its formative stage. Almost completely unknown outside of Winn Parish, Tannehill, like most of the other obscure members of the ticket, was destined to failure. Opposed by Democratic gubernatorial reform candidate Murphy J. Foster, a conservative on matters of economics and politics, and Samuel D. McEnery, the Lottery candidate, Tannehill was buried under a landslide, receiving only 6 percent (9,804) of the state vote in 1892—not an auspicious beginning for the new party. Foster won with a sizable majority of 79,388 votes against 47,037 for McEnery. Two Republican candidates split 41,418 votes. Four Populists were elected to the legislature.[101]

All candidates save Foster claimed—and with some justification, it seems —that gross election frauds had been committed. In the Fifth District, an area containing the highest concentration of blacks in the state, corruption was particularly widespread. Furthermore, it was reported that the "infernal row" within the Democratic Party had "destroyed all interest in life—has poisoned social enjoyment." Warring factions throughout the district were throwing out ballots, and there was a genuine fear that bloodshed would result. The Louisiana Democrats in February 1892 received forty cases of Winchester rifles and thirteen boxes of cartridges. "We are providing ourselves with these simply to protect ourselves against any scheme, armed or otherwise," they explained, "to deny us a 'free ballot and as fair count' in the coming election. . . . [We have heard] that . . . the machinery of the existing State administration was to be used" against their ticket.[102] "Whether it is due to the climate, or to the many races that make up our population, I do not know," a U.S. marshal noted, "but it is a fact that Louisianans never seem to understand when they have had enough of fighting."[103] "Nowhere else in the South," Hair argued, "did Populism encounter so many obstacles or as much brutality" as in Louisiana.[104]

By 1894, certain trends that would undermine black political strength had begun to emerge. Prominent among these obstacles was a proposed change in the suffrage laws that would undercut the party's grassroots supporters. According to the Louisiana Constitution of 1874, "no qualification of any kind for suffrage or office, nor any restraint upon the same, on account of race, color, or previous condition of servitude shall be made by law."[105] Rather than attempt a new constitution, Governor Foster and the Democratic legislature of 1894 passed a bill, to be offered to the voters in the 1896 state election, which would restrict the franchise to adult males on condition that they "shall be able to read the Constitution of the state in his mother tongue, or shall be a bona fide owner of property . . . assessed to him at a cash valuation of not less than $200." A subtle provision attached to this bill allowed, upon endorsement by the voters, the legislature to re-write the existing suffrage amendment in the 1874 constitution without voter approval.[106] Governor Foster's goal was clear: "the mass of ignorance, vice and venality without any proprietary interest in the state" would be totally disenfranchised.[107]

Foster's goal was also to include poor illiterate blacks and whites in this effort. Populists strongly opposed this particular measure but, in turn, en-dorsed ballot reform based upon an Australian (secret) ballot system. They were aware that the Bourbons maintained their power through black votes. It was imperative from their standpoint that some type of reform at the polling place occur, but the Populists lacked the clout to pass such measures. Consider the agrarian's major complaint lodged against the 1894 congres-sional elections, in which they fell short of electing a single congressman. According to the *Louisiana Populist:*

> in all the hill parishes where the white people are in the majority, the Populists polled big majorities, but in the river parishes where the Ne-groes were in the majority the Democrats succeeded in maintaining white supremacy (?) with the Negro votes.[108]

Goodwyn observed that Louisiana's ballot box thievery in 1894 "in sheer arrogance and venality surpassed similar depredations in the rest of the South."[109] The Louisiana Democrats were amazingly candid about their dis-honesty, openly bragging about their plans to manipulate the election ma-chinery. Not a single vote was counted for the Populists in the largely French Catholic Parishes of St. Martin and Lafayette, a highly unlikely event, even though most of the white Populists were Baptist and constantly accused of being anti-Catholic.

To the Populists, by 1894 ballot reform had become necessary to the party's survival. "In the Pelican State," Hair observed, "many Populists [now] put free elections above the cause of free silver."[110] Indeed, the subject shortly took on a militancy that allowed no middle ground:

> The war of ballots will be between Populists and Plutocrats. The Popu-lists will have for allies all honest silverites, prohibitionists and social-ists; while the plutocrats will be divided into Democrats, or Southern Plutocrats and Republicans, or Northern Plutocrats. . . . It will be a

mighty contest between manhood and money—between principles and policy, between freedom and slavery.

There can be no neutrality upon this grave and important question. Those who are not in favor of honest elections are in favor of corrupt elections.[111]

In addition to the more pressing matter of reform and political survival, the third partyites endowed the franchise with a remarkable degree of priority and sanctity: "The ballot box is our highest legal authority."[112] And despite the party's slow start in 1892 and the disappointment in the 1894 congressional election, there were unmistakable signs of growth and interest. However, ballot reform must occur if the party was to transfer its passion for reform into results and out of necessity was moved to the forefront of the political struggle. There is a strong parallel here between the situation in Alabama and Louisiana. Although reform-party expediency and self-interest at bottom had to rule the Populists, as it must any successful political party, and faced with such extreme fraud, the third party was forced to readjust its priorities: political reform must precede economic reform.

Following the 1894 congressional elections a major third-party organ commented that now "this movement is as much a ballot reform move as a silver move."[113] The crucial point was that the party would achieve no other reforms until ballot reform was instituted. "Until we get this we are simply and only political slaves working for the master of election machinery."[114] This particular strain in Louisiana Populist thought did not abate but rather increased with the passage of time.

The same theme again surfaced at the People's Party state convention at Alexandria on January 8, 1896. The party made an appeal for "a perfectly honest and a fair election" to be conducted in the state's forthcoming campaigns. To allow each citizen to "cast his ballot freely and secretly and the vote . . . be fairly counted as they are actually cast" was of the utmost importance. "This is the supreme issue in this campaign." The Populists still denounced the proposed Democratic suffrage amendment, believing that it would not "purify and elevate the ballot box" as claimed but rather disenfranchise "large masses of worthy citizens."[115] The Democrats' proposed use of an educational qualification was also opposed as a move "tending toward the aristocratic form of government."[116] If such measures were passed, they would be used to exclude large numbers of poor whites and blacks, common enemies of the Democrats.

The Populists regarded themselves as the true "white man's party" since, in the main, it was the Democrats who manipulated the black franchise during elections:

The People's Party in this state is a white man's party, as evidenced by
its vote in every election since its organization and by the utterances
of its platform, press and speakers in this state.[117]

The third partyites believed that the money powers through ballot corruption, coercion, and venality "want to extend their dominion over the people
as the slave power did over the blacks."[118] In the face of such omens, it is
understandable that Populists preferred "a white man's government and a
white man's party," although this did not mean that "the negro should not
be allowed to help choose officers." Their major objection was to a party
that must depend on the black parishes for its election success.[119] Blacks
were not only the balance of power in a fair election, but as long as their
votes were bought, converted, or fraudulently manipulated by the Democrats, the Populists were sure to suffer.

By 1894 the shift in Populist attitudes toward the black voter also had
begun to crystallize. By this time Populists in the Fourth District had proposed a white primary to the Democrats, who subsequently rejected the
measure, as did the Republicans in the Third District. To the third partyites,
the reason for the Bourbon opposition to the measure was obvious: it was
"because they wanted to use the Negro." Indeed it had "become very con-
venient in the Southern states to have a *black belt* to rely upon, that never
fails to roll up a big majority in favor of white supremacy." Paradoxically,
Democrats who manipulated the suffrage were unceasing in their cries of
"negro domination" against the Populists. "This old cry of negro domination is kept up by scheming politicians as a pretext to stuff ballot boxes."[120]
Believing strongly in the Jeffersonian sanctity of the ballot for all groups,
the third partyites found these conditions painful, ideally not preferring to
disenfranchise any qualified voter, but the situation required a defensive
posture if the party was to survive. The obvious obstacle was the black vote,
and the answer suggested—at least by some few Populists—was the white
primary, which would "*legally* and *honorably* free the country from the negro
vote."[121]

In 1895 the Populists again decided to "throw down the gauntlet to the
Democrats by inviting them into a white primary." The Bourbons must
now "accept or shoulder all the blame for fraudulent elections." Again, the
Democrats refused for much the same reasons as before. By these actions,
declared the Populists, "the Democratic Party is no longer a party of white
supremacy."[122] The Louisiana election process, Populists contended, had become little more than a "farce." They deplored "this condition of damnable
corruption" that allowed "the politicians and place hunters" to "count negro votes that were never cast nor ever existed." The "rule" in the "black

parishes" was "to count the negro—not to vote him."[123] To aid their cause further the Bourbons reportedly

> made open and secret deals with the negro and brought him into primaries and conventions and caucuses, they have him in office and on their ticket. Not only so, but they deal only with the corrupt and purchasable element of the negro.

In turn, Louisiana Populists averred that they would not stoop to such base tactics. By 1896 their position on working with blacks was clear:

> The Populists have NEVER at any time or place, appointed or empowered any committee man or set of men to see, negotiate or confer with any negro committee, convention or individual, and all these things have the Democrats done at specified times and places, and they cannot or will not deny it.[124]

Such actions accelerated the disenfranchisement movement in Louisiana. Admittedly seeking black votes initially, some Populists had by now shifted their attitudes completely. This polarization was later recalled by a man who had helped resolve the suffrage dilemma:

> The riot of 1868 was white against black—that of 1895 and 1896 was white men against white men, for the negro vote. One side said, "He should not vote. If he does, we go under." The other side said, "He must vote. He will save us."[125]

Other groups were likewise now eager to eliminate blacks from the political scene. By 1895 the Lily-Whites had seized control of the Louisiana Republican party and sought to eliminate black voting power.[126] Whites were reluctant to join the so-called "nigger party." Furthermore, the stiff competition for black votes by the two white factions had increased the prices demanded. In short, it was becoming too expensive even for the more affluent Bourbons to buy up a black majority.[127] Living in an age when wages generally ranged between seventy cents to one dollar a day for "first class" black laborers, some blacks who accepted Democratic bribes probably did so more from efforts to redress their own economic grievances than as acts of demonstrated faith in the Bourbons.[128]

The Louisiana Populists never came close to success through the ballot box except when they fused with the Republicans in 1896. "The year 1896 was easily the most critical in Louisiana political history between the end of Reconstruction and the rise of Huey Long," Kousser has observed.[129] The 1896 Fusion ticket was made up of four Populists, two sugar cane planters, and "Old Swamper" John N. Pharr, himself a rich sugar planter. Pharr, the gubernatorial candidate, was sixty-seven years old and represented something of a contradiction for Populist followers. Probably a millionaire, Pharr at various times in his career had been a Whig, a Democrat, a Prohibitionist, and now a rich Republican. But despite his wealth, Pharr endorsed the Populist planks of free silver and inflation, among others, positions that were normally anathema for such wealthy planters. To the Republicans, with his endorsement of free silver, he seemed like a Populist. To the Populists, being a rich sugar cane planter from South Louisiana, he seemed like a Republican. To the Democrats, his association with "white trash" and blacks, along with being a Republican, marked him as a traitor to his race and the state. In short, his appeal to a cross-section of voters appeared limited at the outset.

Put on the defensive by the hostile Democratic press, Pharr defended his open solicitation of black votes: "I was reared with the Negro and worked side by side with them for twenty odd years," he observed of his political association with blacks. "I have never found him other than a good laborer and as honest as most men. If he has cut a bad figure in politics, we are to blame for it."[130] Bourbon Democrats, also soliciting black votes while promoting white supremacy, were aghast at Pharr's and other white Populists' open fraternization with blacks and solicitation of their vote. "At the Pharr meeting yesterday," a horrified Democrat, William Porcher Miles, exclaimed, "Henry McCall conducted his wife on his arm through the seething mass of black bucks . . . redolent with the genuine African odor (the day being warm) and seated her with the handful of 'ladies' present. Ye Gods! He must be crazy." Yet, Democrats openly solicited black votes and employed a variety of methods to ensure their capture.[131]

Violence, coercion, "bulldozing," vote purchasing, and vilification were common in the 1896 election. Shootings, stink bombs, and the use of rotten eggs were common events at Populist rallies. Several people were killed and others wounded during the campaign. The state militia had to be dispatched to St. Landry Parish to restore order. The Board of Health in one town charged Populists with violating the health laws. A Populist print shop was burned in another town. There were twenty-one lynchings in Louisiana during the year, one-fifth of all the lynchings in the United States. And so it went during the campaign.

Charges of all stripes were made against Pharr. Democrats argued that "John N(igger) Pharr" was "the champion Negro-flogger of South Louisiana," and that "scores of old gray-headed Negroes . . . can testify to the terror of the bullwhip wielded by his lusty arms." He had allegedly sent

Fig. 8. Democrats control of the black vote (*People's Party Paper,* April 24, 1894).

many blacks "to their happy hunting grounds" during his career.[132] Pharr gave "absolute endorsement of the Negro's right to vote and to secure justice in the courts." Pharr and the other two planters on the Fusion ticket raised Democratic alarm that the ticket might pull votes for the party from the wealthy sugar cane areas of South Louisiana, traditional Democratic strongholds. The possible loss of these votes outraged the Democrats. As the election neared, Democrats now feared that this "mongrel ticket," an "utterly impossible" combination of "hayseed and canejuice . . . and malodorous nigger wool" would combine to defeat them in 1896.[133] Enthusiasm for their prospects began to raise Fusionist spirits. Hardy Brian, a Populist legislator from Winn Parish, remarked that it would take "a gigantic piece of stealing" to beat the Populist Republican ticket in the fall election.

But the Democrats had an answer for Brian and this threat to their hegemony. It was the same one they had used against earlier challengers, and it had always worked:

> It is the religious duty of Democrats to rob Populists and Republicans of their votes whenever and wherever the opportunity presents itself and failure to do so will be a violation of true Louisiana Democratic teaching. The Populists and Republicans are our legitimate political prey. Rob them? You bet! What are we here for?[134]

When the dust had settled, incumbent Democratic governor Murphy J. Foster emerged as the victor over Pharr by 116,116 to 87,698 votes. Out of the 206,000 votes cast, Pharr was defeated by more than 28,000 votes. Pharr carried only four black parishes but won in thirty-two predominantly white parishes. Foster had large majorities in the Black Belt. And the suffrage amendment developed in the 1894 legislature went down in defeat. Armed and furious white Populists threatened to march on the state capitol, in much the same manner as Alabama Populists had threatened in 1894. The militia was called out, and Louisiana Populists like their Alabama counterparts decided not to resort to armed rebellion. But the loss in 1896 represented the high point of Louisiana Populism and from then on the party was a mere shadow of itself. The movement never recovered from this heartbreaking loss.

The culmination of the white agrarian "counterrevolution" was reached in the Louisiana constitutional convention of 1898. The new constitution required a voter to demonstrate the ability to read and write or to possess property of not less than three hundred dollars in value. For illiterate, propertyless blacks, the stipulation was fatal. The so-called "grandfather clause" that limited voting to individuals or their descendants who had voted prior to 1867 provided a loophole for the less-affluent white Populists to vote, yet largely eliminated the black.[135] In view of their negative experiences with the black vote, approval by some Populists of the disenfranchisement process is not difficult to comprehend.[136] However, the bulk of the leadership opposed these efforts, believing that they were inconsistent with the principles of Jeffersonian Democracy. Populism at bottom was an idealistic, principled movement, and the ballot was a sacred vehicle that they believed should be extended to all competent voters.

To counteract the loss of black votes, the Bourbons put to best use their remaining constitutional advantages. Principal among these was the use of population—in this case the disenfranchised blacks in the Black Belt—to determine representation in nominating conventions and in the legislature.[137] Populists strongly opposed this Bourbon tactic and spoke out loudly for its restructuring:

> Verily the "nigger" is to remain an important factor in Louisiana politics. He is to be disfranchised but his white neighbors will now make use of him in naming candidates of every political party, instead of using them in the election. The Black Belt can control the policy of every political party in this state and therefore cannot be much interested as to which party wins.[138]

This population advantage would remain with the Bourbons, however, until it was abolished in 1906.[139]

The effect of the new constitution's educational and literacy qualifications on black registration was marked and sharp. During the period 1890 to 1900, black registrants dropped from 127,923 to 5,320. White registrants also decreased but not nearly as sharply, with 126,884 in 1890 as opposed to 125,437 in 1900.[140] For the 1896 national election, the last before the 1898 disfranchisement code, there were 130,344 blacks registered, the majority in twenty-six parishes. But for the 1900 election, there were only the 5,320 blacks registered, a 96 percent decline.[141] Conversely, white registrants dropped by only 30,000.[142]

Paradoxically, perhaps the most immediate effect of the constitutional provision was the increase in voting power for the upland areas where white Populism was strongest. The six alluvial parishes of Red River, Caddo, Concordia, Tensas, Madison, and East Carroll—longstanding Democratic strongholds with large black populations—dropped from 28,498 registrants in 1896 to 5,453 in 1900. In turn the Populist parishes had dropped from 27,702 voters in 1890 to 16,043 by 1896. However, they were able to outvote the Black Belt alluvial parishes by 3–1; the new situation had substantially increased the agrarians' political power, and they were now in a much better position, at least in theory, to outvote the Bourbon strongholds that contained a large black population. With this new state of affairs there was little need now for white men to divide on party lines; Populists slowly returned to the Democratic fold or simply became apathetic about politics as offering any solace for their grievances.

By the end of the century, it was clear that blacks were pretty much excluded from statewide Louisiana politics. The accelerating effect of disenfranchisement was also explicitly manifested in national elections: for the

1896 election black registrants represented an electoral majority in twenty-six parishes. By 1900, two years after the constitutional convention, no parish had a majority of black registrants. This limitation became even more severe in the twentieth century. No blacks were on the voting lists of forty-five of the state's sixty-five parishes as late as 1944. Of the few remaining black registrants during this modern period, approximately three-fourths were concentrated in Baton Rouge and New Orleans and were controlled by Democratic machines.[143]

As a result of the regional and racial cleavages developed or exacerbated during the Louisiana Populist revolt, blacks and not the Bourbons had become the common enemy. There was a need, therefore, for a return to political stability, and disenfranchisement accomplished this. In a perverse sense, disenfranchisement was regarded as a reform of the political process; and the removal of the ignorant, the uneducated, and the propertyless incompetent, according to this view, would help "purify the ballot" and reduce violence. "In effect," Dethloff and Jones have written in their analysis of this period of race relations in Louisiana, "disfranchisement, aside from its racial implications, was a political compromise."[144] It was also a moral compromise, since the increasingly dominant view was that voting was not a natural right but a privilege that should only be exercised by a limited number of people with character, competence, education, and property, which was seen to largely exclude blacks. While the compromise never resulted in consensus over these issues or the agrarian platform, the decline of Populism ushered in a period of relative racial political calm that endured in Louisiana politics until the Civil Rights Era. It had also promised to usher in a period of calm in race relations as well as politics, but race relations became more violent in the one-party Pelican State after the decline of the Populist revolt and the disfranchisement of African Americans. The lack of power left blacks more vulnerable to violence and prejudice than had the late-nineteenth-century Populist movement, with all its violence and corruption.

TEXAS

Late-nineteenth-century Texas was a land of contrasts unlike anywhere else in the South and probably the nation. Proud of its "Six Flags" heritage, the state had been a republic, member of the Confederacy, and member of the Union, with a history of accepting anyone wanting or needing to make a new start in life. Her people were also richly diverse: conservative white Anglo-Saxon Protestants, a large Catholic population, German and Czech immigrants who spoke little English, a large Hispanic population along the

Rio Grande and up toward San Antonio, and a large politically active black population centered in East Texas, the birthplace of the Colored Farmers' Alliance. Third-party politics continually altered the electoral landscape, with blacks cooperating with whites on a variety of issues. Indeed, Populism was far from the first biracial political experiment in the state. As James Ivy has shown in his excellent monograph of the Texas Prohibition movement of the 1880s, black leaders spoke at rallies on both sides of the issue. Although "there was some segregation in the organization of prohibition and anti-prohibition clubs at the precinct level, both sides generally welcomed African Americans in the audience at rallies, and black and white speakers often appeared on the same podium."[145] John Rayner began his third-party career as a Prohibitionist organizer who understood how purchasing black votes would affect the movement's success.[146] But most significantly for the Populist movement, both pro- and anti-Prohibitionists fought for the black vote, which could swing the election.[147] When the 1887 Prohibition Amendment came to a vote, there was an "extraordinarily high level of participation among African American voters." Senator John Reagan complained later that "prohibition was defeated by the votes of the negroes, Germans and Mexicans."[148] In sum, while the Alliance was organizing and gaining momentum to form a third party among agrarians, the prohibition battles of the 1880s demonstrated that biracial coalitions could work at the state level, that the common man (and woman) would accept mixed-race gatherings, and that the black electorate could swing an election. Leaders of the two major parties would have to deal with black voters in one way or the other to survive.

Populism emerged in Texas in the face of competing Democratic and Republican parties not so much because of its superior organization as because of its superior relevance to its members. But the transition from the Democratic to the Populist Party was so painful in Texas, as in Alabama, that discontented agrarians formed the "Jeffersonian Democrats" before finally joining the Populists. Before Populism's appearance, this group coalesced around progressive Democratic governor James S. Hogg, who in his 1890 campaign attracted a varied and impressive backing in the farming regions of central, eastern, and northern Texas. Overthrowing the Bourbon wing of the party, Hogg subsequently became a storm center between Democratic reactionaries and radical Alliancemen. Still, Alliance leaders criticized the governor for being too conservative on such issues as the legal rate of interest, free textbooks, and the subtreasury plan.[149] This growing dissatisfaction with Hogg and the Democrats partly led to the emergence of the Populist Party in Texas.

Given this situation, a third-party convention was scheduled for August

17–18, 1891, during the annual session of the Farmers' Alliance in Dallas. Two blacks, Henry Jennings of Collins County and R. H. Hayes of Tarrant, were elected members of the State Executive Committee.[150] Afterwards, a state People's Party convention assembled in Fort Worth on February 9, 1892.[151] The question of political fellowship with blacks and the party's stance on the race issue surfaced during the first day's session. A black delegate from Grayson County, "Watson," addressing the delegates in a speech mixed with humility and anger, argued that discussions by "the old war horses" in the party, primarily from East Texas, about keeping blacks at arm's length while still expecting to garner their vote would fail. He also challenged Tom Watson's view that the self-interests of blacks and whites were the same:

> I hope it is no embarrassment to you for a colored man to stand before you. I am an emancipated slave of this state. I was emancipated in 1865 and it is now useless to tell you my interest is yours and yours mine. You look over this large assembly and find very few of my people represented in this great movement. It is recognized that the Negro holds the balance of power, and the democrats and republicans are trying to hold him down. You should remember that those parties intend to keep the Negro out of this reform movement if they can, and when you bring up your old war-horses you are putting tools into the democratic and republican hands to help keep the Negro out of your movement.[152]

It was further asserted that "The Negro vote will be the balancing vote in Texas. If you are going to win," R. H. Hayes, black leader from Fort Worth, said, "you *must* take the Negro vote with you. . . . You *must* appoint us by convention and make us feel that we are men" (emphasis added). These sober words made the convention's more progressive whites realize that, whatever their feelings toward blacks, the party must appeal to them. The white convention president agreed. "He is a citizen just as much as we are," it was said of the black voter, "and the party that acts on that fact will gain the colored vote of the South."[153] And the party members proceeded with their efforts, based on this assumption: blacks would be welcomed into the Texas Populist Party.

Efforts at organizing blacks at the grassroots level were made following the 1891 Dallas meeting, and they were fairly substantial for about six months. Several separate black Populist clubs formed. Henry Jennings, the black state committeeman, reported that he "had organized many People's Party colored clubs in Texas and had branded them." From south Texas came reports that "the colored people are coming into the new party in squads and companies. They have third party speakers and are organizing colored clubs." Speakers from the Colored Farmers' Alliance addressed rallies in several counties.[154] In Gonzales County, about one-third of the Populists were black and six of its nineteen delegates to the convention were blacks. These membership drives were illusionary, however, as white Populists expressed little inclination to support black candidates.[155] As in Louisiana, black candidates would provide the Bourbons with propaganda to use against the new party and repel potential white members. The black's role in Texas, then, was to be an organizer and supporter rather than candidate. Black candidates were tolerated to a degree by Republicans but did not appeal to grassroots white agrarians.

Despite optimistic reports, Texas Populists were dissatisfied with their success at the local level, and rightly so, for Governor Hogg had recently shifted again to the left to absorb more of the disaffected farmers. Prominent among Hogg's efforts was a pro-inflation plank that supported free coinage of silver, an issue that had strong Populist support not only in Texas but nationally.[156] Yet the tide of disgruntled farmers leaving the Democratic Party was not stemmed, due in part to the energetic recruiting efforts of the third partyites in the rural areas. By May 1892 "so many Hogg democrats are going into the third party that he will be left in the primaries."[157] The governor's conciliatory efforts were too little and too late to blunt the Populist organizational activity.

A state nominating convention subsequently selected Populist candidates for state office. The gubernatorial nomination went to Judge Thomas L. Nugent, a former Democrat and Confederate officer described by an opposition newspaper as "a quiet, self-contained, intellectual and scholarly man and an accomplished lawyer" whose candidacy would add "dignity and moral elevation to the campaign."[158] A gaunt, soft-spoken, well-read man with a socialist bent, long flowing beard and a bald head, Nugent linked his unorthodox ideas to the teachings of Jesus. He had a strong faith in the improvability of man, wanting to socialize Christianity and make social Christians of men, and he wanted to use the Populist Party as the vehicle to achieve these ends. According to his biographer, he was "a political expression of the social gospel movement." Nugent differed from many of his fellow Populists in that he did not expect to secure complete justice by political action or by institutional reform, although he was convinced that such actions could help.[159]

Like many white Populists leaders, Nugent seemed very traditional in matters of race. A sensitive religious man with a strong humanitarian spirit, he separated blacks from his Christian charity, believing in *noblesse oblige* and separation of the races as a means of maintaining racial harmony. "My idea," he asserted, "is that segregation, as far as possible, is best for the Negro."[160] Nugent also supported segregation in railway cars and in schools where blacks should be "prevented by law from close association with white people."[161] He wanted to extend segregation into the prison system on the premise that blacks' supervision of their own penal system would provide valuable training.[162] Like other Populist leaders and almost all whites of his era, Nugent opposed social equality, believing that it was unattainable as well as unthinkable.[163] Such views did not make Nugent appealing to black voters. His opinions on racial matters were buttressed by the Texas Populist Party's Ku Klux Klan sympathizer James H. "Cyclone" Davis, the renowned orator and 1894 Texas Populist candidate for attorney general. Possessing a wiry, rangy body of some six feet, three inches and superior oratorical abilities, Davis was known nationally as a result of his dominating speaking abilities and presence (he gained his nickname because of the "cyclones" of applause that followed his showmanlike oratories). Davis suggested that a prime motive for reforming the American economy and muting the money power was to prevent white women from being forced into "hoeing cotton" beside "a big burley Negro."[164]

The Texas Populist Party was largely unsuccessful in 1892, winning only eight seats in the legislature and running third behind the other two major parties.[165] Hogg, the candidate of the liberal wing of the Democratic Party, easily won the gubernatorial election, receiving 43.7 percent (190,486) of the vote to Nugent's 108,000 and the "goldbug" (more conservative) faction of the Democratic Party led by conservative railroad lawyer George Clark, who garnered 133,000 votes.[166] During the campaign, Hogg made a concerted bid for the black vote, with a strong anti-lynching stance in particular resonating among black voters. The Populists fatally appear to have tried to appeal directly to the black vote, bypassing black leaders and using the local Colored Farmers' Alliance structure to appeal to blacks. The third partyites also made no overtures for Republican support, which further retarded their black support, since the party still controlled a bloc of some 75–90,000 black votes in the state.[167] With the Democratic Party split into two factions in 1892, a strong showing by blacks for the Populist Party would have made a victory for the new party more attainable. But if Texas Populists did not receive a significant portion of the black vote in 1892 or even the support of many white Alliancemen who remained loyal to the Hogg wing of the Party, their loss seemed assured. And the Populist showing among black voters in 1892 was dismal. According to regression studies completed by Cantrell and Barton and Morgan Kousser, the percentage of black males who voted for the Populists in 1892 was less than 9 percent.[168]

A combination of an appeal directly to the grassroots (bypassing black leaders), Nugent's lack of appeal to blacks, the rapid decline of the Colored Farmers' Alliance, and a healthy dose of fraud, corruption, and coercion of the black vote helps explain in part this dismal failure (Cantrell and Barton, using regression techniques, concluded that "virtually no blacks voted for Nugent and over one third of blacks did not vote"). A subsequent change of tactics in appealing to black votes, using more black leaders such as John Rayner, would result in much better showings in 1894 and 1896.[169] And fusion with the Republicans in 1896 added to the Populist camp a healthy number of blacks who had not been present in earlier campaigns.

It seems reasonably clear that Hogg received the lion's share of the black vote. Like W. J. Northen, his gubernatorial counterpart in Georgia, he was favored by blacks even though he headed the party of white supremacy and his party's faction had initiated the state's first Jim Crow transportation law in 1891. Hogg's popularity was probably related to his well-known record of honesty and fairness to blacks. Like Northen, he took a strong stand against mob action. Consider Hogg's comments:

> Now, I have gone this far, when mobs have become too strong in the State for the local officers to cope with them. I have quelled them by the strong arm of the law without conferring with anybody. I have suppressed more than one mob too. Did you ever hear of an influential and wealthy man being killed by a mob? Let a humble negro or a poor white man commit some crime and a gang of enterprising and wild and wooly fellows will swing him to a tree without a trial.[170]

In contrast, Nugent did not support Hogg's anti-lynching stand.[171] It was logical that blacks, seeking protection of person and the ability to deliver on promises, would vote for Hogg.

Hogg's comments on equal law enforcement were not idle boasts. He subsequently placed "rewards over the heads of all these criminals [lynchers], and propose[d] to let them stay there as long as I hold the office of Governor."[172] He also granted numerous pardons and commuted the sentences of black offenders.[173] His biographer has

> found this theme of abhorrence of mob violence throughout Hogg's addresses and writing, as part of his fundamental concern with and insistence on law enforcement and justice for all manner of man.[174]

Increasing violence and limited opportunities encouraged blacks to be more pragmatic in their politics. This trend was especially prevalent among middle-class black leaders, who were developing sources of support among progressive white Democrats who could and did deliver on their promises. Hogg's black support was further strengthened by such middle-class black leaders as Guadalupe College president David Abner Jr. in Seguin, black attorney W. O. Lewis from Denison, John Anderson, and a host of others.[175] There seems to be massive evidence to document the fact that Hogg received a substantial portion of the black vote in 1892, and it also appears that this support was not based largely on fraud and coercion.[176] Yet the Hoggites had played a decisive role in the enactment of the state's Jim Crow statute in 1891 for separate railroad accommodations.[177] Populists, in turn, had little appeal to either Mexicans or blacks and depended for their success in areas largely devoid of blacks.[178]

It was apparent from the 1892 election that attracting more black leaders to the party would be a key factor in the future success of the Populists among blacks. The Populists early on wanted to appeal directly to the black masses, bypassing leaders who required money to deliver the vote, but that approach proved futile in Texas. Black votes were better garnered through the use of black leaders or black surrogates appealing directly to the masses for the involved party. It was at this point that the third partyites converted the portly John B. Rayner, a former black Republican and person of notable character, to serve as a grassroots organizer and stump speaker.[179] With the aid of "a corps of colored assistants," Rayner roamed the state preaching Populism to blacks.[180] His speaking schedule was arduous, filling three engagements for every one of the white Populist speakers. Rayner's success proved the need for black party leaders, and it was fortunate that his enthusiasm came not from financial gain but his conviction about the positive role of Populism in American society.[181] H. S. P. "Stump" Ashby, chairman of the State Executive Committee, recognized that Rayner was "the most useful speaker [we] can employ to implant our principles among the colored voters." As Ashby indicated, "the work I want Rayner to do no white man can do."[182]

Rayner's career in Texas Populism reads like that of an evangelist. His enthusiasm and ability to endure hardship was remarkable. His salary was minimal, often nonexistent; at one point he was so destitute that he did not have money enough to buy postage stamps.[183] Rayner was later credited with converting at least twenty-five thousand blacks to Texas Populism, and as a reward for his diligent work was appointed to the State Executive Committee in 1895.[184] As with other Southern Populist leaders, his devotion to the cause and zeal for Populist principles were unmatched.

Rayner found fertile ground for his doctrines, for political discontent by Texas black Republicans had reached new heights during the nineties. By

1888, Lily-White clubs formed in opposition to black participation in the party.[185] In Texas, the Republican Party divided over the "Negro question," a rift that manifested itself openly at the state Republican convention at San Antonio in September 1890. The result was a Black and Tan faction led by Norris Wright Cuney that sought to retain black participation, and a Lily-White faction that wanted to attract more whites by reducing the role and presence of blacks. The black faction, according to one unfriendly correspondent, thought they "have got dem white folks where the hair is short."[186] If that was indeed the black faction's sentiment, however, this elation was short-lived, as the Lily-Whites managed to nominate their own candidate.[187] As in other states, race split the Texas Republican Party.

This was merely the beginning of a long series of defeats for black Texas Republicans. By 1894, the Lily-Whites proposed setting up an independent republic for blacks.[188] By 1896, Cuney had lost his place in the party, and the suppression of blacks that followed was even more dramatic.[189] With this change of fortune, blacks would be more open to solicitation from other parties. As previously indicated, a large number of black voters had crossed over and supported James Hogg in both 1890 and 1892. Blacks at the grassroots level, if they were to vote for a non-Republican, were more attracted to personalities and issues than party, as the Prohibition campaigns already demonstrated.

By 1894, Cuney reluctantly advocated fusion between the Populists and the black Republicans, perhaps less as a result of sympathy with Populist principles than, in the words of Cuney's daughter, "the combined vote of the two parties, [which] was far greater than that of the Democrats."[190] But as in other states examined, black Republicans were as a rule not strongly supportive of the idea of fusion. During the 1892 election, a good turnout by blacks and disaffected agrarians for the Populist Party could have resulted in victory. However, Cuney had early opposed fusion with both the Democrats and the Populists, but the Populists in particular. In many ways, the conservative Cuney sounded very much like a contemporary northeastern white Republican who opposed inflation and advocated conservative Republican business principles. These were the very principles Populists opposed, so fusion for Cuney—or with Cuney—was not appealing. Consider Cuney on the Populist gubernatorial candidate and platform:

I objected to Mr. Nugent because he is in line with Mr. Hogg; but a few steps removed toward socialism and communism—for instance, the Government owner ship of railroads and the subtreasury. His principles seek to undermine our whole system of business, which has existed for years, and under which our country has become great and strong, and made itself the foremost among the nations of the world.[191]

Four years later, Cuney still opposed fusion with the more radical Populists, although in practice he was not as adverse to fusion with other political parties.[192] It was during this latter period that his leadership in the Republican Party was challenged and reconciliation with the Lily-Whites was advocated. With Cuney's demise in 1897, new black leaders were more committed to fusion with the Populists.[193] But blacks as a statewide voting block would disappear within a decade, and grassroots blacks were never favorably disposed as a group to fusion, preferring to remain with the Republican Party.

A faction of black Republicans under the aegis of William "Gooseneck Bill" McDonald, a Cuney assistant, continued to oppose fusion because of the fundamental philosophical differences between Republicanism and Populism.[194] McDonald, a slender, wiry black man, some six feet tall with a bronze-brown complexion and a rancorous cigar as his constant companion, was obsessed with gaining wealth. He had earned his sobriquet from the *Dallas Morning News* in 1896, which referred to McDonald as having "an Irish name" but is "a kind of goosenecked Negro." Taking control of the Black and Tan faction after Cuney's death, McDonald was more pragmatic than Cuney—his critics would say mercenary—and would have been more receptive to fusion with other parties, most likely the Democrats, than Cuney. In 1896, for example, McDonald and his faction fused with the Democratic gubernatorial candidate, Charles A. Culberson. It was widely alleged that his fondness for money rather than principle had been the deciding factor in his choice.[195] But some blacks were turning to the Populist movement.

From its near-zero gain of the black vote in 1892, Populism gained an estimated 17 percent of the black vote in 1894 and 42 percent in 1896, despite Cuney's early opposition. Rayner's efforts were also instrumental, and the decline of the Republican Party forced blacks to look for other alternatives. Statewide, the Republican Party had collapsed by 1894. In the 1894 gubernatorial contest, the Democratic gubernatorial candidate received 207,167 votes to Populist Nugent's 152,731—up from his 108,000 votes in 1892. Populism had now become the second party in Texas. Republican Party gubernatorial candidate W. K. Makemson received only 54,520 votes, and Lily-White candidate John Schmitz received an insubstantial 5,036 votes. In 1896 the Populists and the Republicans fused locally, allowing Jerome Kearby (the Populist gubernatorial candidate who replaced the

McDonald - Say Gubner doan you hoal dat bait sech a distance in de future.
Culberson - that's all right Bill. All you have to do is to whoop up the colored vote for the democratic ticket and all will be well.

Fig. 9. Texas Democrats solicit votes in 1896 with black Republican leader, William "Gooseneck Bill" McDonald (*Southern Mercury,* October 22, 1896).

deceased Nugent) to receive 238,692 votes, their best showing, to the winning Democratic candidate C. A. Culberson's 298,528 votes.[196] By this point the increase in black votes for the third party made little difference, for Texas Populism underwent a marked decline after 1896. Always in fragile health, Nugent's death in December 1895 was a serious blow to the party. In 1898, Populist gubernatorial candidate Barnett Gibbs only received 114,955 votes, a drop of 124,000 votes from the 1896 result. Democratic candidate J. D. Savers received 291,548 votes, approximately the same number of votes the party's candidate had received in 1896. The Democrats maintained their vitality despite the Populist challenge, as the third party declined after 1896. By 1900, the Populists only attracted about 6 percent of the adult white male vote and almost no black votes, yet 36 percent of Texas male blacks and 80 percent of whites voted in the 1900 Texas gubernatorial race.[197]

This drop in electoral interest can be largely attributed to Democratic appropriation of Populist policies.[198] This was a common and successful strategy throughout the South: incorporate the Populist platform in the Democratic message, play the race card, and concurrently bring about a decline in the overall number of black votes. Also, there was never a great degree of incompatibility between the Populists and the progressive Democrats under Hogg.[199] Many of the issues advocated early by the Populists had been incorporated by the Hogg Democrats. So the enticement of the grassroots white Populist voter back into the Democratic Party was accom-

THE STORY OF LITTLE RED RIDING HOOD
The Democratic wolf's invitation to the People's Party.

Fig. 10. Populism is absorbed by the Democratic party after 1896 (*Southern Mercury,* October 29, 1896).

plished with relative ease in Texas after 1896. However, as in other states, some disaffected members of both races gave up on politics as a solution to their problems.

The effect of Texas Populism on black suffrage differed from Louisiana and Alabama. In those states, black electoral participation took a sharp drop after the disenfranchising conventions before the turn of the century. But it was not until 1902 that a constitutional amendment enacted a poll tax in Texas and black voting was almost eliminated. As early as the 1875 Texas constitutional convention, three unsuccessful efforts were made to enact a poll tax to eliminate the "irresponsible" voter, meaning "the lazy, purchasable Negro, who pays no taxes," and the "men with white skins" who "don't pay the state a pittance." In general, during the next three decades it was primarily the agrarians who opposed the poll tax. According to Rice's *Negro in Texas,* " 'Black Populism' eventually led to the adoption of the poll tax and the white Democratic primary."[200] Cantrell and Barton agree with Rice, although Kousser is not of the same opinion. Yet blacks were effectively disenfranchised and a substantial portion of the white voters had begun to boycott the polls long before. But 36 percent of adult black males still voted in the 1900 gubernatorial race. The major disenfranchisement measure in Texas was the 1902 constitutional amendment requiring payment of a poll tax as a prerequisite for voting. In 1903 the Terrell Election Law in Texas provided for a noncumulative poll tax and allowed a white county primary. These two efforts largely doomed the black vote and any challenge to the Democratic Party in Texas until the late 1950s. There was also a growing distrust in universal suffrage, believing that voting should be a privilege and not a right, not only in Texas but the South as a whole.[201] More and more it was believed that eliminating the black voter would end ballot box corruption and its corrosive effect on an honest election process.

Perhaps the explanation for the delay in eliminating the black vote in Texas lies partly in the limited number of qualified black voters in the state—approximately 20 percent of the total. In other Gulf Coast states, blacks made up as much as 30–35 percent of the voting population and were perceived as an election threat to the white population. There was a more pressing need, therefore, to quickly eliminate the black vote in states outside Texas, and that elimination did occur earlier. But after 1896, blacks in Texas were never a real threat to white supremacy unless fusion was effected with other parties, and the Republican Party as a vehicle of black protest was also played out.

Fraud also played a role in the dissolution of black voting strength in the state. One of three black majority counties in far northeastern Texas, Harrison County following Reconstruction regularly produced the largest Democratic majorities in the state, despite the fact that 68 percent of its voters were blacks who normally supported the Republican Party or Populists. The answer, in simplest terms, was gross voter fraud. But voter fraud here was more open, more sophisticated, and at a level of manipulation greater than elsewhere, and the term "Harrison County Methods" became synonymous with massive election fraud in Texas. Worth Miller has carefully documented the methods and results used here, which became a prototype not only for election fraud in Texas but elsewhere. Some of the fraud was stunningly blatant. For example, official poll lists in Harrison County during this era carried the names of Ulysses S. Grant, Rutherford B. Hayes, the late James Garfield, Jefferson Davis, Samuel J. Tilden, and Alexander H. Stephens. Populist congressional candidate "Cyclone" Davis wrote in his memoir that in one county election box a dog named Fido Jenkins voted against him five times in 1894! Furthermore, he added, "dead Negroes, mules, and horses" had voted against him in the same year. It will remain unknown how many Populist and Republican candidates in Texas lost because of fraud and how many discouraged voters simply failed to go to the polls.[202]

The black vote in Texas and elsewhere in the South after 1903 remained larger in the city than in the country and on occasion proved of some value to parties during disputes. But even in large cities such as Houston and New Orleans, the black vote was controlled by Democratic machines, although the same could be said for Chicago, New York, and Boston. Black "indifference" occurred primarily in the rural districts, although there were local variations. It appears that the remaining base of power for Southern blacks following the Populist revolt was largely urban.[203] Populism had influenced election alignments in Texas, and it kept the black voter important to the state's politics. As noted earlier, all parties in the early 1890s competed for black votes with varying degrees of success. However, the third-party campaigns in Texas were mild in comparison with other Gulf or Atlantic Coast states, and the level of corruption and violence was never as extreme as in other Southern states.[204] Cantrell and Barton indicate that they found "no evidence" of fraud, intimidation, and particularly violence surrounding the black vote in Texas by Populists. But fraud did occur by all parties. However, nowhere in Texas did Populists approximate the level of intimidation and fraud as in Georgia. Populists in Texas as well as elsewhere were more often the victims rather than the perpetrators of fraud and violence, but on rare occasions Texas Populists did indulge in fraud. Consider the comments of a Democratic observer of the Crockett County Populists in 1892: "But for ten days before the election, the[y] had their dark lantern meetings at night and put their tidy [money] in their [black] hands the morning of the election and marched them to the polls under leaders in droves not blocks of 5's but 25 and 30 at a time, white and black, and voted them like sheep." "More than one Populist Sheriff" according to Martin "enjoyed the reputation of having won office through manipulation of the colored vote."[205]

Alliance and Populist strength in Texas was concentrated in the vast sections of North and West Texas, and dominated certain parts of Central and

East Texas where the state's black population was concentrated. A handful of impoverished white farmers had founded the original Farmer's Alliance movement in 1877 in the hill country's Lampasas County, and the Colored Farmer's Alliance was founded in 1886 on an East Texas farm near Lovelady, in Houston County—both becoming the institutional base for the two major National Alliance organizations. In all, some seven largely rural congressional districts statewide constituted the core strength of the state's Alliance and Populist movement. South of San Antonio, however, in "the Valley" with its cactus and mesquite covering the gently undulating "brush country," extending to the Mexican border—whose predominantly Mexican inhabitants had one of the lowest literacy rates in the United States—Populism never took hold. These inhabitants of the Valley as a whole possessed a long history of serf-like dependence on a *patrón* or *jefe*—a strong local leader with near feudalistic leadership customs. As they migrated to the United States, these Mexican Americans largely continued this custom of unwavering loyalty in their new roles as tenants and ranch hands to the Valley ranch owners, largely Democrats, who now served as their lords and protectors. In return, these inhabitants gave their unquestioning loyalty to these *patrónes* on election day, and the number of votes such conditions could generate were not necessarily limited by the number of voters, but by the need of the candidate. These ranch *patrónes* were ruthless political bosses who retained an iron-fisted control over the Valley precincts.

According to one description of Valley election day events:

> The Mexican voter . . . was marched to the polls, generally by a half-breed deputy sheriff with two six-shooters, a Winchester rifle, and a bandoleer of ammunition, to perform the sovereign act of voting. He entered the polls, one at a time, was handed a folded ballot which he dropped in the box, was given a drink of Tequila, and then was marched out, where he touched the hand of one of the local political bosses or some of his sainted representatives.[206]

Matters were not always handled so crudely, but the results were the same: Democratic ranch bosses controlled the local Mexican American votes, produced the desired results, and controlled their feudal domain through this dependence of the inhabitants. Martin also suggested in his study of the state's movement that Texas Populism possessed fears of a population with a "non-alien makeup" and embraced an "alleged anti-alien program" that "cast about the Third Party a cloud of Knownothingism so that reasoning Mexicans regarded Populism with doubt, while the unthinking masses took fright and stampeded outright when the party was mentioned."[207] Their alleged attitude further deterred Hispanic voters from being attracted to Populism, even when unrestrained.

The methods employed against this particular ethnic group were the same as those used in the plantation black belts of the South, such as Georgia, Alabama, and Louisiana, to produce huge majorities against the Populists: wholesale ballot box stuffing, various forms of intimidation and violence, open bribery, and massive voting by dead or fictitious blacks (or Mexican Americans in the Texas Valley), dogs, or mules. These events run through much of Texas and Southern history until recent years and are strikingly revelatory of the corrupt tendencies in the state's and region's political history. The fact that the methods and results were *more* fraudulent in Georgia, Alabama, and Louisiana than Texas only indicates that the Democratic Bourbons there as a group attacked Populism with a greater lack of limits and morality that justified any maneuver as long as the result was victory. The ruthlessness, cynicism, and aggression that characterized these events, in Texas and elsewhere, became the defining Democratic campaign methods and election day results of the Southern Populist era. Despite the regional or state differences, such events seem to blur together to form a pattern of conduct. To many of these Southwide political despots, votes were a commodity to be bought and sold, like any of the region's other commodities, such as cotton or sugar. As a result of these formidable conditions, the third party in Texas wrote off these Southern districts and their Mexican American inhabitants, which encompassed nearly one-fourth of the state.

For all of these reasons, Mexican Americans did not support the Populist movement in Texas. The Valley's controlled vote, generally estimated to provide a plurality to the favored candidate of between twenty and twenty-five thousand votes, proved a largely insurmountable obstacle for the statewide Populist Party and its quest for power.[208]

Populism's legislative impact in Texas was minor during the 1890s, for the simple reason that the party had not elected enough members to effect change. The state's ethnic diversity complicated the situation more than elsewhere and, despite mixed efforts, Populists never attracted significant support from blacks, Mexicans, Germans, businessmen, or prosperous farmers—and particularly from the leadership of these groups. The two major exceptions in the black community were Melvin Wade, a radical black trade unionist who worked the urban areas, and John B. Rayner and his corps of assistants who worked the rural areas carrying the doctrines of Populist reform. The peak of black support appears to have been in the 1896 gubernatorial election, and this support was due more to fusion with Republicans than black attraction to the party.[209] But in Texas as elsewhere fusion tended to create a fission particularly among its black leadership, while grassroots blacks largely remained loyal to the Republican Party; and the benefits of the black vote to the Populists largely came from fusion and not political conversion. Moreover, improved economic conditions after 1896 worked against Texas Populism as a protest party. Politically, most third partyites returned to the Democratic Party, and several former Populists were elected as legislators.[210] John Rayner eventually gravitated back to the Republican Party and was reduced to poverty, his wife taking in washing from whites to sustain her family. Impoverished and in a status of forced accommodation, he died in 1918 a "very bitter" lonely old man who was buried in a Jim Crow cemetery near Calvert, Texas.[211]

President Lyndon Johnson, a son of the Texas hill country, sometimes seen as a progressive Democrat, a friend to African Americans, and a product of this tapestry, may in reality have been a neo-Populist—representing one of the remaining threads of Texas Populism that ran into the 1960s. His grandfather, Sam Johnson, had been a Texas hill country Populist (where the Alliance Movement began in 1877), and he acknowledged that his "father and grandfather handed down to him a philosophy of life."[212]

SUMMATION

The Populist challenge in the Gulf Coast South differed in some respects from the Atlantic Coast variety. One prominent difference, particularly in Alabama and Louisiana, was the demand for ballot reform. Populism there had started out with economic issues being prominent, but it soon became clear that reform would not be effected at the ballot box with the amount of corruption and fraud existing. By 1894, economics was subordinate to ballot reform as the dominant challenge to the party. Afterward, the Populists placed greater stress on suffrage change: political reform must precede economic reform, for without this no party that sought to work through the established election system could be effective. This problem disappeared with disenfranchisement, but ironically, that also contributed to Populism's decline. In some cases, Democrats incorporated proposed Populist reforms, and ballot box reform long advocated by the Populists was at least partially achieved by black disenfranchisement. But Populists were nervous about disenfranchising voters, fearing not only that blacks but that they themselves would be victims. Viewing the situation from a class perspective, white Populist fears of disenfranchisement were not without some basis in reality.

The Texas pattern was complicated by the existence of a progressive wing within the Democratic Party, with leaders like Governor Hogg incorporating Populist reforms into the party platform. Concurrently, progressive Democrats such as Hogg received substantial portions of the black vote due to their established record on race relations. Also, Populism was unable to attract a substantial following in the black middle-class or Republican leadership to promote its program in the black community. The few converts it did gain, such as John Rayner, were overburdened and underpaid and on occasion threatened with violence. Being a third partyite in the white Democratic South was difficult, and blacks who left the Republican Party also invited peer pressure. The picture for the third party was further complicated by black Republican leaders who did not endorse fusion with the Populists until the party was disintegrating. And grassroots blacks were nowhere, as a group, attracted to the potential for fusion, perhaps fearing this class of men who in earlier days had been in the forefront of black oppression. This picture was a familiar one in both the Atlantic and Gulf Coast South. Black and white farmers of both regions started as discontented economic groups, and that discontent translated into political activism aimed at gaining particular reforms—specifically "a free ballot and a fair count." After 1896 farmers had no national voice, and by 1900 they had no organization of substance left at the state or national level. Also, meaningful black participation had all but ended by the turn of the century. It remains now to make an interpretive summary of Populist actions and interaction with blacks and tally up the balance sheet.

8

The Balance Sheet

A law should be made disfranchising all who buy or sell votes.

Southern history has witnessed a long line of third parties—from the Green-backers to the Reform Party of Ross Perot—all of which have achieved some notable successes at the state level. Their declines came about not so much because of voter rejection, but because they were cut off from the national patronage system under the domination of the two major parties.[1] In this context, Southern Populism was no exception, for it not only spoke for the powerless but suffered the same political failing. Populism was essentially a political defense mechanism of the disinherited. Despairing of substantial reform through the established parties, the agrarians rejected the region's political system, exalted the underprivileged, and tried to cast down the power elite.

The Populists clashed immediately with the South's culture of conformity. As white Southerners, they were tradition-bound to codes of behavior and prejudices, yet their formation of a biracial political movement with an active role for blacks conflicted with these same codes. Although labor groups had achieved limited success with biracial cooperation, such success was localized and unsuccessful for the South as a whole. Southern Alliancemen and Populists similarly achieved some local successes but could not convince the mass of blacks and poor whites to join them. As a result, third-party elected officials were forced to compromise with representatives of the two major parties, and Populist reform diluted. Additionally, the lack of patronage for ambitious followers and recruits weakened the movement at the grassroots level, and even prominent Populist leaders such as Marion Butler, Tom Watson, and John Rayner eventually rejoined one of the two major parties. This political realignment also seems true of the electorate, although many former Populists expressed their disillusionment by abandoning political participation altogether, once the movement vanished.

By about 1905, voting was little more than a memory for most Southern blacks, except in a few urban areas such as New Orleans and Knoxville. And in these areas it was largely under the control of a local political machine. Populism could offer few inducements or, more importantly in the case of blacks, protection of person. Furthermore, many Southern black leaders were openly suspicious of the earlier bitterness and violence manifested toward their race by many of these same men, or class of men, from the dark days of Redemption who now were opting for a class alliance. Given these drawbacks, coupled with white ambivalence, Populism's biracial experiment seemed doomed from the start.

Electoral fraud perpetrated by the Democratic Bourbon class in no small part defeated Southern Populism. The conservatives shared few of the third party's convictions for high sounding principles of democracy and black political participation, and they saw the security of their own position threatened by a combination of lower-class whites and blacks. To retain control, Bourbons sought black votes, some secured honestly but most gained dishonestly through fraud, corruption, and coercion. Seeing these disgraceful events in the South as well as elsewhere in the nation was enough to discourage even the most stout-hearted reformer. Angry Populists charged in the 1892 national platform that "Corruption dominates the Ballot Box, the legislatures, the Congress and touches even the ermine of the bench." Southern Populists, in general, had shifted to a tone of hard-boiled political realism by 1894 and called for a drastic reform of the election process, making "a free ballot and a fair count" two of their primary goals. But these were goals they never achieved, and their inability to eliminate or control voter fraud largely ended the movement. Some third partyites came to regard blacks, who were both the victims and the perpetrators of much of this fraud, as one of the forces challenging the moral legitimacy of their proposed new order. Simultaneously, white supremacy campaigns drove poor white voters to support Democratic candidates and occasionally triggered white-on-black violence. The logical response was a regional deterioration in race relations, a reaction that downplayed the initially proposed program of biracial class measures brought on by the pinch of economic pressures. This shift in attitude was accompanied by a corresponding shift in black support—all of which signaled the discontinuity of Populist class feeling with the blacks.

When Populists and Democrats largely closed ranks, "the main dish at their love feasts was the disfranchisement of the Negro."[2] A series of state election laws in the mid-1890s (e.g., Sayre Election Law in Alabama and the Walton Act in Virginia) eroded black voting power. By 1895, eight of the eleven states of the Old South had adopted secret ballot laws. Georgia and South Carolina had a poll tax and the eight-ballot-box law respectively, which achieved the same end in reducing black votes. Only North Carolina, with a Populist-Republican majority in the legislature, had no such law.[3] The result was a sharp reduction in black votes. And as black votes declined, Populism concurrently declined, and Populist attitudes toward the biracial venture soured.

Populism started with the rhetorical assumption that there could be no progress until there was a consciousness of class interests, and black and white, largely based on profession, fell within this agrarian class. A people must know what it is reasonable to want, and then seek to achieve it through concentrated political effort. The great majority of Populists, black and white, had their aspirations shaped by a society that placed great emphasis on a program of self-help. Blacks in particular emphasized self-help and economic and character development as a means to success and acceptance during the agrarian revolt era. Largely rejected by the Republican Party, which was developing new alignments, blacks were forced to seek new means to prosper. And accommodation with their own worst enemies, the Bourbon Democrats, or abandoning politics altogether, were options being explored.

Reared on this tradition, it is not surprising that the agrarian movement was largely a refurbishing of the Protestant ethic. At bottom, Farmers' Alliance and Populist rhetoric represented an agrarian translation of the traditional Protestant and Jeffersonian concept of achieving wealth through honest hard work and virtue, accompanied by a deep belief that right would ultimately prevail over wrong. Populists admired the days of Jefferson and Jackson, not always correctly, for their ideal economic organization as well as their philosophic underpinnings. The Populist's view of government was also closely related to his belief in a rustic concept of Emersonian self-reliance and virtue, with the development of a new political leadership based on human happiness and social democracy. Its intellectual and ideological foundations combined in religious thought the idea of the social gospel and in politics the idea of a social democracy. Its stated ideal would be a society in which all people, no matter what their race, would be given a chance politically to rise as far as their merits and character ("competency considered") would take them. In theory, theirs was to be a monolithic coalition of special agrarian and labor class interests recognizing no racial or regional boundaries.

Populist rhetoric oversimplified economics and grouped all individuals as either "producers" or "consumers" on the basis of economic grievances—the classic struggle of the have's against the have-not's. The basis of their problem, they believed, was not overproduction of crops but an underproduction of money by the federal government. As debtors and avowed inflationists, they blamed the gold bugs and the railroads, among others, for many of their problems. Ironically, the Republican Party and its black followers, with whom they often fused in elections and enjoyed their greatest successes, represented ideologically the very people that they blamed as the root of their problems. A party of principle was reduced to practical politics in order to prevail. Their bold, idealistic simplifications overlooked the social and sentimental responses that often determine personal needs. Blacks as a largely landless tenant debtor class who aspired largely to greater wages for their *labor* conflicted at bottom with the small landowning white agrarians who wished more for the *products* they and their black tenant labor produced. Class-interest at bottom conflicted with self-interest, which the Alliance and Populists hoped to use to bring the two groups together to defeat their common enemies.

Because black and white agrarians faced similar economic obstacles, Tom Watson and others assumed that the races shared a common and self-interest and would unite under a single occupational and political banner. New Orleans dockworkers and Alabama coalminers had some success along these lines, but that success is attributable to a number of conditions, including the specificity of occupation and a visible identifiable enemy. Southern Populists spoke against the ruling elite, but in most cases the mass of black and poor white voters apparently did not see that general class as detrimental to their well-being. The black agricultural experience was also qualitatively different from that of poor whites despite surface similarities. Local factors of race and class were too different within the South as a whole for Populism's biracial experiment to succeed throughout the region. Consider the following scenario.

On a typical day in the South of the 1890s the lives of black and white Populists may have intersected, but never did they integrate. In matters most intimate to their lives—their faith, their entertainment, their schools, their work, their transportation, and increasingly their neighborhoods—they went their separate ways, or when coming together in political meetings, it was largely a matter of expediency and polite interactions and not as equals. This by no means denies the real and meaningful contact between some black and white Populists, such as the Reverend Walter Pattillo, the Reverend Seb Doyle, Tom Watson, and John Rayner, but these are the conspicuous exceptions rather than the rule in both the Southern Alliance Movement and the Populist Party. Black and white Populists sent their children to separate schools, worshiped separately, had largely supported different political parties, and only briefly interacted in their agrarian professions, largely as laborer and owner, but never as equals. Black and white Populists experienced the world differently, and offering "self-interest" as a common vehicle for political gain was a chasm too wide for the fledgling third party to cross.

While external pressures from the Bourbons and a conformist society severely dissipated the movement, the effort seemed destined from the start to fail because of internal differences too great to overcome. When combined with corruption, coercion, and ballot box stuffing, it is amazing that the movement represented such a formidable challenge to the region's rulers.

Intraracial black class prejudice was also overlooked almost completely by Populists. Although existing prior to emancipation, the black class structure was largely a postbellum phenomenon, initially chronicled by W. E. B. Du Bois and still largely channeled through a light-skinned leadership and the black church. Frederick Douglass also was acutely aware of the class-color problem within the black community. "While the rank and file of our race," he lamented, "quote the doctrine of human equality, they are often among the first to deny it in practice."[4] Within the black class structure, Southern middle-class urban blacks largely sought accommodationist rather than political routes to success, whereas poorer rural blacks either remained loyal to the Republican Party, forsook politics altogether, or flirted with third-party movements. Furthermore, the shared misery that Populism hoped to use to reconcile poor blacks and whites was often muted by an equally passionate racial hatred. In both the abstract and in person the enmity that existed between the poor of both races was captured in a song known to blacks throughout the South:

My name's Sam, I don't give a dam;
I'd rather be a nigger than a poor white man.[5]

Blacks, like whites, were not immune to the racist traditions that clustered around their historical experience. The economic deterioration and despair that the Alliance and Populist movements hoped to use to transcend racial lines did not, at bottom, dissipate long deep-seated racial attitudes among the masses of untutored grassroots blacks and whites. While the agrarian movement attracted distressed elements of both races, they maintained separate organizations in the Alliance and often separate clubs in the Populist movement. As they attempted to form biracial political combinations, they contained within them the seeds of their own destruction. The issues that would attract black support would, as a general rule, repel grassroots white supporters. For example, blacks wanted to serve on juries, supported anti-lynching legislation, and supported such federal legislation as the Blair Bill and the Lodge "Force" Bill—all issues that whites, including the agrarians, generally opposed. Although the pattern was not always sharply delineated, grassroots blacks also seemed more resistant to fusion efforts between Republicans and Populists. In turn, some poor whites had reservations about fusing with Republicans, who were characterized as "the nigger party." These divisions of support and differences in attitude made the Populist biracial effort even more difficult to maintain and sustain. Goodwyn asserts that it was not the "corporate monopolies" and the "money power" that worried blacks, but the "whiteness" of the ravages of these monopolies. Race and condition were more of a repellent than the desire to coalesce against a common external enemy. Blacks were fearful of whites and their power, and so they approached politics from a more cautious perspective than whites, because winning elections would not necessarily mean liberation for them, but losing elections could have devastating results.[6] Chafe points out that blacks and whites came to Populism for different reasons: whites for economic reasons ("corporate monopolies") and blacks seeking protection from prejudice and violence.[7] The whites involved in these biracial combinations were largely of the upland yeoman rural mountain, piney woods, "wool hat boys" variety, whose racial antagonisms toward blacks as a whole dated back to the antebellum period. The economic misery that the Populist leadership, with its sense of *noblesse oblige,* hoped to use to transcend racial feelings was always shrouded with uncertainty. If the anxieties created by these historical sentiments and differences over issues were not enough, the Bourbons' calls for racial solidarity and invectives of "nigger lover" reinvigorated and aroused their racial antipathies and shook their confidence about their biracial coalition. And blacks who sought to defect to this biracial coalition also had reasons to be apprehensive about their allies, and with group peer pressures of their own were equally as reluctant to leave the Republican Party, the psychological home of the black masses, as the whites were to leave the Democratic Party.

The hesitation that the grassroots members had was not as prominent in the more sophisticated and educated leadership who recognized that "self-interest" required them to steer a middle ground to achieve political solutions, black men's votes often being the balance of power in state and local elections. But the Bourbons resorted to massive fraud on a scale not seen since Reconstruction. It was the use and manipulation of the black vote that prompted many Southerners, including some white Populists, to seek to remove blacks as a political force in Southern politics. With this political liability removed, the South's characteristic vice of racial adversity easily undercut any sort of colorblind agrarian egalitarianism promoted by the leadership, based on class and occupation rather than color. And again, at its source, race oftentimes determined economic condition. Despite idealistic allegations that "they are in the ditch just like we are," it cannot be overemphasized that blacks were largely a landless laboring class seeking better wages for their *labor* while white agrarians were often a small landowning class seeking more benefit for the *products* of their labor. The benefit of one group came at the expense of the other. Individual and racial self-interests were not the same interests that the group movement espoused.

In its appeal to both poor blacks and whites, Southern Populism provided a common class and political denominator around which those who felt ignored and bypassed could gather. The mass of blacks who supported Populism were the landless rural poor. The arrogant elitism of the emerging black middle class, largely concentrated in the rising urban areas, generally precluded them from supporting a party of the earthy common man. Du Bois, speaking of Populism, denied that "the conclusions of ages of conscientious research are to be cast away in a moment just because some long beard from the wild woolly west wants to shirk paying his just debts."[8] To Du Bois, "The Populists as a third-party movement beginning during this time [the 1890s] did not impress me."[9] Frederick Douglass likewise expressed little enthusiasm for Populism and for the most part, entirely ignored the movement.[10] "A Republican to the death," his biographer has written of Douglass, "he was aware of the Party's defection from commitments to black Americans, but blind to the energy of the Populist Movement that some courageous hopeful blacks risked entering in the belief that their joint actions with whites caught as they were in poverty could lead to basic economic change."[11] Booker T. Washington also did not support the Populist movement. It is hardly surprising, therefore, that Populism attracted so few black leaders in the South. Indeed, Southern Populism attracted no major black leaders, although devotees such as Rayner, Doyle, Pattillo, Charles A. Roxborough, and L. D. Laurent tried to win over the black masses. Further, most of them were initially Republicans, and later returned to the party, despite the party's increasing abandonment of blacks. Republicans of the period, their own party in decline, were often responsive to fusion maneuvers, seeing them as their only way to defeat the Democrats. Black antipathy toward Populism was further reinforced by strong black loyalty in particular to *national* Republican candidates. At the same time, more and more local black middle-class urban leaders openly supported intrastate Bourbon Democratic candidates to promote local sources of strength and pecuniary benefits, along with stable race relations—a role the Populists were particularly ill equipped to handle. The "better class of blacks" were increasingly looking to "the better class of white people," rather than politics, for solace. And "the better class of white people" were often Democratic and increasingly businessmen.

In practice, Populist racial attitudes showed two distinct strains: economic and political reform and social inequality. Promoting "social equality" was a charge leveled constantly against the Alliance and Populist movements and one they vehemently denied; but their denial was no less a defense than it was probably a true reflection of their inner feelings about blacks. It is often overlooked that blacks of that era also embraced separation in certain cases, seeking their own segregated organizations as avenues of racial pride, confidentiality of action, and social comfort. The Colored Farmers' Alliance, for example, "positively prohibited" the admission of whites to membership. The two attitudes often overlapped, and any crossing of racial lines to bring about a class coalition based on occupation and self-interest created a feeling of ambivalence, a confusion about patterns of race relations that were still in flux. For example, black and white agrarians would commonly meet together, but when food was served blacks would eat by themselves. This ambivalence was further strained by the outcry of the conservatives alleging "social equality" and "Negro rule" against the agrarian coalition. On one hand, Southern white Populism promoted intellectually a class coalition with the agrarian and labor producer class, including blacks. Socially, Southern white Populists believed in an inequality of status between the races, with moral and intellectual capabilities at its center. Blacks were viewed as a race evolving toward maturity, and full political equality and leadership was a role for which they were currently ill equipped to assume, although they could participate. But by the 1890s a growing number of Southerners questioned openly if blacks were "ready" as a people to exercise the ballot. The black masses had emerged from slavery with a lack of skills and education and a tradition lacking independence of action or civic spirit. By the turn of the century, approximately 65 percent of the Southern black population was still illiterate, compared to 16 percent of the white population. An illiterate people not armed with either knowledge, tradition, or resources are highly vulnerable to manipulation by persons of either race. And blacks were manipulated. As such, their ballot was all too often viewed by whites, and sometimes treated by blacks, as an immediate gratification rather than as a means of long-term fulfillment of the democratic promise which Populists advocated. As a result, the concept of universal suffrage was also under attack.

Thus, blacks were not totally blameless in this disfranchising process. Certainly they were vulnerable to coercion and fraud, but many black leaders bought, sold, and directed black votes based not so much on principle but profit and self-interest. Black failure to respond to Populist appeals was largely the result of corruption, coercion, and fraud by both races; but when the black vote was unrestrained, African Americans remained unusually loyal to the Republican Party, often opposing fusion with the Populists. Perhaps they mistrusted the Populists or feared the consequences of the party's failure, but the blind loyalty of the majority of the Southern black masses to the Republican Party resulted in a largely disfranchised black proletariat at the beginning of the new century.

Did the failure of blacks to adequately respond to Populist appeals in fact influence or accelerate the direction the forces of reaction took, within the generally restrictive limits set by the political structure? Clearly black racial and political chauvinism had acted to diminish Southern Populist reform and accelerated a reaction in the form of disfranchisement disguised as ballot reform and "purification of the process." Consider the comments of Democratic representative and later governor Allen D. Candler of Georgia. The ballot, he noted, had been "thrust" upon the black "when he was utterly and totally unprepared for it. He regarded it as a bauble, a plaything, an article of merchandise. He regards election day as a public holiday. He goes to the polls as he goes to the circus or a public execution—as a frolic."[12] This viewpoint gained popularity as the South searched for a solution to blacks' role in politics. Populism only accelerated this search. To their credit, Populist leadership believed that black political participation—not political equality—with "competency" and character as criteria should be tolerated in Southern politics. Blacks were evolving in political maturity as a race, Populists believed, but as respectable citizens they were entitled to vote. Gunner Myrdal noted of this and later eras that white Southerners generally agreed "in principle" that blacks had a right to vote under national ideals sanctioned by the Constitution and the "American Creed." But the illegal practices against the black franchise had what he calls "the sanction of tradition" behind them.[13] The irony of the situation was that black disenfranchisement was now viewed as necessary to prevent corruption—it was not a reaction to, but a necessary reform of the political system. Populists had sought specific election reforms ("a free ballot and a fair count") in their platforms, incorporating blacks, to improve the living conditions of both groups. But as Henry W. Grady, the New South visionary, pointed out, it was not the black man who was the contaminant in the mix but "the baseness of white politicians" who might use the black vote for "nefarious purposes."[14] Disenfranchisement then was viewed as both a necessity and a political reform to purify the election process.

The second strain in Populist racial attitudes, involving pragmatic political relationships, contained many contradictions and complexities depending upon both the state and the individuals involved. However, the more educated and visionary white Populist leaders recognized the necessity of some concessions to blacks in order to enhance their own political role and provided limited political participation to accommodate a racial coalition. The purported catalyst was "self-interest," which would cut across racial lines and bring about a class defense calculated to better one's group and personal status and economic condition. In other words, white Populists, in challenging the South's political traditions, were forced to imagine an alternate line of racial development that to them, whether ethically, politically, or economically, seemed more realistic. In the early 1890s blacks still constituted the balance of power at best and a potent voting bloc at worst in a number of Southern states. To an emerging party that needed voters of all parties and colors, the appeal to blacks was both ideologically pure and a practical necessity. With the failure of the movement, many white Populists such as Tom Watson advocated traditional racist mores and criticized the values they sought earlier to implement. Thus, a reform movement either conspired, acquiesced, or deferred with the forces of reaction to help disenfranchise blacks by the turn of the century, depending on the location and the individuals involved. But as a rule, white Populists viewed with trepidation the understanding and character clauses and literacy tests that the Democratic Party had proposed to reform the voting process, fearing that such tools in the hands of their old Bourbon enemies would be used to disenfranchise undesirable whites as well as blacks from the voting lists. Furthermore, such activities were viewed as contrary to the Jeffersonian principles of American democracy.

At the outset of the Southern Populist revolt, the Populists put major stress on *economic* reform brought about through changes at the ballot box. It soon became apparent, however, that *political* reform and purification of the election process would be necessary before economic reform could be achieved. The result was a shift in priorities by Southern Populists advocating "a free ballot and a fair count" as the first necessity to achieve economic reform. The emerging Populist movement energized black voter turnout, with a 70–80 percent voting rate not uncommon in hotly debated elections involving the three parties. With the sharp increase in black participation in politics, Bourbon anxiety resulted in a turn to massive fraud, coercion, and corruption to maintain and perpetuate their victories. All of this was troubling (and expensive) and distressing to those who wanted to bring about a purification of the ballot. As the Southern Populist movement progressed, the principle of ballot reform received wider audience and was promoted to a position of at least equal importance with economics in most states of the South by 1894. Indeed, one of the distinctions between Western and Southern Populism was the latter's greater emphasis at the state and local level on political reform and the elimination of fraud as necessary to achieve their ends. As a result, a few Populists came to regard blacks as purchasable, corruptible tools of the "money power" rather than as class allies and subsequently regarded elimination of their vote as a reform. "Purchasable [black] votes mean that the dollar and not the man is to rule," a Loui-

siana agrarian organ concluded, "and we think a law should be made disfranchising all who sell or buy votes."[15] Far from being inconsistent with
their principles, these Populists viewed this strategy as a natural realignment
of moral and class interests, one to which the region must accommodate
itself if the political structure was to be consistent with the high-minded
Populistic principles of Jefferson and Jackson. However, it should be emphasized that most white Populists looked askance at methods to eliminate voters. While emphasizing "competency" and character as determinants for
voter participation, they feared the elimination of their own votes by the
Bourbons in the process, leaving them even more vulnerable to the whims
of the entrenched Bourbon aristocracy.

The challenge venality presented to the ideology of Southern Populism
created a major psychic crisis that was felt on all levels. In fact, the association of venality with political rewards threatened to turn the moralistic
political standards of Populism upside down. Every major Southern election
examined during this period was symptomatic of the breakdown of political standards in Southern politics. The corrupt "Harrison County methods"
employed statewide in Texas, elections in Georgia where the combined vote
exceeded the population, and the 1892 and 1894 elections in Alabama show
how flagrant voter fraud had penetrated the election process.[16] These corrupt features of the political system had troubling implications for Democracy. For a reform party that promoted virtue and honesty as necessary for
success, these acts were more than troubling, and Populist literature spoke of
a cataclysm in the system. Unable to muster a defense against fraud, Populists became cynical about the linkage of virtue and political success. They
deplored the widespread corruption of the vote through pressure and pecuniary rewards but in turn could not recover from the Democratic use of the
racial issue and the corruption of the election process. One must remember
that the promotion of Populism took on the passion and urgency of a principled crusade by its idealistic adherents. Populists saw themselves as active
political combatants in the struggle for human dignity, fighting to preserve
moral agrarian traditions that they believed were being undermined by the
Democrats and the money power. They were convinced that right would
prevail over wrong and virtue would lead to success, which was not happening. Such idealism and moral indignation, once blunted, often harbors
an equal or stronger impetus for reaction, and so it was with Southern
Populism.

Populists such as Joseph P. Manning of Alabama endured the bitterness
and brutal campaigning to the end of their days with courage and determination. Others such as Georgia's Tom Watson became embittered and obsessed with race hatred. The contrast in Watson's case was sharp. There was

a time in Watson's early Populist career when blacks would crowd about him, touch his garments with reverence, and go home and tell their families, "I seen him today. I seen him and heard him talk and touched his clothes." Yet in his later years his bitterness toward blacks bordered on the pathological. Still others, such as Reverend Sam Small of Georgia and James "Cyclone" Davis of Texas, were always outspoken white supremacists and remained such until the end of their days.

Both blacks and whites supplied reasons for some of the prejudices that enslaved Populism. The white native Southerners' triumph over Reconstruction was known as Redemption, and leaders of the fight were known as Redeemers. Christianity was used as in the Old South to promulgate the idea that blacks were the Children of Ham, children of darkness. The white Redeemers, which included the upland yeoman "wool hat boys," having early encouraged dishonest election procedures to redeem the political system, now found themselves obliged to continue with the worst products of it against the poor agrarian whites in order to survive politically. The injustices and evils of the system, so plainly seen and condemned by the Populists, affected attitudes toward blacks because of the central role blacks played in the system and the process. Consider the brazen theft in Richmond County, Georgia, where Tom Watson was counted out. "I remember," one inhabitant of the area recalled years later, "seeing the wagonloads of Negroes brought into the wagon yards, the equivalent of our parking lots, the night before the election. There was whisky there for them, and all night many drank, sang and fought. But the next morning they were herded to the polls and openly paid in cash, a dollar bill for each man as he handed in his ballot."[17] Reform-minded Populists who had befriended blacks and demanded that honest elections be honored were understandably affronted by such actions. Populist conclusions were not, of course, exact or even perhaps entirely rational; the truth was more complex and multifaceted than the black's outward appearance of accepting such corrupt practices. Yet, such sights deeply affected the white Populist reform conscience and produced a racial bitterness that some saw as retribution and others as ironic.

Against this regional backdrop of concern over morals and materialism, Southern Populism helped bring forth a consciousness of one of the region's most pregnant dictums, the separate-but-equal philosophy of Booker T. Washington. No one prior to Washington's Atlanta Exposition speech in September 1895 had been able to articulate this dimension of the Southern race system very precisely, and Southern Populism was no exception. Southerners seized upon Washington's philosophy and inverted it with far-reaching implications. Yet Washington had merely reinforced the doctrine that Southern Populists had been proposing all along—minus Populist willingness to grant, out of necessity, black political participation. According to Tom Watson, Washington's plea for vocational education, economic progress, and political accommodation represented "the same opinions as to the Negro question which we were handed down for uttering in 1892."[18] Watson regarded the Tuskegee philosophy of thrift, industry, and encouraging blacks to "cast down your bucket" in the South "as mighty sound doctrine."[19] An Alabama Populist paper likewise endorsed Washington's idea of maintaining a separate "social character" but working together on matters of "material welfare." This was, the Populists agreed, "a solution [to] the race issue." The organ further contended that "the Populists are simply making a practical application of this sentiment."[20] Washington's philosophy of black vocational education largely reflected also what both Populists and non–Populists believed it ought to be. "Make Booker T. Washington manager of negro schools and give him a long tether," an Alabama agrarian suggested. "He would revolutionize our ideas."[21] Southern Populism, then, was a link that connected the ascetic virtues of the Protestant ethic and most political reform with the Washingtonian belief in social separation of the races. This continuity may be likened to a single thread that stretched across the whole of the Southern Populist biracial experience.

It is one of the ironies of Southern history that the solution to the region's race problem was proposed by a black rather than a white man, and that both races accepted this solution, rather than the Populist proposals. Populism had offered related proposals for dealing with the black populace's role in Southern society, but Washington's proved more acceptable by not taking the political route to reform. Already at a tactical disadvantage, both groups were fated to forfeit their ideals to the point where further compromise meant surrender. Unfortunately, the swelling forces of fraud, corruption, and racism ultimately rendered both philosophies impotent.

Appendixes

TABLE I
Pearsonian Coefficients of Correlation between
Pairs of Selected Variables

	Virginia		North Carolina		South Carolina		Georgia		Florida		Alabama	
	% for Harrison	% for Weaver	% for Harrison	% for Weaver	% for Harrison	% for Weaver	% for Harrison	% for Weaver	% for Harrison	% for Weaver	% for Harrison	% for Weaver
A. % for Harrison (GOP) - 1888 Presidential Election	*	.10	*	-48	*	.10	*	-41	*	.29	*	.13
B. % for Weaver (Pop.) - 1892 Presidential Election	-18	*	-36	*	-18	*	-37	*	-25	*	.07	*
C. % of Population Blacks	42	-66	20	-37	-42	-66	.07	-08	34	-31	-29	.13
D. % of Population in Towns of 2,500 or More	.00	-27	20	-09	.00	-27	.14	-28	50	-35	.02	.13
E. % of Farms Operated by Owners	66	.01	-13	-29	66	.01	.18	-22	.06	30	.25	-26
F. Value of Farmland Per Acre	-31	.17	10	-19	-31	.17	-03	.06	-02	-17	.09	.20

* Not on ballot.

TABLE I (continued)

	Mississippi		Louisiana		Arkansas		Texas		Tennessee	
	% for Harrison	% for Weaver	% for Harrison	% for Weaver	% for Harrison	% for Weaver	% for Harrison	% for Weaver	% for Harrison	% for Weaver
A. % for Harrison (GOP) - 1888 Presidential Election	*	-.20	*		*	-.34	*	-.34	*	-.61
B. % for Weaver (Pop.) - 1892 Presidential Election	-.32	*			-.41	*	.38	*	-.58	*
C. % of Population Blacks	.39	-.47	.09		.73	-.23	.59	-.06	-.32	.30
D. % of Population in Towns of 2,500 or More	.09	-.31	.08		.22	-.01	.14	-.20	-.01	-.10
E. % of Farms Operated by Owners	-.33	.27	.19		-.64	.25	-.10	-.13	.24	-.23
F. Value of Farmland Per Acre	.50	-.40	.39		.56	-.25	.08	.03	-.13	.06

*Not on ballot.

TABLE II

Pearsonian Coefficients of Correlation between Selected
Variables and Populist Gubernatorial Elections (by county)

	Virginia		North Carolina		South Carolina*
	% for Cocke (Pop.) - 1893 Gubernatorial Election	% for Cocke (Pop.) - 1897 Lieutenant Gubernatorial Election	% for Exum (Pop.) - 1892 Gubernatorial Election	% for Guthrie (Pop.) - 1896 Gubernatorial Election	
A. % for Harrison (GOP) - 1888 Presidential Election	.42	-.03	-.30	-.54	
B. % for Weaver (Pop.) - 1892 Presidential Election	.46	.29	.93	.81	
C. % of Population Blacks	-.26	-.32	.59	.56	
D. % of Population in Towns of 2,500 or More	-.35	-.23	-.02	-.02	
E. % of Farms Operated by Owners	.47	.02	-.07	-.09	
F. Value of Farmland Per Acre	.25	-.39	-.33	-.29	

*Not on ballot.

TABLE II (*continued*)

	Louisiana		Arkansas	
	% for Tannehill Gubernatorial Election (Pop.) - 1892	% for Pharr Gubernatorial Election (Pop.) - 1896	% for Baker Gubernatorial Election (Pop.) - 1894	% for Morgan Gubernatorial Election (Pop.) - 1898
A. % for Harrison (GOP) - 1888 Presidential Election	-30	.06	-55	-47
B. % for Weaver (Pop.) - 1892 Presidential Election	*	*	.78	.73
C. % of Population Blacks	-21	-08	-04	.02
D. % of Population in Towns of 2,500 or More	-32	-28	-04	-10
E. % of Farms Operated by Owners	.29	-09	.10	.14
F. Value of Farmland Per Acre	-33	-34	-11	-19

*Not on ballot.

TABLE II (*continued*)

	Georgia	Florida	Alabama		Mississippi
	% for Hines Gubernatorial (Pop.) - 1894 Election	% for Weeks Gubernatorial (Pop.) - 1896 Election	% for Kolb Gubernatorial (Pop.) - 1894 Election	% for Goodwin Gubernatorial (Pop.) - 1896 Election	% for Burkitt Gubernatorial (Pop.) - 1895 Election
A. % for Harrison (GOP) - 1888 Presidential Election	-03	-33	-11	.06	-42
B. % for Weaver (Pop.) - 1892 Presidential Election	-70	.70	.19	.02	-16
C. % of Population Blacks	.11	-06	.20	-23	-39
D. % of Population in Towns of 2,500 or More	.22	-28	.02	-23	-43
E. % of Farms Operated by Owners	-40	.59	-13	.08	.02
F. Value of Farmland Per Acre	-01	-48	.05	-14	.02

¹Not on ballot.

TABLE II (continued)

	Texas	Tennessee	
	% for Nugent Gubernatorial (Pop.) - 1892 Election	% for Buchanan Gubernatorial (Pop.) - 1892 Election	% for Mims Lieutenant Gubernatorial (Pop.) - 1894 Election
A. % for Harrison (GOP) - 1888 Presidential Election	-42	-68	-63
B. % for Weaver (Pop.) - 1892 Presidential Election	.94	.94	.89
C. % of Population Blacks	.13	.44	.47
D. % of Population in Towns of 2,500 or More	-21	-04	.04
E. % of Farms Operated by Owners	-22	-21	-16
F. Value of Farmland Per Acre	.07	.17	.25

Not on ballot.

TABLE III
Pearsonian Coefficients of Correlation between Pairs of Selected Variables for Virginia (by county)

	A	B	C	D	E	F	G	H
A. % for Weaver (GOP) - 1888 Presidential Election	*	.05	.39	.06	-.14	-.05	.22	-.20
B. % for Weaver (Pop.) - 1892 Presidential Election	.07	*	.31	.30	-.38	-.35	.24	-.33
C. % for Cocke (Pop.) - 1893 Gubernatorial Election	.42	.46	*	.35	-.26	.35	.47	.25
D. % for Cocke (Pop.) - 1897 Lieutenant Gubernatorial Election	-.03	.29	.32	*	-.32	-.23	.02	-.39
E. % of Population Blacks	.47	.12	.29	-.02	*	.37	-.42	.17
F. % of Population in Towns of 2,500 or More	-.18	-.38	-.43	-.25	-.09	*	-.50	.07
G. % of Farms Operated by Owners	.05	-.06	.25	.04	-.30	-.35	*	.07
H. Value of Farmland Per Acre	-.06	-.41	-.46	-.26	-.21	.23	.20	*

N = 118 counties in the state, 62 with less than 40 percent black population.

*Not on ballot

TABLE IV

Pearsonian Coefficients of Correlation between Pairs of Selected
Variables for North Carolina (by county)

	A	B	C	D	E	F	G	H
A. % for Harrison (GOP) - 1888 Presidential Election	*	-41	-46	-58	-19	-01	.03	.12
B. % for Weaver (Pop.) - 1892 Presidential Election	-36	*	.98	.88	.60	.01	-13	-29
C. % for Exum (Pop.) - 1892 Gubernatorial Election	-30	.93	*	.88	.59	-02	-07	-33
D. % for Guthrie (Pop.) - 1896 Gubernatorial Election	-54	.81	.78	*	.56	-02	-09	-29
E. % of Population Blacks	.20	-37	.40	.28	*	.24	-34	-05
F. % of Population in Towns of 2,500 or More	.20	-09	-10	-11	.25	*	-16	.47
G. % of Farms Operated by Owners	-13	-29	-23	-10	-56	-10	*	.17
H. Value of Farmland Per Acre	.10	-19	-18	-21	-05	.40	-18	*

N = 97 counties in the state, 61 with less than 40 percent black population.
*Not on ballot

TABLE V
Pearsonian Coefficients of Correlation between Pairs of Selected
Variables for South Carolina (by county)

	A	B	C	D	E	F	G
A. % for Harrison (GOP) - 1888 Presidential Election	*	.10	-85	-66	.01	.28	-19
B. % for Weaver (Pop.) - 1892	-18	*	.41	-84	-60	-18	-13
C. % for Tillman (Pop.) - 1890 Gubernatorial Election	-74	.31	*	.30	.15	-FV	.46
D. % of Population Blacks	.42	-66	-49	*	.32	.05	.00
E. % of Population in Towns of 2,500 or More	.00	-27	-18	.09	*	-59	.78
F. % of Farms Operated by Owners	.66	.01	-45	-02	-20	*	-75
G. Value of Farmland Per Acre	-31	.17	.32	-20	.34	-52	*

N = 45 counties in the state, 9 with less than 40 percent black population.
*Not on ballot.

TABLE VI

Pearsonian Coefficients of Correlation between Pairs of Selected Variables for Georgia (by county)

	A	B	C	D	E	F	G
A. % for Harrison (GOP) - 1888 Presidential Election	*	-41	-06	-21	-26	.19	-04
B. % for Weaver (Pop.) - 1892 Presidential Election	-37	*	.74	.10	.22	-51	.14
C. % for Hines (Pop.) - 1894 Gubernatorial Election	-03	.70	*	-11	-22	-40	-01
D. % of Population Blacks	.07	-08	-15	*	.32	-18	.11
E. % of Population in Towns of 2,500 or More	.14	-28	-32	.12	*	-06	.24
F. % of Farms Operated by Owners	.18	-22	-17	.53	-02	*	-36
G. Value of Farmland Per Acre	-03	.06	-04	-06	.25	-20	*

N = 137 counties in the state, 55 with less than 40 percent black population.

*Not on ballot.

TABLE VII

Pearsonian Coefficients of Correlation between Pairs of Selected Variables for Florida (by county)

	A	B	C	D	E	F	G
A. % for Harrison (GOP) - 1888 Presidential Election	*	.29	.34	.55	.36	-.19	.10
B. % for Weaver (Pop.) - 1892 Presidential Election	-.25	*	.76	-.07	-.30	.27	-.39
C. % for Weeks (Pop.) - 1896 Gubernatorial Election	-.33	.70	*	-.06	-.28	.59	-.48
D. % of Population Blacks	.34	-.31	-.30	*	.23	-.01	-.36
E. % of Population in Towns of 2,500 or More	.50	-.35	-.29	.19	*	-.28	.03
F. % of Farms Operated by Owners	.06	.30	.38	-.57	.02	*	-.25
G. Value of Farmland Per Acre	-.02	.17	-.29	-.43	-.00	.10	*

N = 45 counties in the state, 26 with less than 40 percent black population.

*Not on ballot.

TABLE VIII

Pearsonian Coefficients of Correlation between Pairs of Selected Variables for Alabama (by county)

	A	B	C	D	E	F	G	H	I
A. % for Harrison (GOP) - 1888 Presidential Election	*	.13	.22	-.29	-.19	-.18	-.19	-.03	.22
B. % for Weaver (Pop.) - 1892 Presidential Election	.07	*	.10	.19	.09	.18	-.06	-.21	.03
C. % for Kolb (Pop.) - 1892 Presidential Election	.30	-.01	*	.10	.14	.16	-.36	-.24	.10
D. % for Kolb (Pop.) - 1894 Gubernatorial Election	-.11	-.19	-.07	*	.08	.20	.02	-.13	.05
E. % for Goodwyn (Pop.) - 1896 Gubernatorial Election	.06	.02	.20	-.00	*	-.23	-.23	-.08	-.14
F. % of Population Blacks	-.29	.13	-.59	-.00	-.33	*	.25	-.34	.52
G. % of Population in Towns of 2,500 or More	.02	.13	-.35	.30	-.15	.12	*	-.35	.52
H. % of Farms Operated by Owners	.25	-.26	.42	-.04	.22	-.75	-.02	*	.70
I. Value of Farmland Per Acre	.09	.20	-.34	-.03	-.15	.30	.62	-.45	*

N = 66 counties in the state, 34 counties with less than 40 percent black population.
*Not on ballot.

TABLE IX
Pearsonian Coefficients of Correlation between Pairs of Selected
Variables for Mississippi (by county)

	A	B	C	D	E	F	G
A. % for Harrison (GOP) - 1888 Presidential Election	*	-20	-49	.09	.23	.03	.14
B. % for Weaver (Pop.) - 1892 Presidential Election	-23	*	.76	.01	-46	-61	.33
C. % for Burkitt (Pop.) - 1895 Gubernatorial Election	-42	.85	*	-16	-39	-43	.02
D. % of Population Blacks	.39	-47	-62	*	.11	.07	.36
E. % of Population in Towns of 2,500 or More	.09	-31	-21	.11	*	.34	-00
F. % of Farms Operated by Owners	-33	.27	.48	-86	-04	*	-69
G. Value of Farmland Per Acre	.50	-40	-55	.73	.03	-73	*

N = 75 counties in the state, 26 counties with less than 40 percent black population.
*Not on ballot.

TABLE X

Pearsonian Coefficients of Correlation between Pairs of Selected Variables for Louisiana (by county)

	A	B	C	D	E	F	G	H
A. % for Harrison (GOP) - 1888 Presidential Election	*		-50	-27	.14	.52	.03	.58
B. % for Weaver (Pop.) - 1892 Presidential Election	*	*	*	*	*	*	*	*
C. % for Tannehill (Pop.) - 1892 Gubernatorial Election	-30	*	*	.56	-21	-32	.29	-33
D. % for Pharr (Pop.) - 1896 Gubernatorial Election	.06	*	.39	*	-08	-28	-09	-34
E. % of Population Blacks	.09	*	-47	-53	*	.10	-32	.14
F. % of Population in Towns of 2,500 or More	.08	*	-17	.00	-12	*	-15	.97
G. % of Farms Operated by Owners	.19	*	.33	.49	-82	.07	*	-19
H. Value of Farmland Per Acre	.39	*	-31	-05	-01	.73	.07	*

N = 59 parishes in the state, 15 with less than 40 percent black population.
*Not on ballot

TABLE XI
Pearsonian Coefficients of Correlation between Pairs of Selected
Variables for Arkansas (by county)

	A	B	C	D	E	F	G	H	I	J
A. % for Harrison (GOP) - 1888 Presidential Election	*	-.34	.33	.43	-.45	-.39	.28	.18	-.04	.12
B. % for Weaver (Pop.) - 1892 Presidential Election	-.41	*	.15	.12	.79	.73	.08	-.02	.94	-.11
C. % for Norwood (Union Labor) - 1888 Gubernatorial Election	.64	-.06	*	.88	.23	.20	.03	-.03	.01	-.14
D. % for Fizer (Union Labor) - 1890 Gubernatorial Election	.73	-.12	.88	*	.18	.12	.03	.10	-.01	.01
E. % for Barker (Pop.) - 1894 Gubernatorial Election	-.55	.78	-.11	-.17	*	.87	.04	-.04	.10	-.11
F. % for Morgan (Pop.) - 1898 Gubernatorial Election	-.47	.73	-.06	-.14	.87	*	.02	.10	.14	-.19
G. % of Population Blacks	.73	-.23	.46	.56	.40	-.34	*	-.02	-.13	-.15
H. % of Population in Towns of 2,500 or More	.22	-.01	.14	.06	-.04	-.10	.06	*	-.02	.36
I. % of Farms Operated by Owners	-.64	.25	-.42	-.55	.39	.37	-.73	-.07	*	-.57
J. Value of Farmland Per Acre	.56	-.25	.27	.40	-.34	-.31	.48	.27	-.76	*

N = 95 counties in the state, 52 counties with less than 40 percent black population.
*Not on ballot.

TABLE XII
Pearsonian Coefficients of Correlation between Pairs of Selected
Variables for Texas (by county)

	A	B	C	D	E	F	G	H	I
A. % for Harrison (GOP) - 1888 Presidential Election	*	-34	-63	-30	-38	.36	.18	.08	.04
B. % for Weaver (Pop.) - 1892 Presidential Election	-38	*	.27	.29	.94	.09	-20	-20	.07
C. % for Hogg (Prog.) - 1890 Gubernatorial Election	-75	.CB	*	.41	.35	-41	-41	.07	-06
D. % for Railroad Commission 1890	-35	.41	.43	*	.32	-22	-26	.09	-04
E. % for Nugent (Pop.) - 1892 Gubernatorial Election	.42	.94	.37	.33	*	.13	-21	-22	.07
F. % of Population Blacks	.59	-06	.59	-28	-03	*	.23	-41	.40
G. % of Population in Towns of 2,500 or More	.14	-20	-11	-23	-21	.18	*	-22	.40
H. % of Farms Operated by Owners	-10	-13	.09	.15	-15	-47	-22	*	-62
I Value of Farmland Per Acre	.08	.03	.09	-06	-03	.32	.38	-62	*

N = 227 counties in the state, 202 counties with less than 40 percent black population.
'Not on ballot.

TABLE XIII
Pearsonian Coefficients of Correlation between Pairs of Selected
Variables for Tennessee (by county)

	A	B	C	D	E	F	G	H	I
A. % for Harrison (GOP) - 1888 Presidential Election	*	-.61	-1.00	-.71	-.67	-.35	.03	.20	-.15
B. % for Weaver (Pop.) - 1892	-.58	*	.60	.94	.89	.36	-.11	-.22	.08
C. % for Taylor (Prog.) - 1888 Gubernatorial Election	-.99	.57	*	.70	.65	.33	-.03	-.09	.12
D. % for Buchanan (Prog.) - 1892 Gubernatorial Election	-.68	.94	.67	*	.92	.44	-.04	-.21	.17
E. % for Mims (Pop.) - 1894 Gubernatorial Election	-.63	.89	.62	.92	*	.47	.04	-.16	.25
F. % of Population Blacks	-.32	.30	.34	.35	.41	*	.36	-.36	.65
G. % of Population in Towns of 2,500 or More	-.01	-.10	.01	-.01	.04	.41	*	.03	.59
H. % of Farms Operated by Owners	.24	-.23	-.27	-.22	-.22	-.66	-.18	*	-.16
I. Value of Farmland Per Acre	-.13	.06	.10	.16	.23	.44	.56	-.14	*

N = 96 counties in the state, 87 counties with less than 40 percent black population.
*Not on ballot.

TABLE XIV

Voting and Black Population Characteristics for the North
Carolina Congressional Election of 1896*

	Total Vote	Populist Vote	Percentage Populist in Total Vote	Black Population	Percentage Blacks in Total Population
FIRST DISTRICT					
Beaufort	4,636	2,647	57.10	9,203	43.7
Camden	1,141	646	56.62	2,320	40.9
Carteret	2,231	1,094	49.04	2,297	21.2
Chowan	1,934	1,211	62.62	5,156	56.2
Currituck	1,387	620	44.70	2,016	29.9
Dare	877	473	53.93	406	10.8
Gates	1,904	1,046	54.94	4,713	46.0
Hertford	2,677	1,827	68.25	7,944	57.4
Hyde	1,864	993	53.27	3,941	44.3
Martin	3,034	1,608	53.00	7,383	48.5
Pamlico	1,491	990	66.40	2,379	33.3
Pasquotank	2,548	1,688	66.25	5,546	53.2
Perquimans	1,676	1,007	60.08	4,574	49.2
Pitt	5,593	3,133	56.02	12,327	48.3
Tyrrell	788	480	60.91	1,225	20.0
Washington	1,792	1,261	70.37	5,238	51.4
	35,573	*20,724*	*58.26*	*76,668*	*41.4***
SECOND DISTRICT					
Bertie	3,855	216	5.60	11,291	58.9
Edgecomb	4,886	370	7.57	15,599	64.7
Greene	2,217	202	9.11	4,758	47.4
Halifax	6,216	205	3.30	19,293	66.7
Lenoir	3,348	291	8.69	6,362	42.8
Northampton	4,203	144	3.43	12,018	56.6
Warren	3,336	61	1.83	13,480	69.6
Wayne	5,408	438	8.10	10,984	42.1
Wilson	3,979	811	20.38	7,760	41.6
	37,448	*2,738*	*7.31*	*101,545*	*41.2***

TABLE XIV (*continued*)

	Total Vote	Populist Vote	Percentage Populist in Total Vote	Black Population	Percentage Blacks in Total Population
THIRD DISTRICT					
Bladen	2,878	1,522	52.88	8,117	48.4
Craven	4,800	3,078	64.13	13,358	65.1
Cumberland	4,717	2,834	60.08	12,341	45.2
Duplin	3,581	2,043	57.05	7,087	37.9
Harnett	2,738	1,480	54.05	4,220	30.8
Jones	1,512	849	56.15	3,518	47.5
Moore	4,159	2,454	59.00	6,479	31.6
Onslow	2,178	1,011	46.42	2,911	28.3
Sampson	3,962	2,718	68.60	9,316	36.4
	30,525	*17,989*	*58.93*	*67,347*	*41.2***
FOURTH DISTRICT					
Chatham	4,221	2,525	59.82	8,199	32.3
Franklin	5,002	2,750	54.98	10,335	49.0
Johnston	5,284	2,172	41.11	7,322	26.9
Nash	4,505	2,938	65.22	8,521	41.2
Randolph	5,215	2,939	56.36	3,347	13.3
Vance	3,079	2,033	66.03	11,143	63.4
Wake	10,076	5,620	55.78	23,109	47.0
	37,382	*20,977*	*56.12*	*71,976*	*33.8***
FIFTH DISTRICT					
Alamance	4,647	119	2.56	5,583	30.6
Caswell	3,065	6	.20	9,389	58.6
Durham	4,349	36	.83	7,329	40.6
Granville	4,447	155	3.49	12,360	50.5
Guilford	6,989	75	1.07	8,223	29.3
Orange	2,979	67	2.25	5,242	35.1
Rockingham	5,115	40	.78	10,164	40.1
Stokes	3,522	10	.28	2,813	16.4
	35,113	*508*	*1.45*	*61,103*	*37.6***

TABLE XIV (*continued*)

	Total Vote	Populist Vote	Percentage Populist in Total Vote	Black Population	Percentage Blacks in Total Population
SIXTH DISTRICT					
Anson	3,204	1,547	48.28	9,789	48.9
Brunswick	2,141	1,323	61.79	4,761	43.7
Columbus	3,169	1,752	55.29	6,052	33.9
Mecklenburg	8,700	4,378	50.32	19,526	45.8
New Hanover	5,427	3,217	59.28	13,935	58.0
Pender	2,436	1,363	55.95	6,546	52.3
Richmond	4,674	2,859	61.17	12,959	54.1
Robeson	5,777	3,622	62.70	14,672	46.6
Union	3,758	1,990	52.95	5,547	26.1
	39,286	*22,051*	*56.13*	*93,787*	*45.4***
SEVENTH DISTRICT					
Cabarrus	3,240	1,867	57.62	5,459	30.1
Catawba	3,647	1,949	53.44	2,616	14.0
Davidson	4,432	2,611	58.91	3,528	16.3
Davie	2,090	1,491	71.34	2,852	24.5
Iredell	4,889	2,430	49.70	5,939	23.3
Lincoln	2,398	1,292	53.88	2,558	20.3
Montgomery	2,311	1,453	62.87	2,257	20.1
Rowan	4,519	2,089	46.23	6,980	28.9
Stanly	1,842	855	46.42	1,507	12.4
Yadkin	2,590	1,632	63.01	1,368	9.9
	31,958	*17,669*	*55.29*	*35,064*	*19.9***

*United States Department of Commerce, *Bureau of Census, Black Population*, 1790-1915, 784-85; North Carolina Department of Archives and History, "*North Carolina Congressional Election Returns*, 1896." These figures were tabulated from a number of sources, including the official returns, as a part of the University of Michigan's Political Consortium project to gather and tabulate state election returns.

**All district totals of black population are expressed as arithmetic means.

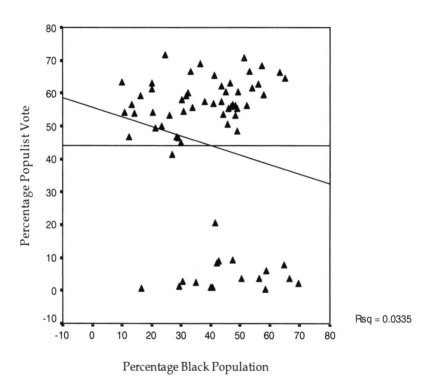

Figure 1.   Relationship between Black Density and Populism in the
           North Carolina Congressional Election of 1896.

TABLE XV
Voting and Black Population Characteristics for the
Alabama Congressional Election of 1896*

	Total Vote	Populist Vote	Percentage Populist in Total Vote	Black Population	Percentage Blacks in Total Population
THIRD DISTRICT					
Barbour	4,518	463	10.25	21,442	61.4
Bullock	2,681	16	.60	21,005	77.6
Coffee	1,619	872	53.86	1,933	15.9
Dale	2,532	1,157	45.70	3,358	19.5
Geneva	1,321	802	60.71	1,026	9.6
Henry	3,801	995	26.18	8,809	35.5
Lee	3,268	422	12.91	16,497	57.5
Russell	2,444	32	1.31	18,279	75.9
	22,184	4,759**	21.45	92,349	44.1***
FIFTH DISTRICT					
Autauga	1,648	399**	24.21	8,418	63.2
Chambers	3,119	1,050	33.66	13,858	52.7
Clay	1,894	895	47.25	1,704	10.8
Coosa	1,954	1,192	61.00	5,354	33.7
Elmore	3,250	1,965	60.46	10,288	47.3
Lowndes	3,679	272	7.39	26,985	85.5
Macon	1,337	268	20.04	14,188	76.9
Randolph	2,075	870	41.93	3,305	19.2
Tallapoosa	3,373	1,831	54.28	8,508	33.4
	22,329	8,742	39.15	92,608	49.1***
SEVENTH DISTRICT					
Cherokee	2,431	1,345	55.33	2,803	13.7
Cullman	1,738	710	40.85	38	0.3
Dekalb	2,949	305	10.34	1,204	5.7
Etowah	2,691	863	32.07	3,755	17.1
Franklin	1,591	531	33.38	1,160	10.9
Marshall	2,476	1,128	45.56	1,279	6.8
St. Clair	2,283	1,228	53.79	3,050	17.6
Winston	1,074	58	5.40	36	0.5
	17,233	6,168	35.79	13,325	9.0***

*Department of Commerce, *Bureau of Census, Black Population, 1790-1915* , 776; Secretary of State, *Official Returns* , 55th Congress, 1896 Congressional Election.

**Democrat affiliated with Populist.
***All district totals of black population are expressed as arithmetic means.

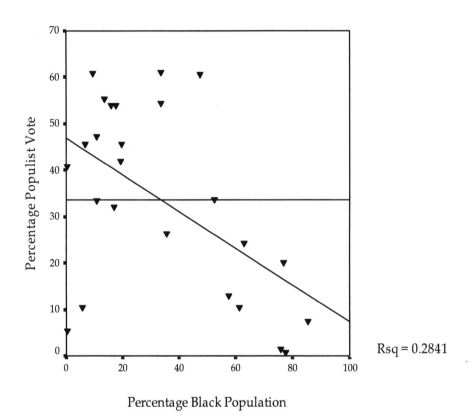

Rsq = 0.2841

Figure 2.   Relationship between Black Density and Populism in the
            Alabama Congressional Election of 1896.

TABLE XVI
Voting and Black Population Characteristics for the
Tennessee Congressional Election of 1896*

	Total Vote	Populist Vote	Percentage Populist in Total Vote	Black Population	Percentage Blacks in Total Population
THIRD DISTRICT					
Monroe	3,248	3	.09	1,247	8.10
Hamilton	8,109	43	.53	17,717	33.10
Warren	2,979	3	.10	2,011	14.00
Franklin	3,382	82	2.42	3,570	18.90
Meigs	1,371	2	.15	698	10.10
	19,089	*133*	*.70*	*25,243*	*12.8***
FIFTH DISTRICT					
Cannon	2,053	2	.10	952	9.4**
SIXTH DISTRICT					
Davidson	13,023	95	.73	41,315	38.2**
SEVENTH DISTRICT					
Williamson	4,465	411	9.20	10,084	38.3
Maury	6,580	385	5.85	15,910	41.7
Giles	6,327	372	5.88	12,320	35.2
Lawrence	2,517	7	.28	779	6.3
Wayne	2,243	42	1.87	884	7.7
Lewis	522	26	4.98	252	6.3
Hickman	2,523	219	8.68	2,744	18.9
Dickson	2,790	334	11.97	2,101	15.4
	27,967	*1,796*	*6.42*	*45,074*	*21.2***
EIGHT DISTRICT					
Henry	4,563	125	2.74	5,853	27.8
Benton	2,235	123	5.50	617	5.5
Perry	1,568	123	7.84	670	8.6
Decatur	1,881	12	.64	1,304	14.5
Hardin	3,506	5	.14	2,401	13.6
McNairy	2,975	69	2.32	1,881	12.1
Henderson	3,346	6	.18	2,365	14.5
Madison	4,716	323	6.85	14,669	48.1
Carroll	4,523	289	6.39	5,664	24.0
Chester	1,690	167	9.88	1,776	19.6
	31,003	*1,242*	*4.01*	*37,200*	*18.8***

TABLE XVI (*continued*)

	Total Vote	Populist Vote	Percentage Populist in Total Vote	Black Population	Percentage Blacks in Total Population
NINTH DISTRICT					
Weakley	5,895	2,199	37.30	4,520	15.6
Gibson	6,181	2,711	43.86	9,337	26.0
Grockett	2,561	933	36.43	4,186	27.6
Haywood	3,024	743	24.57	15,569	66.1
Lauderdale	3,012	1,094	36.32	7,810	41.6
Dyer	3,369	1,174	34.85	4,690	23.6
Obion	4,863	1,733	35.64	4,333	15.9
Lake	947	127	13.41	1,075	20.3
	29,852	*10,714*	*35.89*	*51,520*	*29.5***
TENTH DISTRICT					
Hardeman	3,700	156	4.22	8,787	41.8
Fayette	3,725	54	1.45	20,492	71.0
Shelby	10,430	225	2.16	61,612	54.7
Tipton	4,551	491	10.79	11,770	48.5
	22,406	*926*	*4.13*	*102,661*	*54.0***

*United States Department of Commerce, *Bureau of Census, Black Population, 1790-1915* , 787-88; *Tennessee Election Returns* , November 3, 1896.

**All district totals of black populations are expressed as arithmetic means.*

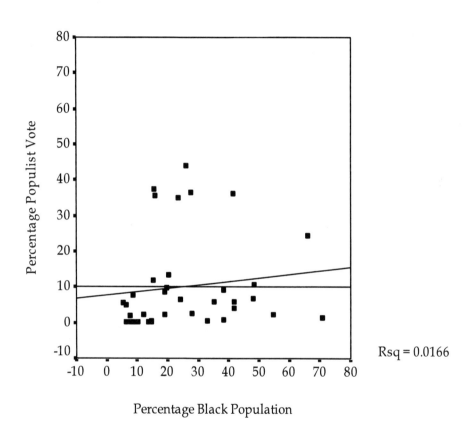

Rsq = 0.0166

Figure 3.   Relationship between Black Density and Populism in the Tennessee
Congressional Election of 1896.

TABLE XVII
*Voting and Black Population Characteristics for the
Mississippi Congressional Election of 1896**

	Total Vote	Populist Vote	Percentage Populist in Total Vote	Black Population	Percentage Blacks in Total Population
FIRST DISTRICT					
Alcorn					26.8
Itawanba					8.4
Lee					37.6
Lowndes					77.8
Monroe					63.0
Oktibbeha					67.4
Prentiss					20.8
Tishomingo					10.7
	8,398	742	8.83	67,450	39.6**
SECOND DISTRICT					
Benton					46.5
DeSota					71.2
LaFayette					43.1
Marshall					62.6
Panola					54.7
Tallahatchie					64.1
Tate					55.9
Tippah					22.6
Union					25.6
	9,884	1,472	14.89	91,917	50.8**
FOURTH DISTRICT					
Calhoun					23.2
Carroll					56.5
Chickasaw					57.3
Choctaw					24.3
Clay					69.8
Grenada					74.0
Kemper					56.0
Montgomery					48.5
Noxubee					82.8
Pontotoc					29.1
Webster					24.7
Yalobushago					53.8
	11,737	3,086	26.29	108,095	50.0**

TABLE XVII (*continued*)

	Total Vote	Populist Vote	Percentage Populist in Total Vote	Black Population	Percentage Blacks in Total Population
FIFTH DISTRICT					
Attala					42.5
Clarke					51.2
Holmes					77.1
Jasper					49.3
Lauderdale					49.3
Leake					33.9
Neshoba					19.5
Newton					37.0
Scott					39.3
Smith					16.1
Wayne					40.9
Yazoo					76.1
	13,051	*2,218*	*16.99*	*115,026*	*44.3***
SIXTH DISTRICT					
Adams					76.4
Amite					58.2
Covington					35.8
Greene					23.9
Hancock					30.2
Harrison					27.2
Jackson					30.5
Jones					15.0
Lawrence					49.3
Marion					31.5
Pearl-River					22.2
Perry					28.9
Pike					50.1
	10,477	*2,683*	*25.60*	*80,757*	*36.8***
SEVENTH DISTRICT					
Claiborne					75.6
Copiah					51.6
Franklin					47.3
Hinds					72.2
Jefferson					81.0
Lincoln					42.4
Madison					77.9

TABLE XVII (*continued*)

	Total Vote	Populist Vote	Percentage Populist in Total Vote	Black Population	Percentage Blacks in Total Population
SEVENTH DISTRICT					
Rankin					58.1
Simpson					38.6
	8,647	898	10.37	116,437	60.0**

*United States Department of Commerce, *Bureau of Census*, *Black Population*, *1790-1915*, 783-84; Office of the Mississippi Secretary of State, *Vote of Mississippi*. November 16, 1896. The vote of Mississippi during this period was expressed as a condensed statement of district totals.

**All district totals of black population are expressed as arithmetic means.*

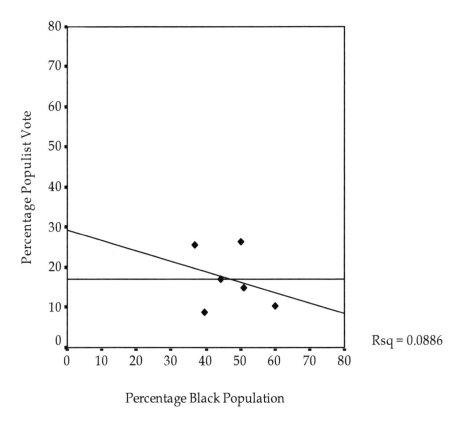

Figure 4. Relationship between Negro Density and Populism in the Mississippi Congressional Election of 1896.

TABLE XVIII
Voting and Black Population Characteristics for the
Georgia Congressional Election of 1896*

	Total Vote	Populist Vote	Percentage Populist in Total Vote	Black Population	Percentage Blacks in Total Population
FIRST DISTRICT					
Bryan	454	16	3.52	2,687	48.7
Bulloch	1,869	465	24.88	4,689	34.2
Burke	1,772	125	7.05	22,680	79.6
Chatham	4,859	253	5.21	34,757	60.2
Effingham	689	111	16.11	2,210	39.5
Emanuel	1,498	485	32.38	5,306	36.1
Liberty	1,204	219	18.19	8,673	67.3
McIntosh	789	2	.25	5,212	80.6
Screven	1,510	614	40.66	7,507	52.0
Tattnall	1,530	378	24.71	3,115	30.4
	16,174	2,668	16.50	96,836	52.9**
SECOND DISTRICT					
Baker	607	65	10.71	4,549	76.2
Berrien	955	196	20.52	2,417	22.6
Calhoun	772	51	6.61	6,199	73.5
Clay	907	179	19.74	4,815	61.6
Colquitt	667	259	38.83	477	9.9
Decatur	1,890	392	20.74	10,811	54.2
Dougherty	521	24	4.61	10,231	83.8
Early	1,174	372	31.69	6,122	62.5
Miller	484	159	32.85	1,574	36.8
Mitchell	848	234	27.59	6,106	56.0
Quitman	499	74	14.83	3,050	68.2
Randolph	1,157	177	15.30	9,473	62.0
Terrell	1,387	171	12.33	9,169	63.2
Thomas	1,453	284	19.55	17,450	57.5
Worth	1,181	398	33.70	8,412	31.0
	14,502	3,035	20.93	100,855	54.6**
THIRD DISTRICT					
Crawford	455	94	20.66	5,156	55.3
Dooly	1,402	458	32.67	8,914	49.1
Houston	1,067	186	17.43	16,341	75.6
Lee	451	161	35.70	7,642	83.5
Macon	871	283	32.49	9,181	63.3

TABLE XVIII (*continued*)

	Total Vote	Populist Vote	Percentage Populist in Total Vote	Black Population	Percentage Blacks in Total Population
THIRD DISTRICT					
(continued)					
Pulaski	927	172	18.55	10,001	60.4
Schley	630	223	35.40	3,205	58.9
Stewart	852	212	24.88	11,484	73.2
Sumter	1,503	390	25.95	15,098	68.3
Taylor	594	354	59.60	4,068	46.9
Twiggs	527	108	20.49	5,447	66.5
Webster	433	201	46.42	3,272	57.5
Wilcox	884	254	28.73	3,155	39.5
	6,350	*1,914*	*30.14*	*55,730*	*61.3***
SIXTH DISTRICT					
Baldwin	977	424	43.40	9,343	64.0
Bibb	2,626	665	25.32	23,336	55.1
Butts	1,002	412	41.12	5,398	51.1
Fayette	980	386	39.39	3,074	35.2
Henry	1,259	503	39.95	7,591	46.8
Jones	890	314	35.28	8,778	69.1
Monroe	1,342	546	40.69	12,516	65.4
Pike	1,766	755	42.75	8,077	49.6
Spalding	881	166	18.84	7,281	55.5
Upson	1,209	525	43.42	6,123	50.2
	12,932	*4,696*	*36.31*	*91,517*	*54.2***
SEVENTH DISTRICT					
Bartow	1,868	287	15.36	6,041	29.3
Catoosa	747	194	25.97	636	11.7
Chattooga	1,483	348	23.47	1,998	17.8
Cobb	2,285	412	18.03	6,774	30.4
Dade	513	105	20.47	1,093	19.2
Floyd	3,275	212	6.47	10,414	36.7
Gordon	1,426	314	22.02	1,727	13.5
Haralson	1,274	640	50.24	1,117	9.9
Murray	931	212	22.77	484	5.7
Paulding	1,654	800	48.37	1,505	12.6
Polk	1,477	477	32.30	4,654	31.1
Walker	1,689	168	9.95	1,932	14.5
Whitfield	1,440	217	15.07	1,930	14.9
	20,062	*4,386*	*21.86*	*40,305*	*19.0***

TABLE XVIII (*continued*)

	Total Vote	Populist Vote	Percentage Populist in Total Vote	Black Population	Percentage Blacks in Total Population
EIGHT DISTRICT					
Clarke	1,194	81	6.78	8,111	9.8
Elbert	1,659	181	10.91	7,884	51.3
Franklin	1,516	696	45.91	3,298	22.5
Greene	1,665	545	32.73	11,719	68.7
Hart	1,352	509	37.65	2,957	27.2
Jasper	785	55	7.01	8,487	61.1
Madison	884	118	13.35	3,662	33.2
Morgan	1,518	87	5.73	10,997	68.6
Oconee	917	316	34.46	3,832	49.7
Oglethorpe	1,426	104	7.29	11,264	66.5
Putnam	459	17	3.70	10,903	73.5
Welkes	1,384	253	18.28	12,464	48.4
	14,759	*2,962*	20.07	*95,578*	*48.4**
NINTH DISTRICT					
Banks	1,147	303	26.42	1,563	18.3
Cherokee	1,597	463	28.99	1,508	9.8
Dawson	634	58	9.15	259	4.6
Fannin	1,418	8	.56	112	1.3
Forsyth	840	231	27.50	1,288	11.5
Gilmer	1,214	17	1.40	69	0.8
Gwinnett	2,424	996	41.09	2,996	15.1
Habersham	1,093	76	6.95	1,589	13.7
Hall	1,886	331	17.55	2,767	15.3
Jackson	2,669	899	33.68	5,396	28.1
Lumpkin	904	41	4.54	414	6.0
Milton	735	246	33.47	672	10.8
Pickens	1,140	26	2.28	349	4.3
Rabun	509	7	1.38	166	3.0
Towns	642	5	.78	74	1.8
Union	1,010	72	7.13	165	2.1
White	523	147	28.11	662	10.8
	20,385	*3,926*	19.26	*20,049*	*9.3**
TENTH DISTRICT					
Columbia	884	619	70.02	8,038	71.3
Glascock	483	320	66.25	1,168	31.4
Hancock	1,153	203	17.61	12,410	72.4

TABLE XVIII (*continued*)

	Total Vote	Populist Vote	Percentage Populist in Total Vote	Black Population	Percentage Blacks in Total Population
TENTH DISTRICT					
(continued)					
Jefferson	1,733	1,008	58.17	10,763	62.5
Lincoln	853	634	74.33	3,673	59.8
McDuffie	822	667	81.14	5,522	62.8
Richmond	5,849	702	12.00	22,818	50.5
Taliaferro	685	472	68.91	4,827	66.2
Warren	1,009	747	74.03	6,756	61.7
Washington	2,565	1,202	46.86	14,925	59.1
Wilkinson	1,188	531	44.70	5,214	48.4
	14,704	*5,963*	40.55	*74,498*	*58.7***
ELEVENTH DISTRICT					
Appling	1,106	593	53.62	2,462	28.4
Brooks	846	125	14.78	7,637	54.6
Camden	412	123	29.85	4,137	67.0
Charlton	No returns listed for any party.				
Clinch	523	146	27.92	2,360	35.5
Coffee	1,333	810	60.77	3,858	36.8
Dodge	939	395	42.07	5,309	46.4
Echols	228	108	47.37	1,020	33.1
Glynn	1,008	162	16.07	7,741	57.7
Irwin	1,044	380	36.40	2,075	32.9
Johnson	592	287	48.48	1,456	23.8
Laurens	1,299	645	49.65	6,093	44.3
Lowndes	1,344	598	44.49	7,974	52.8
Montgomery	1,051	488	46.43	3,658	39.6
Pierce	672	250	37.20	1,983	31.1
Telfair	945	125	13.23	2,335	42.6
Wayne	946	511	54.02	2,195	29.3
Ware	900	262	29.11	3,619	41.1
	15,188	*6,008*	39.56	*65,912*	*41.0***

*United States Department of Commerce, *Bureau of Census, Black Population, 1790-1915*, 778-80; *Atlanta Constitution*, November 4, 1896; *Georgia Consolidated Election Returns*, 55th *Congress*, 1896.

**All district totals of black population are expressed as arithmetic means.*

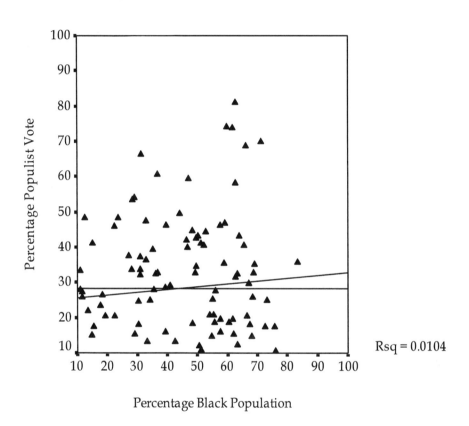

Rsq = 0.0104

Figure 5.   Relationship between Black Density and Populism in the Georgia
Congressional Election of 1896.

TABLE XIX
Voting and Black Population Characteristics for the
Texas Congressional Election of 1896*

	Total Vote	Populist Vote	Percentage Populist in Total Vote	Black Population	Percentage Blacks in Total Population
FIRST DISTRICT					
Chambers	521	92	17.66	757	33.8
Freestone	3,246	1,313	40.45	6,675	41.8
Grimes	4,587	2,392	52.15	11,664	54.7
Harris	11,850	5,033	42.47	13,522	36.3
Leon	3,067	1,508	49.17	5,377	38.8
Madison	1,716	847	49.36	2,070	24.3
Montgomery	2,779	1,209	43.50	5,488	46.6
Trinity	1,615	639	39.57	1,903	24.9
Walker	2,490	1,050	42.17	7,232	56.2
Waller	2,638	1,105	41.89	6,703	61.6
	34,509	*15,188*	*44.01*	*61,391*	*41.9+*
SECOND DISTRICT					
Anderson	4,769	796	16.69	9,502	45.4
Angelina	2,190	823	37.58	601	9.5
Cherokee	4,063	1,522	37.46	7,705	33.4
Hardin	908	122	13.44	967	24
Harrison	3,807	411	10.80	18,191	68.1
Houston	4,500	1,828	40.62	8,467	43.7
Jasper	1,133	428	37.78	2,378	42.5
Jefferson	2,035	184	9.04	2,218	37.9
Nacogdoches	3,829	1,943	50.74	4,257	26.6
Newton	946	204	21.56	1,558	33.5
Orange	1,263	62	4.91	829	17.4
Panola	2,840	598	21.06	9,204	44.3
Polk	2,453	841	34.28	3,837	37.1
Sabine	960	520	54.17	1,084	21.8
San Augustine	1,523	800	52.53	2,131	31.9
San Jacinto	1,670	167	10.00	4,328	58.8
Shelby	3,223	1,125	34.91	2,954	22.6
Tyler	2,062	448	21.73	2,392	22.0
	44,174	*12,822*	*29.03*	*82,603*	*34.5+*

TABLE XIX (*continued*)

	Total Vote	Populist Vote	Percentage Populist in Total Vote	Black Population	Percentage Blacks in Total Population
THIRD DISTRICT					
Greggs	1,865	540	28.95	5,349	56.9
Henderson	3,197	1,510	47.23	2,988	24.3
Hunt	8,344	3,074	36.84	2,953	9.3
Rains	1,058	604	57.09	415	10.6
Rockwall	1,517	380	25.05	216	3.6
Rusk	4,334	2,110	48.68	7,624	41.1
Smith	6,569	3,117	47.45	12,690	44.8
Upshur	2,737	1,245	45.49	3,929	30.9
Van Zandt	4,522	2,216	49.00	1,098	6.8
Wood	3,418	1,555	45.49	3,249	23.3
	37,561	16,351	43.53	40,511	25.2+
FOURTH DISTRICT					
Bowie	4,496	1,477	32.85	7,591	37.5
Camp	1,426	666	46.70	3,296	49.8
Cass	4,226	2,018	47.75	8,512	37.7
Delta	2,225	1,271	57.12	728	8.0
Franklin	1,421	508	35.75	819	12.6
Hopkins	4,496	2,183	48.55	2,838	13.8
Lamar	8,015	2,259	28.18	9,378	25.1
Marion	1,991	594	29.83	6,989	64.4
Morris	1,499	567	37.83	2,610	39.7
Red River	5,112	1,151	22.52	6,628	30.9
Titus	2,204	1,009	45.78	1,760	21.5
	37,111	13,703	36.92	51,149	31.0+
FIFTH DISTRICT					
Collin	9,610	2,353	24.48	2,525	6.9
Cooke	5,207	1,097	21.07	1,351	5.5
Denton	5,431	1,008	18.56	1,707	8.0
Grayson	11,517	2,839	24.65	6,712	12.6
Montague	4,959	1,753	35.35	87	0.5
	36,724	9,050	24.64	12,382	6.7+

TABLE XIX (*continued*)

	Total Vote	Populist Vote	Percentage Populist in Total Vote	Black Population	Percentage Blacks in Total Population
SIXTH DISTRICT					
Bosque	3,347	1,668	49.84	641	4.5
Dallas	15,780	7,151	45.32	11,177	16.7
Ellis	10,390	4,152	39.96	3,376	10.6
Hill	8,544	3,521	41.21	2,096	7.6
Johnson	6,316	2,816	44.59	852	3.8
Kaufman	5,776	2,160	37.40	3,176	14.7
Navarro	8,222	3,762	45.76	6,266	23.8
	58,375	*25,230*	*43.22*	*27,584*	*11.7+*
SEVENTH DISTRICT					
Bell	8,715	2,661	30.53	2,650	7.9
Brazos	3,855	351	9.11	8,433	50.6
Falls	6,672	798	11.96	7,961	38.4
Limestone	6,180	2,047	33.12	4,459	20.6
McLennan	12,014	1,780	14.82	10,381	26.5
Milan	7,040	1,997	28.37	6,220	25.1
	44,476	*9,634*	*21.66*	*40,104*	*28.2+*
EIGHTH DISTRICT					
Brown	2,816	1,371	48.69	73	0.6
Coleman	1,572	679	43.19	69	1.1
Comanche	2,782	1,493	53.67	8	0.1
Coryell	4,026	1,775	44.09	459	2.7
Erath	5,242	2,960	56.47	723	3.3
Hamilton	2,308	1,253	54.29	13	0.1
Hood	1,728	763	44.16	274	3.6
Lampasas	1,421	846	59.54	262	3.5
Mills	1,328	714	53.77	57	1.0
Parker	5,094	2,091	41.05	671	3.1
Runnels	723	327	45.23	31	1.0
Somervell	744	372	50.00	6	0.2
Tarrant	9,413	2,866	30.45	4,316	10.5
	39,197	*17,510*	*44.67*	*6,962*	*2.3+*

TABLE XIX (*continued*)

	Total Vote	Populist Vote	Percentage Populist in Total Vote	Black Population	Percentage Blacks in Total Population
NINTH DISTRICT					
Bastrop	4,677	1,300	27.80	8,898	42.9
Burleson	3,261	358	10.98	5,727	44.1
Burnet	2,033	834	41.02	307	2.9
Caldwell	3,406	1,009	29.62	4,878	30.9
hays	2,534	392	15.47	2,171	19.1
Lee	2,561	472	18.43	3,102	26.0
Travis	8,207	676	8.24	10,090	27.8
Washington	5,931	96	1.62	15,200	52.1
Williamson	7,009	1,650	23.54	2,755	10.6
	39,619	*6,787*	*17.13*	*53,128*	*28.5+*
TENTH DISTRICT					
Austin	3,789	239	6.31	5,185	29.0
Brazoria	2,891	237	8.20	8,523	74.1
Colorado	3,985	395	9.91	8,845	45.3
Fayette	6,695	593	8.86	8,446	26.8
Fort Bend	3,126	221	7.07	8,981	84.8
Galveston	8,613	643	7.47	7,009	22.3
Gonzales	4,413	1,874	42.47	5,869	32.6
Lavaca	4,704	1,262	26.83	4,253	19.4
Matagorda	1,009	12	1.19	2,621	65.8
	39,225	*5,476*	*13.96*	*59,732*	*35.9+*
ELEVENTH DISTRICT					
Aransas	471	65	13.80	137	7.5
Atascosa	1,369	426	31.12	285	4.4
Bee	1,485	196	13.20	317	8.5
Calhoun	374	74	19.79	168	20.6
DeWitt	6,582	249	3.78	3,995	27.9
Dimmit	211	65	30.81	37	3.5
Duval	1,195	1	.08	7	0.1
Frio	832	151	18.15	102	3.3
Goliad	1,421	298	20.97	1,644	27.8
Guadalupe	3,378	206	6.10	4,415	29.0
Jackson	1,061	210	19.79	1,822	55.5
Karnes	1,700	637	37.47	544	15.0
Live Oak	545	162	29.72	49	2.4

TABLE XIX (*continued*)

	Total Vote	Populist Vote	Percentage Populist in Total Vote	Black Population	Percentage Blacks in Total Population
ELEVENTH DISTRICT (*continued*)					
Nueces	2,048	26	1.27	707	8.7
Refugio	324	17	5.25	324	26.2
San Patricio	619	117	18.90	25	1.9
Victoria	2,210	34	1.54	3,519	40.3
Wharton	2,010	112	5.57	6,119	80.7
Wilson	2,426	1,003	41.34	1,053	9.9
Zavala	153	21	13.73	3	0.3
	30,414	*4,070*	13.38	25,272	*18.7+*
TWELFTH DISTRICT					
Bandera	789	161	20.41	126	3.3
Bexar	10,793	382	3.54	5,504	11.2
Blanco	922	300	32.54	210	4.5
Coke	450	173	38.44	none listed**	**
Comal	1,365	14	1.03	180	2.8
Concho	64	1	1.56	14	1.3
Edwards	496	36	7.26	6	0.3
Gillespie	1,542	108	7.00	108	1.51
Kendall	793	41	5.17	216	5.6
Kerr	979	125	12.77	92	2.4
Kimble	418	77	18.42	5	0.2
Llano	1,318	426	32.32	52	0.8
Mason	1,007	278	27.61	31	0.6
McCullock	689	214	31.06	12	1.4
Medina	1,458	125	8.57	283	4.9
Menard	457	103	22.54	23	1.9
Midland	327	9	2.75	3	0.3
Pecos	256	1	.39	8	0.6
Presidio	1,454	520	35.76	26	1.5
San Saba	1,301	520	39.97	53	0.8
Sterling	213	84	39.44	none listed**	**
Sutton	363	2	.55	1	0.2
Tom Green	1,258	30	2.38	202	3.9
	28,712	3,730	12.99	7,155	1.9+

TABLE XIX (*continued*)

	Total Vote	Populist Vote	Percentage Populist in Total Vote	Black Population	Percentage Blacks in Total Population
THIRTEENTH DISTRICT					
Archer	540	79	14.63	12	0.6
Armstrong	199	74	37.19	285	4.4
Baylor	487	142	29.16	6	0.2
Borden	103	42	40.78	5	2.3
Briscoe	175	85	48.57	**	**
Callahan	1,449	595	41.06	31	0.6
Carson	108	3	2.78	1	0.3
Childress	382	74	19.37	2	0.2
Clay	1,734	442	25.49	102	1.4
Collingsworth	189	53	28.04	**	**
Cottle	123	18	14.63	**	**
Crosby	115	22	19.13	1	0.3
Dallam	44	7	15.91	**	**
Deaf Smith	108	19	17.59	**	**
Dickens	112	35	31.25	**	**
Donely	336	116	34.52	40	3.8
Eastland	2,794	1,346	48.17	25	0.2
El Paso	3,685	1,428	38.75	377	2.4
Fisher	500	227	45.40	15	6.5
Floyd	279	110	39.43	**	**
Foard	300	175	58.33	**	**
Hale	275	84	30.55	3	0.4
Hall	300	67	22.33	1	0.1
Hansford	28	10	35.71	**	**
Hardeman	570	131	22.98	21	0.5
Hartley	113	13	11.50	1	0.4
Haskell	332	81	24.40	6	0.4
Hemphill	143	25	17.48	9	1.7
Howard	378	161	42.59	34	2.8
Jack	1,987	915	46.05	97	1.0
Jones	947	490	51.74	7	0.2
Kent	121	70	57.85	**	**
King	91	1	1.10	2	1.2
Knox	306	94	30.72	**	**
Lipscomb	131	31	23.66	**	**
Lubbock	101	9	8.91	2	***
Martin	109	14	12.84	**	**
Mitchell	509	193	37.92	99	4.8

TABLE XIX (*continued*)

	Total Vote	Populist Vote	Percentage Populist in Total Vote	Black Population	Percentage Blacks in Total Population
THIRTEENTH DISTRICT (*continued*)					
Moore	37	21	56.76	**	**
Motley	162	33	20.37	3	2.2
Nolan	384	138	35.94	32	2.0
Ochiltree	38	13	34.21	**	**
Oldham	79	9	11.39	3	1.1
Palo Pinto	2,088	981	46.98	67	.8
Potter	347	118	34.01	14	1.6
Randall	132	39	29.55	**	**
Reeves	597	70	11.73	7	.6
Roberts	141	22	15.60	2	.6
Scurry	373	197	52.82	2	0
Shackelford	515	230	44.66	167	8.3
Stephens	1,224	564	46.08	5	.1
Swisher	204	89	43.63	**	**
Taylor	1,666	834	50.06	174	2.5
Throckmorton	325	144	44.31	11	1.2
Ward	157	51	32.48	3	***
Wheeler	100	17	17.00	16	2.1
Wichita	974	221	22.69	128	2.6
Wilbarger	1,026	287	27.97	26	0.4
Wise	5,584	2,218	39.72	161	0.7
Young	1,205	448	37.18	15	0.3
	37,561	14,225	37.87	2,020	1.2+

*United States Bureau of Commerce, *Bureau of Census, Black Population*, 1790-1915, 789-92; Report of Secretary of State, November 3, 1896, 61-64; *Southern Mercury*, October 29, 1896.

**The census did not report any black population in these counties.

***Percent not shown since the base is less than 100.

+All district totals of black population are expressed as arithmetic means.

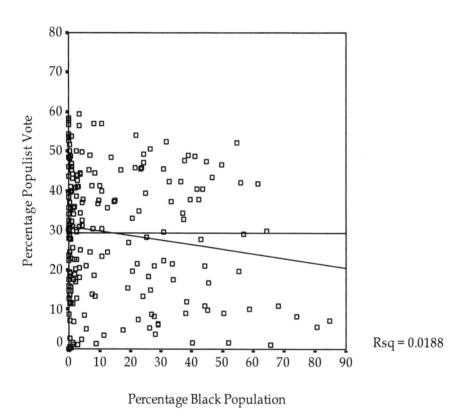

Figure 6.   Relationship between Black Density and Populism in the Texas
Congressional Election of 1896.

TABLE XX
Voting and Black Population Characteristics for the
Florida Congressional election of 1894*

	Total Vote	Populist Vote	Percentage Populist in Total Vote	Black Population	Percentage Blacks in Total Population
FIRST DISTRICT					
Calhoun	183	104	56.83	549	32.7
Citrus	247	39	15.79	304	12.7
DeSoto	706	250	35.41	139	2.8
Escambia	2,013	20	.99	8,706	43.1
Franklin	236	49	20.76	1,358	41.1
Hernando	189	66	34.92	892	36.0
Hillsborough	3,133	216	6.89	2,917	19.5
Holmes	277	156	56.32	184	4.2
Jackson	793	220	27.74	11,211	63.9
Lee	112	1	.89	80	5.7
Leon	937	23	2.45	14,631	82.4
Levy	307	29	9.45	2,129	32.3
Liberty	141	74	52.48	634	43.7
Manatee	333	103	30.93	181	6.3
Monroe	942	16	1.70	5,935	31.6
Pasco	367	78	21.25	376	8.8
Polk	736	280	38.04	784	9.9
Santa Rosa	181	4	2.21	2,192	27.5
Taylor	73	23	31.51	151	7.4
Walton	408	196	48.04	743	15.4
Washington	432	188	43.52	1,339	20.8
	12,746	2,135	16.75	55,435	26.1**
SECOND DISTRICT					
Alachua	652	63	9.66	13,260	57.8
Baker	317	181	57.10	745	22.4
Bradford	435	83	19.08	1,555	20.7
Brevard	352	20	5.68	541	15.9
Clay	243	66	27.16	1,521	29.5
Columbia	581	120	20.65	6,484	50.4
Duval	1,886	366	19.41	14,802	55.2
Hamilton	355	31	8.73	3,170	37.3
Lake	1020	150	14.71	1844	23.0
Marion	1,177	482	40.95	11,485	55.2
Nassau	577	109	18.89	4,338	52.3

TABLE XX (*continued*)

	Total Vote	Populist Vote	Percentage Populist in Total Vote	Black Population	Percentage Blacks in Total Population
SECOND DISTRICT (*continued*)					
Orange	183	104	56.83	549	32.7
Osceola	247	39	15.79	304	12.7
Putman	706	250	35.41	139	2.8
St. Johns	2,013	20	.99	8,706	43.1
Sumter	236	49	20.76	1,358	41.1
Suwannee	189	66	34.92	892	36.0
Volusia	3,133	216	6.89	2,917	19.5
	6,707	744	11.09	14,865	26.1**

*United States Bureau of Commerce, Bureau of Census, Black Population, 1790-1915, 778; Congressional Directory, 54th Congress, 1st Session, 27; Florida National Elections, November 6, 1894, 6-7; *Appletons Annual Cyclopedia*, 1894, 283.
**All district totals of black population are expressed as arithmetic means.

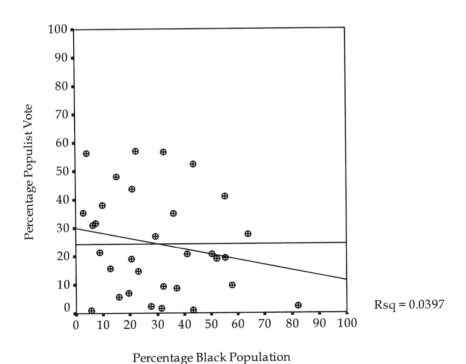

Figure 7.   Relationship between Black Density and Populism in the Florida Congressional Election of 1894.

TABLE XXI
Voting and Black Population Characteristics for the
Arkansas Congressional election of 1894*

	Total Vote	Populist Vote	Percentage Populist in Total Vote	Black Population	Percentage Blacks in Total Population
FIRST DISTRICT					
Randolph	700	45	6.43	595	4.1
Clay	452	134	29.65	43	.4
Greene	777	362	46.59	161	1.2
Lawrence	614	135	21.99	833	6.4
Sharp	637	160	25.12	177	1.7
Jackson	494	57	11.54	4,329	28.5
Craighead	503	121	24.06	519	4.3
Poinsett	201	18	8.96	546	12.8
Cross	286	34	11.89	2,890	37.6
St. Francis	531	207	38.98	8,000	59.1
Lee	676	16	2.37	14,187	75.1
Phillips	668	2	.30	19,640	77.5
Woodruff	566	8	1.41	7,556	53.9
	7,105	1,299	18.28	59,476	27.9**
SECOND DISTRICT					
Lincoln	258	1	.39	8,451	63.1
Drew	544	52	9.56	9,865	56.9
Dallas	343	7	2.04	3,265	35.1
Hot Spring	362	7	1.93	1,249	10.8
Polk	152	3	1.97	46	0.5
Scott	456	18	3.95	31	0.2
	2,115	88	4.16	22,907	27.8**
FOURTH DISTRICT					
Franklin	1,253	204	16.28	677	3.4
Johnson	992	246	24.80	631	3.8
Logan	1,433	190	13.26	1,124	5.4
Pulaski	2,123	216	10.17	21,935	46.3
Conway	1,143	99	8.66	7,671	39.4
Pope	1,537	279	18.15	1,621	8.3
Yell	1,138	166	14.59	1,362	7.6
Perry	502	157	31.27	941	17.0
	10,121	1,557	15.38	35,962	16.4**

TABLE XXI (*continued*)

	Total Vote	Populist Vote	Percentage Populist in Total Vote	Black Population	Percentage Blacks in Total Population
FIFTH DISTRICT					
Benton	2,032	25	1.23	92	.3
Washington	2,089	36	1.72	1,010	3.2
Carroll	1,384	101	7.30	82	.5
Boone	927	2	.22	91	.6
Newton	717	16	2.23	6	.1
Crawford	1,464	14	.96	2,296	10.6
Van Buren	602	135	22.43	162	1.9
Faulkner	1,736	421	24.25	3,348	18.3
Searcy	701	9	1.28	28	0.3
	11,652	759	6.51	7,115	4.0**

*United States Bureau of Commerce, *Bureau of Census, Black Population* , 1790-1915, 777; Biennial Report of the Secretary of State of Arkansas, November, 1894, 65-67; Congressional Directory, 1st Session, 54th Congress, 18-20.
**All district totals of black population are expressed as arithmetic means.

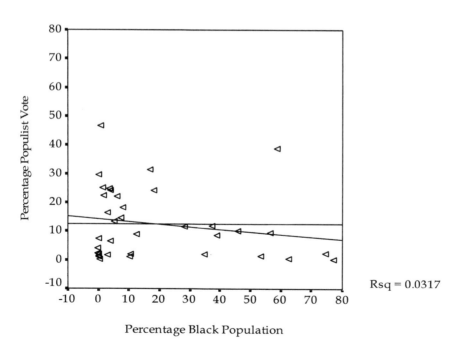

Rsq = 0.0317

Figure 8. Relationship between Black Density and Populism in the Arkansas Congressional Election of 1894.

TABLE XXII
Voting and Black Population Characteristics for the
Louisiana Congressional election of 1892*

	Total Vote	Populist Vote	Percentage Populist in Total Vote	Black Population	Percentage Blacks in Total Population
FIRST DISTRICT					
Orleans	12,859	40	.31	64,491	26.6
St. Bernard	733	12	1.64	1,977	45.7
	13,592	52	.38	66,468	36.2**
THIRD DISTRICT					
Iberville	2,241	595	26.55	15,142	69.3
Assumption	2,003	696	34.75	8,890	45.3
Lafourche	3,160	93	2.94	7,819	35.4
Terrebonne	1,577	346	21.94	9,699	48.1
St. Mary	1,580	249	15.76	14,395	64.2
Iberia	616	28	4.55	10,477	49.9
St. Martin	485	2	.41	7,821	52.5
Lafayette	665	1	.15	6,884	43.1
Vermilion	560	237	42.32	2,899	20.4
Cameron	188	6	3.19	426	15.1
Calcasieu	1,756	692	39.41	3,194	15.8
Ascension	2,319	178	7.68	11,270	57.7
	17,150	3,123***	18.21	98,916	43.1**
FOURTH DISTRICT					
Rapides	3,672	457	12.45	15,800	57.2
Sabine	1,270	760	59.84	2,067	22.0
DeSoto	1,921	346	18.01	13,220	66.6
Natchitoches	1,679	594	35.38	15,551	60.2
Red River	1,241	288	23.21	7,760	68.6
Caddo	2,483	251	10.11	23,541	74.6
Bossier	3,015	72	2.39	16,225	79.8
Winn	992	791	79.74	1,010	14.3
Grant	838	500	59.67	3,416	41.3
Bienville	2,074	443	21.36	6,268	44.4
Vernon	694	369	53.17	540	9.1
Webster	1,720	296	17.21	7,289	58.5
	21,599	5,167+	23.92	112,687	49.7**

TABLE XXII (*continued*)

	Total Vote	Populist Vote	Percentage Populist in Total Vote	Black Population	Percentage Blacks in Total Population
FIFTH DISTRICT					
Caldwell	909	224	24.64	3,106	53.4
Franklin	830	25	3.01	4,040	58.6
Tensas	2,564	11	.43	15,492	93.1
Madison	3,206	3	.09	13,204	93.4
Ouachita	2,964	151	5.09	12,344	68.6
Jackson	866	466	53.81	2,608	35.0
Lincoln	1,753	1,084	61.84	6,269	42.5
Union	2,012	647	32.16	7,403	42.8
Morehouse	1,231	96	7.80	13,267	79.0
East Carroll	1,392	22	1.58	11,360	91.9
West Carroll	416	9	2.16	2,310	61.6
Claiborne	2,574	1,121	43.55	13,512	58.0
Catahoula	1,570	442	28.15	4,976	41.5
	22,287	4,301***	19.29	109,891	63.0**
SIXTH DISTRICT					
Acadia	369	96	26.02	1,629	12.3
St. Landry	2,034	899	44.20	22,274	55.3
Avoyelles	1,609	3	.19	12,161	48.4
East Feliciana	1,427	102	7.15	12,707	71.0
E. Baton Rouge	1,533	287	18.72	16,420	63.3
W. Baton Rouge	1,601	30	1.87	5,964	71.3
St. Helena	382	78	20.42	4,589	56.9
Livingston	567	245	43.21	871	15.1
Tangipahoa	892	114	12.78	4,698	37.1
Washington	541	127	23.48	2,062	30.8
St. Tammany	124	62	50.00	3,702	36.4
	11,079	2,043	18.44	87,077	45.3**

*United States Bureau of Commerce, *Bureau of Census, Black Population*, 1790-1915, 782-83; State of Louisiana, *Report of the Secretary of State*, "Official vote of 1892 Congressional Election, "98-100; *Congressional Directory*, 3rd Session, 53rd Congress, 47-48.

**All district totals of black population are expressed as arithmetic means.

***These candidates represented both the Republican and the Populist Parties in their districts. Only Ross Carlin in the first district ran expressly as a Populist candidate. See Charles W. Dabney Jr., Congressional Directory, 3rd Session, 53rd Congress, 47-48.

+T. J. Guice appears to have been a Farmers' Alliance candidate running against a Democrat, N. C. Blanchard. As such, Guice probably received the Populist, Republican, and Farmers' Alliance vote in the Fourth district since these were the only two candidates. He is, therefore, included as a Populist candidate for this reason. See "Fourth district," Congressional Record, 2nd Session, 52nd Congress, 45; Melvin J. White, "Populism in Louisiana during the Nineties," Mississippi Valley Historical Review 5 (June, 1918), 5-6.

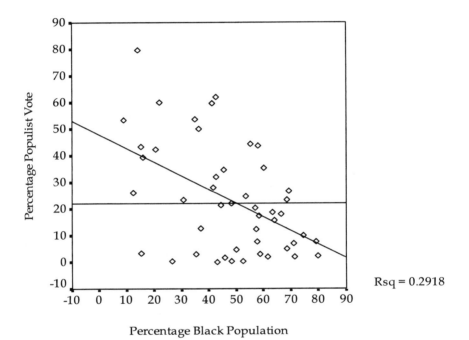

Figure 9.   Relationship between Black Density and Populism in the Louisiana
           Congressional Election of 1892.

TABLE XXIIII
Voting and Black Population Characteristics for the
Virginia Congressional election of 1892*

	Total Vote	Populist Vote	Percentage Populist in Total Vote	Black Population	Percentage Blacks in Total Population
FIRST DISTRICT					
Accomack	5,352	1,630	30.46	9,730	35.7
Caroline	2,742	1,475	53.79	9,322	55.9
Essex	1,839	933	50.73	6,462	64.3
City of Fredericksburg	944	176	18.64	1,682	37.1
Gloucester	2,356	1,440	61.12	6,216	53.3
King & Queen	1,616	55	3.40	5,430	56.2
Lancaster	1,891	874	46.22	4,020	55.9
Mathews	1,565	619	39.55	2,137	28.2
Middlesex	536	255	47.57	4,317	57.9
Northampton	1,622	387	23.86	5,479	53.1
Northumberland	1,791	812	45.34	3,090	39.2
Richmond County	1,328	609	45.86	3,148	44.1
Spotsylvania	1,560	673	43.14	4,395	46.3
Westmoreland	1,561	807	51.70	4,737	56.4
	26,703	10,745	40.24	70,165	48.9**
SECOND DISTRICT					
Charles City	883	4	.45	3,717	73.4
Elizabeth City	2,124	114	5.37	7,774	48.1
Isle of Wight	2,202	80	3.63	5,144	45.5
Nansemond	3,392	226	6.66	10,765	54.7
Norfolk	5,094	62	1.22	19,216	66.5
City of Norfolk	6,050	8	.13	16,244	46.6
Portsmouth	2,751	3	.11	4,018	30.3
Princess Anne	1,077	66	6.13	4,130	43.4
Surry	1,297	139	10.72	5,017	60.8
Southampton	2,571	245	9.53	11,782	58.7
Warwick	1,644	12	.73	1,320	60.0
York	1,355	17	1.25	4,395	57.9
	30,440+	976	3.21	93,522	53.8**

TABLE XXIII (*continued*)

	Total Vote	Populist Vote	Percentage Populist in Total Vote	Black Population	Percentage Blacks in Total Population
THIRD DISTRICT					
Chesterfield	2,982	1,241	41.62	10,811	41.2
Goochland	1,466	811	55.32	5,874	59.0
Hanover	2,833	1,336	47.16	8,211	47.2
henrico	4,318	1,966	45.53	11,265	51.2
King William	1,346	656	48.74	5,685	59.2
New Kent	838	445	53.10	3,545	64.3
Manchester	1,821	574	31.52	***	***
City of Richmond	13,480	3,459	25.66	32,330	39.7
	29,084+	10,488	36.06	77,721	51.7**
FOURTH DISTRICT					
Amelia	1,116	588	52.69	6,045	66.7
Brunswick	2,206	1,122	50.86	10,584	61.4
Dinwiddie	1,649	842	51.06	8,394	62.1
Greensville	802	436	54.36	5,311	64.5
Lunenburg	1,278	457	35.76	6,736	59.2
Mecklenburg	3,179	1,816	57.12	16,030	28.2
Nottoway	1,511	442	29.25	7,623	65.8
Petersburg	3,599	1,023	28.42	12,221	53.9
Powhatan	1,210	816	67.44	4,433	65.3
prince Edward	1,541	764	49.58	9,924	57.5
Prince George	842	569	67.58	5,132	65.2
Sussex	879	587	66.78	7,576	68.3
	19,812	9,462	3.21	100,009	6.07**
SIXTH DISTRICT					
Bedford	4,986	1,731	34.72	11,149	35.7
Campbell	3,467	1,694	48.86	9,998	46.8
Charlotte	2,405	967	40.21	9,361	62.1
Halifax	5,660	2,384	42.12	19,416	56.4
Lynchburg	3,789	1,362	35.95	9,802	49.7
Montgomery	2,643	1,341	50.74	3,515	19.8
Radford	783	185	23.63	***	***
Roanoke City	4,605	1,879	40.80	4,929	30.4
Roanoke County	2,936	1,306	44.48	4,076	29.2
	31,274+	12,849	41.09	72,246	41.3**

TABLE XXIII (*continued*)

	Total Vote	Populist Vote	Percentage Populist in Total Vote	Black Population	Percentage Blacks in Total Population
EIGHTH DISTRICT					
City of Alexandria	3,154	1,153	36.56	5,113	35.7
Alexandria	839	470	56.02	2,123	49.9
Culpeper	2,502	904	36.13	6,085	46.0
Fairfax	3,389	1,187	35.03	5,069	30.4
Fauquier	4,166	1,383	33.20	7,904	35.0
King George	1,027	474	46.15	3,208	48.3
Loudoun	4,186	1,448	34.59	6,578	28.3
Louisan	2,662	1,373	51.58	9,805	57.7
Orange	2,221	883	39.76	6,241	48.7
Prince William	1,791	275	15.35	2,595	26.5
Stafford	1,267	516	40.73	1,469	20.0
	27,204+	10,066	37.00	56,190	38.8**
NINTH DISTRICT					
Bland	945	262	27.72	241	4.7
Buchanan	910	71	7.80	24	.4
Craig	778	73	9.38	149	3.9
Dickenson	779	47	6.03	26	0.5
Lee	2,773	23	.83	1,213	6.7
Russell	2,749	386	14.04	1,203	7.5
Scott	3,540	309	8.73	968	4.5
Smyth	2,314	126	5.45	1,224	9.2
Tazewell	3,432	72	2.10	3,504	17.6
Washington	4,730	138	2.92	2,965	11.4
Wise	1,879	26	1.38	582	6.2
Wythe	3,413	176	5.16	3,170	17.6
	28,242	1,709	3.21	15,269	7.5**
TENTH DISTRICT					
Alleghany	1,193	855	71.67	2,328	25.1
Amherst	1,670	1,161	69.52	7,628	43.5
Appomattox	1,687	905	53.65	4,336	45.2
Augusta	3,645	2,211	60.66	6,112	20.4
Bath	490	374	76.33	761	16.6
Botetourt	1,692	1,188	70.21	3,732	25.1
Buckingham	1,286	1,043	81.10	7,597	52.8
Cumberland	980	554	56.53	6,622	69.8
Flwanna	925	546	59.03	4,457	46.9

TABLE XXIII (*continued*)

	Total Vote	Populist Vote	Percentage Populist in Total Vote	Black Population	Percentage Blacks in Total Population
TENTH DISTRICT (*continued*)					
Highland	607	401	66.06	422	7.9
Nelson	1,431	1,097	76.66	6,303	41.1
Rockbridge	2,209	1,631	73.83	5,131	22.2
Buena Vista	342	83	24.27	***	***
	17,731+	12,049	70.36	55,429	34.7**

*United States Bureau of Commerce, *Bureau of Census, Black Population*, 1790-1915, 792-93, 797; *Congressional Directory*, 3rd Session, 53rd Congress, 115-118; Commonwealth of Virginia, *Election Record*, No. 92, 22-31.

**All district totals of black population are expressed as arithmetic means.*

***Figures not available for these areas.

+The population of the independent cities is not included in the population given for counties.

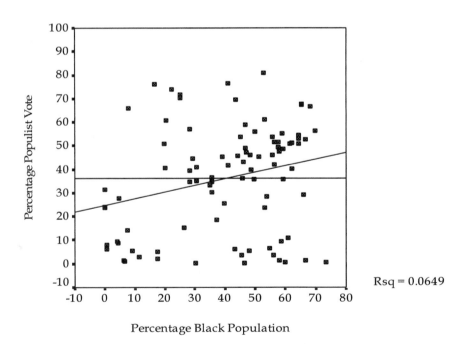

Figure 10.   Relationship between Black Density and Populism in the Virginia Congressional Election of 1892.

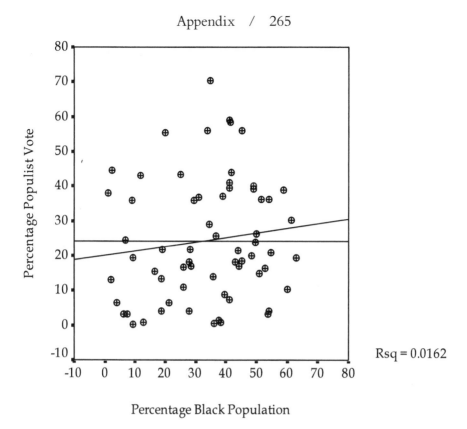

Figure 11. Relationship between Black Density and Populism by Congressional District in the South.

Notes

INTRODUCTION

1. Carl N. Degler, "Racism in the United States: An Essay Review," *Journal of Southern History* 38 (February 1972): 101.

2. Richard Reeves, "The New Populism and the Old: A Matter of Words," *Saturday Review,* 8 April 1972, 46–47.

3. Degler, "Racism in the United States," 102.

4. Robert Sherrill, *Gothic Politics in the Deep South: Stars of the New Confederacy* (New York: Grossman Publishers, 1968), 122.

5. Pat Watters, *The South and the Nation* (New York: Pantheon Books, 1969), 59.

1. BLACKS AND THE FARMERS' ALLIANCE MOVEMENT

1. *People's Party Paper* (Atlanta), 28 August 1896.

2. According to Hicks, "Perhaps half of the members of the [Southern] Alliance gave the new party their support. The rest were unwilling to risk the reality of white supremacy in what might prove to be a vain struggle for a new order." However, under pressure to conform to private principles, ultimately "it was no longer possible to be a good Allianceman unless one also was a good Populist." The initial formation of the Populist Party was probably a catalyst to attract the less aggressive members (John D. Hicks, *The Populist Revolt: A History of the Farmers' Alliance and the People's Party* [Lincoln: University of Nebraska Press, 1931; rpr. Lincoln: University of Nebraska Press, 1961], 243, 270–73). For a study of the germination and growth of such movements, see C. Wendell King, *Social Movements in the United States* (New York: Random House, 1956), 40–48.

3. C. Vann Woodward, *Origins of the New South, 1877–1913* (Baton Rouge: Louisiana State University Press, 1951), 185–86, 269; Melvin Johnson White, "Populism in Louisiana During the Nineties," *Mississippi Valley Historical Review* 5 (June 1918): 3; Lawrence Goodwyn, *Democratic Promise: The Populist Moment in America* (New York: Oxford University Press, 1976), 25–33, 571–81; Barton Shaw, *The Wool-*

Hat Boys: Georgia's Populist Party (Baton Rouge: Louisiana State University Press, 1984), 8–10.

4. Theodore Saloutos, *Farmer Movements in the South: 1865–1933* (Lincoln: University of Nebraska Press, 1960), 70–71; Hicks, *Populist Revolt,* 104–5. A good discussion of the Texas Alliance can be found in Ralph Smith, "The Farmers' Alliance in Texas, 1875–1900," *Southwestern Historical Quarterly* 48 (October 1948): 346–69.

5. For a discussion of the background and plans of C. W. Macune, see Fred Shannon, "C. W. Macune and the Farmers' Alliance," *Current History* 28 (June 1955): 330–35; Ralph Smith, "'Macuneism' or the Farmers of Texas in Business," *Journal of Southern History* 13 (May 1947): 220–44; Annie L. Diggs, "The Farmers' Alliance and Some of Its Leaders," *Arena* 5 (April 1892): 598–99; Charles W. Macune Jr., "The Wellsprings of a Populist: Dr. C. W. Macune before 1886." *Southwestern Historical Quarterly* 90 (October 1986): 139–58.

6. *Progressive Farmer* (Raleigh), 9 September 1887; C. Vann Woodward, *Tom Watson: Agrarian Rebel* (New York: Rinehart and Company, 1938; rpr. New York: Oxford University Press, 1963), 136.

7. William F. Holmes, "The Demise of the Colored Farmers' Alliance," *Journal of Southern History* 41 (May 1975): 191 n.17.

8. Saloutos, *Farmer Movements,* 69; Woodward, *Origins,* 190–91; Ina W. Van Noppen, ed., *The South: A Documentary History* (Princeton, NJ: Van Nostrand, 1958), 404–5. See also Clifton Paisley, "The Political Wheelers," *Arkansas Historical Quarterly* 25 (spring 1966): 3–21; *Appleton's Annual Cyclopedia, 1886* (New York: Appleton, 1887), 42; *Appleton's Annual Cyclopedia, 1890* (New York: Appleton, 1891), 299; Hicks, *Populist Revolt,* 110.

9. James W. Vander Zanden, "The Ideology of White Supremacy," *Journal of the History of Ideas* 20 (June–September 1959): 385–402; Guion Griffis Johnson, "The Ideology of White Supremacy, 1876–1910," in *Essays in Southern History,* ed. Fletcher Melvin Green (Chapel Hill: University of North Carolina Press, 1949), 125–26; Rhett Jones, "Proving Blacks Inferior, 1870–1930," *Black World* 20 (February 1971): 4–19.

10. George Brown Tindall, *South Carolina Negroes, 1877–1900* (Baton Rouge: Louisiana State University Press, 1966), 309; Merline Pitre, *Through Many Dangers, Toils, and Snares: Black Leadership in Texas, 1870–1890* (Austin, TX: Eakin Press, 1985), 223–45.

11. Saloutos, *Farmer Movements,* 72.

12. Fred A. Shannon, *The Farmers' Last Frontier: Agriculture, 1860–1897* (New York: Farrar and Rinehart, 1968), 77–100, 314, 418; Hicks, *Populist Revolt,* 114; Woodward, *Origins,* 205–6.

13. *National Economist,* 4 July 1891. This paper served as the official organ of the Southern Alliance from its beginning. The first copy of the paper was issued on 14 March 1889 from Washington, DC. See also William D. Sheldon, *Populism in the Old Dominion* (Princeton, NJ: Princeton University Press, 1935), 3–4; Paul Lewison, *Race, Class, and Party: A History of Negro Suffrage and White Politics in the South* (New York: Oxford University Press, 1932), 71. A similar "resolution" was adopted in

1889 by the "committee on co-operation" of the National Alliance concerning the "detrimental" effects "to both white and colored to allow conditions to exist that force our colored farmers and laborers to sell their products for less and pay more for supplies than the market justifies" (*Weekly Toiler* [Nashville], 23 January 1889).

14. Saloutos, *Farmer Movements,* 69–70, 74, 77, 79; August Meier, *Negro Thought in America, 1880–1915* (Ann Arbor: University of Michigan Press, 1966), 44; Hicks, *Populist Revolt,* 108; Frank M. Drew, "The Present Farmers' Movement," *Political Science Quarterly* 6 (June 1891): 282–84.

15. Roy Scott, "Milton George and the Farmers' Alliance Movement," *Mississippi Valley Historical Review* 45 (June 1958): 107 n.59.

16. Hicks, *Populist Revolt,* 98; Saloutos, *Farmer Movements,* 69–70, 79.

17. Gregg Cantrell, *Kenneth and John B. Rayner and the Limits of Southern Dissent* (Urbana: University of Illinois Press, 1993), 198.

18. Richard M. Humphrey, "History of the Colored Farmers' National Alliance and Cooperative Union," in *The Farmers' Alliance and Agricultural Digest,* ed. Nelson A. Dunning (Washington, DC: Alliance Publishing Co., 1891), 288. Humphrey, however, failed to recognize George's early effort in his official account. See also Goodwyn, *Democratic Promise,* 218, 229–32, 276–94.

19. Humphrey, "History," 288–90; Woodward, *Origins,* 185–86.

20. Humphrey, "History," 288.

21. Ibid.; *Weekly Toiler,* 27 March 1889; Van Noppen, *The South,* 405. Van Noppen has interwoven details from the *Progressive Farmer* on the 1886 convention with the national convention of 1888.

22. See Meier, *Negro Thought,* 42–58, 121–38; Edwin S. Redkey, *Black Exodus: Black Nationalist and Back-to-Africa Movements, 1890–1910* (New Haven, CT: Yale University Press, 1969), 1–23; Purvis M. Carter, "Robert Lloyd Smith and the Farmers' Improvement Society, a Self-Help Movement in Texas," *Negro History Bulletin* 29 (fall 1966): 175–76, 190–91.

23. Van Noppen, *The South,* 405.

24. Woodward, *Origins,* 192. For further evidence, see *Weekly Toiler,* 4 July 1888.

25. Holmes, "Demise," 190 n.13; William W. Rogers, "The Negro Alliance in Alabama," *Journal of Negro History* 45 (January 1960): 40–41; Robert C. McMath Jr., "Southern White Farmers and the Organization of Black Farm Workers: A North Carolina Document," *Labor History* 18 (winter 1977): 115 n.2.

26. William Edward Spriggs, "The Virginia Colored Farmers' Alliance: A Case Study of Race and Class Identity," *Journal of Negro History* 64 (summer 1979): 194.

27. *Weekly Toiler,* 21 August 1889.

28. Rogers, "The Negro Alliance," 40.

29. Humphrey, "History," 289.

30. This vignette of Humphrey is compiled from a number of sources: Humphrey, "History," 289; *National Economist,* 7 June 1890; *Atlanta Constitution,* 4 December 1890; William J. Northen Scrapbook I, folder 83, in Northen Collection, Georgia Department of Archives and History, Atlanta; Drew, "Present Farmers' Movement," 287–88; Holmes, "Demise," 189; William F. Holmes, "The Arkansas

Cotton Pickers' Strike of 1891 and the Demise of the Colored Farmers' Alliance," *Arkansas Historical Quarterly* 32 (summer 1973): 108, 113; Goodwyn, *Democratic Promise,* 280, 656 n.4; Omar Ali, "R. M. Humphrey," available at *Black Populism in the South, 1886–1898,* http://www.geocities.com/soho/workshop/4275/.

31. Humphrey, "History," 289.

32. Humphrey, "History," 289; Colored Farmers' Alliance Charter, Office of Recorder of Deeds, Corporation Division, Instrument #1606, Incorporation Liber #4, Folio 354, Washington, DC.

33. Lawrence Rice, *The Negro in Texas, 1874–1900* (Baton Rouge: Louisiana State University Press, 1971), 178; Carter, "Robert Lloyd Smith," 175–76, 190–91.

34. Rogers, "The Negro Alliance," 39–40; *Weekly Toiler,* 30 January 1889; William W. Rogers, *The One-Gallused Rebellion: Agrarianism in Alabama, 1865–1896* (Baton Rouge: Louisiana State University Press, 1970), 141–44.

35. Rogers, "The Negro Alliance," 39–44. See also *Appleton's Annual Cyclopedia, 1890,* 301.

36. *Union Springs (AL) Bullock County Reporter,* 18 October 1889, quoted in Rogers, *One-Gallused Rebellion,* 143–44.

37. Rogers, "The Negro Alliance," 43–44; Rogers, *One-Gallused Rebellion,* 144–45. For further information on the agrarian movement in Alabama, see William W. Rogers, "Agrarianism in Alabama, 1865–1896" (Ph.D. diss., University of North Carolina at Chapel Hill, 1959).

38. *Weekly Toiler,* 18 July 1888. The *Weekly Toiler* served as the official state organ of the Tennessee Southern and Colored Farmers' Alliances. J. H. McDowell purchased the paper on 28 August 1888 and thereafter turned it into a major Alliance organ. "The policy of the *Toiler* in the future," said the new editor, "will be conservative" (12 September 1888). Nevertheless, the Colored Farmers' Alliance received extensive coverage under McDowell and L. K. Taylor, who later replaced McDowell, while the major state papers ignored its very existence. Compare Roger L. Hart, *Redeemers, Bourbons, and Populists: Tennessee, 1870–1896* (Baton Rouge: Louisiana State University Press, 1975), 124–25, 283. The current author found the Tennessee black Alliance and black Wheel to generally work closely together, not necessarily the black and white Alliance, as Hart alleges.

39. *Weekly Toiler,* 4 July 1888. Vaughn served as the Tennessee General Superintendent of the Colored Farmers' Alliance in the early years but was later replaced by J. W. Brown of Prospect, Tennessee. As with so many Colored Farmers' Alliance officers, nothing is known of his financial position or race.

40. Ibid., 7 October 1888.

41. Ibid., 1 July 1888.

42. Ibid., 31 July 1889. For evidence of financial difficulties in the white Tennessee Alliance, see *Nashville Banner,* 4 October 1891.

43. Samuel J. Barrows, "What the Southern Negro Is Doing for Himself," *Atlantic Monthly* 67 (June 1891): 805; Covington Hall, *Labor Struggles in the Deep South and Other Writings,* ed. David K. Roediger and Charles H. Kerr (Chicago: Charles H. Kerr Publishers, 1999), 49.

44. Plans were made, however, to establish a local co-op at Fayetteville, Tennessee. See *Weekly Toiler,* 31 July 1889.

45. *National Economist,* 23 August 1890.

46. Woodward, *Origins,* 237.

47. Saloutos, *Farmer Movements,* 113–14; *National Economist,* quoted in *Weekly Toiler,* 2 December 1891. See also James A. Sharp, "The Entrance of the Farmers' Alliance into Tennessee Politics," *East Tennessee Historical Society Papers* no. 9 (1937): 80–84.

48. For a brief discussion of these laws, see Sharp, "Entrance," 85–87; Hart, *Redeemers, Bourbons, and Populists,* 266–73.

49. See Gerald H. Gaither, "The Negro Alliance Movement in Tennessee, 1888–1891," *West Tennessee Historical Society Papers* 27 (1973): 50–62.

50. *Nashville Banner,* 9 August 1892; *National Economist,* quoted in *Weekly Toiler,* 2 December 1891; Corinne Westphal, "The Farmers' Alliance in Tennessee" (master's thesis, Vanderbilt University, 1929), 79–81; *Appleton's Annual Cyclopedia, 1890,* 299–301; Daniel M. Robison, "Tennessee Politics and the Agrarian Movement, 1886–1896," *Mississippi Valley Historical Review* 20 (December 1933): 365; Hart, *Redeemers, Bourbons, and Populists.* For statements of Alliance Democrat Rice Pierce in the Tennessee House of Representatives concerning the race issue, see *National Economist,* 28 February 1891.

51. See Holmes, "Demise," 196–97. See also Dorothy Granbury, "Black Community Leadership in a Rural Tennessee County, 1865–1903," *Journal of Negro History* 83 (autumn 1998): 249–57.

52. Bruce E. Baker, "The 'Hoover Scare' in South Carolina, 1887: An Attempt to Organize Black Farm Labor," *Labor History* 40 (August 1999): 261–82. See also Lacy K. Ford, "Rednecks and Merchants: Economic Development and Social Tensions in the South Carolina Upcountry, 1865–1900," *Journal of American History* 71 (September 1984): 294–318; Martin Dann, "Black Populism: A Study of the Colored Farmers' Alliance through 1891," *Journal of Ethnic Studies* 2 (fall 1974): 58–71.

53. Meier, *Negro Thought,* 46; Baker, "The 'Hoover Scare,'" 261.

54. Tindall, *South Carolina Negroes,* 114–19; Saloutos, *Farmer Movements,* 80.

55. Baker, "The 'Hoover Scare,'" 273–75.

56. Tindall, *South Carolina Negroes,* 115–19.

57. Ibid., 117–18. The year 1890 appears to have been one of continued growth for the South Carolina Colored Farmers' Alliance.

58. Ibid., 117.

59. Ibid., 118–19; Francis Butler Simkins, *The Tillman Movement in South Carolina* (Durham, NC: Duke University Press, 1926), 128–29, 132–33. A contemporary agrarian sympathizer believes the Colored Alliance did support Tillman (Joseph C. Manning, *The Fadeout of Populism* [New York: T. A. Hebbons Co., 1928], 17).

60. Tindall, *South Carolina Negroes,* 118–19.

61. Woodward, *Origins,* 184–87; John D. Hicks and John D. Barnhart, "The Farmers' Alliance," *North Carolina Historical Review* 6 (July 1929): 268.

62. *Ottawa (KS) Journal,* quoted in *National Economist,* 15 August 1891.

63. Barrows, "What the Southern Negro Is Doing for Himself," 814.

64. *National Economist,* 28 February 1891.

65. William F. Holmes, "Colored Farmers' Alliance," in *The New Handbook of Texas,* ed. Ron Taylor (Austin: Texas State Historical Society Association, 1996), 2:231; see also Holmes, "Arkansas Cotton Pickers' Strike," 119.

66. Holmes, "Colored Farmers' Alliance," 231; Dann, "Black Populism," 58–71.

67. *National Economist,* 13 June 1891.

68. Ibid., 16 August 1890.

69. Ibid., 12 July 1890. See also J. H. Turner, "The Race Problem," in *The Farmers' Alliance and Agricultural Digest,* 272–79. Turner was the Secretary-Treasurer of the Southern Alliance.

70. *National Economist,* 20 June 1891.

71. *Ottawa (KS) Journal,* quoted in *National Economist,* 15 August 1891.

72. *Congressional Record,* 51st Cong., 2nd sess.: 158. J. J. Shuffer was the first elected president, from December 1886. The bulk of the CFA was concentrated in the South Atlantic and Gulf states, with the remainder scattered in Delaware, Ohio, Illinois, Indiana, Missouri, and Nebraska. Historians have assessed CFA membership between 800,000 and 1,300,000, although in all probability membership peaked at 1,000,000. Evidence from both primary and secondary sources suggests the peak was reached in early 1890. Regardless of the exact figures, the CFA appears to have been up to that time the largest nonpolitical black organization on record in the United States.

73. Humphrey, "History," 290.

74. *Progressive Farmer,* 23 December 1890.

75. A member would be suspended automatically if he failed to pay dues for six months; he was then in theory forced to wear his badge backwards until he paid his delinquent dues.

76. Jack Abramowitz, "Accommodation and Militancy in Negro Life, 1876–1916" (Ph.D. diss., Columbia University, 1950), 50.

77. Ibid.

78. Cantrell, *Kenneth and John B. Rayner,* 207, 321 n.12.

79. Ibid., 188–89, 191–93, 204–5, 238–40, 244–45.

80. Ibid.; Gregg Cantrell, "John B. Rayner: A Study in Black Populist Leadership," *Southern Studies* 24 (winter 1985): 432–43; Jack Abramowitz, "John B. Rayner —A Grass Roots Leader," *Journal of Negro History* 36 (April 1951): 160–93.

81. Pitre, *Through Many Dangers,* 195–205; Rice, *Negro in Texas,* 79, 110–11, 180–81; Cantrell, *Kenneth and John B. Rayner,* 267.

82. Saloutos, *Farmer Movements,* 80; Holmes, "Demise," 188; *National Economist,* 25 January 1890.

83. Saloutos, *Farmer Movements,* 80; Holmes, "Arkansas Cotton Pickers' Strike," 111–12.

84. Tindall, *South Carolina Negroes,* 118.

85. Spriggs, "Virginia Colored Farmers' Alliance," 191–204.

86. W. E. B. Du Bois, "The Negroes of Farmville, Virginia" (1888), in *W. E. B. Du Bois: A Reader,* ed. David Levering Lewis (New York: Henry Holt, 1995), 233–35. See also Barrows, "What the Southern Negro Is Doing for Himself," 804–5.

87. Spriggs, "Virginia Colored Farmers' Alliance," 198.

88. Pitre, *Through Many Dangers,* 231–38.

89. Spriggs, "Virginia Colored Farmers' Alliance," 199; Holmes, "Demise," 189, 197. The conflict of interest between better educated landowning leaders and less educated tenant farmer members occurred not only in the Colored Farmers' Alliance but in the Southern Alliance as well. Michael Schwartz, Naomi Rosenthal, and Laura Schwartz, "Leader-Member Conflict in Protest Organizations: The Case of the Southern Farmers' Alliance," *Social Problems* 29 (October 1981): 22–36. See also Hart, *Redeemers, Bourbons, and Populists,* 114, 126–28.

90. An example of this was the National Headquarters' establishment of trading posts and exchanges in the cities of Houston, New Orleans, Mobile, Charleston, and Norfolk. A two-dollar fee was charged each member for trading privileges. Humphrey, "History," 289–90; Rogers, "The Negro Alliance," 42; Rogers, *One-Gallused Rebellion,* 143; Holmes, "Demise," 187.

91. See in particular Thomas D. Clark, "The Furnishing and Supply System in Southern Agriculture Since 1865," *Journal of Southern History* 12 (February 1946): 24–44; John Samuel Ezell, *The South Since 1865* (New York: Macmillan, 1963), 115–35.

92. *National Alliance,* quoted in *National Economist,* 21 June 1890.

93. Dr. James Sparkman, "The Negro" (1889), in *The Origins of Segregation,* ed. Joel Williamson (New York: D. C. Heath, 1968), 67.

94. *National Economist,* 7 June 1890.

95. Barrows, "What the Southern Negro Is Doing for Himself," 805, 808.

96. Hall, *Labor Struggles,* 49.

97. Rice, *Negro in Texas,* 173.

98. Tindall, *South Carolina Negroes,* 98–99.

99. Carl H. Moneyhon, "Black Politics in Arkansas During the Gilded Age, 1876–1900," *Arkansas Historical Quarterly* 44 (autumn 1985): 228.

100. *Cleveland Gazette,* 26 September 1891, in Herbert Aptheker, *A Documentary History of the Negro People in the United States* (New York: Citadel Press, 1951), 2:810; Holmes, "Demise," 196–97; Holmes, "Arkansas Cotton Pickers' Strike," 107–19.

101. *National Economist,* 7 June 1890; United States Bureau of the Census, *Negro Population in the United States, 1790–1915* (Washington, DC: GPO, 1918), 459–61, 503–6.

102. The debtor class of blacks reportedly paid interest rates as high as 100 percent, which prevented any annual realization of profit. Humphrey, "Colored Alliance," 290. See also Woodward, *Origins,* 180–81; Clark, "Furnishing and Supply System," 24–44.

103. See for example Hall, *Labor Struggles,* 25–30; Granbury, "Black Community Leadership," 249–57; Baker, "The 'Hoover Scare,'" 261–82; M. Langley Biegert,

"Legacy of Resistance: Uncovering the History of Collective Action by Black Agricultural Workers in Central Arkansas from the 1860s to the 1930s," *Journal of Social History* 32 (fall 1998): 73–100.

104. Gerald Grob, "Terence V. Powderly and the Knights of Labor," *Mid-America* 39 (January 1957): 51–53; Roger Wallace Shugg, "The New Orleans General Strike of 1892," *Louisiana Historical Quarterly* 11 (April 1938): 550; Sidney H. Kessler, "The Organization of Negroes in the Knights of Labor," *Journal of Negro History* 27 (July 1952): 248–76; William W. Rogers, "Negro Knights of Labor in Arkansas: A Case Study of the 'Miscellaneous Strike,' " *Labor History* 10 (summer 1969): 498–505; William I. Hair, *Bourbonism and Agrarian Protest: Louisiana Politics, 1877–1900* (Baton Rouge: Louisiana State University Press, 1969), 171–85, 227; Woodward, *Origins,* 229–31. These actions would seem to suggest a reinterpretation of the stereotyped docile Southern laborer. Also, these studies cast doubt on the traditional view that the Knights were not fomenters of strikes. While the overt stages of strikes were black efforts, the role of the Knights as promoters of these actions is implicit in several of these studies.

105. William F. Holmes, *The White Chief: James Kimble Vardaman* (Baton Rouge: Louisiana State University Press, 1970), 35; William Holmes, "The Leflore County Massacre and the Demise of the Colored Farmers' Alliance," *Phylon* 34 (September 1973): 267–74. See also *Leavenworth Advocate,* 28 September 1889; *Washington, D.C., Bee,* 27 September 1889 for further indications of Colored Farmers' Alliance efforts in Mississippi during this same period.

106. Woodward, *Origins,* 206. See also Clark, "Furnishing and Supply System," 24–44.

107. Aptheker, *Documentary,* 2:810. A copy of one such circular was reprinted in the black-owned *Topeka American Citizen,* 11 September 1891.

108. Tindall, *South Carolina Negroes,* 117–18; Holmes, "Arkansas Cotton Pickers' Strike," 111–12.

109. Tindall, *South Carolina Negroes,* 117–18; Abramowitz, "Accommodation and Militancy," 43; Holmes, "Arkansas Cotton Pickers' Strike," 107–19.

110. For a brief bibliography of major works on the strike, see Holmes, "The Colored Farmers' Alliance," 231. The number of fatalities according to Holmes *supra* and Holmes, "Demise," 195, differ slightly.

111. *National Economist,* 26 September 1891. Emphasis added. The text of the column indicates that the strike remained minor, receiving little publicity—favorable or unfavorable—from the major newspapers of the region.

112. See Holmes, "Demise," 187–200.

113. Quoted in Abramowitz, "Accommodation and Militancy," 43.

114. *National Economist,* 26 September 1891.

115. *Weekly Toiler,* 14 October 1891; John Hope Franklin, *From Slavery to Freedom,* 3rd ed. (New York: Knopf, 1967), 36; Woodward, *Tom Watson,* 219; *Atlanta Constitution,* 23 September 1891; William J. Northen Scrapbook, No. 1, 213, Northen Papers; a good discussion of the strike is found in Abramowitz, "Accommodation and Militancy," 42–49.

116. Pitre, *Through Many Dangers,* 197–98; Holmes, "Demise," 260.

117. See and compare J. H. Turner, "The Race Problem," 272–92, and Thomas E. Watson, "The Negro Question in the South," *Arena* 6 (October 1892): 544–48, for a concept of "self interest" in biracial unions, such as the Alliance and Populists.

2. THE SEARCH FOR POLICY

1. Philip Dray, *At the Hands of Persons Unknown: The Lynching of Black America* (New York: Random House, 2002), ix, 47, 73–80.

2. Dray, *At the Hands,* ix, 5, 79.

3. Ida Barnett Wells, *Autobiography,* quoted in William S. McFeely, *Frederick Douglass* (New York: Norton, 1991), 302; Ida Barnett Wells, *Mob Rule in New Orleans: Robert Charles and His Fight to the Death* (1900), reprinted in *Southern Horrors and Other Writings: The Anti-Lynching Campaign of Ida B. Wells, 1892–1900,* ed. Jacqueline Jones Royster (Boston: Bedford Books, 1997), 203.

4. See particularly Benjamin O. Flower, "The Burning of Negroes in the South," *Arena* 7 (April 1893): 630–40.

5. See Gunnar Myrdal, *An American Dilemma: The Negro Problem and Modern Democracy* (New York: Harper and Row, 1944), 561; James Inverarity, "Populism and Lynching in Louisiana, 1889–1896: A Test of Erickson's Theory of the Relationship between Boundary Crises and Repressive Justice," *American Sociological Review* 41 (April 1976): 262–78; Sarah A. Soule, "Populism and Black Lynching in Georgia, 1880–1900," *Social Forces* 71 (December 1992): 431–49; Ira Wasserman, "Southern Violence and the Political Process," *American Sociological Review* 42 (April 1977): 359–62. Lynching figures vary from source to source; in some cases "hangings" are not considered "lynchings," causing some inconsistency.

6. Quoted in Myrdal, *American Dilemma,* 1438 n.34.

7. Ibid., 511–15.

8. For a state study utilizing this viewpoint, see in particular William H. Chafe, "The Negro and Populism: A Kansas Case Study," *The Journal of Southern History* 34 (August 1968): 402–19.

9. See for example Leslie H. Fishel, "The Negro in Northern Politics, 1870–1900," *Mississippi Valley Historical Review* 42 (December 1955): 466–89; Vincent P. De Santis, "The Republican Party and the Southern Negro, 1877–1897," *Journal of Negro History* 45 (April 1960): 71–87; Carl Degler, *The Other South: Southern Dissenters in the Nineteenth Century* (New York: Harper and Row, 1974), 265–69; Moneyhon, "Black Politics in Arkansas," 222–45.

10. Booker T. Washington to John Elbert McConnell, 17 December 1885, *Booker T. Washington Papers,* ed. Louis R. Harlan (Urbana: University of Illinois Press, 1972), 2:284.

11. De Santis, "Republican Party," 71–87.

12. Woodward, *Origins,* 220.

13. Ibid. On T. Thomas Fortune and his efforts with the Afro-American League,

see Emma Lou Thornbrough, "The National Afro-American League, 1887–1908," *The Journal of Southern History* 27 (November 1961): 494–512.

14. For the example of John B. Rayner, the black populist leader from Texas, see Cantrell, *Kenneth and John B. Rayner,* 203–5.

15. *National Economist,* 24 May 1890.

16. Cantrell, *Kenneth and John B. Rayner,* 204; Hicks, *Populist Revolt,* 110, 116–17.

17. *Weekly Toiler,* 8 January 1890.

18. Hicks, *Populist Revolt,* 119–20.

19. *National Economist,* 6 September 1890; Hicks, *Populist Revolt,* 108, 119–27. See also *Weekly Toiler,* 11 December 1889; 18 December 1889; 15 January 1890.

20. Hicks, *Populist Revolt,* 112; Drew, "Present Farmers' Movement," 285, citing *Proceedings of Farmers' and Laborers' Union, 1889,* 57. Quote from Ford, "Rednecks and Merchants," 315.

21. Woodward, *Origins,* 201; Shaw, *The Wool-Hat Boys,* 8.

22. Humphrey, "History," 291; *Weekly Toiler,* 18 December 1889.

23. Humphrey, "History," 291; *Weekly Toiler,* 23 January 1889.

24. Scott, "Milton George," 107–8.

25. Woodward, *Origins,* 201.

26. Lord Bryce, *American Commonwealth,* quoted in Clement Eaton, *The Waning of the Old South Civilization, 1860–1880's* (Athens: University of Georgia Press, 1968), 137.

27. Woodward, *Origins,* 201. On the size of the Southern Alliance, see Michael Schwartz, "An Estimate of the Size of the Southern Farmers' Alliance," *Agricultural History* 51 (October 1977): 759.

28. *National Economist,* 31 May 1890.

29. *Weekly Toiler,* 23 January 1889; *Appleton's Annual Cyclopedia, 1890,* 301.

30. Barrows, "What the Southern Negro Is Doing for Himself," 805–6.

31. Dann, "Black Populism," 58–71.

32. *National Economist,* 12 April 1890.

33. In North Carolina, for example, blacks were specifically excluded from the Farmers' Alliance. Alliance membership was open to "white persons only, with the exception of Cherokee Indians in Clay, Graham, Haywood, Jackson, Macon and Swain Counties if they are of pure Indian blood and not less than half white." Croatan Indians located on the eastern shore were also included in the same category. Helen G. Edmonds, *The Negro and Fusion Politics in North Carolina, 1894–1901* (Chapel Hill: University of North Carolina Press, 1951), 24; Schwartz, Rosenthal, and Schwartz, "Leader-Member Conflict," 33.

34. Gerald Grob, *Workers and Utopia: A Study of Ideological Conflict in the American Labor Movement, 1865–1900* (Evanston, IL: Northwestern University Press, 1969), 54; *Weekly Toiler,* 25 December 1889; Gerald Grob, "Terence V. Powderly," 53.

35. *Greensboro Herald,* quoted in Clark, "Furnishing and Supply System," 39–40.

36. Kathryn T. Abbey, "Florida Versus the Principles of Populism, 1896–1911," *Journal of Southern History* 4 (December 1938): 463.

37. Jamie Lawson Reddick, "The Negro in the Populist Movement in Georgia,"

(master's thesis, Atlanta University, 1937); Saloutos, *Farmer Movements*, 18; Jack Abramowitz, "The Negro in the Populist Movement," *Journal of Negro History* 38 (July 1953): 258. See also James O. Knauss, "Farmers' Alliance in Florida," *South Atlantic Quarterly* 25 (July 1926): 300–315; Samuel Proctor, "National Farmers' Alliance Convention of 1890 and its Ocala Demands," *Florida Historical Quarterly* 18 (January 1950): 167–69.

38. Humphrey, "History," 291–92; Dunning, *Farmers' Alliance and Agricultural Digest*, 153.

39. Humphrey, "History," 292.

40. *National Economist*, 10 January 1891.

41. Dunning, *Farmers' Alliance and Agricultural Digest*, 153–54; *Progressive Farmer*, 9 December 1890.

42. *Philadelphia Times*, 5 December 1890, in *Public Opinion* 10, no. 10 (1890): 220; *Atlanta Constitution*, 4 December 1890; *Augusta Chronicle*, 4 December 1890; Dunning, *Farmers' Alliance and Agricultural Digest*, 153–54.

43. Woodward, *Origins*, 254. See also Richard E. Welch Jr., "The Federal Elections Bill of 1890: Postscripts and Preludes," *Journal of American History* 52 (December 1965): 511–20.

44. *Boston Journal*, 8 December 1890, in *Public Opinion* 10 no. 10 (1890): 220.

45. *National Economist*, 7 March 1891, in Aptheker, *Documentary*, 2:807–9.

46. *Congressional Record*, 51st Cong., 2nd sess.: 158. The full text of a telegram to the Senate Committee on Agriculture is included in the record.

47. Woodward, *Origins*, 200; Holmes, "The Colored Farmers' Alliance," 231; Sharp, "Entrance," 92; Drew, "Present Farmers' Movement," 298–99; Herman C. Nixon, "The Cleavage within the Farmers' Alliance Movement," *Mississippi Valley Historical Review* 15 (June 1928): 28–30; Holmes, "Arkansas Cotton Pickers' Strike," 109–10.

48. *Atlanta Constitution*, 7 December 1890; Northen Scrapbook, No. I, 83–84, in Northen Papers; Drew, "Present Farmers' Movement," 285, 298; Holmes, "Demise," 193 n.24.

49. Woodward, *Origins*, 220; Holmes, "Arkansas Cotton Pickers' Strike," 110. See also Grob, "Terence V. Powderly," 39–55, for additional details on Powderly's views.

50. Drew, "Present Farmers' Movement," 285–86; Holmes, "Demise," 193; Humphrey, "History," 290–92; *National Economist*, 13 December 1890; Hart, *Redeemers, Bourbons, and Populists*, 114–16, 126–28.

51. Holmes, "Colored Farmers' Alliance," 231.

52. Saloutos, *Farmer Movements*, 119.

53. Woodward, *Origins*, 217–22; Turner, "The Race Problem," 277.

54. *Atlanta Constitution*, 4 December 1890; Northen Scrapbook, No. I, 83, Northern Papers; Turner, "The Race Problem," 277; Drew, "Present Farmers' Movement," 288.

55. Dunning, *Farmers' Alliance and Agricultural Digest*, 95, 142; Hicks, *Populist Revolt*, 217; Hair, *Bourbonism and Agrarian Protest*, 211.

56. *National Economist*, 11 April 1891, in Aptheker, *Documentary*, 2:808–10; Woodward, *Origins*, 202–4.

57. *Atlanta Constitution*, 13 January 1890, quoted in Woodward, *Tom Watson*, 144; Shaw, *Wool-Hat Boys*, 22–34.

58. Hicks, *Populist Revolt*, 178, 208; Woodward, *Origins*, 203–4; William F. Holmes, "The Southern Farmers' Alliance and the Georgia Senatorial Election of 1890," *Journal of Southern History* 50 (May 1984): 197–224; Holmes, "Demise," 194; Hart, *Redeemers, Bourbons, and Populists*, 266–73; Rice, *Negro in Texas*, 147–48. See also Drew, "Present Farmers' Movement," 302–3.

59. *National Economist*, 7 March 1891, in Aptheker, *Documentary*, 2:805, 890.

60. Woodward, *Origins*, 193. See also C. Vann Woodward, *The Burden of Southern History* (Baton Rouge: Louisiana State University Press, 1960), 153; Edna Bonacich, "A Theory of Ethnic Antagonism: The Split Labor Market," *American Sociological Review* 37 (October 1972): 547–59.

61. Barnhart, "The Farmers' Alliance," 271; Drew, "Present Farmers' Movement," 286; Hicks, *Populist Revolt*, 115. On the white farmers as landowners, see Woodward, *Origins*, 193; Holmes, "Southern Farmers' Alliance," 206–10; Stephen Kantrowitz, "Ben Tillman and Hendrix McLane, Agrarian Rebels: White Manhood, 'The Farmers,' and the Limits of Southern Populism," *Journal of Southern History* 66 (August 2000): 517–18; Cantrell, *Kenneth and John B. Rayner*, 198, 201; Baker, "The 'Hoover Scare,'" 270–82; Schwartz, Rosenthal, and Schwartz, "Leader-Member Conflict," 22–36; Hart, *Redeemers, Bourbons, and Populists*, 114–15, 126–28. The question as to whether the white Alliance largely comprised landowners is still open to debate. The present writer believes that, as a group, white Alliance members, particularly the leadership, were primarily small landowners, while the Colored Farmers' Alliance was composed largely of landless blacks. However, it appears that a considerable segment of the CFA leadership were also black small landowners. Texas and Virginia leaders stand as small landowner prototypes for the CFA.

62. Loren Schwenginger, *Black Property Owners in the South, 1790–1915* (Urbana: University of Illinois Press, 1990), 162–63.

63. See for example Barrows, "What the Southern Negro Is Doing for Himself," 805–8; Du Bois, "The Negroes of Farmville, Virginia," in Lewis, *W. E. B. Du Bois*, 233–35.

64. Meier, *Negro Thought*, 60; August Meier and Elliot Rudwick, *From Plantation to Ghetto: An Interpretive History of American Negroes* (New York: G. P. Putnam and Sons, 1960), 158–59. For other reports of such open conflicts of interest between black and white Alliancemen, see *Atlanta Constitution*, 11 September 1889; *New York Age*, 4 January 1890; Schwartz, Rosenthal, and Schwartz, "Leader-Member Conflict," 33–34.

65. Daniel W. Crofts, "The Black Response to the Blair Education Bill," *Journal of Southern History* 37 (February 1971): 41–65.

66. Welch, "The Federal Elections Bill," 511–26; Allen J. Going, "The South and the Blair Education Bill," *Mississippi Valley Historical Review* 44 (September 1957): 267–90.

67. Meier, *Negro Thought,* 20–23.

68. *Booker T. Washington Papers,* 2:259.

3. TIME OF TRIAL, TIME OF HOPE

1. Rogers, *One-Gallused Rebellion,* 142.

2. See Degler, *Other South,* 1, 288–91; Clifton Paisley, "The Political Wheelers and the Arkansas Election of 1888," *Arkansas Historical Quarterly* 25 (spring 1966): 3–21; Theodore Saloutos, "The Grange in the South, 1870–1877," *Journal of Southern History* 19 (November 1953): 473–87; Hall, *Labor Struggles,* 48–50.

3. Degler, *Other South,* 1. See also *The Populist Mind,* ed. Norman Pollack (Indianapolis: Bobbs-Merrill, 1967), xxx–xxxiii. The history of these movements has been adequately chronicled elsewhere and need not be repeated here in abbreviated form. A list of the more significant studies can be found in ibid., lx. See also Saloutos, *Farmer Movements,* 1–68.

4. *People's Party Paper,* 28 August 1896.

5. Ibid., 28 June 1895.

6. Abramowitz, "John B. Rayner," 193.

7. *Greensboro Daily Record,* 7 March 1892, 19 August 1892, quoted in Hicks, *Populist Revolt,* 239.

8. *Atlanta Constitution,* 13 January 1890, quoted in Woodward, *Tom Watson,* 144.

9. George Washington Cable, "The Freedman's Case in Equity," *Century Magazine* 29 (January 1885): 417.

10. Degler, *Other South,* 247–48.

11. Turner, "The Race Problem," 272–73.

12. W. E. B. Du Bois, "Social Equality and Racial Intermarriage," in Lewis, *W. E. B. Du Bois,* 372–74.

13. *People's Party Tribune,* 28 May 1896, in Pollack, *Populist Mind,* 387–88.

14. Cantrell, *Kenneth and John B. Rayner,* 212.

15. Maud Cuney Hare, *Norris Wright Cuney: A Tribune of the Black People,* intro. Tera W. Hunter (Austin, TX: Steck-Vaughan Co., 1913; reprint, New York: G. K. Hall, 1968), xv–xviii; Dray, *At the Hands,* 55–56.

16. Richard Newman, *African-American Quotations* (Phoenix, AZ: Oryx Press, 1998), 250.

17. Degler, *Other South,* 7.

18. Ezell, *The South Since 1865,* 223.

19. Woodward, *Origins,* 80. For similar descriptions of attitudes in two southern states, see John B. Clark, *Populism in Alabama, 1874–1896* (Auburn, AL: Auburn Printing Co., 1927), 80; Albert D. Kirwan, *Revolt of the Rednecks: Mississippi Politics, 1876–1925* (New York: Harper, 1965), 95.

20. Quoted in David Alan Harris, "The Political Career of Milford W. Howard, Populist Congressman from Alabama" (master's thesis, Auburn University, 1957), 57–58.

21. Ibid.

22. Woodward, *Tom Watson,* 223. In Alabama, a comparable situation occurred with Joseph Manning, whose brother edited a newspaper that opposed him. Likewise, his father and brother remained staunch Democrats. The salient fact here is that politics, like "the late war," literally turned brother against brother. Jerrell H. Shofner and William Warren Rogers, "Joseph C. Manning: Militant Agrarian, Enduring Populist," *Alabama Historical Quarterly* 29 (spring–summer 1967): 36.

23. Quoted in Woodward, *Tom Watson,* 239. For a description of one such event, see Ralph McGill, *The South and the Southerner* (Boston: Little, Brown, 1964), 126–27.

24. Thomas K. Hearn, "The Populist Movement in Marshall County [Alabama]" (master's thesis, University of Alabama, 1935), 66.

25. *People's Party Paper,* 29 September 1893.

26. See Frederick A. Bode, "Religion and Class Hegemony: A Populist Critique of North Carolina," *Journal of Southern History* 37 (August 1971): 417–38.

27. For a summary of religious views in the southern states, see Ezell, *The South Since 1865,* 340–58.

28. Quoted in Helen M. Blackburn, "The Populist Party in the South" (master's thesis, Howard University, 1941), 51.

29. Smith, *Wool-Hat Boys,* 94.

30. *Raleigh Biblical Recorder,* 3 January 1894, quoted in Bode, "Religion and Class Hegemony," 425.

31. Quoted in ibid., 427.

32. *Raleigh Caucasian,* 25 July 1895, quoted in ibid., 433.

33. *People's Party Paper,* 3 June 1892.

34. See Chafe, "Negro and Populism," 402–19; *Lynchburg (VA) Daily Advance,* 10 October 1893, in Charles E. Wynes, *Race Relations in Virginia, 1870–1902* (Charlottesville: University of Virginia Press, 1961), 40; Meier, *Negro Thought,* 166–69, 208–11.

35. Janet Brenner Franzoni, "Troubled Tirader: A Psychobiographical Study of Tom Watson," *Georgia Historical Quarterly* 57 (winter 1973): 493–510.

36. William H. Skaggs, *The Southern Oligarchy: An Appeal in Behalf of the Silent Masses of Our Country against the Despotic Rule of the Few* (New York: Devin-Adair, 1924), 126, 424; Rayford W. Logan, *Negro in American Life and Thought* (New York: Dial, 1954), 61–64, 67–73; Welch, "The Federal Elections Bill," 511–26.

37. For discussion of the Lodge Bill, see *Congressional Record,* 51st Cong., 1st sess.: 5789–93, 6538–45, 6851, 6869. On Degler, see *Other South,* 192–93.

38. Reddick, "The Negro in the Populist Movement," 25.

39. Frenise A. Logan, *The Negro in North Carolina, 1876–1894* (Chapel Hill: University of North Carolina Press, 1964), 61.

40. For the case against the bill's being logically tagged as a "Force Bill," see Welch, "The Federal Elections Bill," 511–26.

41. For a discussion of the role the Republican "silverites" played in the defeat of the Lodge Bill, see Fred Wellborn, "The Influence of the Silver-Republican Senators, 1889–1891," *Mississippi Valley Historical Review* 14 (March 1928): 402–80.

42. Ibid, 402–80.

43. *Birmingham People's Weekly Tribune,* 28 May 1896; *People's Party Paper,* 26 August 1892.

44. Wilbur J. Cash, *The Mind of the South* (New York: Knopf, 1941), 174.

45. Hicks, *The Populist Revolt,* 243.

46. Degler, *Other South,* 9. See also Kirwan, *Revolt of the Rednecks,* 95.

47. *People's Party Paper,* 28 August 1896.

48. Hicks, *The Populist Revolt,* 243.

49. *National Economist,* 26 July 1890.

50. Ibid., 18 April 1891.

51. *Progressive Farmer,* 9 December 1890; *National Economist,* 26 July 1890.

52. *National Economist,* 10 January 1891. For further information on the Lodge Bill, see Ruth E. Byrd, "The History of the Force Bill of 1890 and its Effect upon State Constitutions" (master's thesis, University of North Carolina at Chapel Hill, 1939); Hoke Smith, "Disastrous Effects of the Force Bill," *The Forum* 13 (August 1892): 686–92; Henry Cabot Lodge and Terence V. Powderly, "The Federal Election Bill," *The North American Review* 151 (September 1890): 257–73; A. W. Shaffer, "A Southern Republican on the Lodge Bill," *The North American Review* 151 (November 1890): 601–9; Thomas B. Reed, "The Federal Control of Elections," *The North American Review* 151 (June 1890): 671–80; *Progressive Farmer,* 27 January 1891; H. D. Hutchison to L. L. Polk, 15 April 1892, Leonidas L. Polk Papers, Southern Historical Collection, University of North Carolina at Chapel Hill. See also Daniel Wallace Crofts, "The Blair Bill and the Federal Elections Bill: The Congressional Aftermath to Reconstruction" (Ph.D. diss., Yale University, 1968).

53. *Booker T. Washington Papers,* 2:259.

54. The use of the "Force Bill" as a measure to create political conformity in the South can be very aptly traced in the newspapers and periodicals of the day. To follow the issue, see *Public Opinion* 8 (1889–90): 551–53; 9 (1890–91): 330–31; 13 (1893): 420–21; 14 (1893): 103–4, 223; 15 (1893): 377–78, 614–15; 16 (1893–94): 43–44, 71.

55. On this philosophy, see Meier, *Negro Thought,* 42–46, 62–63, 74–96, 80–99, 105–6, 119–57, 208–47; Robert L. Factor, *The Black Response to America: Men, Ideals, and Organization from Frederick Douglass to the NAACP* (Reading, MA: Addison-Wesley, 1970), 109–16.

56. "An Open Letter from Charles A. Roxborough Resigning from the Republican Committee, with his Reasons Therefore, July 31, 1891." Charles A. Roxborough Letter, Louisiana State University Archives, Baton Rouge. Roxborough was a black leader of the Republican Party in Louisiana during the 1880s. In the above letter, he hints that blacks should support the Democrats rather than the Republicans. The black lawyer's quote can be found in *Charleston News and Courier,* 12 September 1892, in De Santis, "The Republican Party," 86.

57. Rayford W. Logan, *Betrayal of the Negro* (New York: Da Capo, 1997), 80; Donald J. Calista, "Booker T. Washington: Another Look," *Journal of Negro History* 49 (October 1964): 246.

58. Meier, *Negro Thought,* 77. Interviewed by the *Atlanta Constitution,* a white

Democratic paper, Professor Meier said he believed that blacks made such statements "for white ears." However, I am of the opinion that the views of middle-class
prosperous blacks differed little from whites of the same class level on the Lodge Bill.

59. Quoted in Meier, *Negro Thought,* 192.

60. Ibid., 80–82; W. E. B. Du Bois, *The Souls of Black Folk: Essays and Sketches*
(Greenwich, CT: Fawcett, 1961), 47; *Progressive Farmer,* 27 January 1891. See also
Thornborough, "The National Afro-American League," 494–512; Jeffrey J. Crow,
Paul D. Escott, and Flora J. Hatley, *A History of African Americans in North Carolina*
(Raleigh: Division of Archives and History, North Carolina Department of Cul-
tural Resources, 1992), 102–4.

61. Meier, *Negro Thought,* 38.

62. Earl E. Thorpe, *The Mind of the Negro: An Intellectual History of Afro-Americans*
(Westport, CT: Negro University Press, 1970), 275.

63. Spriggs, "Virginia Colored Farmers' Alliance," 191–204.

64. *National Economist,* 15 August 1891.

65. Hicks, *Populist Revolt,* 207–12.

66. Ibid., 212–13; Blackburn, "Populist Party in the South," 15–16; Sheldon,
Populism in the Old Dominion, 66. Out of the estimated 1,400 delegates, the two
states of Kansas and Ohio had over 700 representatives. It also appears that blacks
were not viewed as "Southern delegates" by some members of the press.

67. Quoted in Hicks, *Populist Revolt,* 212.

68. Clipping in Tom Watson Scrapbook #22, 24, Tom Watson Papers, Southern Historical Collection, University of North Carolina at Chapel Hill. See also
Henry D. Lloyd, "The Populists at St. Louis," *Review of Reviews* 14 (September
1896): 299–300.

69. Reddick, "Negro in the Populist Movement in Georgia," 30; De Santis,
"Republican Party," 71–87.

70. Blackburn, "Populist Party in the South," 16–17.

71. Grob, "Terence V. Powderly," 52–53.

72. *New York Times,* 21 May 1891.

73. Reddick, "Negro in the Populist Movement in Georgia," 92; Blackburn,
"Populist Party in the South," 16.

74. Quoted in Hicks, *Populist Revolt,* 215.

75. Ibid., 213–18.

76. Quoted in Stuart Noblin, *Leonidas LaFayette Polk: Agrarian Crusader* (Chapel
Hill: University of North Carolina Press, 1949), 269–70; Lloyd, "Populists at St.
Louis," 299.

77. The Cincinnati platform can be found in Hicks, *Populist Revolt,* 433–35.

78. Various newspaper opinions on the third party question as well as the region's attitude toward its chance of success are discussed in *Public Opinion* 11 (1891):
167–71.

79. *National Economist,* 11 April 1891.

80. Ibid., 13 June 1891. "The first distinctive political body known as the People's

party" was not formed until nearly six months later at Indianapolis (*People's Party Paper,* 17 December 1891).

81. *Alliance Vindicator,* quoted in *National Economist,* 27 June 1891. On Asberry and the *Alliance Vindicator,* see Cantrell, *Kenneth and John B. Rayner,* 207, 321 n.12. Cantrell indicates the paper was founded in February 1892, but this citation suggests an earlier founding.

82. Degler, *Other South,* 191–316.

83. *People's Party Tribune,* 28 May 1896, in Pollack, *Populist Mind,* 389.

84. Saloutos, *Farmer Movements,* 123; Holmes, "Demise," 193 n.24; Abramowitz, "Negro in the Populist Movement," 261–62.

85. *People's Party Paper,* 17 March 1892.

86. Ibid.

87. Spriggs, "Virginia Colored Farmers' Alliance," 195; Abramowitz, "Negro in the Populist Movement," 261.

88. Blackburn, "Populist Party in the South," 22.

89. A list of the number of seats allotted to each individual can be found in Hicks, *Populist Revolt,* 226.

90. Reddick, "Negro in the Populist Movement in Georgia," 34–35; Blackburn, "Populist Party in the South," 22–23.

91. *People's Party Paper,* 17 March 1892.

92. Ibid.

93. Spriggs, "Virginia Colored Farmers' Alliance," 191–202; see also Floyd J. Miller, "Black Protest and White Leadership: A Note on the Colored Farmers' Alliance," *Phylon* 33 (June 1972): 169–74.

94. Saloutos, *Farmer Movements,* 124

95. *National Economist,* 5 March 1892.

96. The events of the St. Louis Convention can be found in *People's Party Paper,* 25 February 1892; *National Economist,* 27 February 1892, 5 March 1892.

97. *National Economist,* 5 March 1892.

98. Ibid., 27 February 1892; *People's Party Paper,* 25 February 1892.

99. *Nashville Banner,* 4 October 1891; *Philadelphia Press,* 24 October 1891, quoted in *Public Opinion* 12 (1891–92): 99.

100. Degler, *Other South,* 191–316.

101. Tom Watson Scrapbook, #27, 1; *National Economist,* 5 March 1892. These two accounts, both from newspapers, differ little in their reporting of the actions that occurred. However, the difference involved a portrayal of attitudes and motivations that surrounded this event, one indicating self-interest, the other humane intentions. Probably the event was a mixture of the two. See also Abramowitz, "Negro in the Populist Movement," 263.

102. Robert M. Saunders, "The Southern Populists and the Negro in 1892," *University of Virginia Essays in History* 12 (1966–67): 10.

103. Saloutos, *Farmer Movements,* 139. See also Sheldon, *Populism in the Old Dominion,* 1–21; *Southern Mercury,* 29 January 1897; Logan, *Negro in North Carolina,* 76–78.

104. Hicks, *Populist Revolt,* 243.

105. Hicks, *Populist Revolt,* 229; Lloyd, "Populists at St. Louis," 278–79.

106. Stanley P. Hirshson, *Farewell to the Bloody Shirt: Northern Republicans and the Southern Negro, 1877–1893* (Bloomington: Indiana University Press, 1962), 18.

107. Hicks, *Populist Revolt,* 229.

108. Hicks, *Populist Revolt,* 230. Anna Rochester agrees that eight representatives were elected at large, but states that eight, rather than four, additional delegates were selected from each congressional district (*The Populist Movement in the United States* [New York: International Publishers, 1943], 66).

109. James H. "Cyclone" Davis, for example, when speaking to an audience, would keep several volumes of Jefferson's works nearby to use in buttressing the principles of Populism. See Woodward, *Origins,* 245. See also, "Jefferson on the Race Question," *Progressive Farmer,* 21 October 1890; Thomas E. Watson, "The Creed of Jefferson, the Founder of Democracy," in *The Life and Speeches of Thomas E. Watson* (Nashville, TN: [n.p.], 1908); R. M. Goodman to Robert Felton, 18 September 1892, in Rebecca Latimer Felton Collection, University of Georgia Library, Athens, Georgia.

110. Hicks, *Populist Revolt,* 230–31.

111. Blackburn, "Populist Party in the South," 27.

112. Simkins, *Tillman Movement,* 111–13, 180–81.

113. Blackburn, "Populist Party in the South," 27; Saunders, "Southern Populists, 1892," 10.

114. *Columbus Advocate,* quoted in Abramowitz, "Negro in the Populist Movement," 278.

115. *Kansas City American Citizen,* 2 October 1891, quoted in Chafe, "Negro and Populism," 410.

116. *Omaha Daily Bee,* quoted in Abramowitz, "Accommodation and Militancy," 34.

117. *People's Party Paper,* 21 January 1892.

118. Hicks, *Populist Revolt,* 439–45.

119. *National Economist,* 9 July 1892. The rest of the platform can be found in Hicks, *Populist Revolt,* 439–44.

120. C. Vann Woodward, *The Strange Career of Jim Crow* (New York: Oxford University Press, 1957), 13–48.

121. See Noblin, *Leonidas LaFayette Polk,* 284–88; Hicks, *Populist Revolt,* 232–33; Lloyd, "Populists at St. Louis," 278–79; Woodward, *Tom Watson,* 30. Polk died on 11 June 1892.

122. Undated newspaper clipping in Tom Watson Scrapbook, #27, 1.

123. Noblin, *Leonidas LaFayette Polk,* 28, 199.

124. *People's Party Paper,* 30 September 1892. While Tom Watson described this plan to a black audience during his 1892 campaign, it seems unlikely, in view of his great admiration for the man, that he would have invented such a scheme which would discredit the memory of Polk. See Noblin, *Leonidas LaFayette Polk,* 155, 285, 291, 297.

125. The Alabama Jeffersonian Democrats–Populist Party advocated a similar plan in their 1894 platform. While calling for a separate state, the declaration favored relocating only those blacks who voluntarily agreed to leave. The wording of the measure indicates that this was a humanitarian and paternalistic move designed to protect blacks from recent white violence, rather than any expression of hostility toward blacks. The text of the declaration can be found in *Appleton's Annual Cyclopedia, 1894,* 4. See also Benjamin Quarles, *Negro in the Making of America* (New York: Macmillan, 1965), 157, concerning black sentiment in Texas for a separate state.

126. The relevant literature on this subject has been collected in John H. Bracey Jr., August Meier, and Elliott Rudwick, ed., *Black Nationalism in America* (Indianapolis: Bobbs-Merrill, 1970), lxi–lxx.

127. Meier, *Negro Thought,* 63.

128. See, for example, Roy Graham, "Benjamin, or 'Pap,' Singleton and His Followers," *Journal of Negro History* 33 (January 1948): 7–23.

129. *Afro-American Encyclopedia,* ed. and comp. James T. Haley (Nashville, TN: Haley and Florida, 1895), 9. A copy of this rare volume is available in the Special Collections Department, Franklin Library, Fisk University, Nashville, Tennessee.

130. Cantrell, *Kenneth and John B. Rayner,* 188–89; Abramowitz, "John B. Rayner," 163.

131. The Reverend Garland H. White to Governor W. J. Northen, 29 March 1894, in "The Negro at the South: Letters by Governor W. J. Northen," Northen Papers, State of Georgia Archives, folder marked "Speeches 1889–1891," 9–10. The best narrative of Bishop Turner's role in the movement can be found in Redkey, *Black Exodus.*

132. *Afro-American Encyclopedia,* 9.

133. *Natchitoches Louisiana Populist,* 29 November 1895.

134. *Birmingham Daily News,* 8 July 1894, in Pollack, *Populist Mind,* 391–92.

135. Meier, *Negro Thought,* 62.

136. Hicks, *Populist Revolt,* 235. Judge Gresham declined the nomination, threw his support to Cleveland, and later became his secretary of state (Sheldon, *Populism in the Old Dominion,* 83).

137. For newspaper opinions of Weaver's chance to break the solid South in 1892, as well as his presidential campaign, see *Public Opinion* 13 (1892): 319–25; 14 (1892–1893): 78–79.

138. Sheldon, *Populism in the Old Dominion,* 83–85; Alex M. Arnett, *The Populist Movement in Georgia,* Columbia University Studies in History, Economics, and Public Law, 104, No. 1 (New York: Columbia University Press, 1922), 141–42; *National Economist,* 9 July 1892; *People's Party Paper,* 8 July, 22 July 1892. "General" James Field never attained any rank above major; his title was purely honorary.

139. Smith, *Wool-Hat Boys,* 36, 55–57, 69–71.

140. *Montgomery Advertiser,* 16 September 1892; *Birmingham Daily News,* 16 September 1892, quoted in Mary A. Boras, "A Case Study of the Speeches of the Birmingham, Alabama Populist Party Convention, September 15–16, 1892" (master's thesis, University of Alabama, 1952), 113.

141. *Louisiana Populist,* 24 January 1896.

142. See Inverarity, "Populism and Lynching in Louisiana," 262–79.

143. "The Negro Heart," n.d., John B. Rayner Papers, Barker History Center, The University of Texas, Austin.

144. *People's Party Paper,* 3 June 1892.

145. Quoted in Calista, "Booker T. Washington," 242.

146. The circumstances distinguishing the growth and motivation of such movements can be found in King, *Social Movements,* 39–64; *People's Party Paper,* 3 June 1892.

147. *National Economist,* 17 September 1892.

148. The myth of the liberating proletariat has been soundly disproved by sociologist Seymour Lipset, who views this type of individual as prone to express ethnic prejudice, political authoritarianism, and fundamentalist religious beliefs. See Seymour Lipset, "Workingclass Authoritarianism," in his *Political Man* (New York: Doubleday, 1963), 86–126. This essay is also found in *American Sociological Review* 24 (August 1959): 482–501. For other evidence that disputes this myth, see Morris Jamowitz and Dwaine Marvick, "Authoritarianism and Political Behavior," *Public Opinion Quarterly* 47 (summer 1953): 185–201; Louis Wirth, "Race and Public Policy," *Scientific Monthly* 68 (April 1944): 304; William MacKinnon and Richard Centers, "Authoritarianism and Urban Stratification," *American Journal of Sociology* 61 (May 1966): 616.

149. Sheldon, *Populism in the Old Dominion,* 83.

150. *People's Party Paper,* 7 July 1893.

4. THE MINORITY TEMPER

1. Woodward, *Origins,* 245, 249–50; Lloyd, "Populists at St. Louis," 279–80. For additional use of the Jacksonian-Jeffersonian doctrine, see the statements of Davis and Milford W. Howard, the Populist congressman from Alabama, in Pollack, *Populist Mind,* 203–30.

2. Copy of an untitled speech, 1896, Box 3, folder 19, Marion Butler Papers, Southern Historical Collection, University of North Carolina. For a similar assertion by "Stump" Ashby of Texas, see Pollack, *Populist Mind,* 226.

3. Cantrell, *Kenneth and John B. Rayner,* 2–15, 16–18, 25, 28, 201–2.

4. Historians are divided over the question of whether or not Populism's utopia was in the future or the past. The present writer accepts the thesis of Richard Hofstadter: "The utopia of the Populists was in the past, not the future"; Richard Hofstadter, *Age of Reform: From Bryan to FDR* (New York: Knopf, 1955), 62.

5. Woodward, *Strange Career,* 43. A similar comment can be found in Ignatius Donnelly's *Doctor Huguet* (Chicago: F. J. Schulte and Co., 1891), a novel of the post–Civil War South (Pollack, *Populist Mind,* 491). See also Hair, *Bourbonism and Agrarian Protest,* 193–94.

6. Thomas E. Watson, "The Negro Question in the South," *Arena* 6 (October 1892): 540–50.

7. Woodward, *Origins,* 252. See also Hofstadter, *Age of Reform,* 64–65.

8. *Progressive Farmer,* 28 April 1887.

9. Marion Butler to J. A. Simms, 17 February 1896, Box 2, Butler Papers.

10. B. S. Heath, *Labor and Finance Revolution* (1892), quoted in Hofstadter, *Age of Reform,* 63.

11. *Louisiana Populist,* 18 October 1895.

12. "National People's Party Platform," in *The World Almanac, 1893* (New York: Press Pub. Co., 1893), 83–84.

13. Wayne Alvord, "T. L. Nugent, Texas Populist," *Southwestern Historical Quarterly* 57 (July 1953): 65–81.

14. Shofner and Rogers, "Joseph C. Manning," 7–37; Charles Grayson Summersell, "The Alabama Governor's Race of 1892," *Alabama Review* 8 (January 1955): 22.

15. The roots and subsequent development of the Social Gospel have been traditionally assumed to be of a non-Southern, urban, clerical focus. Although the movement was "not unknown" in the South, according to Woodward, it had but "few spokesmen" in the region (Woodward, *Origins,* 452–53). The present writer's examination of the literature of Southern Populism has convinced him that the principles of the Social Gospel were more widely incorporated into the movement and had wider circulation in the South than previously acknowledged. The studies of individuals, such as those conducted by Professors Alvord ("T. L. Nugent"), Bode ("Religion and Class Hegemony"), and Shofner and Rogers ("Joseph C. Manning"), reveal that individual Southern Populists, however rustic and ineffective, sympathetically presented the Social Gospel. Another individual who must be included in the group of Southern Social Gospelers is Milford Howard (Elmer F. Suderman, "The Social Gospel Novelists' Criticisms of American Society," *Midcontinent American Studies Journal* 7 [spring 1966]: 60). Such a movement deserves more treatment in depth than I have been able to accord it here. For traditional surveys of the Social Gospel movement that exclude the South's role, see Charles Howard Hopkins, *The Rise of the Social Gospel in American Protestantism, 1866–1915* (New Haven, CT: Yale University Press, 1940); Sidney Fine, *Laissez Faire and the General Welfare State* (Ann Arbor: University of Michigan Press, 1966): 169–97.

16. Alvord, "T. L. Nugent," 72, 78.

17. Bode, "Religion and Class Hegemony," 421–23.

18. *Louisiana Populist,* 6 December 1895.

19. Ibid., 7 February 1896. For a similar comment by W. Scott Morgan, see ibid., 12 July 1895.

20. George Tindall, ed., *A Populist Reader* (New York: Harper Torchbooks, 1966), x.

21. Tindall, *A Populist Reader,* xi–xii.

22. Mary A. Boras, "A Case Study of the Speeches of the Birmingham, Alabama, Populist Party Convention, September 15–16, 1892" (master's thesis, University of Alabama, 1952), 85, 110.

23. *Dallas Morning News,* 25 June 1892, quoted in Woodward, *Origins,* 247.

24. *Montgomery Advertiser,* 16 September 1892; *Birmingham Daily News,* 16 September 1892, quoted in Boras, "Birmingham's Populist Party Convention," 85, 110.

25. *People's Weekly Tribune,* 14 May 1896, 21 May 1896.

26. Shofner and Rogers, "Joseph C. Manning," 9.

27. Woodward, *Origins,* 245–46.

28. Letter from W. R. Elmore, 6 July 1894, printed in *West Alabama Breeze,* 12 July 1894, quoted in Charles Grayson Summersell, "A Life of Reuben Kolb" (master's thesis, University of Alabama, 1930), 108–9.

29. J. H. Buchanan to Marion Butler, 27 August 1896, Box 3, folder 33, Butler Papers.

30. Summersell, "Reuben Kolb," 111.

31. W. J. Pearson to Marion Butler, 18 May 1896, Box 2, folder 27, Butler Papers. For an example of "an Alliance lay sermon," which further shows the religious tinge and moral attitude of the Southern agrarian revolt, see the letter of Linn Tanner of Cheyneyville, Louisiana, in *National Economist,* 13 June 1891.

32. Goodwyn, *Democratic Promise,* 47–51, 56, 58–60, 62–66, 71–85.

33. *Town Talk,* 17 January 1896, quoted in Hofstadter, *Age of Reform.*

34. Hofstadter, *Age of Reform,* 23–59; Paul Gaston, *The New South Creed: A Study in Southern Mythmaking* (New York: Knopf, 1970), 7–13; "The Agrarian Myth in American History," in their *Myth and Reality in the Populist Revolt,* ed. Edwin C. Rozwenc and John C. Matlon (Boston: D. C. Heath and Co., 1967), 1–6.

35. Hostadter, *Age of Reform,* 62.

36. *Facts and Figures,* quoted in *Louisiana Populist,* 14 December 1894.

37. Quoted in Hofstadter, *Age of Reform,* 64.

38. Ibid.

39. *Louisiana Populist,* 14 December 1894.

40. *Oneonta (AL) Star,* quoted in *People's Weekly Tribune,* 3 December 1896.

41. *Louisiana Populist,* 24 August 1894.

42. John Sparkman, "The Kolb-Oates Campaign of 1894" (master's thesis, University of Alabama, 1924), 2.

43. *People's Weekly Tribune,* 21 May 1896.

44. The "opulent theme" exalted in the New South can be traced in Gaston, "The Opulent South," in *The New South Creed,* 43–80.

45. Dorothy Scarborough, *In the Land of Cotton* (New York: Macmillan, 1923), 162.

46. The most complete study of these ideas can be found in Irvin G. Wyllie, *The Self-Made Man in America* (New Brunswick, NJ: Rutgers University Press, 1954).

47. Quoted in Hofstadter, *Age of Reform,* 74; Hicks, *Populist Revolt,* 162 n.46.

48. *Louisiana Populist,* 10 January 1896.

49. Joel A. Tarr, "Goldfinger, the Gold Conspiracy, and the Populists," *Midcontinent American Studies Journal* 7 (fall 1966): 49–52. Populist conspiracies, both Right and Left, have blossomed since the advent of the Internet. See, for example, Mark Fenster's *Conspiracy Theories: Secrecy and Power in American Culture* (Minneapolis: University of Minnesota Press, 2001), Robert S. Robins and Jerrold M. Post, *Political Paranoia: The Psychopolitics of Hatred* (New Haven: Yale University Press, 1997), and Daniel Pipes's *Conspiracy: How the Paranoid Style Flourishes and Where It Comes From* (New York: Free Press, 1997)

50. Hofstadter, *Age of Reform*, 71.

51. *Congressional Record*, quoted in William Loren Katz, ed., *Eyewitness: The Negro in American History* (New York: Pittman, 1967), 339.

52. M. A. M'Cardy, "Duty of the State to the Negro," in *Afro-American Encyclopedia*, 143–44.

53. Tindall, *South Carolina Negroes*, 248.

54. Ibid., 247. For various opinions, black and white, on "federal interference," see Open Letter Correspondence, folder 5, State of Tennessee Archives, Nashville.

55. See particularly George Wilson to Marion Butler, 30 May 1896, Box 2, folder 27, Butler Papers; John B. Brownlow to Oliver P. Temple, 19 December 1897, Box 14, folder 2; Brownlow to Temple, 29 July 1894, Box 12, folder 5, Temple Papers. For two perceptive interpretations of southern Republicanism and northern attitudes on the race question during the period, see Vincent P. De Santis, *Republicans Face the Southern Question: The New Departure Years, 1877–1897* (Baltimore: Johns Hopkins University Press, 1959) and Hirshson, *Farewell to the Bloody Shirt*.

56. Reverend A. L. Phillips, "God's Problem for the South," in *Afro-American Encyclopedia*, 23.

57. "Choice Thoughts and Utterances of Wise Colored People," in ibid., 527; Charles W. Chestnutt, Letter No. 2, Open Letter Club Correspondence.

58. "Choice Thoughts," 527.

59. Meier, *Negro Thought*, 35, 40; Bracey et al., *Black Nationalism*, 223.

60. Clarence A. Bacote, "Negro Proscriptions, Protest and Proposed Solutions," in *Understanding Negro History*, ed. Dwight Hoover (Chicago: Quandrangle Books, 1968), 202.

61. Wynes, *Race Relations in Virginia*, 117. See also Logan, *Negro in North Carolina*, 175.

62. *Richmond Planet*, 6 April 1895, in Wynes, *Race Relations in Virginia*, 118.

63. *Voice of Missions*, 1 December 1900, in Bracey et al., *Black Nationalism*, 227. This comment was made by William Hooper Councill, president of the State Normal School at Huntsville, Alabama, who was "an even more extreme accommodator" than Booker T. Washington (ibid., 223). For additional information on Councill, see Meier, *Negro Thought*, 72, 77, 110, 209–10, 233, 260, 267.

64. Quoted in Aptheker, *Documentary*, 2:757.

66. Ridgely Torrence, *The Story of John Hope* (New York: Macmillan, 1948), 114–15.

66. Gaston, *New South Creed*, 129–35.

67. Meier, *Negro Thought*, 101. For a discussion of "the contrast between a natural legend of moral innocence, in which Southerners always claimed to share, and the reality of Southern determination to maintain a master class," see Gaston, "The Innocent South," *New South Creed*, 119–50.

68. *Weekly Toiler*, 17 April 1889. See also Summersell, "Alabama Governor's Race," 34 n.59.

69. Quoted in Wynes, *Race Relations in Virginia*, 45.

70. Ibid., 45–46.

71. Quoted in Woodward, *Origins,* 219. The story of the Texas Lily-White Republican movement can be found in Paul Douglas Casdorph, "Norris Wright Cuney and Texas Republican Politics, 1883–1896," *Southern Historical Quarterly* 68 (January 1965), 455–64; Maud Cuney Hare, "The Lily Whites," in *Norris Wright Cuney,* 92–104.

72. Quoted in Woodward, *Origins,* 220. See also Joseph F. Steelman, "Vicissitudes of Republican Party Politics: The Campaign of 1892 in North Carolina," *North Carolina Historical Review* 43 (autumn 1966): 436–42.

73. John Roy Lynch, *Reminiscences of an Active Life: The Autobiography of John Roy Lynch,* ed. John Hope Franklin (Chicago: University of Chicago Press, 1970), 334. Lynch's comments on the motivations behind the Lily-White movement seem sound. However, his attempt to downplay their role and scope would appear to this writer to be open to question. As a black Mississippi Republican, perhaps his intentions were honorable. The author of the standard biography of L. Q. C. Lamar, Wirt Armstead Cate, has challenged the accuracy of Lynch's case: "Generally speaking, little or no dependence can be placed on the writings of the Mississippi Negro ex-Congressman, John R. Lynch. . . . [He] perverted the facts . . . in all cases that suited his purpose and in some where falsifying apparently brought him no advantage" (ibid., 318).

74. Quoted in Woodward, *Origins,* 220.

5. PRINCIPLES, PREJUDICE, AND POPULISM

1. Woodward, *Strange Career,* 46. Woodward has repeated the essence of this statement in his earlier and later works on Populism. See Woodward, *Tom Watson,* 222; "The Populist Heritage and the Intellectual," in *Burden of Southern History,* 157; "Tom Watson and the Negro in Agrarian Politics," *Journal of Southern History* 4 (February 1938): 21. This stimulating statement, which was largely responsible for the initiation of this study, has received wide acceptance by many and discussion by other historians studying the period. For example, see Hair, *Bourbonism and Agrarian Protest,* 241. See Williamson, *Origins of Segregation,* v–ix, for a discussion of the Woodward thesis. See also special issue of *Journal of Southern History* 67 (November 2001), "C. Vann Woodward's *Origins of the New South, 1877–1913:* A Fifty-Year Retrospective." Woodward moderated his stance considerably in his later years. See particularly C. Vann Woodward, *American Counterpoint: Slavery and Racism in the South Dialogue* (Boston: Little, Brown and Co., 1971); Woodward, "Strange Career Critics: Long May They Persevere," *Journal of American History* 75 (December 1988): 857–68.

2. See particularly Woodward, "Tom Watson and the Negro."

3. Abramowitz, "Negro in the Populist Movement," 288.

4. Goodwyn, *Democratic Promise,* 297. See also McGill, *The South and the Southerner,* 128.

5. *National Economist,* 10 September 1892; *People's Party Paper,* 12 August 1892.

6. Hair, *Bourbonism and Agrarian Protest,* 218–19.

7. *National Economist,* 26 November 1892. This was a part of Loucks's presiden-

tial address to the Supreme Council of the Southern Alliance at Memphis on 16 November 1892.

8. August Meier and Elliot Rudwick, introductory note to Herbert Shapiro, "The Populists and the Negro: A Reconsideration," *Making of Black America* (New York: Atheneum, 1969), 2:27. Professor Shapiro's essay also examines this viewpoint, reaching a similar conclusion.

9. Gerald H. Gaither, "The Negro in the Ideology of Southern Populism, 1889–1896" (master's thesis, University of Tennessee, 1967), 172–215, examines the inverse linear relationship between the black population and the Populist congressional vote in the various Southern states. See also Kirwan, *Revolt of the Rednecks,* 96.

10. Roscoe C. Martin, *The People's Party in Texas: A Study in Third Party Politics,* University of Texas *Bulletin* No. 3308 (Austin: University of Texas Press, 1933), 93–94; Rice, *Negro in Texas,* 86–87; Abramowitz, "Negro in the Populist Revolt," 267–68.

11. Edmonds, *Fusion Politics,* 17, 225–27; Dray, *At the Hands,* 112.

12. For statistical evidence on this phenomenon, see Gaither, "Negro in the Ideology of Southern Populism," 172–215.

13. *Richmond State* [n.d.], quoted in *Public Opinion* 13 (1892): 320.

14. For example, see statements in the *National Economist,* 26 March 1892; H. S. Scomp to W. H. Felton, 11 September 1894, Felton Collection. See also Woodward, "Populist Heritage," 150–51.

15. Psychologists, unlike many historians, have long been acutely aware of the inconsistency between verbal attitudes and inner commitment. For further information on this subject, see Richard T. La Piere, "Attitudes vs. Actions," *Social Forces* 13 (December 1934): 230–37; Bernard Kutner, Carol Wilkins, and Penny Yarrow, "Verbal Attitudes and Overt Behavior Involving Racial Prejudice," *Journal of Abnormal and Social Psychology* 47 (July 1952): 649–52; Lawrence S. Linn, "Verbal Attitudes and Overt Behavior: A Study of Racial Discrimination," *Social Forces* 45 (March 1965): 353–64; Milton Malof and Albert Lott, "Ethnocentrism and the Acceptance of Negro Support in a Group Situation," *Journal of Abnormal and Social Psychology* 65 (October 1962): 254–58.

16. Woodward, *Origins,* 254. See also T. Harry Williams, *Romance and Realism in Southern Politics* (Baton Rouge: Louisiana State University Press, 1966), 53.

17. Carl Carmer, *Stars Fell on Alabama* (New York: Farrar and Rinehart, 1934), 67.

18. Mrs. William H. Felton, *My Memoirs of Georgia Politics* (Atlanta: Index Printing Co., 1911), quoted in Francis M. Wilhoit, "An Interpretation of Populism's Impact on the Georgia Negro," *Journal of Negro History* 52 (April 1967): 123. William H. Felton was a candidate of the earlier Independents and later unsuccessful Populist movement in north Georgia. For the careers of W. H. Felton and his wife, see William P. Roberts, "The Public Career of Dr. William Harrell Felton" (Ph.D. diss., University of North Carolina, 1952); John E. Talmadge, *Rebecca Latimer Felton: Nine Stormy Decades* (Athens: University of Georgia Press, 1960).

19. *Richmond Sun,* 20 December 1894, quoted in Woodward, *Origins,* 258.

20. *Louisiana Populist,* 31 August 1894. See also *Capitol Item* quoted in ibid., 31 August 1894; and ibid., 21 September 1894, for similar comments.

21. Ibid., 24 August 1894.

22. *Progressive Farmer,* 3 May 1892, quoted in Florence E. Smith, "Populist Party in North Carolina" (Ph.D. diss., University of Chicago, 1929), 77–78.

23. Quoted in Thomas K. Hearn, "The Populist Movement in Marshall County [Alabama]" (master's thesis, University of Alabama, 1935), 56.

24. Alwyn Barr, *Reconstruction to Reform: Texas Politics, 1876–1901* (Austin: University of Texas Press, 1971), 152.

25. *Greensboro Watchman,* quoted in *People's Weekly Tribune,* 28 May 1896.

26. *Atlanta Constitution,* 19 August 1896, 3 October 1896, quoted in Olive Hall Shadgett, *The Republican Party in Georgia: From Reconstruction through 1900* (Athens: University of Georgia Press, 1964). 117.

27. Quoted in Logan, *Negro in North Carolina,* 19.

28. *Welsh (LA) Crescent,* quoted in *Baton Rouge Daily Advocate,* 4 March 1890, in Hair, *Bourbonism and Agrarian Protest,* 187.

29. *People's Party Paper,* 26 August 1892.

30. See Alvord, "T. L. Nugent," for a discussion of Nugent as a Social Gospeler.

31. Catherine Nugent, ed., *Life Work of Thomas L. Nugent* (Stephenville, TX, 1890), quoted in Saunders, "Southern Populists, 1892," 17 n.59.

32. Ibid.

33. *Dallas Morning News,* 31 July 1892, quoted in ibid.

34. Hackney, *Populism to Progressivism in Alabama,* 45–47.

35. Robert L. Saunders, "The Transformation of Tom Watson, 1894–1895," *Georgia Historical Quarterly* 54 (fall 1970): 350.

36. Charles Crowe, "Tom Watson, Populists, and Blacks Reconsidered," *Journal of Negro History* 55 (April 1970): 102. See also Lawrence J. Friedman, *The White Savage: Racial Fantasies in the Postbellum South* (Englewood Cliffs, NJ: Prentice-Hall, 1970), 80, for additional primary evidence to support this viewpoint.

37. Crowe, "Tom Watson," 107–8.

38. See particularly Woodward, *Tom Watson,* 408–86.

39. Wilhoit, "Populism's Impact on the Georgia Negro," 117.

40. *People's Party Paper,* 28 September 1894; Clarence A. Bacote, "Negro Proscriptions, Protests, and Proposed Solutions in Georgia, 1886–1908," *Journal of Southern History* 25 (August 1959): 202–3; E. Merton Coulter, *Georgia: A Short History* (Chapel Hill: University of North Carolina Press, 1960), 392. See also Bonner, "Alliance Legislature of 1890," and Holmes, "Georgia Senatorial Election of 1890," 147–224.

41. Shaw, *Wool-Hat Boys,* 83; Crowe, "Tom Watson," 99–116; Bacote, "Negro Proscriptions in Georgia," 200–223.

42. *People's Party Paper,* 28 September 1894; Robert L. Saunders, "Southern Populists and the Negro, 1893–1895," *Journal of Negro History* 54 (July 1969): 252.

43. For black and white opinion on the bill, see Bacote, "Negro Proscriptions in Georgia," 202–4.

44. *Savannah Tribune,* 17 October 1891, quoted in ibid., 203.

45. Unidentified newspaper clipping in Frederick Douglass Papers, marked 20 July 1892, quoted in McFeely, *Frederick Douglass,* 365, 718.

46. Shaw, *Wool-Hat Boys,* 59–60.

47. Hair, *Bourbonism and Agrarian Protest,* 196–97. See also Henry C. Dethloff and Robert R. Jones, "Race Relations in Louisiana, 1877–1898," *Louisiana History* 9 (fall 1968): 314–16.

48. Wynes, *Race Relations in Virginia,* 47.

49. *Virginia Sun,* 26 October 1892, quoted in Saunders, "Southern Populists, 1892," 7–8 n.2.

50. Wynes, *Race Relations in Virginia,* 47–50; Wynes, "Charles T. O'Ferrall and the Virginia Gubernatorial Election of 1893," *Virginia Magazine of History and Biography* 64 (October 1956): 449–53. Cf. Saunders, "Southern Populists, 1892," 12–13, for a contrasting interpretation of Virginia Populism and blacks on the local level. See also Sheldon, *Populism in the Old Dominion,* 102. On the Colored Farmers' Alliance, see Spriggs, "Virginia Colored Farmers' Alliance."

51. Hall, *Labor Struggles,* 49.

52. Barrows, "What the Southern Negro Is Doing for Himself," 809.

53. Woodward, *Strange Career,* 45–46; Goodwyn, "Populist Dreams," 1435–56; Gregg Cantrell and D. Scott Barton, "Texas Populists and the Failure of Biracial Politics," *Journal of Southern History* 55 (November 1989), 659–92.

54. Quoted in Abramowitz, "Negro in the Populist Movement," 267–68.

55. Cf. Saunders, "Southern Populists, 1892," 11; Wynes, *Race Relations in Virginia,* 48.

56. John William Graves, "Negro Disfranchisement in Arkansas," *Arkansas Historical Quarterly* 26 (autumn 1967): 203.

57. Quoted in Saunders, "Southern Populists, 1892," 11.

58. Ibid.; Saunders, "Southern Populists, 1893–1895," 241.

59. Lucia E. Daniel, "The Louisiana People's Party," *Louisiana Historical Quarterly* 26 (October 1943): 1080.

60. Saunders, "Southern Populists, 1893–1895," 243. Minority participation was clearly not one of the distinguishing features of all Populist conventions. Amid a heady cynicism it would be easy at this point to wax eloquent about how a self-professed reform movement failed to achieve proportional representation for oppressed minorities. However, on examination, our contemporary standard does not appear to be significantly better than the Populist model. The Democratic Party has been the primary political vehicle for minorities since the Great Depression period of the 1930s, and yet, as recently as the 1968 Democratic convention in Chicago, blacks made up only 5.5 percent of the delegates, although they were 20 percent of the total who eventually voted for Hubert Humphrey, the party's presidential candidate. Although they eventually provided 52 percent of the Democratic vote in 1968, women made up only 13 percent of the delegates. On examination, the convention delegates were predominantly middle-aged middle-class white males. The persistence through time of this pattern reveals the problems of using the American

party system as an instrument of reform by individuals seeking surcease from their discontents. "Democrats: Trying for Party Reform," *Time,* 6 December 1971, 17.

61. Saunders, "Southern Populism, 1893–1895," 243.

62. *New York Times,* 23 March 1965, 28; Willie Morris, *North toward Home* (New York: Delta, 1970), 398–99. Twenty history professors, including Woodward, were involved in the march on Montgomery. At one point, Woodward and several fellow historians gathered in a circle and gave three cheers for Martin Luther King Jr.

63. In 1891, blacks and whites lived on the same street, occasionally alternating "like the squares on a checkerboard" on "some of the streets" of Montgomery, Alabama. Barrows, "What the Southern Negro Is Doing for Himself," 809. Yet, during Woodward's march on Montgomery in 1965, residential segregation was solid.

64. Woodward, *Strange Career,* 46.

65. *Augusta Chronicle,* 12 August 1886, in Watson Papers, Box 1, folder 2; Philip S. Foner, *Frederick Douglass: A Biography* (New York: Citadel Press, 1964), 341–42, 431 n.20. There is the same telling force of directness and fervor in Populist press coverage of the Douglass episode that is found in later Southern press coverage of another famous "dinner at the White House" episode in 1901. See Dewey W. Grantham Jr., "Dinner at the White House: Theodore Roosevelt, Booker T. Washington, and the South," *Tennessee Historical Quarterly* 17 (June 1958): 112–30. Transposing the two names across time, there is illustrated in the language of the press an attitude so similar as to approach something akin to plagiarism. This example further illustrates the homogeneity in racial attitudes of Southern whites, be they Populist or Democrat.

66. *National Economist,* 17 September 1892. See also *Caucasian,* 21 March 1895; *People's Party Paper,* 12 April 1895; Abramowitz, "Negro in the Populist Movement," 95.

67. *Progressive Farmer,* 18 September 1894; *People's Party Paper,* 28 October 1892, 24 August 1894, 31 August 1894; *Weekly Toiler,* 2 November 1892. Many Populists advocated and openly supported education for blacks on a segregated basis. See *Progressive Farmer,* 7 August 1894; *Southern Mercury,* 26 July 26, 1894; Kirwan, *Revolt of the Rednecks,* 98; Edmonds, *Fusion Politics,* 35; William D. McCain, "The Populist Party in Mississippi" (master's thesis, University of Mississippi, 1931), 46–48; *Appleton's Annual Cyclopedia, 1892,* 740.

68. Saunders, "Transformation of Tom Watson," 350; Saunders, "Southern Populists, 1893–1895," 245. For Frederick Douglass's viewpoint on "mixed schools," see Philip S. Foner, ed., *The Life and Writings of Frederick Douglass* (New York: Citadel Press, 1955), 4:288–90.

69. *People's Party Paper,* 25 May 1894, quoted in Friedman, *White Savage,* 79. See also *People's Party Paper,* 22 July 1892, for a similar statement issued by the Georgia People's Party.

70. *Caucasian,* 4 April 1895.

71. *People's Party Paper,* 13 March 1896, quoted in Friedman, *White Savage,* 79–80.

72. *People's Party Paper,* 22 September 1893, 29 September 1893, 13 October 1893, quoted in ibid., 81.

73. *Progressive Age,* quoted in *Louisiana Populist,* 14 September 1894. Taylor was found guilty later of soliciting election funds from black government employees. The penalty was three years in prison, five thousand dollars, or both. It does not appear that the sentence was carried out (ibid.; Bacote, "Negro Proscriptions in Georgia," 223 n.71). On Taylor, see Randall B. Woods, "C. H. J. Taylor and the Movement for Black Political Independence, 1882–1896," *Journal of Negro History* 67 (summer 1982): 122–35.

74. Meier, *Negro Thought,* 32, 36, 50; Redkey, *Black Exodus,* 54–55, 80, 188; Bacote, "Negro Proscription in Georgia," 214, 233 n.71.

75. Quoted in Meier, *Negro Thought,* 32.

76. *Southern Mercury,* 9 August 1894; *People's Party Paper,* 5 April 1895; Meier, *Negro Thought,* 32, 36, 50.

77. *People's Weekly Tribune,* 18 June 1896.

78. Friedman, *White Savage,* 81.

79. *People's Weekly Tribune,* 4 June 1896.

80. Ibid., 22 March 1895.

81. Saunders, "Southern Populists, 1893–1895," 252, 260 n.49.

82. *People's Party Paper,* 22 May 1895.

83. Ibid., 22 March 1895, quoted in Saunders, "Transformation of Tom Watson," 352. Emphasis added.

84. For other such volatile incidents, see Edmonds, *Fusion Politics,* 42–43; *Louisiana Populist,* 15 March 1895, 1 November 1895; *Alliance Farmer,* quoted in *Louisiana Populist,* 22 March 1895; *Progress,* quoted in ibid., 22 March 1895; *People's Weekly Tribune,* 11 June 1896, 25 June 1896, 2 July 1896; *Birmingham State Herald,* 5 June 1896. The first set of citations relates to an 1895 incident in North Carolina over legislative adjournment in honor of Frederick Douglass; the second concerns a contested congressional election case (*Murray v. Elliot* [1896]) in South Carolina. Murray, a black, was seated over Elliot, a white, who had resorted to fraud in order to win his seat. On Murray, see *Congressional Record,* 53rd Cong., 1st Sess.: 2147–50.

85. *Kansas City American Citizen,* 23 December 1892, quoted in Chafe, "Negro and Populism," 415.

86. Ibid.

6. THEORY AND PRACTICE OF POPULISM

1. Joseph Howard Gerteis, "Class and the Color Line: The Sources and Limits of Interracial Class Coalition, 1880–1896" (Ph.D. diss., University of North Carolina at Chapel Hill, 1999), 187–247.

2. Quoted in Sheldon, *Populism in the Old Dominion,* 222. Serving as president of the Virginia Alliance for three years, Page was subsequently elected presi-

dent of the National Alliance. In addition, he was a major leader in the Virginia Populist Party.

3. *Virginia Sun,* 20 July 1892, quoted in Saunders, "Southern Populists, 1892," 12.

4. Ibid., 12–13.

5. For a good study of Virginia Populism's change of heart on this issue, see Gerteis, "Class and the Color Line," 187–247.

6. Quoted in Sheldon, *Populism in the Old Dominion,* 86.

7. Allen W. Moger, *Virginia: Bourbonism to Byrd, 1870–1925* (Charlottesville: University Press of Virginia, 1968), 95–98.

8. J. Morgan Kousser, *The Shaping of Southern Politics: Suffrage Restriction and the Establishment of the One-Party South, 1880–1910* (New Haven, CT: Yale University Press, 1974), 173.

9. Richard L. Morton, *The Negro in Virginia Politics, 1885–1910* (Charlottesville: University of Virginia Press, 1919), 98–132; Moger, *Virginia,* 47–75.

10. Quoted in Sheldon, *Populism in the Old Dominion,* 87–88. In the Southern ideological system, whites sharply distinguished themselves from blacks, conceiving the latter in terms of a marked physical contrast. Under this system, "blue" cuticles were considered black physical characteristics, or were regarded as a measure of black blood in one's heritage. Conversely, white cuticles were properties of the white man and stood as the antithesis of the character and properties of the black man. In substance, white cuticles were pure and desirable; "blue" cuticles were inferior and undesirable.

11. *Norfolk (VA) Public Ledger,* 30 December 1893, quoted in Moger, *Virginia,* 115.

12. *Richmond Planet,* 11 November 1893, 25 November 1893, quoted in Saunders, "Southern Populists, 1893–1895," 240.

13. Wynes, *Race Relations in Virginia,* 84.

14. Gerteis, "Class and the Color Line," 188.

15. Sheldon, *Populism in the Old Dominion,* 92.

16. *Virginia Sun,* 16 November 1892, quoted in Woodward, *Origins,* 261. In early December 1896, the *Virginia Sun,* "the populist [*sic*] organ of this state, gave a loud wail of anguish . . . and 'kicked the bucket.'" *Southern Mercury,* 17 December 1896.

17. Woodward, *Origins,* 261; Sheldon, *Populism in the Old Dominion,* 90–92. See also *Southern Mercury,* 17 December 1896.

18. *Richmond Times,* 6 February 1894, quoted in Moger, *Virginia,* 98.

19. Ibid., 108.

20. Quoted in Morton, *Negro in Virginia Politics,* 133.

21. Wynes, "Charles T. O'Ferrall," 437.

22. Kousser, *Southern Politics,* 297.

23. Sheldon, *Populism in the Old Dominion,* 102.

24. Edmund Randolph Cocke to H. St. George Tucker, 25 January 1891, quoted in Wynes, *Race Relations in Virginia,* 47. Cocke, grandson of Edmund Randolph, is an excellent example of the many distinguished families involved in the leadership of Virginia Populism.

25. Kousser, *Southern Politics,* 173 n.56.

26. Quoted in Sheldon, *Populism in the Old Dominion,* 101.

27. Kousser, *Southern Politics,* 173 n.56.

28. Wynes, "Charles T. O'Ferrall," 437, 450; Sheldon, *Populism in the Old Dominion,* 102.

29. Kousser, *Southern Politics,* 173.

30. Henry M. Field, *Bright Skies and Dark Shadows,* quoted in Morton, *Negro in Virginia Politics,* 145.

31. Morton, *Negro in Virginia Politics,* 137, 144–45.

32. Wynes, "Charles T. O'Ferrall," 437, 451.

33. Kousser, *Southern Politics,* 173 n.56.

34. Wynes, *Race Relations in Virginia,* 49; Sheldon, *Populism in the Old Dominion,* 103–5; Wynes, "Charles T. O'Ferrall," 451.

35. Kousser, *Southern Politics,* 171–75.

36. Ibid., 174.

37. Morton, *Negro in Virginia Politics,* 131.

38. See Table 6.9 in Kousser, *Southern Politics,* 174.

39. *Lynchburg (VA) Daily Advance,* 10 October 1893, quoted in Wynes, *Race Relations in Virginia,* 49.

40. Kousser, *Southern Politics,* 173.

41. *Lynchburg (VA) Daily Advance,* 10 October 1893, quoted in Wynes, *Race Relations in Virginia,* 49.

42. *Appleton's Annual Cyclopedia, 1896,* 813; Sheldon, *Populism in the Old Dominion,* 150. Despite the Populists' exaggerated claim that "there are 80,000 populist [*sic*] in Virginia" as of December 1896, and "the populist party is stronger in Virginia today than ever," the movement was in decline throughout the state. Further evidence of this was the death of the *Virginia Sun,* the major Populist paper in late 1896. *Southern Mercury,* 17 December 1896.

43. Steelman, "Vicissitudes of Republican Party Politics," 438–42; Theron Paul Jones, "The Gubernatorial Election of 1892 in North Carolina" (master's thesis, University of North Carolina at Chapel Hill, 1949), 63–69. Helen Edmonds, however, has concluded that the North Carolina Populists were "in the main, dissatisfied Democrats" (Edmonds, *Fusion Politics,* 221).

44. Kousser, *Southern Politics,* 183.

45. Logan, *Negro in North Carolina,* 22–23.

46. Edmonds, *Fusion Politics,* 221; T. L. Jones to Marion Butler, 19 May 1896, Box 2, folder 27, Butler Papers.

47. Edmonds, *Fusion Politics,* 37–38; *Progressive Farmer,* 11 October 1892; Robert Wayne Smith, "A Rhetorical Analysis of the Populist Movement in North Carolina, 1892–1896" (Ph.D. diss., University of Wisconsin, 1957), 83–84.

48. Quoted in William Alexander Mabry, "Negro Suffrage and Fusion in North Carolina," *North Carolina Historical Review* 12 (April 1955): 91.

49. Edmonds, *Fusion Politics,* 37–38; *Progressive Farmer,* 11 October 1892; Smith, "Rhetorical Analysis of the Populist Movement," 83–84.

50. *Progressive Farmer,* 24 March 1896. Ironically, it appears that a large segment of the Colored Farmers' Alliance probably voted against the Populists in the 1892 election in North Carolina. J. D. Thorne to L. L. Polk, 20 April 1892, Polk Collection; Edmonds, *Fusion Politics,* 26; "Proceedings of the Eleventh Annual Session of the North Carolina Farmers' State Alliance, 1897," in *Proceedings of the North Carolina Farmers' State Alliance, 1888–1906* (n.p., n.d.), 5.

51. Omar Ali, "The Making of a Black Populist: A Tribute to the Rev. Walter A. Pattillo," *Oxford (NC) Public Ledger,* 28 March 2002. Available online at http://www.geocities.com/salika4/ OxfordPublicLedgerRevWAP.html.

52. One observer, writing in 1929 of North Carolina politics, noted that not a single political campaign had taken place in the state since the Civil War without the cry of "nigger" by some speakers and newspapers. Smith, "Populist Party in North Carolina," 30. See also Logan, *Negro in North Carolina,* 22–24; *National Economist,* 1 October 1892; "The South Under the Lash," circular in Marmaduke J. Hawkins Papers, North Carolina State Library and Archives, Raleigh, North Carolina.

53. Hugh Talmadge Lefler and Albert Ray Newsome, *North Carolina: The History of a Southern State* (Chapel Hill: University of North Carolina Press, 1963), 514–15. The North Carolina Populist platform for 1892 can be found in *Progressive Farmer,* 23 August 1892.

54. *Progressive Farmer,* 21 August 1894, 28 August 1894; Joseph F. Steelman, "Republican Party Strategists and the Issue of Fusion with Populists in North Carolina, 1893–1894," *North Carolina Historical Review* 47 (July 1970): 251, 264–65; Edmonds, *Fusion Politics,* 37–38. The North Carolina Populist platform for 1894 can be found in *Progressive Farmer,* 16 October 1894.

55. *Progressive Farmer,* 4 December 1894.

56. *Caucasian,* 4 January 1894.

57. *Charlotte News and Observer,* 18 August 1894, quoted in Smith, "Populist Party in North Carolina," 112.

58. Joseph Gregoire de Roulhac Hamilton, *North Carolina Since 1860* (Chicago: University of Chicago Press, 1919), 248–49.

59. Ibid., 249.

60. W. A. Guthrie to Marion Butler, 7 June 1896, Box 2, folder 29, with clipping from *Charlotte Observer* (n.d.) attached, Butler Papers. Guthrie was a former Republican who had joined the Populist Party and was chosen as gubernatorial candidate in 1896. For an analysis of Guthrie's campaign, see Edmonds, *Fusion Politics,* 56–57.

61. A. J. Nage to Marion Butler, 30 April 1896, Box 2, folder 26(a), Butler Papers.

62. J. H. Wilson to Marion Butler, 4 November 1896, Box 4, folder 46, Butler Papers.

63. Ibid., clipping, *Charlotte Observer,* 31 October 1896, Box 4, folder 45, Butler Papers.

64. Walter R. Henry to Marion Butler, 20 October 1896, Box 4, folder 43–44,

J. H. Wilson to Butler, October 24, 29, 31, 1896, Box 4, folder 45; clipping, *Charlotte Observer,* 31 October 1896, Box 4, folder 45, Butler Papers.

65. Charles H. Martin to Marion Butler, 11 December 1896, Box 4, folder 50, Butler Papers.

66. B. F. White to Marion Butler, 28 June 1896, Box 2, folder 29, Butler Papers.

67. T. L. Jones to Marion Butler, 19 May 1896, Box 2, folder 27, Butler Papers.

68. B. F. White to Marion Butler, 28 June 1896, Box 2, folder 29, Butler Papers. Russell was the successful Republican gubernatorial candidate in 1896. The Populist gubernatorial candidate was William A. Guthrie.

69. Edmonds, *Fusion Politics,* 37, 231.

70. Steelman, "Republic Party Strategists and the Issue of Fusion," 245.

71. Andrew D. Cowles should not be confused with William H. H. Cowles, a Democrat from the Eighth District. For a sketch of William H. H. Cowles, see *Congressional Directory,* 1st sess., 52nd Congress, 88.

72. Andrew D. Cowles, "A Card to the Republican Party of Iredell County," Statesville, North Carolina, 29 October 1894, in Marmaduke J. Hawkins Collection, State Archives and Library, Raleigh, North Carolina. Emphasis added. Cowles's letter opposing fusion was widely disseminated. As a former chairman of the Republican Executive Committee from Iredell County, his voice carried considerable weight with the following. Steelman, "Republican Party Strategists and the Idea of Fusion," 268.

73. Hal W. Ayer to Marion Butler, 6 October 1896, Box 4, folder 41, Butler Papers. Ayer was the Populist candidate for auditor in 1896.

74. Campaign pamphlet, "An Appeal to Populists and Defense of Mr. Thos. Watson, Washington, October 20, 1896," Box 4, folder 45, Butler Papers.

75. Woodward, *Origins,* 286.

76. Lefler and Newsome, *North Carolina,* 519–20.

77. James H. Sherrill to Marion Butler, 13 September 1896, Box 3, folder 36, Butler Papers.

78. A. J. Moyr to Marion Butler, 7 September 1896, Box 3, folder 35, Butler Papers.

79. H. S. Shufen to Marion Butler, 8 September 1896, Box 3, folder 35, Butler Papers.

80. James R. Happs to Marion Butler, 11 September 1896, Box 3, folder 36, Butler Papers.

81. W. A. Guthrie to Marion Butler, 26 September 1896, Box 3, folder 39, Butler Papers.

82. R. R. Krusey to Marion Butler, 1 May 1896, Box 2, folder 26, Butler Papers.

83. Elsie M. Lewis, "The Political Mind of the Negro," *Journal of Southern History* 21 (May 1955): 189–202.

84. Meier, *Negro Thought,* 26–41.

85. Quoted in Logan, *Negro in North Carolina,* 22.

86. Quoted in Meier, *Negro Thought,* 33.

87. J. C. Price, "Does the Negro Seek Social Equality?" *The Forum* 14 (1891): 558, rpt. in William Jacob Walls, *Joseph Charles Price: Educator and Race Leader* (Boston: Christopher Publishing House, 1943), 476–77.

88. Quoted in Carter G. Woodson, *Negro Orators and Their Orations* (Washington, DC: Associated Publishers, Inc., 1925), 500, rpt. in Walls, *Joseph Charles Price,* 477.

89. Y. C. Morton to Marion Butler, 30 April 1896, Box 2, folder 26(a), Butler Papers.

90. A. H. Paddison to Marion Butler, 23 April 1896, Box 2, folder 26(a), Butler Papers.

91. Williard H. Smith, "William Jennings Bryan—A Reappraisal," *Indiana Academy of Social Sciences Proceedings, new series* 10 (1965): 56–69; Smith, "William Jennings Bryan and the Social Gospel," *Journal of American History* 53 (June 1966): 41–60; Smith, "William Jennings Bryan and Racism," *Journal of Negro History* 54 (April 1969): 127–49.

92. *The Afro-American Sentinel* (Omaha), 29 August 1896, quoted in Aptheker, *Documentary,* 2:818–19. This editorial was by Philip H. Brown, an official of the Afro-American Associated Press. See also Thornbrough, "The National Afro-American League," 494–512; Lefler and Newsome, *North Carolina,* 518.

93. Smith, "Bryan and Racism," 137–39.

94. Ibid., 136.

95. A. J. Moyr to Marion Butler, 7 September 1896, Box 3, folder 35, Butler Papers.

96. W. A. Guthrie to Marion Butler, 6 October 1896, Box 4, folder 41, Butler Papers.

97. The events of the "Fusionist" victory are detailed in Edmonds, *Fusion Politics.* The 1894 North Carolina Fusion legislature divided in the following manner: in the Senate, eight Democrats, twenty-four Populists, and eighteen Republicans; in the House, forty-six Democrats, thirty-eight Republicans, and thirty-six Populists. *Appleton's Century Cyclopedia, 1895,* 556.

98. Kousser, *Southern Politics,* 187.

99. Ibid.

100. Lefler and Newsome, *North Carolina,* 393–97, 517–19.

101. Ibid.

102. See particularly the handbill "To the People of North Carolina" (dated 2 July 1896), distributed and endorsed by some of the state's major black leadership. Prominent "anti-Russell" blacks included R. B. Russell of Maxton; W. H. Quick of Rockingham; R. B. Fitzgerald, A. M. Moore, and J. E. Shepherd of Durham; R. W. H. Leak, L. A. Scruggs, E. A. Johnson, and Bruce Capehart, all of Raleigh. Black leadership reportedly supported W. A. Guthrie, the former Republican turned Populist. W. A. Guthrie to Marion Butler, 7 June 1896, 11 July 1896; clipping from *Charlotte Observer* (n.d.), Box 2, folders 29–30, Butler Papers.

103. Kousser, *Southern Politics,* 185–87.

104. Edmonds, *Fusion Politics,* 222. A similar view can be found in William Alexander Mabry, *The Negro in North Carolina Politics Since Reconstruction* (Durham,

NC: Duke University Press, 1940), 34–35; Mabry, "Negro Rule and Fusion Politics," 85–86.

105. Quoted in Lefler and Newsome, *North Carolina*, 518.

106. *Progressive Farmer*, 23 August 1892.

107. Ibid., 16 October 1894.

108. M. C. Birmingham to Marion Butler, 19 December 1896; *Charlotte Observer*, 29 October 1896, 31 October 1896, Box 4, folder 50, Butler Papers.

109. Kousser, *Southern Politics*, 54; Lefler and Newsome, *North Carolina*, 518.

110. Lefler and Newsome, *North Carolina*, 528–29.

111. Ibid.

112. The "eight ballot box" law passed in 1882 "was in effect, a literacy test for voting," with the intent of reducing black voting, and had along with trickery and fraud bitten deeply into the political ranks of blacks. In the mid-1890s before the 1895 constitutional convention, there were only about 120,000 potential legal black voters remaining in the state. Ernest M. Lander Jr., *A History of South Carolina, 1865–1960* (Chapel Hill: University of North Carolina Press, 1960), 28, 40.

113. Kousser, *Southern Politics*, 50, 55.

114. The classical study of the Tillman movement is Simkins, *Tillman Movement*.

115. The Populists supported Tillman, who accepted many of the Alliance and Populist doctrines and incorporated them into the Democratic platform. Like Tennessee, an organized party of considerable strength never existed in South Carolina. In 1892, for example, the South Carolina Populists remained content to nominate presidential electors only. See Simkins, *Tillman Movement*, 172, 180–81; Hicks, *Populist Revolt*, 246; Joseph Church, "The Farmers' Alliance and the Populist Movement in South Carolina, 1887–1896" (master's thesis, University of South Carolina, 1953), 50–52, 75–76.

116. Simkins, *Tillman Movement*, 136–37, 318, 325, 327. See also Francis Butler Simkins, "Ben Tillman's View of the Negro," *Journal of Negro History* 3 (May 1937): 161–74.

117. *National Economist*, 8 October 1892.

118. For a discussion of blacks and South Carolina Republicanism, see Tindall, *South Carolina Negroes*, 41–68; James W. Patton, "The Republican Party in South Carolina, 1876–1895," in *Essays in Southern History*, 91–111. Tindall quote in Tindall, *South Carolina Negroes*, 73.

119. Tindall, *South Carolina Negroes*, 73; Meier, *Negro Thought*, 33, 40, 112–13, 164–65.

120. Tindall, *South Carolina Negroes*, 49, 54, 56–58, 78, 89–90.

121. See Church, "Farmers' Alliance and Populist Movement in South Carolina," 24–33.

122. *Georgia Baptist*, quoted in *Progressive Farmer*, 30 October 1894.

123. Watson, "The Negro Question," 547; *People's Party Paper*, 16 September 1892. Emphasis added.

124. The following discussion is based primarily on Watson, "The Negro Question," 541–49. This same article also appeared in Watson's personal newspaper,

People's Party Paper, 16 September 1892, and C. H. Pierson's *Virginia Sun,* 19 October 1892, just prior to the elections in Georgia and Virginia. It further illustrates the white Populist efforts to acquaint the black voter with their basic philosophy of "self interest."

125. *People's Party Paper,* 16 September 1892. The Louisiana People's Party, which met on 17 February 1892, adopted almost verbatim this same proposal into their platform. Ibid., 10 March 1892.

126. Watson, "The Negro Question," 546. Author's emphasis added.

127. See for example Shaw, *Wool-Hat Boys,* 109–10, for Georgia, and Gerteis, "Class and the Color Line," 223; *People's Party Paper,* 17 June 1892, 15 September 1893.

128. Hofstadter, *Age of Reform,* 83.

129. Watson, "The Negro Question," 550. For similar statements by Watson, see Watson, *Life and Speeches,* 127–65; *People's Party Paper,* 16 September 1892, 17 March 1892. The Georgia People's Party Convention also endorsed the viewpoint that "there is no southern man who will advocate social equality." Ibid., 22 July 1892. For a summary of this same philosophy in Alabama, see *People's Weekly Tribune,* 28 May 1896.

130. *Caucasian,* 4 April 1895. See also Smith, "Rhetorical Analysis of the Populist Movement," 85.

131. Norman Pollack, "Ignatius Donnelly on Human Rights: A Study of Two Novels," *Mid-America: An Historical Review* 47 (1965): 105–12. The quotes are selected from Pollack's analysis of the Donnelly work.

132. *Georgia Baptist,* quoted in *Progressive Farmer,* 30 October 1894. Emphasis added.

133. *Southern Alliance Farmer* (Atlanta), 2 August 1892, quoted in Pollack, *Populist Mind,* 386–87; Arnett, *Populist Movement,* 151–53; Shadgett, *Republican Party in Georgia,* 105–21; Thomas E. Watson to W. H. Felton, 16 September 1894, Felton Collection.

134. For comments on Doyle, see Woodward, *Tom Watson,* 239–40; Woodward, "Tom Watson and the Negro," 48–49, *People's Party Paper,* 28 October 1892, 27 October 1893, 25 October 1895.

135. Shaw, *Wool-Hat Boys,* 58–59.

136. *People's Party Paper,* 17 March 1892.

137. L. Moody Sims Jr., "A Note on Sidney Lanier's Attitude Toward the Negro and Toward Populism," *Georgia Historical Quarterly* 52 (September 1968): 305–7.

138. Additional evidence of this view is found in Saunders, "Southern Populists, 1892," 8–9.

139. *People's Party Paper,* 22 July 1892. This issue contains events of Georgia's first People's Party Convention, held in Atlanta on 20 July 1892.

140. *Southern Alliance Farmer,* 2 August 1892, quoted in Pollack, *Populist Mind,* 386–87.

141. Crowe, "Tom Watson," 109.

142. *Atlanta Journal,* 7–8 December 1893, quoted in Crowe, "Tom Watson." The

Populist record is also examined by Crowe in "Tom Watson." See also Shadgett, *Republican Party in Georgia,* 117, for the hostile comment of Henry Lincoln Johnson, a black Republican leader in Georgia.

143. Shadgett, *Republican Party in Georgia,* 35–36, 216.

144. *Atlanta Constitution,* 1 October 1892, quoted in Shadgett, *Republican Party in Georgia,* 111.

145. Crowe, "Tom Watson," 110.

146. Ibid., 109.

147. Shadgett, *Republican Party in Georgia,* 110–11.

148. *Atlanta Constitution,* 1 October 1892, quoted in Shadgett, *Republican Party in Georgia,* 111.

149. Shaw, *Wool-Hat Boys,* 72–77, 90, 91; Kousser, *Southern Politics,* 215; Coulter, *Georgia,* 293.

150. Crowe, "Tom Watson," 116; Meier, *Negro Thought,* 28. Although Northen sought to protect blacks from violence, he was considerably resistant to "social equality" between the races. See particularly the folder marked "Mob Violence," Northen Collection.

151. In conjunction with his promise, Northen advocated, and the Georgia Legislature subsequently approved, an "anti-lynch" bill on 20 December 1893. *Georgia Law, 1893,* 128. See also Northen's "The Negro at the South" address before the Congregational Club, Boston, Massachusetts, 22 May 1899, in "Speeches, 1889–91," Northen Collection; David Godshalk, "William J. Northen's Public and Personal Struggles against Lynching," in *Jumpin' Jim Crow: Southern Politics from Civil War to Civil Rights,* ed. Jane Dailey, Glenda Elizabeth Gilmore, and Bryant Simon (Princeton, NJ: Princeton University Press, 2000), 140–61.

152. Meier, *Negro Thought,* 170.

153. Shaw, *Wool-Hat Boys,* 46, 83, 100.

154. Goodwyn, *Democratic Promise,* 305–16.

155. Woodward, *Origins,* 259.

156. Coulter, *Georgia,* 393–94. Emphasis added. See also Arnett, *Populist Movement,* 153–54; Woodward, *Tom Watson,* 241.

157. Shaw, *Wool-Hat Boys,* 93–94. For a comparable description of such activities in Texas, see Martin, *People's Party.*

158. *People's Party Paper,* 30 January 1893. A similar story is told by a North Carolina black in *Progressive Farmer,* 24 January 1893.

159. Shaw, *Wool-Hat Boys,* 75–77.

160. Reddick, "Negro in the Populist Movement in Georgia," 58–59. See also Woodward, *Tom Watson,* 208, 241; Shaw, *Wool-Hat Boys,* 76; Arnett, *Populist Movement,* 154–55, 183–84, 209; Clarence A. Bacote, "Negro in Georgia Politics, 1880–1908" (Ph.D. diss., University of Chicago, 1956), 181, 193–94.

161. *People's Party Paper,* 14 October 1892.

162. Ibid., 28 October 1892.

163. Quoted in Crowe, "Tom Watson," 109.

164. *National Economist,* 1 October 1892. For an example of the type of "Force

Bill" propaganda used against the Georgia Populists, see "The Force Bill, the Farmer and the Tariff," a circular distributed by Democrat Charles F. Crisp "in his usual forcible style." Marmaduke J. Hawkins Collection. For similar tactics, see the full print of a "Rape Circular" issued by W. Y. Atkinson, a prominent Georgia Democrat, in *People's Party Paper,* 18 September 1896.

165. Shaw, *Wool-Hat Boys,* 117–18; Bascom O. Quillian Jr., "The Populist Challenge in Georgia in the Year 1894" (master's thesis, University of Georgia at Athens, 1948), 60–61.

166. Coulter, *Georgia,* 395.

167. Arnett, *Populist Movement,* 183.

168. Shaw, *Wool-Hat Boys,* 116.

169. Kousser, *Southern Politics,* 40–43.

170. Coulter, *Georgia,* 394.

171. Quillian, "The Populist Challenge," 60–61.

172. *People's Party Paper,* 18 October 1894.

173. Ibid., 1 June 1894. See also Arnett, *Populist Movement,* 183.

174. *People's Party Paper,* 29 March 1895. See also Shadgett, *Republican Party in Georgia,* 117.

175. *People's Guide,* quoted in *People's Party Paper,* 28 October 1895; Woodward, *Tom Watson,* 269–71. If the price is correct, this was a bargain, as votes normally sold for a dollar each.

176. H. S. Scomp to W. H. Felton, 9 November 1894, Felton Collection. Felton, a former Democrat and Whig, ran as a Populist Congressional candidate from the Seventh District in 1894 against John W. Maddox, an incumbent Democrat.

177. J. D. Cunningham to W. H. Felton, 8 November 1894, Felton Collection. Using unfriendly newspaper accounts, one student has concluded that blacks voted for Populist candidates in 1894. Abramowitz, "Negro in the Populist Movement," 275–76.

178. W. H. Hidell to Rebecca Felton, 15 October 1894; W. H. Hidell to W. H. Felton, 7 November 1894, Felton Collection. Rebecca Felton, the wife of W. H. Felton, was a reformer and advocate of temperance and women's rights.

179. Arnett, *Populist Movement,* 184. See also Manning, *Fadeout of Populism,* 22, 25. Despite the fraudulence, 1894 represented the apex of Georgia Populism, as the party garnered 44.5 percent of the total vote; Quillian, "Populist Challenge in Georgia," 112.

180. *People's Party Paper,* 14 October 1892.

181. This practice appears to have been widespread. See Arnett, *Populist Movement,* 154; Coulter, *Georgia,* 83; Woodward, *Tom Watson,* 241; *Southern Mercury,* 29 October 1896; *People's Party Paper,* 28 September 1894, 5 October 1894, 29 July 1892, 14 October 1892. Democrats were not alone in having sufficient pressure to force blacks to vote according to their wishes. "It is undoubtedly true," Woodward has written, "that the Populist ideology was dominantly that of the landowning farmer who was, in many cases, the exploiter of landless tenant labor" (Woodward, *Tom Watson,* 218).

182. Ralph Wardlaw, *Negro Suffrage in Georgia, 1867–1930,* Phelps-Stokes Fellowship Studies, Number 11, Bulletin of the University of Georgia 33 (1932): 45–46, 79–80.

183. Coulter, *Georgia,* 395.

184. Kousser, *Southern Politics,* 216.

185. Ibid., 216–23.

186. Murphy [?] to W. H. Felton, 4 December 189?. See also H. [?] to Rebecca Felton, 13 December 1894, Felton Collection.

187. Kousser, *Southern Politics,* 42–43.

7. THEORY AND PRACTICE OF POPULISM

1. Clark, *Populism in Alabama,* 182, 26. The governor is not identified by name.

2. William G. Brown, "The South and the Saloon," *Century Magazine* 76 (1908), quoted in Woodward, *Origins,* 452.

3. Clark, *Populism in Alabama,* 21, 162–63, 180.

4. Quoted in ibid., 76.

5. Clark, *Populism in Alabama,* 11–20, 172–74; Manning, *Fadeout of Populism,* 60.

6. For earlier examples in Alabama, see Daniel Letwin, "Interracial Unionism, Gender, and 'Social Equality' in the Alabama Coalfields," *Journal of Southern History* 61 (August 1995): 519–54; Daniel Letwin, *The Challenge of Interracial Unionism: Alabama Coal Miners, 1878–1921* (Chapel Hill: University of North Carolina Press, 1998); Herbert Gutman, "Black Coal Miners and the Greenback-Labor Party in Redeemer Alabama, 1878–1879," *Labor History* 10 (summer 1969): 506–35; Brian Kelly, "Policing the 'Negro': Racial Paternalism in the Alabama Coalfields, 1908–1921," *Alabama Review* 51 (July 1998): 163–83.

7. Rogers, *One-Gallused Rebellion,* 55; Allen J. Going, *Bourbon Democracy in Alabama, 1874–1890* (University: University of Alabama Press, 1951), 47–49, 54–56. Cotton prices in Alabama declined as follows: 1 December 1880, 10 cents; 1 December 1888, 8.5 cents; 1893, 7 cents; 1894, 4.8 cents; 1896, 6.5 cents. Clark, *Populism in Alabama,* 35, 68.

8. Rogers, "The Negro Alliance," 41.

9. Quoted in ibid., 174.

10. Woodward, *Origins,* 244–45.

11. Cash, *Mind of the South,* 165.

12. Shofner and Rogers, "Joseph C. Manning," 7–37.

13. *Louisiana Populist,* 30 November 1894.

14. *Louisiana Populist,* 30 November, 1894; Hackney, *Populism to Progressivism,* 22, 49, 70–71, 87–88.

15. Goodwyn, *Democratic Promise,* 403.

16. Samuel Webb, "From Independents to Populists to Progressive Republicans: The Case of Chilton County, Alabama, 1880–1920," *Journal of Southern History* 59 (November 1993): 708.

17. William Warren Rogers, "Reuben F. Kolb: Agricultural Leader of the New South," *Agricultural History* 32 (April 1958): 109–19.

18. Hackney, *From Populism to Progressivism*, 18.

19. Rogers, *One-Gallused Rebellion*, 221.

20. Summersell, "Alabama Governor's Race," 5.

21. Ibid., 21.

22. Leah R. Atkins, "Populism in Alabama: Reuben F. Kolb and the Appeals to Minority Groups," *Alabama Historical Quarterly* 32 (fall and winter 1970): 169–70, 173–74.

23. *Huntsville (AL) Gazette*, 2 January 1892, quoted in Saunders, "Southern Populists, 1892," 15.

24. Atkins, "Populism in Alabama," 174.

25. Clark, *Populism in Alabama*, 144; Rogers, *One-Gallused Rebellion*, 233.

26. Atkins, "Populism in Alabama, 174.

27. Ibid., 173.

28. Hackney, *From Populism to Progressivism*, 40; Rogers, *One-Gallused Rebellion*, 238.

29. Saunders, "Southern Populists, 1893–1895," 240–42, 257.

30. *Butler (AL) Choctaw Advocate*, 13 July 1892, quoted in Atkins, "Populism in Alabama," 173; Rochester, *Populist Movement in the United States*, 59. Emphasis added. As in other states previously examined, the emphasis here was on "political rights" and moral elevation, not social rights.

31. Quoted in Rogers, *One-Gallused Rebellion*, 213.

32. Hackney, *From Populism to Progressivism*, 38.

33. Ibid., 22.

34. Ibid., 25–26. A listing of blacks who supported Jones is included in Summersell, "Alabama Governor's Race."

35. Summersell, "Alabama Governor's Race," 27.

36. Clark, *Populism in Alabama*, 136.

37. Kousser, *Southern Politics*, 138.

38. For an investigation of these charges, see "The Alabama Election," *Public Opinion* 12 (1892): 442–44; Albert Burton Moore, *History of Alabama and Her People* (Tuscaloosa: Alabama Supply Store, 1927), 624; Rogers, *One-Gallused Rebellion*, 221–27.

39. Hackney, *From Populism to Progressivism*, 22–23; Rogers, *One-Gallused Rebellion*, 226.

40. Clark, *Populism in Alabama*, 26–27, 80.

41. Summersell, "Alabama Governor's Race," 27.

42. Woodward, *Origins*, 262.

43. Summersell, "Alabama Governor's Race," 19.

44. Summersell, "Alabama Governor's Race," 29–30.

45. Factor, *Black Response to America*, 158.

46. Ibid. Additional analyses of the voting in black belt counties can be found in Abramowitz, "Negro in the Populist Movement," 280.

47. Summersell, "Alabama Governor's Race," 5; Clark, *Populism in Alabama*, 175.

48. Webb, "From Independents," 716.

49. Goodwyn, *Democratic Promise*, 404.

50. Ibid., 177–78. Populists in both Alabama and North Carolina generally used the term "co-operation" rather than "fusion" in their literature. The theme projected was that this effort was a necessary cooperative venture to secure fair elections.

51. Hackney, *From Populism to Progressivism*, 33–34; Clark, *Populism in Alabama*, 142, 152. As an example of how contorted Alabama politics had become, the Lily-Whites had some black members. Hackney, *From Populism to Progressivism*, 33; Rogers, *One-Gallused Rebellion*, 280.

52. Hackney, *From Populism to Progressivism*, 34; Saunders, "Southern Populists, 1893–1895," 256.

53. Allen J. Going, "Critical Months in Alabama Politics, 1895–1896" *Alabama Review* 5 (October 1952): 276 n.26.

54. Summersell, "Reuben Kolb," 102–3; Sparkman, "Kolb-Oates Campaign," 33; Clark, *Populism in Alabama*, 153.

55. *Appleton's Annual Cyclopedia, 1894*, 5.

56. *Birmingham Daily News*, 8 February 1894, in Pollack, *Populist Mind*, 391.

57. Skaggs, *The Southern Oligarchy*, 120. Skaggs played a prominent role in Alabama Populism and his conclusions herein are largely based on his personal observations of the political situation in his state. His conclusions should be balanced against more objective accounts.

58. Atkins, "Populism in Alabama," 179–80.

59. Skaggs, *The Southern Oligarchy*, 121; Rogers, *One-Gallused Rebellion*, 280–82.

60. Skaggs, *The Southern Oligarchy*, 121.

61. Rogers, *One-Gallused Rebellion*, 289.

62. Houston Cole, "Populism in Tuscaloosa County" (master's thesis, University of Alabama, 1927), 77–80.

63. Skaggs, *The Southern Oligarchy*, 119; Rogers, *One-Gallused Rebellion*, 281–82.

64. Clark, *Populism in Alabama*, 175.

65. Kousser, *Southern Politics*, 138.

66. Hackney, *Populism to Progressivism*, 62.

67. Goodwyn, *Democratic Promise*, 406.

68. David Ashley Bagwell, "The Magical Process: The Sayre Election Law of 1893," *Alabama Review* 25 (April 1972): 101.

69. *Birmingham Daily News*, 29 January 1894.

70. Hicks, *Populist Revolt*, 335; Cole, "Populism in Tuscaloosa County," 77–80.

71. Clark, *Populism in Alabama*, 175.

72. Accounts of black disenfranchisement can be found in Joseph H. Taylor, "Populism and Disfranchisement in Alabama," *Journal of Negro History* 34 (October 1949): 410–27; and Hackney, *From Populism to Progressivism*, 147–208. In my estimation, Taylor overemphasizes the Populists' proposal for black disenfranchisement while Hackney probably minimizes their contribution.

73. *Tallapoosa (AL) New Era*, in *People's Weekly Tribune*, 3 December 1896.

74. *People's Weekly Tribune,* 26 November 1896, 14 January 1897.

75. Ibid.

76. I. L. Brock to Oliver D. Street, 13 September 1902, quoted in Hackney, *From Populism to Progressivism,* 203.

77. Ibid., 176. *People's Weekly Tribune,* 10 December 1896. For a contrasting interpretation of Manning, see Shofner and Rogers, "Joseph C. Manning," 7–37.

78. *Birmingham Daily News,* 8 February 1894, in Pollack, *Populist Mind,* 391–92.

79. *Birmingham News,* 8 February 1894; Redkey, *Black Exodus,* 193–94; Alfred W. Reynolds, "The Alabama Negro Colony in Mexico, 1894–1896," *Alabama Review* 5 (October 1952): 243–68, and 6 (January 1953): 31–58; *Appleton's Annual Cyclopedia, 1894,* 4. "Plans" to put "all negroes in one place and all whites in another" were absurd, according to Tom Watson. Parting from one's black mammy would be sufficient reason to reject such a proposal. Friedman, *White Savage,* 83.

80. Kousser, *Southern Politics,* 32, 139–81, 239; William A. Mabry, "Disfranchisement of the Negro in Mississippi," *Journal of Southern History* 4 (August 1938): 318–33; Frank B. Williams Jr., "The Poll Tax as a Suffrage Requirement in the South, 1870–1901," *Journal of Southern History* 18 (November 1952): 469–96.

81. Hackney, *From Populism to Progressivism,* 206.

82. Dethloff and Jones, "Race Relations in Louisiana," 306, 308. A table indicating voter registration by race can be found in Ezell, *The South Since 1865,* 176.

83. Hair, *Bourbonism and Agrarian Protest,* 113–14, 234, 237, 241–43, 247, 262–65; Dethloff and Jones, "Race Relations in Louisiana," 305; Woodward, *American Counterpoint,* 212–13; Ezell, *The South Since 1865,* 175–76.

84. Dale A. Somers, "Black and White in New Orleans: A Study in Urban Race Relations, 1865–1900," *Journal of Southern History* 40 (February 1974): 19–42.

85. Gilbert L. Dupre, *Political Reminiscences,* quoted in Dethloff and Jones, "Race Relations in Louisiana," 308.

86. Ibid., 307–8; Kousser, *Southern Politics,* 28, 42, 154, 241.

87. Hair, *Bourbonism and Agrarian Protest,* 186–92; Woodward, *Strange Career,* 29–31. For a description of a pattern of aristocratic paternalism in nearby Arkansas, see Graves, "Negro Disfranchisement in Arkansas," 200–201.

88. *Opelousas (LA) Courier,* 11 February 1888, quoted in Dethloff and Jones, "Race Relations in Louisiana," 308.

89. Melvin J. White, "Populism in Louisiana during the 'Nineties," *Mississippi Valley Historical Review* 5 (June 1918): 14–15.

90. "Town Talk" in *Louisiana Populist,* 4 January 1895. Like any complex movement, Populism cannot be sharply defined, but suffice it to say that this portrait formed a central theme of the membership's view of its recent past.

91. Hair, *Bourbonism and Agrarian Protest,* 244, 248. See also Hofstadter, *Age of Reform,* 101–2.

92. Ibid., 216–17.

93. *National Economist,* 17 October 1891. Emphasis added.

94. Ibid.

95. White, "Populism in Louisiana," 11.

96. Daniel, "The Louisiana People's Party," 1080.

97. *National Economist*, 20 December 1890; Abramowitz, "Negro in the Populist Movement," 94–95.

98. Roxborough, "An Open Letter."

99. Hair, *Bourbonism and Agrarian Protest*, 223; Daniel, "The Louisiana People's Party," 1055.

100. Pollack, *Populist Mind*, 386. This same philosophy was being expressed almost verbatim by Tom Watson in Georgia. See particularly *People's Party Paper*, 17 March 1892.

101. Hair, *Bourbonism and Agrarian Protest*, 225. Woodward is clearly wrong in his statement that "Louisiana Populists in combination with Anti-Lottery allies of the Democratic party won an easy victory over the regular Democrats in the state election of 1892" (Woodward, *Origins*, 261).

102. Paul Lewinson, *Race, Class and Party* (New York: Oxford University Press, 1932; rpr. 1965), 77.

103. N. T. N. Robinson (Marshall, U.S. Circuit Court of Appeals, 5th District, Louisiana) to Henry Wise Garrett, Washington, DC, 7 April 1892. Robinson Letter, Tulane University Library and Archives, Tulane University, New Orleans.

104. Hair, *Bourbonism and Agrarian Protest*, 234.

105. Quoted in Ezell, *The South Since 1865*, 175.

106. Hair, *Bourbonism and Agrarian Protest*, 235.

107. Ibid., 234.

108. *Louisiana Populist*, quoted in Woodward, *Origins*, 276.

109. Goodwyn, *Democratic Promise*, 334.

110. Hair, *Bourbonism and Agrarian Protest*, 241.

111. *Louisiana Populist*, 29 March 1895, 17 May 1895.

112. Ibid., 7 September 1894.

113. Ibid., 21 June 1895, 5 July 1895.

114. Ibid., 6 December 1895.

115. Ibid., 17 January 1896, 24 January 1896, 31 January 1896.

116. Ibid., 17 May 1895.

117. Ibid., 31 August 1894. See also ibid., 24 August 1894 and 21 September 1894.

118. Ibid., 20 September 1895.

119. Ibid., 13 September 1895.

120. *Louisiana Populist*, 31 August 1894, 19 October 1894; *Shreveport (LA) Progress*, in *Louisiana Populist*, 19 October 1894.

121. Ibid., 14 May 1894. See also ibid., 1 November 1895.

122. Ibid., 11 October 1895, 25 October 1895.

123. Ibid., 16 August 1895. White, "Populism in Louisiana," 13–14.

124. *Louisiana Populist*, 21 February 1896.

125. Quoted in Williams, *Romance and Realism in Southern Politics*, 50.

126. Dethloff and Jones, "Race Relations in Louisiana," 307; Hair, *Bourbonism and Agrarian Protest*, 274.

127. Williams, *Romance and Realism in Southern Politics,* 57.

128. Hair, *Bourbonism and Agrarian Protest,* 175.

129. Kousser, *Southern Politics,* 157.

130. Quoted in Perry Howard, *Political Tendencies in Louisiana* (Baton Rouge: Louisiana State University Press, 1957), 98–99.

131. Degler, *Other South,* 334.

132. Hair, *Bourbonism and Agrarian Protest,* 256.

133. Ibid., 257.

134. *Shreveport (LA) Evening Judge,* 15 December 1895, quoted in Hair, *Bourbonism and Agrarian Protest,* 260.

135. Lewinson, *Race, Class, and Party,* 91; Hair, *Bourbonism and Agrarian Protest,* 276–77; White, "Populism in Louisiana," 18–19.

136. Dethloff and Jones, "Race Relations in Louisiana," 317. A different viewpoint of Populist attitudes can be found in Hair, *Bourbonism and Agrarian Protest,* 274.

137. Dethloff and Jones, "Race Relations in Louisiana," 317. These objections sound strangely reminiscent of Northern objections to Southern congressional representation based on slave population prior to the Civil War.

138. *Louisiana Populist,* 22 April 1898, quoted in ibid.

139. Ibid.

140. Ibid., 316.

141. Ibid., 81. There is a slight discrepancy between the figures of Lewinson and of Dethloff and Jones. However, on one point all authors agree: a sharp decline in black registrants followed the 1898 constitutional convention.

142. Lewinson, *Race, Class, and Party,* 81.

143. V. O. Key Jr., *Southern Politics in State and Nation* (New York: Vintage, 1949), 519. An enclosed table indicates voter registration by race and sex.

144. Dethloff and Jones, "Race Relations in Louisiana," 316. See also White, "Populism in Louisiana," 16–19.

145. James D. Ivy, *No Saloon in the Valley: The Southern Strategy of Texas Prohibitionists in the 1880s* (Waco, TX: Baylor University Press, 2003), 60.

146. Ibid., 61.

147. Ibid., 59.

148. Ibid., 92–93.

149. Barr, *Reconstruction to Reform,* 117–22; Robert C. Cotner, *James Stephen Hogg: A Biography* (Austin: University of Texas Press, 1959), 250–51.

150. Ernest W. Winkler, ed., *Platforms of Political Parties in Texas* (Austin: University of Texas, 1916), 293. The origin of the Texas Populist party can be traced to the formation of a county ticket in Navarro County, February 1888. E. G. Sessions to Marion Butler, 11 June 1896, Box 2, folder 29, Butler Papers.

151. Winkler, *Platforms,* 297–99.

152. Quoted in Abramowitz, "Negro in the Populist Movement," 267–68.

153. *Southern Mercury,* 30 June 1892, quoted in Goodwyn, *Democratic Promise,* 288–290.

154. Saunders, "Southern Populists, 1892," 11 n.28; Abramowitz, "Negro in the Populist Movement," 262–68; *Southern Mercury*, 30 June 1892, 7 July 1892.

155. Rice, *Negro in Texas*, 70.

156. Winkler, *Platforms*, 316–26; Barr, *Reconstruction to Reform*, 129–37. National Populist platforms supporting free silver can be found in Hicks, *Populist Revolt*, 432–44.

157. Quoted in Barr, *Reconstruction to Reform*, 136.

158. *Dallas Morning News*, 25 June 1892, quoted in Woodward, *Origins*, 246.

159. Alvord, "T. L. Nugent," 65–81.

160. Catherine Nugent, ed., *Life Work of Thomas L. Nugent*, quoted in Saunders, "Southern Populists, 1892," 17 n.59.

161. *Dallas Morning News*, 9 August 1892, quoted in Saunders, "Southern Populists, 1892."

162. Ibid., 17.

163. Ibid.

164. Ibid.

165. Woodward, *Origins*, 261–62; Abramowitz, "Negro in the Populist Movement," 268.

166. Cotner, *James Stephen Hogg*, 313.

167. Rice, *Negro in Texas*, 72; Goodwyn, *Democratic Promise*, 328.

168. Cantrell and Barton, "Texas Populists," 662–63; Kousser, *Southern Politics*, 199. Kousser estimates that 8.3 percent of black males voted for the Texas Populists in 1892; Cantrell and Barton believe "virtually none" voted Populist.

169. Cantrell and Barton, "Texas Populists," 662–63.

170. Cotner, *James Stephen Hogg*, 312–13.

171. Saunders, "Southern Populists, 1893–1895," 248.

172. Robert Cotner, ed., *Addresses and State Papers of James Stephen Hogg* (Austin: University of Texas Press, 1951), 432. See also Harrell Budd, "The Negro in Politics in Texas, 1867–1898" (master's thesis, University of Texas at Austin, 1929), 108; Rice, *Negro in Texas*, 75.

173. Ibid., 76.

174. Cotner, *James Stephen Hogg*, 313.

175. Rice, *Negro in Texas*, 74. A partial list of other black leaders who supported Hogg is included. A speech by Henry Clay Gray, a black who supported Hogg, can be found in Douglass Geraldyne Perry, "Black Populism: The Negro in the People's Party in Texas" (master's thesis, Prairie View University, 1945), 58–64.

176. Rice, *Negro in Texas*, 72–77; Barr, *Reconstruction to Reform*, 138–39; Hare, *Norris Wright Cuney*, 163.

177. Goodwyn, *Democratic Promise*, 328.

178. Rice, *Negro in Texas*, 80; Martin, *People's Party*, 73, 76, 78, 90, 96–97. A map illustrating the voting patterns for the various candidates can be found in Cotner, *James Stephen Hogg*, opposite 313.

179. Abramowitz, "John B. Rayner," 160–93.

180. Abramowitz, "Negro in the Populist Movement," 270; Girard T. Bryant, "J. B. Rayner, a Negro Populist," *Negro History Bulletin* 3 (May 1940): 125.

181. Cantrell, *Kenneth and John B. Rayner*, 208–12, 215–20, 226–39, 242–43.

182. Abramowitz, "Negro in the Populist Movement," 270; Bryant, "J. B. Rayner, A Negro Populist," 125.

183. Ibid. *Southern Mercury*, 4 October 1894, 29 March 1895, 18 August 1898, 9 June 1898.

184. Rice, *Negro in Texas*, 79.

185. Lewinson, *Race, Class, and Party*, 110.

186. *Galveston Daily News*, quoted in Paul Douglas Casdorph, "Norris Wright Cuney and Texas Republican Politics, 1883–1896," *Southwestern Historical Quarterly* 68 (January 1965): 457.

187. Ibid.

188. Ibid., 460; Quarles, *Negro in the Making of America*, 157.

189. Casdorph, "Norris Wright Cuney," 460–64; Hare, *Norris Wright Cuney*, 127–230.

190. Ibid., 204.

191. Ibid., 158.

192. Rice, *Negro in Texas*, 82.

193. Ibid., 83; Casdorph, "Norris Wright Cuney," 460.

194. Rice, *Negro in Texas*, 82–84; Perry, "Black Populism" 28–29.

195. Cantrell and Barton, "Texas Populists," 684–85.

196. Ibid., 663.

197. Key, *Southern Politics*, 534; Kousser, *Southern Politics*, 207–8, 240; Paul Casdorph, *A History of the Republican Party in Texas, 1865–1965* (Austin, TX: Pemberton Press, 1965), 64, 68, 72. An enclosed map in Key traces the rise and decline of Texas Populism.

198. Key, *Southern Politics*, 534.

199. Rice, *Negro in Texas*, 138.

200. Ibid., 83, 136; Kousser, *Southern Politics*, 200–209; Cantrell and Barton, "Texas Populists," 684–86.

201. Key, *Southern Politics*, 534–35; Kousser, *Southern Politics*, 207–8, 240.

202. Rice, *Negro in Texas*, 138–39; Worth Robert Miller, "Harrison County Methods: Election Fraud in Late Nineteenth Century Texas," *Locus: Regional and Local History* 7 (spring 1995): 111–28. For another example of election fraud, see Robert Shook, "The Texas 'Election Outrage' of 1886," *East Texas Historical Journal* 10 (spring 1972): 20–30.

203. Lewinson, *Race, Class, and Party*, 104, 121, 147.

204. Shaw, *Wool-Hat Boys*, 83–87; Cantrell and Barton, "Texas Populists," 689.

205. Cantrell and Barton, "Texas Populists," 689 n.67; Rice, *Negro in Texas*, 81–82; Martin, *People's Party*, 136 n.26.

206. Robert Caro, *The Years of Lyndon Johnson: Means of Ascent* (New York: Vintage Books, 1991), 180–84.

207. Martin, *People's Party*, 100–102.

208. Robert Caro, *The Years of Lyndon Johnson: The Path to Power* (New York: Vintage Books, 1983), 33–36.

209. Barr, *Reconstruction to Reform,* 141–42, 149–50, 174; Martin, *People's Party,* 69–87, 105–11, 252–60.

210. Barr, *Reconstruction to Reform,* 173.

211. Cantrell, *Kenneth and John B. Rayner,* 287, 290; Goodwyn, *Democratic Promise,* 304.

212. Barr, *Reconstruction to Reform,* 174; Caro, *Path to Power,* 33–34.

8. THE BALANCE SHEET

1. Joseph A. Schlesinger, *Ambition and Politics: Political Careers in the United States* (Chicago: Rand McNally, 1966), 4–5, 57–58.

2. Myrdal, *American Dilemma,* 452.

3. Kousser, *Southern Politics,* 54.

4. Quoted in Factor, *Black Response to America,* 59.

5. Quoted in Vernon Lane Wharton, *The Negro in Mississippi, 1865–1890* (New York: Harper Torchbooks, 1965), 216.

6. Goodwyn, *Democratic Promise,* 281.

7. Chafe, "Negro and Populism," 404. For a discussion of the "wedge issues" that divided black and white in the Populist movement, see Girard Thompson Bryant, *The Colored Brother: A History of the Negro and the Populist Movement* (Kansas City, MO: Maple Woods Community College Press, 1981), 76–79.

8. Quoted in Francis L. Broderick, *W. E. B. Du Bois, Negro Leader in a Time of Crisis* (Stanford, CA: Stanford University Press, 1966), 86.

9. W. E. B. Du Bois, *Dusk of Dawn: An Essay toward an Autobiography of a Race Concept* (New York: Harcourt, Brace, 1940), 29. In later years Du Bois "began to believe" that Populism was a party of "deep significance," and its failure was caused by "the established election frauds of the South, of which I knew." Ibid., 54.

10. Factor, *Black Response to America,* 103.

11. McFeely, *Frederick Douglass,* 359–61.

12. Kousser, *Southern Politics,* 20?, 218–20, 250, 255.

13. Myrdal, *American Dilemma,* 449.

14. Ibid., 454.

15. *Tallapoosa (AL) New Era,* quoted in *People's Weekly Tribune,* 3 December 1886. See also Joseph B. Taylor, "Populism and Disfranchisement in Alabama," 410–27.

16. See in particular Worth Robert Miller, "Harrison County Methods," 111–28.

17. Quoted in McGill, *The South and the Southerner,* 123–24.

18. *People's Party Paper,* 27 September 1895, quoted in Saunders, "Southern Populists, 1893–1895," 251.

19. Ibid., 260 n.47.

20. *People's Weekly Tribune,* 38 May 1896.

21. Ibid., 31 December 1896.

Selected Bibliography

This bibliography is selective rather than exhaustive. Only those materials—primary and secondary—that proved especially valuable and might serve as research aids for future historians of Southern Populism and African Americans are listed below. Other materials utilized can be found in the footnotes of the various chapters and appendices. The many sources, primary and secondary, consulted for this volume were so voluminous that they became a separate bibliographic volume on blacks and the Populist Movement, edited by myself and a colleague, Anthony Adam, and published by Greenwood Press. Readers interested in the topic and this era of Southern history should consult this additional volume.

A. PRIMARY MATERIALS

1. Manuscript Collections

Marion Butler Papers, Southern Historical Collection, University of North Carolina at Chapel Hill.
   A huge, invaluable collection, the Butler papers contain much political correspondence from various Populists throughout the South. The major portion consists of letters from little-known local political leaders who injected comments about the grassroots tactics of the Democrats. Generally erudite and comprehensive in scope, the Butler papers proved to be perhaps the most valuable collection examined during this study.

Rebecca Latimer Felton Collection, University of Georgia Archives, Athens.
   Generally composed of memoranda and personal letters, these papers contain major and controversial correspondence about the 1894 political campaign in Georgia. They were immensely useful for a balanced treatment of the state's political history during this period, especially in the Seventh District. Bearing heavy emphasis on beliefs about the black man's venality, these manuscripts exhibit the characteristic unevenness of various individual accounts and should be approached with caution.

Marmaduke J. Hawkins Papers, North Carolina State Library and Archives, Raleigh, North Carolina.
   This small collection contains several prominent examples of the type of politi-

cal propaganda used during the Populist revolt. Since their circulation was vigorously pushed by Democrats as "inflammatory" material, they were of particular value in assessing the opposition's psychological attack against Populist racial ideology in the South. The two dominating issues of the "Force Bill" and "Negro domination" are animated by several particulars within the collection. Ostensibly written as propaganda items, their factual merit must be balanced against more objective sources.

William J. Northen Papers, Georgia State Archives and Library, Atlanta, Georgia.
Northen, although a Democratic governor, was particularly critical about the use of violence against blacks. But as a conservative he accepted the white dictum that "social equality" was highly undesirable to both races. This is a valuable collection for understanding why blacks would vote for a man whose party was very hostile toward African Americans. Individual agents of political reform such as Northen acted as a magnetic force for middle-class black leaders who attempted to adapt to local conditions.

Open Letter Club Correspondence, Tennessee State Library and Archives, Nashville.
A small but valuable collection of papers with several interesting pieces debating the "Force Bill" and its possible effects on the South and blacks. Beyond that, the collection is of little value to a study of this nature.

Leonidas L. Polk Collection, Southern Historical Collection, University of North Carolina at Chapel Hill.
The Polk papers provide a rich source of information about the Farmers' Alliance movement in the larger context of agrarian reform. The comments of Polk's contemporaries concerning political conditions and the progress of the agrarian movement proved to be of particular value in analyzing the South's slow philosophical shift toward independent political activity. Also, these same references provided an illuminating insight into the ideological struggle taking place in Southern minds over the African American question and the consequences of a third party.

John B. Rayner Papers, Barker History Center, The University of Texas, Austin.
Although the material here covers Rayner's history after 1904 and omits his earlier experience with Populism, the papers are worth examining to understand the mind of a black Populist leader struggling to reach accommodation after years of fighting discrimination. It is a tribute to Gregg Cantrell's research abilities that he so ably recreated Rayner's earlier career in his biography, for the Rayner papers were of little assistance.

N. T. N. Robinson Letter, Tulane University Library and Archives, Tulane University, New Orleans.
Robinson was a United States Marshall in Louisiana's Fifth District. This letter contains his description of the widespread fraud and violence that was occurring during the state elections in April, 1892.

Charles A. Roxborough Letter, Louisiana State University, Archives, Baton Rouge.
A letter of resignation from a black Republican leader from Louisiana. Roxbor-

ough includes some interesting reasons for possible black defection from the Republican party. By way of innuendo and nuance, he hints that blacks should support the Democrats. He subsequently joined the Louisiana Populist Party and was nominated for the office of state treasurer at the party's first convention in 1892.

Oliver P. Temple Papers, Special Collections, University of Tennessee Library, Knoxville.

Outside of some interesting material on Southern white Republican attitudes toward blacks, the collection is of little value to a study of this nature. The Temple papers are primarily concerned with the political activities of the two major parties. The absence of correspondence concerning the third party in Tennessee is largely indicative of the state's minor role in the Populist revolt.

Tom Watson Papers, Southern Historical Collection, University of North Carolina at Chapel Hill.

Unusually disappointing for a collection with a reputation as a source of information on Populist activities. Because of Watson's prominence as a Southern liberal in race relations, it is regrettable that the collection, despite its size, contains so little of use for the period before 1900. "It is a testimony to C. Vann Woodward's thoroughness," Norman Pollack has written, "that he was able to reconstruct so ably Watson's activities in the 1890s, for the papers themselves were of little help." Despite this weakness, however, these papers constitute an indispensable starting point for any study of Southern Populist racial attitudes.

2. Official Government Records and Documents

Bureau of the Census. *Negro Population, 1790–1915*. Washington, DC: Government Printing Office, 1918.

Congressional Directory, 1891–1896. Washington, DC: Government Printing Office.

Congressional Record, 1890–1896. Washington, DC: Government Printing Office.

Office of Recorder of Deeds, Corporation Division, Instrument No. 1606, *Incorporation Liber 4,* Folio 354, Washington, D.C. (Colored Farmers' Alliance Charter).

State of Georgia. *Georgia Laws,* 1889–1894.

3. Election Returns

All election data (1891–1900) were unselfishly supplied by Dr. Sheldon Hackney. Dr. Hackney's computerized compilation includes all eleven states of the Old Confederacy. All economic and racial statistics were taken from the 1900 census. These data were supplemented by my earlier analysis in a master's thesis, which used 1890 census data. Due to the fraudulent nature of Southern politics, particularly during this period, any conclusions drawn should be balanced against manuscript material. The reader should also consult the works by Kousser, Key, and Cantrell and Barton for additional quantitative data about the period.

4. Newspapers

Banner (Nashville, Tennessee). 1891–1896.

An independent daily which provided objective coverage on Farmers' Alliance and Populist activities as they occurred in the Nashville vicinity. An indispensable aid to any study of the Tennessee order despite its almost total neglect of blacks' role in the state movement.

The Caucasian (Clinton and Raleigh, North Carolina). 1892–1897.

Under the tutorage of Marion Butler, a former Republican turned Populist, this paper, ironically, was not as sympathetic in tone to blacks as its counterpart in the state, *The Progressive Farmer*. It was, however, exceedingly valuable as an aid in gleaning the state's conservative white Populist opinion toward African Americans.

Constitution (Atlanta, Georgia). 1890–1896.

Daily News (Birmingham, Alabama). February 8, 1894.

This issue contains the 1894 state platform of the Alabama Jeffersonian-Populist party. Of particular interest, is the proposal to "set apart sufficient territory to constitute a state, given exclusively to the colored race."

Louisiana Populist (Natchitoches, Louisiana). 1894–1899.

Under the editorship of Hardy Brian, the Populist state secretary, this paper served as the official organ of the Louisiana movement. Brian was particularly vituperative, making hostile comments about Bourbons and blacks alike.

National Economist (Washington, DC). 1890–1893.

The official organ of the Southern Alliance, this weekly quoted extensively from various grassroots Populist papers in a "reform press" section, thereby providing a good insight into the diversity of racial attitudes within the region.

People's Party Paper (Atlanta, Georgia). 1891–1896.

The personal organ of Tom Watson, providing an illuminating example of the white Populist liberal ideology toward the black community. Except during political campaigns, however, other states received only superficial commentary on racial and social conditions.

People's Weekly Tribune (Birmingham, Alabama). 1894–1897.

With John W. DuBose as editor and Reuben Kolb as business manager, this was easily the most influential Populist newspaper in the state. Of all the newspapers examined, the *Tribune* was the most hostile toward blacks—an attitude perhaps prompted by its readership, which seemed less interested in banding together politically with blacks than did other Southern states.

The Progressive Farmer (Raleigh, North Carolina). 1890–1895.

Founded by L. L. Polk, president of the Southern Alliance, this weekly is of particular interest for its broad critical evaluation of the South's contributions to the agrarian movement. In the course of perusing it, the current author also gathered important data due to its wavering between a conservative and conciliatory line toward African Americans.

Public Opinion (New York, Public Opinion Quarterly Press). 1889–1895.

This is a collection of newspaper excerpts arranged topically. The use of these volumes gave a wide geographical and philosophical overview of the Farmers' Alliance and third-party movement. Coverage for political events in the Gulf Coast South was particularly good.

The Southern Mercury (Dallas, Texas). 1893–1897.

> The official organ of Texas Populism, this newspaper is valuable for its regional perspective of the South's political history. Exceedingly important in evaluating the Populists' psychology toward black voters in the South.

Times (New York). May 21, 1891; March 23, 1965.

Weekly Toiler (Nashville, Tennessee). 1888–1892.

> The Tennessee Farmers' Alliance organ under the editorship of J. H. McDowell, this paper was almost the sole source of information on the history of the state's Colored Alliances and Wheels. Despite the *Toiler's* official connotation, the Nashville *Banner* provided a more intricate study of the white Alliance movement during this period.

5. Periodical Articles

Cable, George W. "The Convict Lease System in the Southern States." *Century Magazine* 27 (February 1888): 582–99.

———. "The Freedman's Case in Equity." *Century Magazine* 29 (January 1885): 409–18.

———. "The Silent South." *Century Magazine* 30 (September 1895): 679–91.

———. "A Simpler Negro Question." *Forum* 6 (December 1888): 392–403.

———. "What Shall the Negro Do?" *Forum* 5 (August 1888): 627–39.

Diggs, Annie L. "The Farmers' Alliance and Some of Its Leaders." *Arena* 5 (April 1892): 590–604.

Flower, Benjamin O. "The General Discontent of America's Wealth Creators as Illustrated in Current Cartoons." *Arena* 16 (1896): 298–304.

Lloyd, Henry D. "The Populists at St. Louis." *Review of Reviews* 14 (September 1896): 278–83.

Lodge, Henry Cabot, and Terrence V. Powderly. "The Federal Election Bill." *North American Review* 151 (September 1890): 257–73.

"National People's Party Platform." *The World Almanac 1893* (New York: Newspaper Enterprise Association, 1893): 83–85.

Reed, Thomas B. "The Federal Control of Elections." *North American Review* 151 (June 1890): 671–80.

Shaffer, A. W. "A Southern Republican on the Lodge Bill." *North American Review* 51 (November 1890): 601–9.

Smith, Hoke. "Disastrous Effects of the Force Bill." *Forum* 13 (August 1892): 686–92.

Watson, Thomas E. "The Negro Question in the South." *Arena* 6 (October 1892): 540–50.

6. Edited Documents and Letters

Aptheker, Herbert, ed. *A Documentary History of the Negro People in the United States.* 2 vols. New York: Citadel Press, 1964.

Bracey, John H., Jr., August Meier, and Elliot Rudwick, eds. *Black Nationalism in America.* Indianapolis: Bobbs-Merrill, 1970.

Cotner, Robert C., ed. *Addresses and State Papers of James Stephen Hogg.* Austin: University of Texas Press, 1951.

Foner, Philip S., ed. *Life and Writings of Frederick Douglass.* 4 vols. New York: Citadel Press, 1955.

Hendrick, Burton J. *The Training of an American: The Earlier Life and Letters of Walter Hines Page, 1855–1913.* New York: Houghton Mifflin, 1938.

Katz, William Loren. *Eyewitness: The Negro in American History.* New York: Pittman, 1967.

Pollack, Norman, ed. *The Populist Mind.* New York: Bobbs-Merrill, 1967.

Tindall, George B., ed. *A Populist Reader.* New York: Harper Torchbooks, 1966.

Van Noppen, Ina W., ed. *The South: A Documentary History.* Princeton, NJ: Van Nostrand, 1958.

Williamson, Joel, ed. *The Origins of Segregation.* Boston: D. C. Heath, 1968.

Winkler, Ernest William, ed. *Platforms of Political Parties in Texas.* University of Texas *Bulletin* No. 53. Austin: University of Texas, 1916.

7. Miscellaneous

Cable, George W. *The Negro Question.* New York: Scribner, 1890.

——. *The Silent South.* New York: Scribner, 1890.

Dunning, Nelson A., ed. *The Farmers' Alliance and Agricultural Digest.* Washington, DC: The Alliance Publishing Company, 1891.

Frank, Thomas. *What's the Matter with Kansas? How Conservatives Won the Heart of America.* New York: Metropolitan Books, 2004.

Haley, James T., ed. and comp. *Afro-American Encyclopaedia.* Nashville, TN: Haley and Florida, 1895.

Manning, Joseph. *The Fadeout of Populism.* New York: T. A. Hebbons Company, 1928.

Otken, Charles H. *The Ills of the South; or, Related Causes Hostile to the General Prosperity of the Southern People.* New York: G. P. Putnam and Sons, 1894.

Skaggs, William H. *The Southern Oligarchy: An Appeal in Behalf of the Silent Masses of Our Country against the Despotic Rule of the Few.* New York: Devin-Adair, 1924.

Watson, Thomas E. *The Life and Speeches of Thomas E. Watson.* Nashville, TN: n.p., 1908.

B. SECONDARY SOURCES

1. Biographies

Barr, Alwyn, Robert Calvert, eds. *Black Leaders: Texans for their Times.* Austin: Texas State Historical Society, 1981; rpr. 1994.

Broderick, Francis L. *W. E. B. DuBois: Negro Leader in a Time of Crisis.* Stanford, CA: Stanford University Press, 1966.

Cantrell, Gregg. *Feeding the Wolf: John B. Rayner and the Politics of Race, 1850–1918.* Wheeling, WV: Harlan-Davidson, 2001.

——. *Kenneth and John B. Rayner and the Limits of Southern Dissent.* Urbana: University of Illinois Press, 1993.

Cotner, Robert C. *James Stephen Hogg: A Biography*. Austin: University of Texas Press, 1959.

Foner, Philip S. *Frederick Douglass: A Biography*. New York: Citadel Press, 1964.

Hare, Maud Cuney. *Norris Wright Cuney: A Tribune of the Black People*. Intro. Tera W. Hunter. Austin, TX: Steck-Vaughan Co., 1913; rpr. New York: G. K. Hall, 1968.

Harlan, Louis R. *Booker T. Washington: The Making of a Black Leader, 1865–1901*. New York: Oxford University Press, 1972.

Holmes, William F. *The White Chief: James Kimble Vardaman*. Baton Rouge: Louisiana State University Press, 1970.

Lynch, John Roy. *Reminiscences of an Active Life: The Autobiography of John Roy Lynch*, ed. John Hope Franklin. Chicago: University of Chicago Press, 1970.

Noblin, Stuart. *Leonidas Lafayette Polk*. Chapel Hill: University of North Carolina Press, 1949.

Robison, Dan M. *Bob Taylor and the Agrarian Revolt*. Chapel Hill: University of North Carolina Press, 1935.

Simkins, Francis Butler. *Pitchfork Ben Tillman: South Carolinian*. Baton Rouge: Louisiana State University Press, 1944.

Talmadge, John E. *Rebecca Latimer Felton: Nine Stormy Decades*. Athens: University of Georgia Press, 1960.

Torrence, Ridgely. *The Story of John Hope*. New York: Macmillan, 1948.

Walls, W. J. *Joseph Charles Price*. Boston: Christopher Publishing House, 1943.

Woodward, C. Vann. *Tom Watson: Agrarian Rebel*. New York: Rinehart and Company, 1938; rpr. 1963.

2. State Studies

Arnett, Alex M. *The Populist Movement in Georgia*. Columbia University Studies in History, Economics, and Public Law, 104, No. 1. New York: Columbia University Press, 1922.

Barr, Alwyn. *Reconstruction to Reform: Texas Politics, 1876–1906*. Austin: University of Texas Press, 1971.

Brewer, J. Mason. *Negro Legislators of Texas and Their Dependents*. Dallas, TX: Mathis Publishing Company, 1935.

Casdorph, Paul. *A History of the Republican Party in Texas, 1865–1965*. Austin, TX: The Pemberton Press, 1965.

Clark, John B. *Populism in Alabama, 1874–1896*. Auburn: Auburn Printing Company, 1927.

Coulter, E. Merton. *Georgia: A Short History*. Chapel Hill: University of North Carolina Press, 1960.

Crow, Jeffrey J., Paul D. Escott, and Flora J. Hatley. *A History of African Americans in North Carolina*. Raleigh: Division of Archives and History, North Carolina Department of Cultural Resources, 1992.

Edmonds, Helen. *The Negro and Fusion Politics in North Carolina, 1895–1901*. Chapel Hill: University of North Carolina Press, 1961.

Going, Allen J. *Bourbon Democracy in Alabama, 1874–1900.* University: University of Alabama Press, 1951.

Hackney, Sheldon. *Populism to Progressivism in Alabama.* Princeton, NJ: Princeton University Press, 1969.

Hair, William Ivy. *Bourbonism and Agrarian Protest: Louisiana Politics, 1877–1900.* Baton Rouge: Louisiana State University Press, 1969.

Hamilton, Joseph G. de R. *North Carolina Since 1860.* Chicago: University of Chicago Press, 1919.

Hart, Roger L. *Redeemers, Bourbons, and Populists: Tennessee, 1870–1896.* Baton Rouge: Louisiana State University Press, 1975.

Kirwan, Albert D. *Revolt of the Rednecks: Mississippi Politics, 1876–1925.* New York: Harper, 1951.

Lander, Ernest M., Jr. *A History of South Carolina, 1865–1960.* Chapel Hill: University of North Carolina Press, 1960.

Lefler, Hugh Talmadge, and Albert Ray Newsome. *North Carolina: The History of a Southern State.* Chapel Hill: University of North Carolina Press, 1963.

Logan, Frenise A. *The Negro in North Carolina, 1876–1894.* Chapel Hill: University of North Carolina Press, 1964.

Mabry, William A. *The Negro in North Carolina Politics Since Reconstruction.* Durham, NC: Duke University Press, 1940.

Martin, Roscoe C. *The People's Party in Texas: A Study in Third Party Politics.* University of Texas *Bulletin* No. 3308. Austin: University of Texas Press, 1933.

Moger, Allen W. *Virginia: Bourbonism to Byrd, 1870–1925.* Charlottesville: University of Virginia Press, 1968.

Moore, Albert Burton. *History of Alabama and Her People.* Tuscaloosa: University of Alabama Supply Store, 1934.

Morton, Richard L. *The Negro in Virginia Politics, 1865–1902.* Charlottesville: University of Virginia Press, 1919.

Pitre, Merline. *Through Many Dangers, Toils, and Snares: Black Leadership in Texas, 1870–1890.* Austin, TX: Eakin Press, 1985.

Rice, Lawrence D. *The Negro in Texas, 1874–1900.* Baton Rouge: Louisiana State University Press, 1971.

Rogers, William Warren. *The One-Gallused Rebellion: Agrarianism in Alabama, 1865–1896.* Baton Rouge: Louisiana State University Press, 1970.

Scott, Mingo, Jr. *The Negro in Tennessee Politics and Government Affairs, 1865–1965.* Nashville, TN: Rich Printing Company, 1964.

Shadgett, Olive Hall. *The Republican Party in Georgia: From Reconstruction through 1900.* Athens: University of Georgia Press, 1964.

Shaw, Barton. *The Wool-Hat Boys: Georgia's Populist Party.* Baton Rouge: Louisiana State University Press, 1984.

Sheldon, William DuBose. *Populism in the Old Dominion: Virginia Farm Politics, 1885–1900.* Princeton, NJ: Princeton University Press, 1935.

Simkins, Francis Butler. *The Tillman Movement in South Carolina.* Durham, NC: Duke University Press, 1926.

Tindall, George B. *South Carolina Negroes, 1877–1900.* Columbia: University of South Carolina Press, 1952.

Wardlaw, Ralph W. *Negro Suffrage in Georgia, 1867–1930.* University of Georgia *Bulletin,* 33. Athens: University of Georgia Press, 1932.

Wharton, Vernon Lane. *The Negro in Mississippi, 1865–1890.* New York: Harper Torchbooks, 1965.

Wright, George C. *Racial Violence in Kentucky, 1865–1940.* Baton Rouge: Louisiana State University Press, 1990; 1996.

Wynes, Charles E. *Race Relations in Virginia, 1870–1902.* Charlottesville: University of Virginia Press, 1961.

3. Miscellaneous

Allport, Gordon W. *The Nature of Prejudice.* New York: Doubleday, 1958.

Appleton's Annual Cyclopedia, 1886–1898. New York: Appleton and Company.

Bell, Daniel, ed. *The Radical Right.* New York: Anchor, 1964.

Brawley, Benjamin. *A Short History of the Negro American.* New York: Macmillan, 1950.

Brown, William Garrott. *The Lower South in American History.* New York: Macmillan, 1902.

Bryant, Girard Thompson. *The Colored Brother: A History of the Negro and the Populist Movement.* Kansas City, MO: Maple Woods Community College Press, 1981.

Carmer, Carl. *Stars Fell on Alabama.* New York: Farrar and Rhinehart, 1934.

Cash, Wilbur J. *The Mind of the South.* New York: Knopf, 1941.

Degler, Carl N. *Out of Our Past.* New York: Harper Colophon Books, 1970.

De Santis, Vincent P. *Republicans Face the Southern Question: The New Departure Years, 1877–1897.* Baltimore: Johns Hopkins Press, 1959.

Dollard, John. *Caste and Class in a Southern Town.* New York: Doubleday, 1949.

Dray, Philip. *At the Hands of Persons Unknown: The Lynching of Black America.* New York: Random House, 2002.

DuBois, William E. B. *Dusk of Dawn: Essay Toward an Autobiography of a Race Concept.* New York: Harcourt Brace, 1940.

———. *The Souls of Black Folk: Essays and Sketches.* Greenwich, CT: Fawcett, 1961.

Elkins, Stanley M. *Slavery: A Study in American Institutional and Intellectual Life.* New York: Grosset's University Library, 1961.

Factor, Robert L. *The Black Response to America: Men, Ideals, and Organization from Frederick Douglass to the NAACP.* Reading, MA: Addison-Wesley, 1970.

Fine, Sidney. *Laissez Faire and the General-Welfare State: A Study of Conflict in American Thought, 1865–1901.* Ann Arbor: University of Michigan Press, 1950; 1966.

Frazier, E. Franklin, *The Negro in the United States.* New York: Macmillan, 1949.

Friedman, Lawrence J., ed. *The White Savage: Racial Fantasies in the Postbellum South.* Englewood Cliffs, NJ: Prentice Hall, 1970.

Gaston, Paul. *New South Creed: A Study in Southern Myth Making.* New York: Knopf, 1970.

Goodwyn, Lawrence. *Democratic Promise: the Populist Moment in America.* New York: Oxford University Press, 1976.

Green, Fletcher, ed. *Essays in Southern History.* Chapel Hill: University of North Carolina Press, 1949.

Grob, Gerald. *Workers and Utopia.* New York: Quadrangle Books, 1969.

Hicks, John D. *The Populist Revolt: a History of the Farmers' Alliance and the People's Party.* Lincoln: University of Nebraska Press, 1931; rpr. 1961.

Hirshson, Stanley P. *Farewell to the Bloody Shirt: Northern Republicans and the Southern Negro, 1877–1893.* Bloomington: Indiana University Press, 1962.

Hofstadter, Richard. *The Age of Reform: From Bryan to F. D. R.* New York: Knopf, 1955.

Hopkins, Charles Howard. *The Rise of the Social Gospel in American Protestantism.* New Haven, CT: Yale University Press, 1940.

Ivy, James D. *No Saloon in the Valley: The Southern Strategy of Texas Prohibitionists in the 1880s.* Waco, TX: Baylor University Press, 2003.

Kelsey, Carl. *The Negro Farmer.* Chicago: Jennings and Pye, 1903.

Key, V. O., Jr. *Politics, Parties and Pressure Groups.* New York: Crowell, 1964.

———. *Southern Politics in State and Nation.* New York: Vintage, 1949.

King, C. Wendell. *Social Movements in the United States.* New York: Random House, 1969.

Kousser, J. Morgan. *The Shaping of Southern Politics: Suffrage Restriction and the Establishment of the One-Party South, 1880–1910.* New Haven, CT: Yale University Press, 1974.

Lewinson, Paul. *Race, Class, and Party.* New York: Oxford University Press, 1932; rpr. 1965.

Lipset, Seymour. *Political Man: The Social Basis of Politics.* New York: Doubleday, 1963.

Logan, Rayford W. *The Negro in American Life and Thought.* New York: Dial, 1954.

McMath, Robert C., Jr. *The Populist Vanguard: A History of the Southern Farmers' Alliance.* Chapel Hill: University of North Carolina Press, 1975.

Meier, August. *Negro Thought in America, 1880–1915.* Ann Arbor: University of Michigan, 1966.

———, and Elliot Rudwick. *From Plantation to Ghetto.* New York: G. P. Putnam and Sons, 1960.

Morris, Willie. *North Toward Home.* New York: Delta, 1970.

Quarles, Benjamin. *The Negro in the Making of America.* New York: Macmillan, 1965.

Raper, Arthur F. *The Tragedy of Lynching.* Chapel Hill: University of North Carolina Press, 1933.

Redkey, Edwin S. *Black Exodus: Black Nationalist and Back-to-Africa Movements, 1890–1910.* New Haven, CT: Yale University Press, 1969.

Rochester, Anne. *The Populist Movement in the United States.* New York: International Publishers, 1943.

Rose, Arnold. *The Negro in America.* New York: Harper and Row, 1948.

Rozwenc, Edwin C., and John C. Malton, eds. *Myth and Reality in the Populist Revolt.* Boston: D. C. Heath and Company, 1967.

Saloutos, Theodore. *Populism: Reaction or Reform?* New York: Rinehart and Winston, 1968.

Scarborough, Dorothy. *In the Land of Cotton.* New York: Macmillan 1923.

Schlesinger, Joseph A. *Ambition and Politics: Political Careers in the United States.* Chicago: Rand, McNally, 1966.

Sherrill, Robert. *Gothic Politics in the Deep South: Stars of the New Confederacy.* New York: Grossman Publishers, 1968.

Simpson, George Eaton, and J. Milton Yinger. *Racial and Cultural Minorities.* New York: Harper and Row, 1965.

Stampp, Kenneth M. *The Peculiar Institution.* New York: Vintage, 1965.

Swann, William F. G., et al. *Essays on Research in the Social Sciences: Papers Presented in a General Seminar Conducted by the Committee on Training of the Brookings Institution, 1930–31.* New York: Steiger and Company, 1931.

Thorpe, Earl E. *The Mind of the Negro: An Intellectual History of Afro-Americans.* Westport, CT: Negro University Press, 1970.

Vander Zanden, James W. *American Minority Relations.* New York: Ronald Press, 1963.

Watters, Pat. *The South and the Nation.* New York: Pantheon Books, 1969.

Williams, T. Harry. *Romance and Realism in Southern Politics.* Baton Rouge: Louisiana State University Press, 1966.

Woodward, C. Vann. *American Counterpoint: Slavery and Racism in the South Dialogue.* Boston: Little, Brown and Company, 1971.

———. *Origins of the New South, 1877–1913.* Baton Rouge: Louisiana State University Press, 1951; rpr. 1966.

———. *The Strange Career of Jim Crow.* New York: Oxford University Press, 1957.

Wyllie, Irwin G. *The Self-Made Man in America.* New Brunswick, NJ: Rutgers University Press, 1954.

Wynes, Charles E., ed. *Forgotten Voices: Dissenting Southerners in an Age of Conformity.* Baton Rouge: Louisiana State University Press, 1966.

4. Essays and Periodical Articles

Abramowitz, Jack. "Agrarian Reformers and the Negro Question." *Negro History Bulletin* 11 (March 1974): 138–39.

———. "John B. Rayner—Grass-Roots Leader." *Journal of Negro History* 26 (April 1951): 160–93.

———. "The Negro in the Agrarian Revolt." Agricultural History 24 (April 1950): 89–95.

———. "The Negro in the Populist Movement." *Journal of Negro History* 38 (July 1953): 257–89.

Alvord, Wayne. "T. L. Nugent, Texas Populist." *Southwestern Historical Quarterly* 57 (July 1953): 65–81.

Atkins, Leah R. "Populism in Alabama: Reuben F. Kolb and the Appeals to Minority Groups." *Alabama Historical Quarterly* 32 (fall and winter 1970): 167–80.

Bacote, Clarence A. "Negro Proscriptions, Protest and Proposed Solutions in Georgia, 1886–1908." *Journal of Southern History* 25 (August 1959): 200–223.

Barnhart, John D. "Rainfall and the Populist Party in Nebraska." *American Political Science Review* 19 (August 1925): 527–40.

Bode, Frederich A. "Religion and Class Hegemony: A Populist Critique in North Carolina." *Journal of Southern History* 37 (August 1971): 417–38.

Bryant, Girard T. "J. B. Rayner, a Negro Populist." *Negro History Bulletin* 3 (May 1940): 125–26.

Carter, Purvis M. "Robert Lloyd Smith and the Farmers' Improvement Society, a Self Help Movement in Texas." *Negro History Bulletin* 29 (fall 1966): 175–76, 190–91.

Casdorph, Paul Douglas. "Norris Wright Cuney and Texas Republican Politics, 1883–1896." *Southwestern Historical Quarterly* 68 (January 1965): 455–64.

Chafe, William H. "The Negro and Populism: A Kansas Study." *Journal of Southern History* 34 (August 1968): 402–19.

Clark, Thomas D. "The Furnishing and Supply System in Southern Agriculture Since 1865." *Journal of Southern History* 12 (February 1946): 22–44.

Crowe, Charles. "Tom Watson, Populists and Blacks Reconsidered." *Journal of Negro History* 55 (April 1970): 99–116.

Daniel, Lucia E. "Louisiana People's Party," *Louisiana Historical Quarterly* 26 (October 1943): 1055–1149.

Degler, Carl N. "Racism in the United States: An Essay Review." *Journal of Southern History* 38 (February 1972): 101–9.

De Santis, Vincent P. "Negro Dissatisfaction with Republican Policy." *Journal of Negro History* 26 (April 1951): 148–59.

Dethloff, Henry C., and Robert R. Jones. "Race Relations in Louisiana, 1877–1898." *Louisiana History* 9 (fall 1968): 301–23.

Drew, Frank M. "The Present Farmers' Movement." *Political Science Quarterly* 6 (June 1891): 282–310.

Fishel, Leslie H., Jr. "The Negro in Northern Politics, 1877–1900." *Mississippi Valley Historical Review* 42 (December 1955): 466–89.

Franklin, John Hope. "History of Racial Segregation in the United States." *Annals of the American Academy of Political and Social Science* 304 (March 1956): 1–7.

Godshalk, David. "William J. Northen's Public and Personal Struggles against Lynching." In *Jumpin' Jim Crow: Southern Politics from Civil War to Civil Rights,* ed. Jane Dailey, Glenda Elizabeth Gilmore, and Bryant Simon. Princeton, NJ: Princeton University Press, 2000.

Going, Allen J. "Critical Months in Alabama Politics, 1895–1896." *The Alabama Review* 5 (October 1952): 269–81.

Grantham, Dewey W., Jr. "Dinner at the White House: Theodore Roosevelt, Booker T. Washington and the South." *Tennessee Historical Quarterly* 17 (June 1958): 112–30.

———. "Georgia Politics and the Disfranchisement of the Negro." *Georgia Historical Quarterly* 32 (March 1948): 1–21.

Graves, John William. "Negro Disfranchisement in Arkansas." *Arkansas Historical Quarterly* 26 (autumn 1967): 199–255.

Grob, Gerald. "Terence V. Powderly and the Knights of Labor." *Mid-America* 39 (January 1957): 39–55.

Hammond, Marcus B. "The Southern Farmer and Cotton." *Political Science Quarterly* 12 (September 1897): 450–75.

Hicks, John D., and John D. Barnhart. "The Farmers' Alliance." *North Carolina Historical Review* 6 (July 1929): 254–79.

Holmes, William F. "The Demise of the Colored Farmers' Alliance." *Journal of Southern History* 41 (May 1975): 187–200.

Hovland, Carl Iver, and Robert R. Sears. "Minor Studies of Aggression: VI. Correlation of Lynchings with Economic Indices." *Journal of Psychology* 9 (1940): 301–10.

Ingle, Larry H. "A Southern Democrat at Large: William Hodge Kitchin and the Populist Party." *North Carolina Historical Review* 45 (spring 1968): 169–84.

Janowitz, Morris, and Dwaine Marvick. "Authoritarianism and Political Behavior." *Public Opinion Quarterly* 47 (summer 1953): 185–201.

Jones, Rhett. "Proving Blacks Inferior, 1870–1930." *Black World* 20 (February 1971): 4–19.

Kantrowitz, Stephen. "Ben Tillman and Hendrix McLane, Agrarian Rebels: White Manhood, 'The Farmers,' and the Limits of Southern Populism." *Journal of Southern History* 66 (August 2000): 497–524.

Kendrick, Benjamin B. "Agrarian Discontent in the South, 1880–1900." *Annual Report of the American Historical Association* (1920): 267–72.

Kessler, Sidney H. "The Organization of Negroes in the Knights of Labor." *Journal of Negro History* 37 (July 1952): 248–76.

Krauss, James O. "The Farmers' Alliance in Florida." *South Atlantic Quarterly* 25 (July 1926): 300–315.

Kutner, Bernard, Carol Wilkins, and Penny Yarrow. "Verbal Attitudes and Overt Behavior Involving Racial Prejudice." *Journal of Abnormal and Social Psychology* 47 (July 1952): 649–52.

Le Piere, Richard T. "Attitudes vs. Actions." *Social Forces* 13 (December 1934): 230–37.

Linn, Lawrence S. "Verbal Attitudes and Overt Behavior; A Study of Racial Discrimination." *Social Forces* 45 (March 1965): 353–64.

Lipset, Seymour. "Working-Class Authoritarianism." *American Sociological Review* 24 (August 1959): 482–502.

Mabry, William A. "Negro Suffrage and Fusion Rule in North Carolina." *North Carolina Historical Review* 12 (April 1935): 79–102.

MacKinnon, William, and Richard Centers. "Authoritarianism and Urban Stratification." *American Journal of Sociology* 61 (May 1956): 610–20.

Macune, Charles W., Jr. "The Wellsprings of a Populist: Dr. C. W. Macune before 1886." *Southwestern Historical Quarterly* 90 (October 1986): 139–58.

Malof, Milton, and Albert Lott. "Ethnocentrism and the Acceptance of Negro Support in a Group Situation." *Journal of Abnormal and Social Psychology* 65 (October 1962): 254–58.

Marshall, R. "Precipitation and Presidents." *Nation* 124 (March 1927): 315–16.

Miller, Robert Worth. "Harrison County Methods: Election Fraud in Late Nineteenth Century Texas." *Locus: Regional and Local History* (spring 1995): 111–28.

Paisley, Clifton. "The Political Wheelers and the Arkansas Election of 1888." *Arkansas Historical Quarterly* 25 (spring 1966): 3–21.

Powdermaker, Hortense. "The Channeling of Negro Aggression by the Cultural Process." *American Journal of Sociology* 48 (May 1943): 750–58.

Proctor, Samuel. "National Farmers' Alliance Convention of 1890 and Its 'Ocala Demands.'" *Florida Historical Quarterly* 28 (January 1950): 161–81.

Reeves, Richard. "The New Populism and the Old: A Matter of Words." *Saturday Review* (8 April 1972): 46–47.

Reynolds, Alfred W. "The Alabama Negro Colony in Mexico, 1894–1896." *The Alabama Review* 5 (October 1952): 243–68.

———. "The Alabama Negro Colony in Mexico, 1894–1896." *The Alabama Review* 6 (January 1953): 31–58.

Robinson, Dan M. "Tennessee Politics and the Agrarian Movement, 1886–1896." *Mississippi Valley Historical Review* 20 (December 1934): 365–80.

Rogers, William Warren. "The Negro Alliance in Alabama." *Journal of Negro History* 45 (January 1960): 38–44.

———. "Negro Knights of Labor in Arkansas: A Case Study of the 'Miscellaneous' Strike." *Labor History* 10 (summer 1969): 210–17.

———. "Reuben F. Kolb: Agricultural Leader of the New South." *Agricultural History* 32 (April 1958): 109–19.

Saunders, Robert M. "The Southern Populists and the Negro in 1892." *University of Virginia Essays in History* 12 (1966–1967): 7–25.

———. "Southern Populists and the Negro, 1893–1895." *Journal of Negro History* 54 (July 1969): 240–61.

———. "The Transformation of Tom Watson, 1894–1895." *Georgia Historical Quarterly* 54 (fall 1970): 339–56.

Scott, Roy V. "Milton George and the Farmers' Alliance Movement." *Mississippi Valley Historical Review* 45 (June 1958): 90–109.

Shannon, Fred A. "C. W. Macune and the Farmers' Alliance." *Current History* 28 (June 1955): 330–35.

Shapiro, Herbert. "The Populists and the Negro: A Reconsideration." In *The Making of Black America,* 2 vols., ed. August Meier and Elliot Rudwick, 2:27–36. New York: Atheneum, 1969.

Sharp, J. A. "Entrance of the Farmers' Alliance into Tennessee Politics." East Tennessee Historical Society's *Publications* No. 9 (1937): 72–92.

Shoftner, Jerrell H., and William Warren Rogers. "Joseph C. Manning: Militant Agrarian, Enduring Populist." *Alabama Historical Quarterly* 29 (spring and summer, 1967), 7–37.

Shugg, Roger Wallace. "The New Orleans General Strike of 1892." *Louisiana Historical Quarterly* 21 (April 1938): 117–24.

Simkins, Francis Butler. "Ben Tillman's View of the Negro." *Journal of Southern History* 3 (May 1937): 161–74.

Simms, L. Moody, Jr. "A Note on Sidney Lanier's Attitude Toward the Negro and Toward Populism." *Georgia Historical Quarterly* (September 1968): 305–7.

Smith, Ralph. "The Farmers' Alliance in Texas, 1875–1900." *Southwestern Historical Quarterly* 48 (October 1948): 346–69.

———. "'Macuneism' or the Farmers of Texas in Business." *Journal of Southern History* 13 (May 1947): 220–44.

Smith, Willard H. "William Jennings Bryan and Racism." *Journal of Negro History* 54 (April 1969): 127–49.

——. "William Jennings Bryan—A Reappraisal." Indiana Academy of the Social Sciences, *Proceedings*, n.s. 10 (1965): 56–69.

——. "William Jennings Bryan and the Social Gospel." *Journal of American History* 53 (June 1966): 41–60.

Spriggs, William Edward. "The Virginia Colored Farmers' Alliance: A Case Study of Race and Class Identity." *Journal of Negro History* 64 (summer 1979): 191–209.

Steelman, Joseph H. "Republican Party Strategists and the Issue of Fusion with Populists in North Carolina, 1893–1894." *North Carolina Historical Review* 47 (July 1970): 244–69.

——. "Vicissitudes of Republican Party Politics: The Campaign of 1892 in North Carolina." *North Carolina Historical Review* 33 (autumn 1966): 430–44.

Suderman, Elmer F. "The Social Gospel Novelists' Criticisms of American Society." *Midcontinent American Studies Journal* 7 (spring 1966): 68–74.

Summersell, Charles G. "The Alabama Governor's Race of 1892." *The Alabama Review* 8 (January 1955): 5–35.

——. "Kolb and the Populist Revolt as Viewed by Newspapers." *Alabama Historical Quarterly* 19 (fall and winter 1957): 375–95.

Tarr, Joel A. "Goldfinger, the Gold Conspiracy and the Populists." *Midcontinent American Studies Journal* 7 (fall 1966): 49–52.

Taylor, Joe B. "Populism and Disfranchisement in Alabama." *Journal of Negro History* 34 (October 1949): 410–27.

Taylor, Joe Gray. "The Democratic Idea and the Deep South: An Historical Survey." *Mississippi Quarterly* 18 (fall 1965): 76–83.

Turner, Arlin. "George Washington Cable's Beginning as a Reformer." *Journal of Southern History* 17 (May 1951): 135–61.

——. "George Washington Cable, Novelist and Reformer." *South Atlantic Quarterly* 48 (October 1949): 539–45.

Vander Zanden, James W. "The Ideology of White Supremacy." *Journal of the History of Ideas* 20 (June–September 1959): 385–402.

Weatherford, W. D. "Race Relationship in the South." *Annals of the American Academy of Political and Social Science* 48 (September 1913): 164–72.

Welch, Richard E. "The Federal Elections Bill of 1890. Postscripts and Preludes." *Journal of American History* 52 (December 1965): 511–26.

Wellborn, Fred. "The Influence of the Silver-Republican Senators, 1889–1891." *Mississippi Valley Historical Review* 14 (March 1928): 402–80.

White, Melvin V. "Populism in Louisiana during the 'Nineties." *Mississippi Valley Historical Review* 5 (June 1918): 3–19.

Wilhoit, Francis M. "An Interpretation of Populism's Impact on the Georgia Negro." *Journal of Negro History* 52 (April 1967): 116–27.

Wirth, Louis. "Race and Public Policy." *Scientific Monthly* 68 (April 1944): 302–12.

Woods, Randall B. "C. H. J. Taylor and the Movement for Black Political Independence, 1882–1896." *Journal of Negro History* 67 (summer 1982): 122–35.

Woodward, C. Vann. "Tom Watson and the Negro in Agrarian Politics." *Journal of Southern History* 4 (February 1938): 14–33.

Wynes, Charles E. "Charles T. O'Ferrall and the Virginia Gubernatorial Election of 1893." *Virginia Magazine of History and Biography* 64 (October 1956): 437–53.

———. "Lewis Harvie Blair, Virginia Reformer: The Uplift of the Negro and Southern Prosperity." *Virginia Magazine of History and Biography* 72 (January 1964): 3–18.

5. Theses and Dissertations

Abramowitz, Jack. "Accommodations and Militancy in Negro Life, 1876–1916." Ph.D. diss., Columbia University, 1950.

Blackburn, Helen M. "The Populist Party in the South." Master's thesis, Howard University, 1941.

Boras, Mary A. "A Case Study of the Speeches of the Birmingham, Alabama Populist Party Convention, September 15–16, 1892." Master's thesis, University of Alabama, 1952.

Budd, Harrel. "The Negro in Politics in Texas, 1867–1898." Master's thesis, University of Texas, 1925.

Byrd, Ruth E. "The History of the Force Bill of 1890 and Its Effect upon State Constitutions." Master's thesis, University of North Carolina, 1932.

Cartwright, Joseph Howard. "The Negro in Tennessee Politics, 1880–1891." Master's thesis, Vanderbilt University, 1968.

Church, Joseph. "The Farmers' Alliance and the Populist Movement in South Carolina, 1887–1896." Master's thesis, University of South Carolina, 1953.

Gaither, Gerald. "The Negro in the Ideology of Southern Populism, 1889–1896." Master's thesis, University of Tennessee, 1967.

Gerteis, Joseph Howard. "Class and the Color Line: the Sources and Limits of Interracial Class Coalition, 1880–1896." Ph.D. diss., University of North Carolina at Chapel Hill, 1999.

Harris, David Alan. "The Political Career of Milford W. Howard, Populist Congressman from Alabama." Master's thesis, Auburn University, 1957.

Hearn, Thomas K. "The Populist Movement in Marshall County Alabama." Master's thesis, University of Alabama, 1935.

Jones, Theron Paul. "The Gubernatorial Election of 1892 in North Carolina." Master's thesis, University of North Carolina, 1949.

Lewis, Robert David. "The Negro in Agrarian Uprisings, 1865–1900." Master's thesis, State University of Iowa, 1938.

McCain, William D. "The Populist Party in Mississippi." Master's thesis, University of Mississippi, 1931.

McKay, Herbert S. "Convict Leasing in North Carolina." Master's thesis, University of North Carolina, 1947.

Perry, Douglass Geraldyne. "Black Populism: The Negro in the People's Party in Texas." Master's thesis, Prairie View University, 1945.

Quillian, Bascom Osborne, Jr. "The Populist Challenge in Georgia in the Year 1894." Master's thesis, University of Georgia, 1948.

Reddick, Jamie Lawson. "The Negro in the Populist Movement in Georgia." Master's thesis, Atlanta University, 1937.

Roberts, William P. "The Public Career of William Harrel Felton." Ph.D. diss., University of North Carolina, 1952.

Rogers, William Warren. "Agrarianism in Alabama, 1865–1896." Ph.D diss., University of North Carolina, 1959.

Smith, Florence. "The Populist Movement and Its Influence in North Carolina." Ph.D. diss., University of Chicago, 1928.

Smith, Robert Wayne. "A Rhetorical Analysis of the Populist Movement in North Carolina, 1892–1896." Ph.D. diss., University of Wisconsin, 1957. (A microfilm copy of this dissertation is available in the North Carolina Collection, University of North Carolina.)

Sparkman, John. "The Kolb-Oates Campaign of 1894." Master's thesis, University of Alabama, 1924.

Summersell, Charles G. "A Life of Reuben Kolb." Master's thesis, University of Alabama, 1930.

Westphal, Corinne. "The Farmers' Alliance in Tennessee." Master's thesis, Vanderbilt University, 1929.

Zimmerman, Helen J. "Penal Systems and Penal Reforms in the South Since the Civil War." Ph.D. diss., University of North Carolina, 1947.

Index

Abner, David, Jr., 187

Abramowitz, Jack, x, 97

Afro-American League, 61

Agassiz, Louis, 103

agricultural overproduction, 85–86, 200

Agricultural Wheel: Colored Agricultural Wheels, 9, 10; experiment with biracial coalitions, 1, 49; union with Southern Alliance, 3, 9

Alabama: biracial preludes to Populism, 156; class order, 156, 157; coalminers, 201; Constitution of 1875, 156; Constitution of 1901, 167–68; disenfranchisement of blacks, 167–68; early white support for black Alliance movement, 10; gubernatorial election of 1892, 158; Jim Crow seating bill of 1891, 102; sectionalism between Black Belt and white hill-country, 156, 157, 161; theory and practice of populism, 156–68

Alabama Colored Farmers' Alliance, 9–10; conflict with landless black group, 49; decline of by 1892, 10; membership in 1889, 156

Alabama congressional election of 1896: relationship between black density and Populism in, 234; voting and black population characteristics for, 233

Alabama Democrats: adoption of Populist issues, 165; election fraud, 160, 165–66; race-baiting, 156, 162–63

Alabama Jeffersonian Democratic-Populists: attempts to prevent loss of potential white voters, 162; 1894 platform, 164, 285n125; sought black vote, 158, 159–60; support for black colonization, 77, 167; voted along Populist lines, 157

Alabama Populist Party: appeal to blacks to stay away from the polls, 165; appeal to impoverished white farmers, 156; candidates elected to legislature in 1892, 161–62; charges of election fraud, 161; 1892 election results, 160, 161–62; "free ballot and fair count" theme, 157–58, 166–67; 1892 gubernatorial candidate, 158–59; loss of 1892 supporters and almost all of black votes in 1894, 165; origin of, 155; pitted lower-class agrarian population against urban industrial society, 155; political participation by blacks limited to exercise of the suffrage, 159; theory and practice of populism, 156–68

Alabama Republicans: black members of Lily-Whites, 307n51; factional dispute between the Lily-Whites and the Black and Tans, 163

"Alliance" legislatures, 44, 72

worker's unions, 105, 139, 201; Southern Populist core philosophy, 97–98
Ivy, James, 182

Jackson, Andrew, 70, 81
Jackson, J. S., 19, 41
Jefferson, Thomas, 70, 81
Jennings, Henry, 183
Jim Crow laws, 102, 103
Johnson, Charles, 32
Johnson, E. A., 300n102
Johnson, Henry Lincoln, 101
Johnson, James Weldon, 140
Johnson, Lyndon, 196
Johnson, Sam, 196
Johnson, S. W., 103
Johnson's Island, 77
Jones, Thomas G., 158, 160, 161, 181
Judson, 77

Kazin, Michael, xi
Kearby, Jerome, 189–90
Keys, Isaac, 170
King, Martin Luther, Jr., 108, 294n62
Knights of Labor: biracial experiments, 1, 9, 49; decline in the South, 13; efforts toward working alliance with agrarians, 27; limited success in class coalitions, 139; promotion of strikes, 274n104
Knoxville Gleaner, 93
Kolb, Reuben F.: and 1890 and 1892 elections, 44, 112, 161, 166; approach of Republicans for campaign contribution, 164; and black vote, 158–59; in 1894 election, 163, 165; on need for honest elections, 157, 158–59; and "purifying the ballot," 167
Kousser, Morgan, 120, 151–52, 153, 177, 185, 192

Lamar, L. Q. C., 290n73
Lanier, Sidney, 142

Laurent, L. D., 171, 204
Leak, R. W. H., 300n102
Lease, Mary Elizabeth, 149
Leflore County, Mississippi, attempt to organize Colored Alliance and boycott of white merchants, 27
Lewis, Elsie, 130
Lewis, W. O., 187
liberating proletariat, myth of, 286n148
Liberia, black leaders' plans for colonization, 76
lien system, 71
Lily-Whites: in Alabama, 164, 165; black members of in Alabama, 307n51; control of Louisiana Republican party, 176; Lynch on, 290n73; and purging of blacks from Republican Party, 47, 71, 72, 95, 137, 154; in Texas, 188
Lipset, Seymour, 286n148
literacy requirements, 167, 179, 180
Livingstone, Leonidas F., 67
Livingstone College, 130
Lloyd, Henry Demarest: on Cyclone Davis, 81; *Wealth against Commonwealth,* 72
Lodge, Henry Cabot, 55–56
Lodge "Force" Bill: black division over, 60–61, 202; defeat by coalition of Western free silver Republicans and Southern Democrats, 55–56; disagreement of Southern and Colored Farmers' Alliance over, 47; Du Bois's stand against, 61; effect on agrarian organization in South, 17; propaganda about used against Populism, 56, 149, 303n164; revival of Reconstruction fears of black domination, *58;* Southern Alliance's opposition to, 103; Washington's stand against, 61
Loucks, H. L., 98
Louisiana: black voter registration up to 1890, 168; Constitution of 1898,